THE PUNJABIS IN BRITISH COLUMBIA

McGill-Queen's Studies in Ethnic
History
Series One: Donald Harman
Akenson, Editor

McGill-Queen's Studies in
Ethnic History
Series Two: John Zucchi, Editor

THE PUNJABIS IN BRITISH COLUMBIA

Location, Labour, First Nations, and Multiculturalism

KAMALA ELIZABETH NAYAR

McGill-Queen's University Press

Montreal & Kingston | London | Ithaca

ISBN 978-0-7735-4070-5 (cloth)
ISBN 978-0-7735-4071-2 (paper)

Legal deposit fourth quarter 2012
Bibliothèque nationale du Québec

Printed in Canada on acid-free paper that is 100% ancient forest free (100% post-consumer recycled), processed chlorine free

This book has been published with the help of a grant from the Canadian Federation for the Humanities and Social Sciences, through the Awards to Scholarly Publications Program, using funds provided by the Social Sciences and Humanities Research Council of Canada. Funding has also been received from Kwantlen Polytechnic University.

McGill-Queen's University Press acknowledges the support of the Canada Council for the Arts for our publishing program. We also acknowledge the financial support of the Government of Canada through the Canada Book Fund for our publishing activities.

Library and Archives Canada Cataloguing in Publication

Nayar, Kamala E. (Kamala Elizabeth), 1966–
The Punjabis in British Columbia : location, labour, First Nations, and multiculturalism / Kamala Elizabeth Nayar.

(McGill-Queen's studies in ethnic history. Series two ; 31)
Includes bibliographical references and index.
ISBN 978-0-7735-4070-5 (bound). – ISBN 978-0-7735-4071-2 (pbk.)

1. Panjabis (South Asian people) – British Columbia – Skeena River Region – Economic conditions – 20th century – Case studies. 2. Panjabis (South Asian people) – British Columbia – Skeena River Region – Social conditions – 20th century – Case studies. 3. Immigrants – British Columbia – Skeena River Region – History – 20th century – Case studies. 4. Panjabis (South Asian people) – British Columbia – Migrations – Case studies. 5. Rural-urban migration – British Columbia – Case studies. 6. Multiculturalism – British Columbia – Case studies. 7. British Columbia – Ethnic relations – Case studies. 8. British Columbia – Emigration and immigration – Case studies. I. Title. II. Series: McGill-Queen's studies in ethnic history. Series 2 ; 31

FC3850.P36N39 2012   305.891'4210711   C2012-904921-2

Set in 10.5/12.5 Minion Pro with Trade Gothic and FF Din
Book design & typesetting by Garet Markvoort, zijn digital

For those who have the courage to change our lives for the better

CONTENTS

MAPS AND TABLES

Maps

Tables

PHOTOGRAPHS

ACKNOWLEDGMENTS

In conducting research for and writing this study, I have benefited from the help of many, for which I am very grateful. First and foremost, I would like to express my gratitude to all the interviewees, who took the time to share their experiences, ideas, and insights. Without the interviewees, this project would not have been feasible. Their enthusiasm for the project resulted in many illuminating discussions on the establishment of the Punjabi community in British Columbia. Many members of the Punjabi communities in Prince Rupert, Terrace, and BC's Lower Mainland were of great assistance in helping me network with the community, both through participant observation in cultural and religious events and by suggesting the names of people to interview.

The non-Punjabi citizens of the Skeena region were also welcoming and supportive, especially with regard to my investigation into the intercultural dynamics of the region. I am especially grateful to Simone Emily Stewart, whom I met by chance one day when I had lost my way in the large Canadian Fishing Company plant located right beside Prince Rupert's Old Dry Dock area. Her kind and helpful efforts extended to her inviting me to join her for lunch. Our discussion subsequently inspired me to further explore the intercultural dynamics of the region. Worthy of special mention are the valuable conversations I had with Julius Komlos and the late Ellis Benson Young about the Skeena community's socio-cultural issues and concerns. I am also thankful to George Sampson for welcoming me to the Elders' Group at the Prince Rupert Friendship House. Extremely helpful in the tedious search for archival data for this project were Jean Eiers-Page and Tianna Wright at the Prince Rupert City & Regional Archives, Judi Clark and Monica Lamb-Yorski at the *Prince Rupert Daily News*, Rod Link at the *Terrace Standard*, and Leah Cuthbert at the Prince Rupert Public Library. I would also like to express my gratitude to members of the First Nations for their gifts of appreciation, including Mona and Leonard Alexcee for the bouquet of cedar-crafted flowers, Arnie Nagy for the two eagle feathers, and Lorene Potornay for the cedar friendship pendant.

I am grateful to Sam Migliore of Kwantlen Polytechnic University for his genuine encouragement of my research pursuits in general and of this study in particular; my colleagues Bob Fuhr and Colin Green have similarly been supportive. Thanks are also due to Donald Attwood of McGill for his help, especially in the initial stage of conceptualizing the theoretical framework for the project; Tom Thorner of Kwantlen for sharing his expertise on the history of British Columbia; and Greg Jenion of Kwantlen for enlightening me on qualitative research methodology. Jerome Black of McGill offered me his expertise on Canadian politicians' electioneering for the ethnic vote, while Elisabeth Gidengil of McGill shared her knowledge on voting behaviour and public opinion in Canada. I am also grateful to Jagat Singh Uppal (CEO, Goldwood Industries) for sharing with me his experiences in both the forestry industry and the BC Punjabi community.

The Social Sciences and Humanities Research Council of Canada financed my research through the standard research grant program, and I am very thankful for this assistance. Thanks are also owed to the Office of Research and Scholarship (Kwantlen) for two research grants that allowed me to carry out the preliminary fieldwork. I would like to express my gratitude to both David Atkinson, during his tenure as president at Kwantlen, and Robert Adamoski, former dean of social sciences, for their efforts in providing me with the resources required to successfully pursue and complete the present research project. I am also grateful to the two blind peer reviewers for their positive feedback and suggestions for refining the manuscript. McGill-Queen's University Press editors Kyla Madden, Joanne Pisano, and Ryan Van Huijstee provided excellent support. I also wish to thank Judith Turnbull for her thoughtful copy editing.

Thanks as well to my husband, who has been a constant source of support, especially in terms of helping me balance family life and academic career, and to my two daughters – Shardha and Sangeeta – who have been extremely patient with their mother. As always, I am indebted to my father, Baldev Raj Nayar, who had to contend with the harsh realities of life during the Partition of India. At the young age of sixteen – with a mother nursing a newborn baby and sheltering his younger siblings – he found himself a political refugee, both displaced and mourning the loss of his father. Amid this suffering, he maintained a forward-looking attitude without forgetting the fragility of life. In doing so, my father taught me to value self-reliance, fairness, and respect. Lastly, I would like to acknowledge wholeheartedly the HIV/AIDS patients and Holocaust survivors whom I cared for during my former career as a nurse at St Mary's Hospital in Montreal; it was with them that I learned the art of listening.

Although indebted to many, I alone bear the responsibility for the final analysis.

PREFACE

In this study, I investigate the pattern of social and cultural transformation of the Punjabi community, both in its initial settlement in the Skeena region of northwestern British Columbia and after its shift to large urban centres as a result of the globalization-driven decline of Canada's forestry and fishery industries. In effect, the study examines the "twice-migration" of the Punjabi community – the migration from India to rural Canada and then the internal migration from rural to urban Canada. In doing so, the study sheds light on the contrasting experiences of Punjabi immigrants – the cultural synergy in the small remote towns of Canada and the ethnic insularity in the large urban centres of Canada.

After completing the first set of preliminary interviews for this study, I came to see that the most productive framework for the study would be – in view of the complex nature of the social and cultural transformations involved in the relocation process – the contrast between the consequences of settlement in the different locations as well as a combination of agency and structure. Therefore, in this study, we see Punjabi immigrants in the "foreground" as social actors and active contributors to their own social and cultural transformation as they engage with the new and changing social, economic, and political structures of Canadian society. At the same time, we should also consider these structures as comprising one set of determinants in the "background," helping us to understand place-making and displacement as well as continuity and change.

An investigation of the Punjabi community in the Skeena region constitutes a significant advance in the literature on ethnic group formation, since earlier studies have more commonly been pursued in metropolitan settings.

Besides, studies concerned with immigrant communities have tended to investigate race relations as though they essentially constituted interactions between the particular ethnic group and the Anglo-mainstream. In reality, a significant and much more complex intercultural dynamic is involved; in the Skeena region, this intercultural dynamic encompasses the complex relations among the Punjabis, First Nations people, the Anglo-mainstream, and the many other ethnic communities in the region.

Scholars who have studied immigrant communities in the postwar period have given primary attention to the male's story and have often overlooked the female worker. Thus, little is known of the subculture that emerged among Punjabi women working in the salmon canneries of the Skeena region. Their voices as women immigrants need to be documented and underlined, especially since their entry into the Canadian labour force had a significant impact on their traditional social patterns of behaviour. Moreover, it is noteworthy that their decision to work in the salmon canneries was made for the sake of survival – economic, but also social and psychological – in the course of their adaptation to a remote setting in Canada.

The extant literature does not assess the impact of the declining forestry and fishery industries on the Punjabi communities in remote milieus. In fact, many Punjabis were forced to leave the small towns and resettle in metropolitan areas. As a result, the Punjabi communities of the Skeena region have been shrinking, even as the oral tradition among them has also been vanishing, which means that their "stories," with the passage of time, are more likely to go unheard. Not only do these internal migrants now face the heterogeneity of the Vancouver Punjabi community, but they also encounter a different experience of multiculturalism from the one they encountered in the Skeena. In the case of the children of Skeena Punjabis, the shift to urban centres has led to a re-evaluation of what it means to be Canadian.

Insofar as it addresses these issues, this study should prove useful not only to members of the Punjabi community in Canada, but also to Canadians in general because it provides a more comprehensive understanding of the sociocultural and economic dynamics of the Punjabi community in the Skeena region of northwestern BC and Metro Vancouver. Importantly, as an empirically based and in-depth analysis of one ethnic community, it should be of interest to social scientists who teach or do research on comparative studies on immigrant communities in the multicultural environments of countries such as Canada, especially those affected by the globally driven decline in resource industries and the resulting shift in population from remote towns to urban centres.

Although this study focuses specifically on the twice-migration of the Punjabi community, the issues it examines are relevant as well to the experiences of other immigrant communities, especially visible ethnic minorities that migrated to Canada when the dominion was in need of manual labour. Moreover, given Canada's multicultural mosaic and the current, yet pressing, issues surrounding religious and cultural pluralism, the First Nations, and citizenship, the study can help policy-makers and professionals in related fields understand the complexity of intercultural relations and the process of becoming Canadian in the light of Canada's practice of multiculturalism.

Lastly, this study should be of interest to general readers of Canadian history, especially since the multi-ethnic dynamics of remote towns in British Columbia have rarely been examined, even as the "histories" of these forestry towns have been fading.

THE PUNJABIS IN BRITISH COLUMBIA

CHAPTER 1

Setting the Stage: Ethnicity, Labour, and Multiculturalism

The process of adapting to a new country can become a special challenge for immigrant communities when, after adapting to their new environment, they are then forced to relocate to a new setting. The immigrant experience in this instance involves a "twice-migration," where people are forced to move out of the place where they had made their new home after their initial, overseas migration.[1] The twice-migration experience can be complex even when it occurs internally, such as when the shift occurs from a remote context to an urban one within the receiving country. This relocation process may not only involve socio-economic re-adaptation, but may also require socio-cultural readjustment, during the course of which differences in the application of a country's multicultural policies in small remote towns as opposed to large urban settings may stand revealed.

In carrying forward this line of inquiry, this study examines the patterns of social and cultural transformation of immigrant communities, both in their initial settlement in remote regions of Canada and after their move to large urban centres as a result of the globalization-driven economic decline in several of the resource industries of rural Canada. More specifically, the study investigates the impact that the decline of British Columbia's forestry and fishery industries has had and is having on the Punjabi community in the Skeena region of northwestern British Columbia; many have been forced, in a sense, to readjust as an immigrant group through re-migration to urban locations. The "readjustment" of the Punjabi community reveals sharp differences in the way immigrants experience Canada's practice of multiculturalism, depending on whether the experience occurs in small remote towns or in large urban centres.

At the same time, the process of initial migration and readjustment reveals the role of agency in the social and cultural transformation of the Punjabi immigrant community. With the rise of post-colonial, post-modernist, and feminist challenges to the earlier structural-functional paradigms of "ethnographic maps,"[2] there emerged much theoretical discussion around the issues of heterogeneity in immigrant communities, the porosity of borders, and the negotiability of identities, all of which have, in turn, made for greater importance and value being accorded to the role of agency in the study of immigrant groups. This recent emphasis on agency stands in contrast to a long-standing orientation in scholarship towards immigrants as the "homogeneous Other," according to which external social, economic, and political forces – that is, *structure* – are the determining factors shaping the adjustment of immigrants, as if they were mere passive recipients of change.[3] However, ethnic group formation is a complex and dynamic process during which immigrants as minority groups are themselves, in essence, "social actors" in the course of their social and cultural transformation.[4]

Minority groups have traditionally been studied in terms of ethnicity and class. Recent studies, however, have argued that this approach is empirically mistaken, since the immigrant experience is gender specific.[5] While women are often viewed as the essential medium through which traditional culture is transmitted, it is likely that transformations in their roles and behaviour may occur during migration and modernization.[6]

In investigating the social and cultural aspects of immigrant communities, social anthropologists and historians have, for the most part, situated their research in large urban field sites,[7] even though the immigrant experience has not been limited to metropolitan areas. Moreover, these studies have often included investigations into race relations, largely focusing on the interactions between a particular ethnic community and the Anglo-mainstream. This linear view of race relations can, however, be misleading or limited regarding the actual experience of immigrants, as is made evident in the case of the Punjabis of BC's Skeena region. A new environment often entails a multifaceted range of cultural interactions that immigrants have to contend with, including relations with people belonging to various other ethnic immigrant communities and, more significantly, people of the First Nations. Perhaps more evident and detectable in smaller towns or rural areas, this type of intercultural interaction is very significant, since it reflects the actual complexity of an ethnically diverse milieu.

Another important aspect of immigrant communities relates to the creation or emergence of social spaces in a diasporic setting. Of course, in the contemporary period of globalization, such emergence of social spaces among diasporic communities takes place in the context of porous borders and transnationalism.[8] Diasporic communities now not only interact with, and are embedded in, their local situation, but are also linked to a considerable extent through various mechanisms with their original homeland communities and their related diasporas elsewhere in the world.[9] Consequently, ethnic identification today is much more complex, since the process of identification is fluid, situational, and negotiable according to the shifting contexts of ethnic groups.[10] However, this multi-locality or multiplicity of identities in trans-local spaces[11] can also be viewed as a source of adaptive strength.[12]

The complexity in ethnic identification is further amplified when the ethnic community, after establishing itself in a remote setting, is forced to relocate to an urban site. With this second migration, there occurs a shift from relationships with the broader local community in the small remote towns of Canada to ethnic insularity in the large urban centres. In the course of this shift, the children of immigrants, after having formed their identity in the social context of Canada's practice of multiculturalism in remote settings, find themselves having to renegotiate their ethnic identity and their national identity as they move to metropolitan centres. Significantly, the shift to urban centres has resulted in a re-evaluation of what it means to be Canadian.

Punjabi immigrants have been social actors in and active contributors to their own social and cultural transformation as they engaged with the new and changing social, economic, and political structures of Canadian society. Therefore, the initial migration of the Punjabi community to the Skeena region of British Columbia and its subsequent relocation to urban Canada must be investigated from a broader perspective that incorporates both agency and structure. Accordingly, the larger analytical framework for this study is based, in effect, on three key variables: (1) the characteristics of *Punjabi ethnicity*, (2) the circumstances surrounding *British Columbian labour*, and (3) the policy and practice of *Canadian multiculturalism*. In sum, the explanation of the process of social and cultural adaptation and transformation of the Punjabi community lies in these three variables, as well as in the critical intervening variable of geographic location – that is, the difference between the remote towns and urban settings of British Columbia.

Punjabi Ethnicity

Punjabi is a term that is used to refer to people who are originally from the geographic region of the Punjab in present-day India and Pakistan and who live either in their homeland or in the diaspora. The term *Punjab* (five waters) was first used by the Persians to refer to the geographic region of the northwestern part of the Indian subcontinent, where five rivers (Jhelum, Chenab, Ravi, Beas, and Sutlej) merge into the Indus River, the major river flowing into the Arabian Sea. Punjabi culture grew out of the settlements situated along these five rivers, which served as an important trade route to the Near East as early as the ancient Indus Valley civilization (ca. 3000 BCE).[13] Agriculture has been the major economic feature of the Punjab and has therefore formed the foundation of Punjabi culture, with one's social status being determined by landownership.

The Punjab emerged as an important agricultural region. In fact, the state of Punjab in present-day India, especially following the Green Revolution during the period from the mid-1960s to the mid-1970s,[14] has been described as the "bread basket of India," albeit with adverse environmental and social consequences. Certainly, the state of Punjab has been responsible for producing 23 per cent of India's wheat and 10 per cent of India's rice. The Green Revolution is often attributed, in part, to British colonial initiatives, especially during the late nineteenth century. The British instituted structural and policy changes to enhance agricultural productivity, the structural developments being mainly in terms of canal irrigation and rail transport systems.[15] The expansion of both the rural road system and the railway network was beneficial for both agriculture and trade.

Besides being known for agriculture and trade, the Punjab is also a region that over the centuries has experienced many foreign invasions and consequently has a long-standing history of warfare. Punjabis are often referred to as *Sher Punjabi* (Punjabi Lions); they have similarly been regarded as the "shield and sword arm of India." These references hold true, given that because the Punjab is situated on the principal route of invasions through the northwestern frontier of India, Punjabis have a long history of guarding the "gateway to India."[16] The Punjab even had to contend with Alexander the Great (356 BCE–323 BCE), who successfully extended his military reach as far as the Punjab (326 BCE).[17] The Punjab is vulnerably situated, being the location where foreigner invaders first arrived after crossing the mountain passes of northwest India, and thus it has had to deal with the results of those invasions: "Until the eighteenth century all foreign invaders – the Aryans, the Persians, the Greeks, the Scythians, the Parthians, the Huns, the Turks, and the Mongols – came to India through the northwest, and the brave Punjab had always to bear the brunt of the foreign invasions."[18]

India was invaded frequently via the Punjab up to the eighteenth century. Thus, out of necessity, Punjabis had to adopt a lifestyle that entailed engaging in warfare to protect their land. Warrior culture typically elevates the value of the community's honour (*izzat*), and it is clear that *izzat* was highly esteemed by Punjabis, especially those belonging to the warrior castes. And, as a result, Punjabis have developed a character of resiliency: "Consequently, a great part of the Punjabi's life was spent in fighting and gaining perfection in the art of war, and in building up his physique. It was, therefore, natural for the Punjabis to become sturdy, exuberant, and adventurous people."[19] Even when the Punjab was under British rule (1849–1947), the Punjabis continued to serve in large numbers in the army, and they fought in both the First and Second World Wars; 20 per cent of the British Indian army consisted of Punjabi-Sikhs,[20] with the Jat (farmer) caste group particularly favoured by the British.[21] In line with their renowned brave character, Punjabis were also willing to travel to faraway places under challenging conditions in the hope of finding better employment.[22] Indeed, it is precisely this adventurous and resilient character of the Punjabi people that has aided them in migrating to, and settling in, Canada, especially during the period when Canada was nativist in its immigration policy.

While Punjabis share a common territory, ethnicity, and language, they are likely to be followers of one of several religions, most often Hinduism, Sikhism, or Islam. Regardless of the religious background of the Punjabis, much of their culture has been shaped by Punjabi folk traditions and the pan-Indian social religious customs based on law books like the *Manusmrti* (Code of Manu), which is a collection of the rules of life compiled by Hindu Brahmin priests around 200 BCE.[23] While these law books may have originally been sanctified by the Hindu religion, they have served more generally to form the mores characteristic of traditional Indian society, even as regional cultures and other religions have played an integral role in the development of the various communities in India.

Hinduism is the oldest of the religions practised by the Punjabis; however, the term *Hindu* – also first used by the Persians – was applied to a vast territory that contained much diversity and regional variety. Although Hinduism encompasses a very broad spectrum of beliefs and practices, the unifying concept among its various sects has been the cycle of birth, death, and rebirth (*samsara* in Sanskrit; *sansar* in Punjabi). In contrast to Hinduism, a religion born out of Indian soil, the Islamic presence in the Punjab is a result of the various waves of Muslim invasions and their consequent rule, such as that of the Sultans (1206–1526) and the Mughals (1526–1757). With their empire-building goals, some Mughal rulers conquered large numbers in northern India and converted them to Islam, and in that way, Islamic concepts such as monotheism, iconoclasm, and the precept that one ought to follow or submit to the will of God were brought to India from the Middle East.

Sikhism grew out of Indian soil and shares a number of features with Hinduism (e.g., *karma*, *sansar*, and liberation); it also shares a number of elements with Islam (e.g., the emphasis on a personal formless God, denunciation of icon worship, and equality).[24] Nonetheless, Sikhism has developed its own distinct set of beliefs and practices, one example being the belief that suffering, as understood by the Sikh gurus, is a result of both inner forces (ego-centredness) and external forces (social and political oppression).[25] For the inner forces, one should follow the path shown by Guru (God without form) through the devotional recitation of the Divine Name (*naam*), while for the external forces, one should perform selfless service for the betterment of humanity, such as by helping those in need or fighting against social injustice and political oppression.

There is a complex relationship between the Sikh religion and Punjabi culture. Historically, the culture preceded the religion. Punjabi culture, which is over two millennia old, has a strong hold over Punjabis. In contrast, the Sikh religion emerged in the sixteenth century in reaction to the contemporaneous pan-Indian and Punjabi cultural values and practices (such as asceticism, the caste system, and the subordination of women). As such, Sikhism grew out of Punjabi soil, and it was therefore inevitably a bearer of Punjabi culture, which it shared with the much more numerous Punjabi Hindus. It also grew in the struggle against Mughal rule, and in the course of that struggle, it found common cause with Punjabi Hindus.

With the eventual decline of the Mughal Empire, Sikh *misls* (militia units) came to exercise control over much of the Punjab; by 1799, a Sikh political leader, Maharaja Ranjit Singh, had consolidated the *misls* and become the ruler of the Punjab. Maharaja Ranjit Singh was a secular ruler in that he did not impose Sikhism on his citizens and was tolerant of religious diversity in his rule over Punjab's large Sikh, Hindu, and Muslim populations. Perhaps as a result, by the time Sikh rule ended with the British capturing the Punjab in 1849, the boundaries between Punjabi-Sikhs and Punjabi-Hindus had become "blurred,"[26] especially since during Maharaja Ranjit Singh's leadership the *gurdwaras* (Sikh places of worship) were administered by non-Khalsa (not orthodox) Sikhs.

It was during the Singh Sabha (Assembly of the Lions [Sikhs]) movement under British colonial rule (1849–1947) that a distinct Sikh identity re-emerged and formally began to crystallize; that is, under the threat of Christian missionaries and Hindu revivalist movements, new stirrings within the community signalled the wish to establish a separate Sikh identity. From the last quarter of the nineteenth century, the movement to distinguish the Sikhs from the Hindus became apparent and strengthened over time.[27] The British were eager to encourage this development in order to thwart what they saw as a rising nationalism under the leadership of the Hindus.

At the advent of India gaining its independence in 1947, the Punjab was divided as a result of the partition of India and the creation of Pakistan. This was a tragic turn of events for the Punjab, since not only was the geographic region divided into two, but the largest mass migration in history took place as a result of approximately six million people shifting in each direction,[28] during which over one million people lost their lives.[29] Almost all of the Hindus and Sikhs who had been in Pakistan left to settle in India, while many Muslims left India to live in Pakistan. After independence, many Sikhs became disenchanted with the ruling Congress Party, which was viewed as "short-changing" the Sikhs by not granting them "special consideration as a minority group."[30] This has been an ongoing contentious issue in the Punjab, leading to militant insurgency from the 1980s to the mid-1990s.[31]

It is interesting to note that, in the BC Lower Mainland (Vancouver and surrounding municipalities, including Burnaby, New Westminster, Richmond, and Surrey), Sikhs raised outside the Punjab refer to themselves as Punjabi and use the term interchangeably with "Sikh," understanding the two as synonymous. In reality, there is an ironic reversal of ethnic identification here: on the one hand, "Hindoo" was the term used by Anglo-Canadians to refer to all Sikhs, Hindus, and Muslims during the early years of "East Indian" migration to Canada in order to distinguish "East Indians" from the "Native Indians"; on the other hand, "Punjabi" has now come to be used by Sikhs to refer to themselves alone, even though there are also Hindu and Muslim Punjabis in Canada.[32] That said, it bears acknowledgment that the research on Punjabis in Canada has been primarily based on the Sikhs, especially those in British Columbia, owing to the fact that the first Sikh immigrants to Canada settled in BC and that the Lower Mainland Sikh community continues to be a large and vibrant one, actively involved in the social, political, and economic fabric of BC society. Though its roots in Canada go back to the early 1900s, the Sikh community did not emerge as an important immigrant group until the postwar period, and it has now become the largest non-Christian group in the Lower Mainland.[33]

Previous work on the Sikh community has focused on the history of the various waves of migration.[34] Much has been written about ethnic group formation within the receiving society,[35] including analyses that underscore the factors of racism, discrimination, and unfair labour policies as challenges faced by Sikh immigrants,[36] as well as the pursuit of upward social mobility.[37] In addition, studies have investigated the relations between the Sikh communities abroad and Sikhs in the Punjab in terms of the Sikh quest for an independent religious state[38] and the flow of remittances.[39] Other studies of the Sikh diaspora focus on the growing importance of religion in the formation of group identity[40] and intergenerational relations among its members.[41] Besides work on the Sikh community, research on the Punjabis in Canada has also been carried out in the broader context of South Asian immigration.[42]

In the matter of Punjabi ethnicity, there are important questions to explore regarding the immigration experience and the process of relocation.

This study attempts to address several key issues: What has been the role of agency in the establishment of the Punjabi community in the Skeena region and in its relocation to the Lower Mainland? Which Punjabi cultural elements facilitated the initial adaptation process of the Punjabi community? How did the "gutsy" and resilient character of Punjabis affect their relations with Canadian society? Which Punjabi cultural elements fostered resilience in the relocation process?

British Columbian Labour

British Columbia is a province rich in natural resources – minerals, metals, energy, timber, and fisheries. Despite this abundance, the development of the region was relatively slow because of its geographic location, with four-fifths of the province situated west of the Rocky Mountains.[43] It was not until the last quarter of the eighteenth century that Europeans first came into contact with the First Nations in BC's coastal regions through approaches by sea, and not until the early nineteenth century that they reached them through the land-based fur trade.[44] It was, however, only with the advent of the gold rushes in the Fraser (1858–60) and Cariboo (1860–63) regions of central interior BC that there was a noticeable European migration to, and settlement in, the province.[45] The influx of miners, who arrived hoping to become rich instantly, marked the beginning of conflict over the extraction of resources between Europeans and the First Nations.[46]

Even though the Fraser and Cariboo gold rushes were short-lived, most authorities argue that the two gold rushes and their fleeting prosperity served as a major catalyst for the establishment of the region's economy and infrastructure.[47] As it developed, the region gained greater presence on the map of Canada. In 1871 – when 73.6 per cent of BC's population were First Nations people and a mere 26.4 per cent were European settlers[48] – British Columbia joined Confederation. Four years earlier, in 1867, the Federal Dominion of Canada had been formed, at which time three British colonies became four provinces (Ontario, Quebec, Nova Scotia, and New Brunswick).[49]

The development of British Columbia was undoubtedly linked to the industrialization of the region. With the decline in gold mining, BC's economy expanded into other resource industries, such as forestry and fisheries. Indeed, political leaders now focused on land settlement and the industrialization of the province through the extraction and processing of natural resources. Even as BC became more industrialized, this was accomplished at the cost of the devastation of the First Nations.[50] No doubt, the First Nations subsistence economy of small-scale hunting, fishing, and food gathering was seen by Anglo industrialists as inefficient for a capitalist economy.

Alongside the political initiatives they took to industrialize the province, industrialists were determined both to find cheap labour and to produce large quantities of goods for the global market for profit.[51] The assembly line mode was used for mass production, and this type of production required the hiring of marginal groups for manual or semi-skilled jobs.[52] With a limited Anglo-Canadian labour force, employers – out of necessity – sought out First Nations people and visible minority immigrants to work for them.[53]

British Columbia's two major capitalist ventures were the forestry and fishery industries. With BC's considerable dense growth of timber – especially along the coast and the southern half of the province where the temperature is mild and rainfall abundant – the mills obtained their timber through crown land grants, which then gave title to the land on which the trees grew.[54] The first of the temporary crown land grant tenures were distributed in 1865 and only gave rights to cut timber. This allowed contractors to log and sell the timber in the open market, whether for domestic mills or export business. In effect, government separated landownership from timber-cutting privileges.[55] As a consequence, a pattern of many small locally owned mills emerged along the coast. These mills produced lumber for the domestic market, which consisted of rapidly developing urban centres and the growing farming communities in the Fraser Valley and on Vancouver Island.[56]

The construction of the Canadian Pacific Railway during the period from 1881 to 1885 – connecting the province with prairie and eastern markets – led to a crucial phase in the forestry industry.[57] In fact, the establishment of the railway allowed the province to become a leading exporter of timber.[58] By the turn of the century, two distinct markets emerged: first, the shipment market, which operated on the coast, including export mills in Vancouver's Burrard Inlet and on Vancouver Island; and second, the rail market, which involved the mills in the Vancouver area and BC's interior, serving the local economy and the Canadian prairies.[59] Moreover, railway lands were also leased to some small-scale mill operations for timber.

With the development of the forestry industry, the concern for logging was over private land. In 1896 the BC provincial government passed legislation prohibiting the sale of public land,[60] but it was not until 1912 that the BC government adopted the province's first Forest Act for the systematization of forestry business and government interests.[61] Growth in the forestry industry continued up to the First World War. The industry diversified further with the opening of coastal pulp mills in 1909 and 1912, and the first plywood plant opened at Fraser Mills in 1913.[62] In the 1920s, the forestry industry experienced high growth fuelled by strong local and global markets. With advances in logging and milling technology, the industry became more mechanized, which allowed it to expand further. On the other hand, during the Great

Depression of the 1930s, it became difficult to sell wood in both domestic and world (especially US) markets; production bottomed out in 1932 to half what it had been in 1929.[63] However, with the onset of the Second World War, wood products for fuel became very expensive.

During the 1930s, there was a notable decline in the logging of the large, high-grade Douglas firs in the coastal region. As a result, concern grew over the long-term sustainability of forestry; this concern was, however, interrupted by the Second World War. After the war, the BC government established in 1947 the contentious FML (Forest Management License) system in order to regulate deforestation and maintain systematic control over its land tenures.[64] Subsequent to the decline in Douglas fir in the coastal regions, logging shifted into the interior for the smaller low-grade species like cedar. The peak years in logging operations in the north-central region were from 1946 to 1964. During this time, the industry also experienced the consolidation of mills. By the 1970s, BC was primarily a producer of commodity lumber.[65]

Besides the forestry industry, the fish industries also emerged as a major capitalist venture. Fish catching was the traditional livelihood of many First Nations, and during the 1880s, when the fish-canning industry was established in BC, people of the First Nations – who depended heavily on the fisheries, especially in the coastal areas – had to adjust to the newly imposed Anglo-Canadian capitalist economy. With the building of fish canneries, the fishery industry had become established. The first commercial cannery plant in BC was opened on the Fraser River in 1871. The first cannery on the Skeena River was built in 1877, and the first one on the Nass River was established in 1881.[66]

The Anglo-Canadian industrialists began canning fish in large quantities for export to the United Kingdom and elsewhere. A large majority of the workers in the fish industries came from the First Nations, as well as from the Chinese and Japanese communities. The size of the labour force in these industries declined after the 1920s, however, as a result of technological change. The introduction of gasoline-powered boats in the 1920s meant that canneries could be built further apart; similarly, the introduction of refrigeration in the 1930s meant that fish could be transported long distances before being processed. As a result, the small dispersed canneries were now consolidated in Vancouver and Prince Rupert.[67]

From 1940 to the 1970s, resource industries like forestry and fisheries benefited from the Fordist boom and the model of assembly line production. Increasingly, automatic power-driven machinery was used for the expanding production intended for national and international markets. The mass-production model provided a stable and structured system for resource exploitation.[68] In spite of its resource exploitation, the model was also based on a social contract with labour, providing stable wages and benefits to the workers. Thus, accompanying the boom in production came the strengthening of trade unions, whose leaders engaged in collective bargaining over wages, job protection, and safer workplace conditions.[69]

Unionism became widespread in BC's resource industries. The fisheries were among the most organized and were especially prone to striking, given the seasonal nature of the work, the intense business competition, and uneasy relations between operators and workers. Unions were an asset to labour in negotiating aspects of the fishery business; interestingly, while fishermen were typically on the periphery of the canning industry, they identified with the labour movement.[70] In the early part of the twentieth century, unions excluded non-white workers from their ranks. In 1945, however, the main labour organizations in the fisheries, the United Fishermen Allied Workers' Union (UFAWU), allowed women and Chinese labourers to sign up. In fact, after the Second World War, unions had come to the realization that they needed ethnic support in order to build their bargaining power.[71]

Labour unions were also established in the forestry industry. Woodworkers had begun to organize themselves prior to the First World War (Industrial Workers of the World, est. 1905; BC Loggers' Union, est. 1918)[72] and matured during the 1930s (International Woodworkers of America, est. 1937).[73] With the rise in logging and sawmilling strikes and the drive towards industrial unionization during the 1930s, the International Woodworkers of America moved into BC and absorbed the earlier unions (such as the Lumber Workers Industrial Union), and in 1937 established the IWA in BC.[74] In the late 1940s and early 1950s, an intense internal struggle erupted in the International Woodworkers of America, but once rid of its militant leftist orientation, the union became a more mainstream institution. In the 1960s, however, there emerged once again considerable internal and inter-union politicking. For instance, in 1963 the International Brotherhood of Pulp, Sulphite and Paper Mill Workers split into the Pulp, Paper and Woodworkers of Canada (PPWC) and the Canadian Paperworkers' Union (CPU).[75] Meanwhile, the International Woodworkers of America (IWA) continued to organize and support labour in the woods and sawmills, particularly the latter, since there was a higher concentration of workers in the sawmills.[76]

While the various labour unions gained bargaining power from the 1950s to the 1970s, they have since been struggling for their relevancy in the more competitive globalized economy of recent times. During the 1970s, the energy crisis induced by OPEC (Organization of Petroleum Exporting Countries) was accompanied by serious stagflation as a result of long-term problems with the Fordist production model. Productivity fell, and international competition associated with globalization and technological advancement rose. The Fordist boom from 1940 to the 1970s had created an environmental crisis,[77] and in reaction, post-Fordism emerged, with an emphasis on flexibility in international regulations and production systems.[78] In the post-Fordist period, not only was there a change in trade relations with the United States (e.g., the Free Trade Agreement) and intensified global competition, but there also arose new challenges in the face of a rising environmentalist movement and the reawakening of Aboriginal consciousness in opposition to resource exploitation.[79] The gradual decline of the forestry and fishery industries, beginning in the mid-1980s and continuing throughout the 1990s up until the eventual bust in the early 2000s, resulted in the need to remap the resource industries in BC.[80] The BC Liberal government's repeal of the local processing regulation in order to generate business in a global market has also had a detrimental impact on BC's forestry and fishery labour force.

While rural-to-urban migration is a common theme in the developing world, it is also a phenomenon that occurs in the developed world, including countries like Canada. The general trend of out-migration from remote towns in BC's Skeena region began during the mid-1980s as a result of the globalization-driven decline of natural resource industries.[81] Since BC's resource industries have been the primary mechanism used by Punjabi immigrants in their economic adaptation to Canada, this study specifically looks at BC labour from the perspective of the primary importance of socio-economic security in the adaptation process for immigrants, the relationship that the Punjabi community has had with the labour unions, and the impact that the decline in the forestry and fishery industries is having on the Punjabi community. In the process, several questions emerge for analysis: How have the resource industries been intimately connected with the migration patterns and socio-economic adaptation of Punjabis in BC? What roles did the unions and the labour movement play with respect to minority groups like the Punjabis? How did the Punjabis navigate through socio-economic structures to achieve upward mobility in Canadian society? Since BC labour has been connected with the socio-economic adaptation of Punjabis, how have Punjabis been affected by the globalization-driven decline in resource-based industries? What role has socio-economic security played in the process of Punjabi immigrants becoming Canadian?

Canadian Multiculturalism

The process of immigrant group formation and adaptation is largely influenced by the manner in which the receiving country manages its ethnic diversity. Apart from its First Nations peoples, Canada has been – and continues to be – built on the migration and settlement of people from diverse cultural and religious backgrounds. While Canada has in recent decades defined itself as multicultural, based on the fact that it consists of citizens originating from over 170 countries and speaking over 100 languages,[82] it has not always celebrated cultural and ethnic diversity. At the beginning of the twentieth century, Canada was not receptive to welcoming certain ethnic groups and only permitted some visible minorities in order to fill its labour needs. In fact, the federal government imposed various discriminatory measures in immigration law, such as the head tax on the Chinese (1885–1923),[83] the continuous journey clause for East Indians (1908–47),[84] and the internment of the Japanese during the Second World War.[85] In addition, BC took away the right to vote from the Chinese in 1874, the Japanese in 1895, and the East Indians in 1908. Interestingly, no federal legislation disenfranchised these groups; however, because the federal voters list was made up from the provincial lists, federal disenfranchisement also took place.

Despite the challenges of living in a "receiving" country that was not receptive towards various visible minority groups, these immigrants fought for changes in the Canadian immigration and citizenship laws. In 1947 Asian immigrants were granted both the right to become Canadian citizens and the right to vote in BC. Soon after, the sponsorship of immediate family members – such as one's sibling or prospective spouse – was also permitted. For East Indians, there was a quota of fifty immigrants a year, and then a quota of three hundred until 1962.[86] Although the immigration and citizenship laws had improved for Asians, Canada was also following a policy of assimilation – the process through which minority groups are absorbed into the dominant group (also known as Anglo-conformity) – as a way to manage ethnic diversity. There existed immense pressure on visible minorities to give up their ethnic heritage in order to assimilate into Canada's dominant Anglo society. The predominant sentiment among many immigrants was that they had to adopt the Western lifestyle if they wished to be accepted as members of mainstream Canadian society. Assimilation, with the resulting disconnectedness from their heritage, was a great challenge for many immigrants, especially second-generation members of visible minority groups. Such immigrants often experienced confusion and anxiety in the face of having to reject or deny their background in order to "fit in" or to be accepted, even as they encountered racial and cultural discrimination.

Based on the growing recognition that immigrants need not or should not lose their cultural distinctiveness, assimilation had begun to lose popular appeal by the 1960s. Interestingly, it was at this time that the notion of integration – which held that ethnic barriers should be removed so that the dominant Anglo community and the minority groups could interact and thereby create a new integrated society – began to garner greater interest. In reality, however, integration amounted to conformity with the dominant Anglo culture. Moreover, while the Anglo community was the dominant group in Canada, the French community increasingly demanded that it be recognized as the dominant group in Quebec. Subsequently, in 1965 the Canadian Liberal government made English and French the two official languages of Canada, giving recognition to the British and the French as the two founding nations of Canada. In need of semi-skilled labour and professionals, Canada in 1967 widened its doors to the immigration of various non-European ethnic groups, including East Indian.[87] Afterwards, the federal Liberal government under Pierre Elliott Trudeau made a dramatic gesture to accommodate other communities. In 1971 it established the Multiculturalism Policy, within the context of official bilingualism, to promote a positive attitude towards ethnic diversity. While the government attempted to effect change through its Multiculturalism Policy, many visible ethnic minority groups still encountered a great deal of hostility, prejudice, and racial stereotyping. In theory, the policy was intended to provide Canada with the means to manage its ethnic diversity without pursuing full assimilation.[88] Paradoxically, on 25 June 1969, Trudeau had released a white paper on Indian policy that proposed to abolish the Indian Act in order to eliminate special status for Canada's Aboriginals and to advance instead a policy of cultural assimilation.[89]

Some have argued that the Trudeau's Liberal government instituted the policy of multiculturalism as a means of winning the ethnic vote. In response to the "first phase" of multiculturalism (from the early 1970s to the mid-1980s),[90] some critics maintained that the policy had been instituted to mobilize political support among ethnic organizations and to appeal for the ethnic vote, notwithstanding the argument that multiculturalism hindered the upward socio-economic mobility of ethnic minority groups.[91] In other words, fostering cultural preservation did not translate into equal opportunity.

The "second phase" of multiculturalism in Canada (from the mid-1980s to the early 1990s) involved explicit government initiatives focused on the issue of discrimination in federal institutions. In the interest of social equality, Canada adopted the Charter of Rights and Freedoms (1982), the Employment Equity Act (1986), and the Canadian Multiculturalism Act (1988). The Canadian Multiculturalism Act specifically was intended to achieve the goal of curtailing discrimination through (1) affirmative action and (2) institutional mainstreaming. These government initiatives were undertaken to ensure that ethnic minority groups would be integrated into the mainstream and to accomplish this by providing adequate representation for, and equal treatment of, such groups. Along with its interest in addressing discrimination, multiculturalism also came to be viewed as an opportunity to establish economic bridges in an increasingly globalizing world.

Notwithstanding the government's expectations for the policy of multi-culturalism, some people still viewed it merely as an appeal for the ethnic vote, a form of tokenism, and, more significantly, potentially divisive.[92] For instance, Reginald Bibby maintains that it is naive to assume that "fragments of the mosaic will somehow add up to a healthy and cohesive society … To encourage individual mosaic fragments may well result in the production of individual mosaic fragments and not much more."[93] Similarly, Neil Bissoon-dath, in his passionate but one-sided critique of multiculturalism, argues that the policy promotes a "government-sanctioned mentality" that is divisive, as it "encourages a feeling of ethnic pride and belonging in narrowed commun-ities" by asking "immigrants to conserve their past and make it their only identity."[94]

While government programs associated with multiculturalism have en-couraged cultural diversity and equal opportunity, the practice of multicul-turalism has continued to be critiqued, especially for encouraging ethnic insularity in its appeal for the ethnic vote, to the detriment of developing a Canadian national identity. In response to such criticism, the "third phase" of multiculturalism (1990s–2000s) has been oriented towards fostering a civic-oriented, inclusive society, one with a shared citizenship. For instance, Will Kymlicka argues that multiculturalism calls for the integration of ethnic groups into a common "societal culture," thus creating a national identity.[95] Meanwhile, Ian Angus argues that diversity does not require a rejection of universality or unity; rather, it should be viewed as a new hegemonic concep-tion of unity that is articulated through diversity.[96]

With the tremendous growth in culturally and religiously diverse popula-tions in the West over the last three to four decades, along with the terrorist attacks of 9/11 in New York City, concerns over immigration laws, the role of multiculturalism, and homeland security have intensified. The experi-ence of Quebec is instructive in this respect. In reaction to the perceived "reasonable accommodation" crisis in Quebec, the provincial government commissioned Gérard Bouchard and Charles Taylor to make recommenda-tions on the practice of the reasonable accommodation of different religious and cultural groups. The Bouchard-Taylor commission understood that the practice needed to be based on three major principles: (1) interculturalism (distinguished from English Canada's multiculturalism), which is oriented towards the reconciliation of ethno-cultural diversity with the preservation of the social link or continuity of the French-speaking core of Quebec cul-ture; (2) secularism, which is foundational to Quebec's model of liberal dem-ocracy; and (3) harmonization, which revolves around the legal redress of cultural and religious grievances of different immigrant groups, especially relating to the educational and health sectors of society.[97]

Whether one looks at Quebec or English Canada, serious consideration needs to be given today to ethno-cultural diversity in Canada's urban centres, because by 2017 one out of every five people in Canada is likely to be a member of a visible minority group. Indeed, in Vancouver the majority of the population may be from visible minority groups, which means that there would be a "visible minority majority."[98] At the present time, however, the adaptation process of immigrants and their children is more affected by whether they have settled in small remote towns or in large urban centres. People belonging to a visible minority group may have a different experience in small towns than they would have in large urban centres.[99]

In analysing the twice-migration of the Punjabi community in British Columbia, this study explores the policy and practices of multiculturalism as one set of determinant structures of Canadian society. In focusing on the different immigrant experiences with multiculturalism, depending on whether they take place in remote towns or in urban Canada, this study addresses the following questions: How has the Punjabi community's process of adaptation been influenced by Canada's policy of multiculturalism? What role has multiculturalism played in the progress or betterment of the Punjabi community? What is the difference in the multiculturalism experience between immigrants who settle in a remote area and those who settle in an urban one? Do Punjabis – whether living in remote towns or in large urban Canadian centres – have a sense of shared citizenship with other communities in Canada? How does location influence the manner in which Punjabis develop a sense of shared citizenship?

Aims of the Study

This study examines the patterns of social and cultural transformation of the Punjabi community, both in its initial settlement in the small towns of the Skeena region and after its relocation to the Lower Mainland. The forestry and fishery industries were the primary reason for Punjabi migration to the Skeena region, but the decline of BC's forestry and fishery industries forced the Punjabi community, in a sense, to readjust as an immigrant group through re-migration to an urban location. The study further investigates this process of twice-migration against the wider canvas of Canada's official policy of multiculturalism and its varying outcomes, depending on the location of the remote towns and urban centres settled by Punjabis. Accordingly, in the light of three key variables – Punjabi ethnicity, British Columbian labour, and Canadian multiculturalism – along with the critical intervening variable of geographic location, this study first looks at the initial or first migration of Punjabis, who, after leaving their homeland of Punjab (India), settled in the remote Skeena region of northwestern British Columbia (Canada). In doing so, it not only focuses on the migration process in a remote location in terms of labour, social structure, and political power, but it also examines the gender-specific immigrant experiences in small remote towns and the inter-cultural dynamics in these towns, especially in relation to the First Nations.

Second, this study analyses the impact of the decline in BC's forestry and fishery industries on the Punjabi immigrant community. The second migra-tion, or the relocation, of the Punjabi community – from Canadian remote towns to urban centres – sheds light on the external structural factors and the various internal ethno-cultural values that influence the survival of Punjabis and their community as they exist outside the Punjab. The study also delin-eates the contrasting experiences of the practice of multiculturalism in both the small remote towns and the large urban centres, and further advances our understanding of what it means to be Canadian.

The study evaluates the role of agency in the social and cultural transform-ation of the Punjabi community without losing sight of the implications of the structures of society for the adaptation of immigrants. In sum, the study (1) sheds light on the formation of the Punjabi community in the Skeena re-gion, (2) advances knowledge of the specific immigrant experience of Pun-jabi women, (3) examines the complex intercultural dynamics between the Punjabis and the First Nations, and (4) analyses the contrasting experiences with multiculturalism in rural and urban Canada. Indeed, the study seeks to enhance our understanding of the complexity of social and cultural adapta-tion in one of the largest immigrant communities in Western Canada, and to demonstrate how geographical location fundamentally shapes the experience of settlement and of integration into Canadian society.

I must enter a word of caution before I proceed to discuss these issues. No single study can cover all facets of the Punjabi community or include every voice in the community. This study nonetheless attempts to explore import-ant issues in the hope that its explorations at the very least take us forward to some tentative answers. The aim is to impart greater understanding of some of the major issues that one immigrant community, the Punjabis, confronts as it readjusts after its initial adaptation to remote Canadian towns and to the subsequent shift to large urban centres. In doing so, the study hopes to fur-ther our understanding of the workings of multiculturalism in Canada and how it relates to the cultivation of a spirit of shared citizenship.

Methodology

The research methodology for the study encompasses a qualitative analysis of empirical data consisting of three main components. First of all, given the nature of the research project, there is heavy reliance on interview data based on 105 semi-structured interviews. The second component consists of a longitudinal analysis based on archival data available through various labour and governmental organizations. Lastly, the third component relies on participant observation by the present author in several socio-religious and political centres and programs for Punjabis, Punjabi-Hindus, and Punjabi-Sikhs in the Skeena region and the Lower Mainland.

The first component mentioned above entailed listening to the human story "on the ground" through an analysis of semi-structured interviews designed to uncover the issues that members of the Punjabi community regard as most pertinent to their immigrant experience in remote towns and urban centres. The study therefore involved researching and collecting ethnographic data from different field sites. This approach is critical in any study of "social actors" in a rapidly changing world.[100] Ethnographic data was collected in the two main towns of northwestern BC (Prince Rupert and Terrace) and also from various locations in the Lower Mainland and the Fraser Valley.

The field research was conducted from 2006 to 2011, a period during which actual events were unfolding. For example, in the spring of 2006, interviews were conducted with Punjabi men working at the Terrace Lumber Company (the old Pohle Mill Lumber Company); however, by the spring of 2007 the mill had been completely dismantled, which resulted in the relocation of a number of Punjabis. As a consequence, some follow-up interviews were conducted in the Lower Mainland. The breakdown of interviews was determined by the location of the initial interview, although the official residing place has been used in a few cases where the participants intermittently moved between the Skeena region and a large urban centre.

The interview data are based on (1) twenty-eight interviews with Punjabis living in the major towns of the Skeena region and (2) twenty-eight interviews with Punjabis who have migrated from the above-mentioned towns to the Lower Mainland. The data have been gathered through face-to-face interviews using open-ended questions. Punjabi and English were used during the interviews, depending on the interviewee's capability or preference. The interviews conducted in Punjabi were translated into English, with particular care for nuance. In order to avoid awkward construction, in some places a loose translation is provided, not strictly following the literal pattern of Punjabi grammar.

The qualitative data for the study draw on the experience of the members of the Punjabi community who lived in the Skeena region during the heyday of the forestry and fishery industries, from the late 1960s to the mid-1980s. The breakdown of the 56 Punjabi participants in the interview process is, in terms of gender, 35 males and 21 females and, in terms of generation, 40 immigrants and 16 children of immigrants. Since the Punjabi community tends to be a closed community,[101] the participants were selected on a voluntary basis by using the "snowball" sampling method.[102] The participants were encouraged to share with the researcher their stories and experiences relating to the socio-cultural issues they encountered as immigrants or as children of immigrants in Canada. Special attention was given in the interviews to the areas of (1) migration processes and factors related to settlement, particularly employment and gender concerns; (2) social structure and political power, especially as they relate to the role of labour and multiculturalism; (3) religious and cultural life; and (4) inter- and intra-cultural relations.

Furthermore, three members of the Punjabi Skeena community were chosen to provide their stories in the form of in-depth ethnographic narratives in order to effectively make evident the complexities of the experiences of male and female Punjabi immigrants in adapting to the small towns of the Skeena region and of the experiences of the Canadian-born youth in the shift from remote towns to urban centres. The ethnographic narratives were based on extensive semi-structured interviews conducted with each of the three narrators. Although the narrators gave their stories in English, there was a tendency for the two Punjabi immigrant narrators to speak in Punjabi when sharing stories of a personal nature. While some grammatical changes have been made and some material has had to be translated from Punjabi to English, I have tried to keep true to the spirit of the narrators. Once the narratives were composed, they were read to the narrators as well as shared with at least one family member in order to assure reliability.

The qualitative data also draw on the experience of non-Punjabi members of the Skeena community, including ten interviews with members of the First Nations (two of the Haida Nation, four of the Nisga'a Nation, three of the Tsimshian Nation, and one of the Haisla Nation) and twelve interviews with non-Punjabi residents of the Skeena region (four Italian-Canadians, as well as one each from the Anglo-Canadian, Chinese-Canadian, French-Canadian, Hungarian-Canadian, Lebanese-Canadian, Parsee-Canadian, Polish-Canadian, and Yugoslavian-Canadian communities). The interviews with these individuals focused on (1) social structure and political power, especially as they relate to the role of multiculturalism, (2) intercultural relations, and (3) intercultural development in the Skeena region.

First Nations interviewees were recruited from the fishery labour force and Prince Rupert Friendship House. In cases where the interviewee – or a relative of the interviewee – had attended an Indian Residential School, the exact details of his or her experiences were not explored. Moreover, these interviewees were either aware of, or already connected with, Aboriginal social service programs in their area of residence. The analysis of the First Nations experience involved careful consideration of the historical and socio-political context of First Nations peoples in Canada. Once the project was completed, First Nations interviewees were invited to see how their voices were incorporated in the analysis.

Apart from these interviews, the qualitative data are also based on interviews with seven professionals in the fields of social work, education, and law enforcement; with five businesspeople; and with fifteen public figures in government and labour organizations. These interviews focused on (1) the evolution of the Punjabi community in the Skeena region or the Lower Mainland, (2) the relationship of various political and labour organizations with the Punjabi community, and (3) the impact of the decline in the forestry and fishery industries on both the Punjabi community and the larger community in general.

The second component focuses on a longitudinal analysis of archival information that serves as corroborative evidence and provides a broader context for the qualitative material. The various fish cannery, sawmill, and pulp and paper mill companies have not kept extensive records, as any change of ownership – a common occurrence – resulted in the loss or destruction of previous company histories and records. Therefore, the archival information was primarily gathered from various union offices (e.g., IWA, PPWC, UFAWU-CAW) located in the Skeena region as well as their central offices based in the Lower Mainland. The analysis of this archival information allowed for the delineation of trends relating to (1) the employment patterns according to gender, age, and ethnicity; (2) type of employment (seasonal, part-time, full-time); and (3) barriers to, and changes in, job mobility. Several local Skeena newspapers (*Prince Rupert Daily News, Terrace Standard, Northern Sentinel*) and Vancouver newspapers (*Sun, Province*), available in the regional and Vancouver public libraries, proved useful in substantiating the facts and the personal experiences narrated by the participants. Lastly, ethnic newspapers as well as personal archives were also examined.

The third component comprised participant observation by the author of the present study in several socio-religious and political centres and programs for the Punjabis, as well as observation of Punjabi involvement in mainstream events. This activity was particularly helpful in gathering data regarding the central role that religion and ethnicity have played in the collective experience and community formation of the Punjabis in the context of Canada's practice of multiculturalism.

It is important to note here that I have attempted to ensure that as far as possible the entire community was represented in the study; that is, I endeavoured to include Punjabi immigrants from different religious backgrounds (Hindu and Sikh) and who came to Canada at different times, encompassing the spectrum from the educated to the illiterate and from the semi-skilled labourer to the enterprising business person. When cited in this study, the interviewees are identified by a code in order to maintain confidentiality. They are labelled as P for Punjabi; their gender is marked by M for male and F for female; and each is given a number representing his or her generation and then a number specific to the individual. For instance, "PF 2.5" refers to a Punjabi female belonging to the second generation and listed as number 5. In the case of other interviewees, participants belonging to labour organizations are marked as "Organized Labour"; public figures in government are indicated as "Political"; people in managerial positions are indicated as "Business"; professionals in primary or secondary education are indicated as "Educators"; professionals in law enforcement or social work are indicated as "Social"; First Nations people are marked by the specific nation they belong to; and the members of other immigrant communities are identified by their hyphenated heritage Canadian group, which is then followed by the number given to the specific individual.

Organization of the Study

This study has ten chapters. This present one (chapter 1) has introduced the study by providing the theoretical and general background on the three key variables relevant to the research project: Punjabi ethnicity, British Columbian labour, and Canadian multiculturalism. The chapter has also set out the aims of the study and discussed the research methodology employed. Chapters 2 to 9 are based on intensive field research and seek to investigate the role of agency and structure in relation to the patterns of social and cultural transformation of the Punjabi community, both in the remote context of BC's Skeena region and in urban Canada, especially after its shift to the Lower Mainland.

Chapter 2 specifically focuses on the Punjabi male immigrant experience, especially in relation to the forestry industry in the Skeena region, and examines how – despite the existing barriers – members of the community increasingly moved into skilled labour jobs and business. The chapter then explores the economic and psychological impact that the decline of the forestry industry had on the Punjabi labourer, especially after the mid-1990s when a significant out-migration occurred. Chapter 3 comprises an analysis of the first journey, from a village in the Punjab to the small remote towns of British Columbia, and of the initial process of socio-economic survival and adaptation in the Skeena region during the 1960s and early 1970s. This is accompanied by the ethnographic narrative of a young, single Punjabi man, who arrived in the Skeena region in 1961 and lived in the Prince Rupert Sawmills bunkhouse. The analysis makes evident how the Punjabi cultural ethos fostered resiliency during socio-economic adaptation in Canada.

Chapter 4 focuses on the specific immigrant experience of Punjabi women, especially with respect to their active participation in the fishery industry. It examines the entry of Punjabi women into the Canadian labour force and the significant impact of this new life on their previous traditional social patterns of behaviour. The decline in the fisheries further underscores how, in fact, Punjabi women's entry into the workforce was about reaping not only economic, but also social and emotional benefits. Chapter 5 investigates how Punjabi women made the transition from staying at home and practising *pardah* (the custom of placing a scarf low over the forehead) to joining the Canadian workforce and engaging with the public. It is done through the ethnographic narrative of the journey of one Punjabi woman who, during the mid-1960s, after settling in Prince Rupert, became the first Punjabi immigrant woman to work in the Skeena fishery industry. The chapter demonstrates how the cultural value of respect (*izzat*) is a source of strength and resiliency even though its meaning has undergone transformation as a result of economic change.

Chapter 6 investigates the workplace-related discrimination that Punjabis experienced upon entering the Skeena multi-ethnic workforce, and shows how the labour unions played the role of an intercultural mediator. The chapter makes evident the prominent role of the labour unions as a voice for Punjabi immigrants in the 1970s and 1980s. That role began to diminish, however, in the 1990s and 2000s when the unions were struggling for their own relevancy in a more competitive globalized economy. The investigation reveals the unifying thread of labour in social interactions in the Skeena region and shows how the industrial decline affected everyone, though in different ways, depending on ethnicity.

Chapter 7 examines the intercultural dynamics encountered by Punjabis when they were in the midst of seeking and establishing a social, cultural, religious, and political space for themselves and the Punjabi community. The chapter explores the complex intercultural dynamics among the various immigrant communities and the First Nations in the Skeena region. It also discusses the difficulties that the Punjabis initially faced in attempting to connect with the broader Skeena community. Chapter 8 analyses the Punjabi community's relocation to large urban centres and looks at the contrasting experiences of Punjabis with multiculturalism in the Skeena region and the Lower Mainland, which involved a shift from cultural synergy to ethnic insularity. The chapter then explores how – unlike in the Skeena region – political parties in the Lower Mainland validate the "Punjabi bubble" as a means to win the ethnic vote.

Chapter 9 investigates the issue of ethnic identification as experienced by the children of Punjabi immigrants in their shift from small remote towns to large urban centres in Canada. The investigation is conducted through the ethnographic narrative of a Canadian-born Punjabi who, after growing up in the Skeena region, moved to Metro Toronto in the mid-1980s after the onset of the forestry industry's decline and then moved to the Lower Mainland to pursue post-secondary education. In the course of this investigation, critical issues emerge with respect to the experience of both inter- and intra-cultural dynamics in an urban location as well as with respect to the renegotiation of one's identity as a Canadian.

Chapter 10 provides the main conclusions of the study regarding the role of agency and structure in the transformation of the Punjabi community as it finds itself first settling in small remote towns in the Skeena region and then relocating to metropolitan or large urban centres. The chapter examines the role of agency by investigating Punjabi ethnicity and resilience, and studies the role of structure by looking at multiculturalism. The study ends by looking at what Canadians can learn about themselves by becoming familiar with the Punjabi community's experience with multiculturalism as practised in BC's remote towns and urban centres, and by reflecting on what it means to be Canadian in an increasingly globalizing world in the twenty-first century.

CHAPTER 2

Men, Labour, and Family Economics in the Skeena Region

Canada has been largely built on the immigration and settlement of people from diverse backgrounds, many of them seeking greater economic opportunity. Following this pattern, the Punjabi pioneers of the early decades of the twentieth century migrated to British Columbia, as the country was in need of manual labour in its natural resource industries and Canada had become known in India as an attractive place for making money. Certainly, Canada's colonial ties with the British Empire also played a role in the initial migration of people from South Asia, especially from the Indian state of Punjab. The majority of Punjabi immigrants were young single men who sought work in order to earn money,[1] which they sent back to their families in the Punjab. Many of them initially had the intention of eventually returning and reuniting with their families in the Punjab. With limited English-language and occupational skills, the Punjabis found jobs in logging camps and sawmills, in railway construction, on cattle farms, and in fruit orchards.[2] The work available to Punjabis was primarily the kind of manual labour that non-immigrants in the sawmills in BC's Lower Mainland or on Vancouver Island would not want.

The sawmills in the Lower Mainland (e.g., Alberta Lumber Company on False Creek and Fraser Mills in Burquitlam) and on Vancouver Island (e.g., Hillcrest Lumber Company near Duncan and Mayo Company Mill in Paldi) had been popular places for Punjabis to find employment. However, by the 1950s, many of these sawmills had reached a saturation point or were in decline because of changes in BC's forestry industry.[3] Post-1947 Punjabi immigrants were therefore forced to move to more isolated areas in the northern interior of the province to find work. Moreover, in 1958 a Punjabi lumber industrialist established Prince Rupert Sawmills Ltd, which served as a major catalyst for the initial wave of Punjabi migration to Prince Rupert and to the Skeena region of northwestern BC in general.

During the late 1960s and early 1970s, Punjabi settlement in the Skeena region saw steady growth as a result of the thriving forestry and fishery industries there. The prosperous – albeit unsteady – period for the resource industries in the 1970s and early 1980s coincided with the gradual consolidation of the Punjabi community in the Skeena region. However, the increasing mechanization and globalization-driven decline in job opportunities in the forestry industry, beginning in the mid-1990s, had an adverse impact on Punjabi migrant labourers and the Punjabi community in general. Along with the economic and emotional distress associated with employment uncertainty and loss, the decline in the forestry industry (1990s) and the eventual lumber bust (2000–03) forced many Punjabis to leave the Skeena region and resettle in large urban centres. In fact, the decline in the forestry industry has been a major factor in the out-migration of Punjabis from small, remote BC towns to large urban centres.

The focus of this chapter is twofold. First, it investigates the process of initial Punjabi settlement in the Skeena region, where the Punjabis took manual or semi-skilled labour jobs in the forestry industry, although some members of the community increasingly engaged in skilled labour and business activity from the 1970s onwards. Second, it analyses the economic, but also the psychosocial, impact that the decline of the lumber and pulp and paper mills, beginning in the mid-1990s, had on Punjabi labour, especially when the pulp and paper mill on Watson Island officially shut down in 2003.

The chapter has three parts. The first provides a critical historical look at the Punjabi community's intimate relationship with the forestry industry and examines the settlement pattern of single male Punjabis, who, from the early 1900s until Sohen Gill, a Punjabi, established Prince Rupert Sawmills in 1958, were usually engaged in manual labour. The second part analyses the initial migration and settlement of Punjabis in the Skeena region in the early 1960s, drawn by the Punjabi-owned sawmill, and then the broadening of the Punjabi employment niche into skilled labour jobs and business, especially from the 1970s onwards. The third part examines the impact that the decline of the forestry industry (mid-1990s to 2006) has had on the Punjabi community. In sum, the chapter makes evident the challenges faced by Punjabis in their initial socio-economic adaptation to remote towns in the Skeena region, their psychological and financial stress stemming from job loss, and their having to engage in the forced process of re-establishing themselves. In effect, the chapter demonstrates that while Punjabi male immigrants have been intimately linked with sawmill labour in British Columbia, they have been able to progress to skilled jobs and business. And, despite the occupational barriers, Punjabi men have even been successful in re-establishing themselves in their new homeland after the resource industries declined in the region.

Punjabi Labour and the Sawmills

During the first half of the twentieth century, most work that was available to Punjabis was in the forestry industry. In effect, the Punjabi male immigrant living in British Columbia became equated with manual sawmill labour. This long-standing association persisted into the 1960s. In turn, Punjabi settlement patterns reflected the changes in BC's forestry industry, important among them being the arrival of Punjabis in the Skeena region.

Lumber, Labour, and the Punjabi Male

The initial wave of Punjabi immigrants in the early 1900s comprised young men who were considered to be transients, since they came to Canada at a time when Canadian immigration law did not allow them to bring their families.[5] Since they had come to Canada to work, they took on the only jobs available to them – that is, those jobs that others did not want. The Punjabi immigrant's priority was to make as much money as quickly as possible. Earning higher wages was more important than finding more long-term or secure employment.[6] The Punjabis readily did seasonal outdoor work because it paid slightly more than indoor work. Contractors hired Punjabis to clear building lots, work on the roads, and be part of railway gangs; farmers hired them as fruit pickers and field hands.[7]

The Punjabis were quick to discover that sawmills and shingle mills offered slightly better pay for yard work (the stacking and loading of lumber or shingles). In fact, early in the twentieth century, when many Chinese and Japanese men were working in sawmills, lumber labour had become associated with ethnicity.[8] Industrialists faced a significant shortage of Anglo-Canadian workers as a result of the latter's disinterest in hard labour: "Prejudice, as well as wage rates, discouraged whites from taking laboring jobs in the mills."[9] Lumber work became the main type of employment for Punjabis during the period of rapid growth in the forestry industry, from 1903 to 1913.[10] By 1907, the majority of Punjabis were pulling, packing, and loading lumber in sawmills. By 1908, more Punjabis than ever before were employed in sawmills throughout the Vancouver area.[11]

Soon after their arrival in Canada, some Punjabis, in order to survive, turned to "collective entrepreneurship" by assuming leases of farms and sawmills through partnerships or co-operative ventures.[12] Having acquired shares in a sawmill, the Punjabi mill workers banded together to assume its lease. A Punjabi man whose father arrived in Canada in 1907 made the following comment: "My father arrived in Vancouver in 1907. Sawmills was the only real industry for Punjabis to get a job. There was some farm work, but not too much. My father had a share in a sawmill at Ladysmith [on Vancouver Island]. Several Punjabi men would band together and invest in a sawmill. This was common."[13] The forestry industry was fragmented and decentralized. There were many short-lived, small-scale operations that ran as long as timber was available in the vicinity of the sawmill. Since labour was the main expense in running a sawmill, mill workers would take over sawmill operations in order to minimize the risk of losing their own income. Moreover, taking shares in a group enterprise allowed Punjabis to build assets, especially through the acquisition of real estate.[14]

Being able to assume managerial roles in Punjabi-operated mills provided some relief from the loss of labour jobs during recessions.[15] In the recession of 1913–15, a group of about thirty Punjabis lost their jobs at Fernbridge Lumber, a mill that supplied lumber and shingles to the Rosedale area, a rural community about ninety kilometres east of Vancouver. This group leased a forty-acre farm in the Chilliwack area for potato farming. Despite the failure of the potato venture, these Punjabis banded together and took over the lease of the Cheam Lumber Company at Rosedale, just thirteen kilometres from Chilliwack.[16] Among this group were Kapoor Singh,[17] Mayo Singh,[18] and Doman Singh,[19] three successful Punjabi lumber industrialists.

The group ran the sawmill at a profit for three years until all of the timber had been cut on their leased land. Then, it leased another sawmill, the Markham Lumber Company, at Strawberry Hill in present-day Surrey.[20] In 1916 Mayo and Kapoor, along with three other investors, put $4,000 into the Mayo Lumber Company for timber extraction and lumber production "at places to be selected."[21] By 1917, these investors had expanded the number of shareholders to thirty-five Punjabi immigrants from their respective villages. This expansion allowed the group to purchase a timber tract in the Lake Cowichan area of Vancouver Island, where they built the Mayo Lumber Company mill and eventually established the Paldi mill colony.[22]

In the later stages of the First World War and in the early 1920s, many Punjabis found themselves jobless, and as a result, half of the Punjabi population returned to India.[23] The Punjabis increasingly worked in remote areas at either logging camps or in sawmills on Vancouver Island.[24] During the Great Depression of the 1930s, many sawmills once again shut down. Unemployment rose, forcing another out-migration of many Punjabis. With this exodus, the Punjabi employment niche shrank substantially.[25] Some Punjabis nonetheless continued to work in a few sawmills, especially those owned and operated by Punjabis. By the early 1930s, Mayo Singh and Kapoor Singh were major stakeholders in their sawmill operations on Vancouver Island. However, in 1934–35, these two Punjabi industrialists reached a parting of the ways; while Mayo maintained the Mayo Lumber Company, Kapoor Singh and his partners took over the Pacific Lumber Company (Kapoor Lumber Company) on Sooke Lake outside of Victoria.[26] As a Punjabi pioneer states:

> During the Depression, they [Anglo-Canadians] did not want to give
> us jobs. They [Canadian White Pine] had an advertisement where they
> wanted contractors to haul sawdust for them. However, when we went
> to the office, they told us, "We're sorry that we can't hire you because
> people will think it is an East Indian company." And this of course was
> very hard, menial work, and yet we couldn't even get that.
>   We mainly got our jobs in sawmills run by Punjabis ... My first job
> was working on the green chain at Kapoor Singh's sawmill at Sooke
> Lake [1939], but then it ran out of timber [1940]. I managed to work at
> the planar mill a couple of months. Kapoor Singh then gave me a job
> at his newly established Barnet Mills in Burnaby. I worked there for
> four years.[27]

The Punjabis not only found work more readily in Punjabi-operated saw-mills, but they were also more likely to engage in labour that required specialized skill and paid slightly higher wages. For instance, archival information from one of the largest sawmills on Vancouver Island, situated outside Port Alberni – Great Central (Lake) Sawmills (1932–42) – shows that the number of "East Indians" (Punjabis) in the total workforce was 32 (31.3%) in July 1932; 49 (32.7%) in April 1936;[28] 31 (26.9%) in June 1940; and 36 (33.6%) in April 1942.[29] The Punjabi workforce was highly concentrated at Great Central (Lake) Sawmills, where they worked either in the sawmill or out in the yard. Not a single Punjabi worked in the kilns, sheds, the planar mill, or in power and maintenance.[30] Indeed, Punjabis at the Anglo-operated Great Central (Lake) Sawmills did not engage in skilled labour or trades at all during the 1930s and 1940s.

Following the post-Depression trend in BC's forestry industry in general, the Punjabi-operated sawmills peaked in the 1940s and 1950s. Kapoor Singh and Mayo Singh were successful Punjabi lumber industrialists, but their sawmill operations declined in the late 1950s as the industry became more concentrated and automated and the workers increasingly unionized.[31] Notwithstanding that decline, the success of these industrialists reflected Punjabi entrepreneurship in an environment where skilled and managerial positions were given primarily to Anglo-Canadians. Other Punjabis followed the example of these entrepreneurs, including Sohen Singh Gill, who, in line with the changing trends in the forestry industry during the 1950s, established a sawmill in Prince Rupert, a remote town in the Skeena region of northwestern BC.

Sohen Singh Gill: A Punjabi Lumber Industrialist

Sohen Singh Gill (1911–1971) was born in the Punjab and arrived in Canada in 1931 at the age of twenty-one. He had no formal education and became a naturalized Canadian citizen in 1947.[32] Sohen Gill began work at a wood-fuel company called Dryland Fuels, which was owned and operated by the Johl family.[33] The company's business centred on hauling wood pieces away from the sawmills and then selling them door-to-door for firewood. Prior to the coming of mechanical trucks, some Punjabis transported dry wood and wood by-products by horse and buggy. One Punjabi pioneer commented: "Punjabis got into the trucking business in the 1930s to transport fuel. In those days, fuel was wood or coal for heating. My father had a truck. It was a horse and buggy, selling wood and wood fuels. The Johl family had a big trucking company with quite a few trucks. It was called Dryland Fuels."[34] By the 1920s and 1930s, a number of Punjabis had bought trucks with which they transported unwanted wood pieces or chips.[35] The wood-fuel trucking business was a small – and modest – business available to Punjabis. Some sawmills, like the Cedar Cove Sawmill on False Creek, gave contracts to Punjabi wood-fuel trucking companies even though they had never hired Punjabis to work at their mills.

After a period of about one and a half years, Sohen Gill decided to quit working for Dryland Fuels and start his own family business. He and his brother purchased a truck and began their fuel trucking business under the firm name of Sohen Brothers Co. From 1931 to 1940, the company gradually acquired more contracts, with sawmills in New Westminster and Vancouver. With the onset of the Second World War – when wood fuel was in greater demand and also very expensive – Sohen Brothers Co. increased its operation by adding a fleet of trucks to the business. The company was profitable and was regarded as the largest dry wood–fuel company in Vancouver.[36]

Later, Sohen Gill ventured into the forestry industry; he purchased property on Manitoba Street in South Vancouver (1945), where he built a sawmill called Yukon Lumber Co.[37] The sawmill began its operations in 1946. Following his success with Yukon Lumber Co., Sohen Gill decided to pursue only the sawmill business; meanwhile, his brother took control over the fuel trucking company. Sohen Gill established two more sawmills in British Columbia, building a second sawmill – Pine Lake Lumber (1954) – in BC's interior at

Spuzzum and a third – Prince Rupert Sawmills (1958) – in Prince Rupert. Given the absence of Punjabis in the Skeena region at that time and the limited transportation to and from the area, it was quite a remarkable venture for Sohen Gill to have built a sawmill in the remote town of Prince Rupert and to have acquired timber throughout northwestern BC. As mentioned by the former general manager of Yukon Lumber Co., it was Sohen Gill who began logging in the Northwest: "Sohen Gill's lumber industry in the 1950s and early 1960s had thirteen logging camps in northern British Columbia up to Prince Rupert and the Skeena River. Sohen Singh's forestry empire was the first to open northern BC for Canadians to work in the field."[38]

Upon seeing a report on the forestry potential of northwestern BC,[39] Sohen Gill, though based in Vancouver, acquired a timber quota for logging in the area. His Yukon Lumber Co. became interested in Prince Rupert as a location for a sawmill, since according to the provincial forestry regulations at that time, timber had to be processed in the area where it was logged so that the region would derive some economic benefit. Sohen Gill subsequently formed Prince Rupert Sawmills Ltd on 6 February 1958[40] and leased ten acres of Prince Rupert's "Old Dry Dock" site and surrounding area.[41]

Prince Rupert's "Old Dry Dock"

Prince Rupert's Old Dry Dock dates as far back as the establishment of the town itself. The general manager of the Grand Trunk Pacific Railway (GTPR) – Charles Mayville Hays – founded Prince Rupert. The town is situated on the northwestern shore of Kaien Island, which is north of the mouth of the Skeena River, 42 kilometres south of the Alaskan border, and 770 kilometres north of Vancouver (1,502 kilometres road distance).[42] Hays had "grand plans" to develop Prince Rupert as the major seaport on the west coast, selecting the town as the western terminus for the railway in 1905. Prince Rupert was incorporated on 10 March 1910,[43] the same year the GTPR began building the Dry Dock to function as a shipyard and floating dock. It is plausible that Hays had the necessary resources to develop Prince Rupert into a world-class port city and a rival to Vancouver's seaport.[44] Unfortunately, his plans evaporated when he tragically died on the Royal Mail Steamer *Titanic* on 15 April 1912. Despite Charles Hays's death, the GTPR completed the Dry Dock.[45]

In 1918 the Dry Dock received an order to build five steel ships for the Canadian government.[46] After the First World War, the Dry Dock remained idle until the outbreak of the Second World War. Throughout the Second World War, the shipyard was regarded as the largest in British Columbia, and it reached its peak in the years 1943–45.[47] Not only was the dock needed for constructing ships, but Prince Rupert was regarded as a strategic location

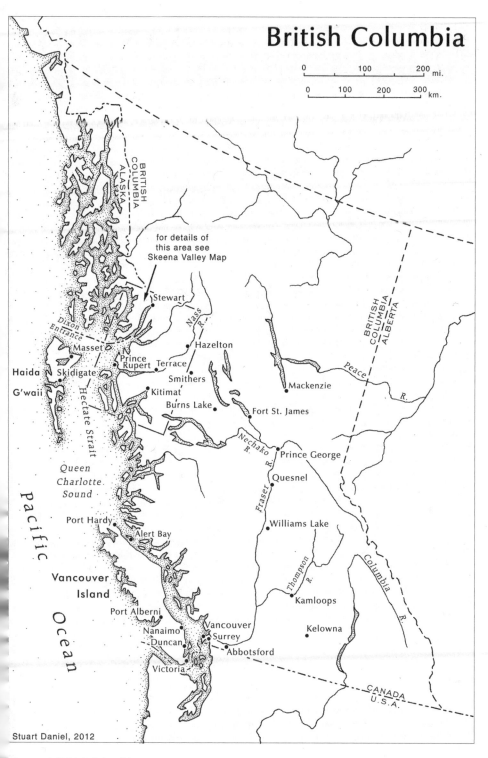

British Columbia

0   100   200 mi.

0   100   200   300 km.

ALASKA

BRITISH COLUMBIA

for details of
this area see
Skeena Valley Map

Stewart

BRITISH COLUMBIA
ALBERTA

Nass R.

Dixon Entrance

Hazelton

Masset

Prince Rupert

Terrace

Peace

Haida

Skidigate

Smithers

R.

G'waii

Kitimat

Mackenzie

Hectate Strait

Burns Lake

Fort St. James

Nechako R.

Prince George

Queen Charlotte Sound

Fraser R.

Quesnel

Pacific

Port Hardy

Williams Lake

Alert Bay

Columbia R.

Thompson R.

Vancouver Island

Kamloops

Ocean

Port Alberni

Nanaimo

Vancouver

Kelowna

Duncan

Surrey

Abbotsford

Victoria

CANADA
U.S.A.

Stuart Daniel, 2012

Map 2.1 | British Columbia

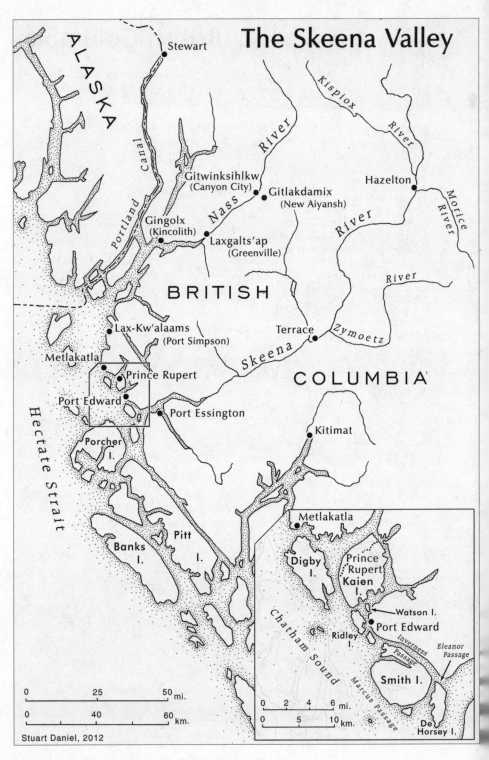

The Skeena Valley

ALASKA

Stewart

Kispiox River

Hazelton

Gitwinksihlkw
(Canyon City)

Gitlakdamix
(New Aiyansh)

Morice River

Portland Canal

Nass River

Gingolx
(Kincolith)

Laxgalts'ap
(Greenville)

River

BRITISH

River

Lax-Kw'alaams
(Port Simpson)

Terrace

Zymoetz

Skeena

Metlakatla

COLUMBIA

Prince Rupert

Port Edward

Port Essington

Kitimat

Porcher I.

Hectate Strait

Banks I.

Pitt I.

Metlakatla

Digby I.

Prince Rupert
Kaien I.

Watson I.

Port Edward

Chatham Sound

Ridley I.

Inverness Passage

Eleanor Passage

Smith I.

Marcus Passage

De Horsey I.

| 0 | 25 | 50 mi. |
| 0 | 40 | 60 km. |

| 0 | 2 | 4 | 6 mi. |
| 0 | 5 | 10 km. |

Stuart Daniel, 2012

Map 2.2 | The Skeena Valley

for a military naval base, given the "perceived threat" from Japan during the war. After the Japanese attacked Pearl Harbor on 7 December 1941, the United States used Prince Rupert as a major staging area for troops being dispatched to Alaska in the spring of 1942. The US Army also built a road along the Skeena River connecting Prince Rupert and Terrace.[48] After the Second World War, the dock once again became idle. By 1947, the facility was non-operational, and in 1955 the floating Dry Dock was sold to a business in Seattle.[49] For many Prince Rupert residents, this put an end to their hope of their town ever becoming a major Canadian seaport. After the sale of the Dry Dock, the area began to be referred to as the "Old Dry Dock."

With the end of military activity in the area, Prince Rupert returned to its main business – the fisheries. Indeed, Prince Rupert was regarded as the halibut capital of the world until the early 1980s.[50] But there was also forestry. Columbia Cellulose, a Canadian subsidiary of the Celanese Corporation of America, was formed in 1946, and then, in May 1948, as part of federal and BC government initiatives to tap into the resources of BC's Northwest during the post–Second World War era, Columbia Cellulose was granted a No. 1 Tree Farm Licence for 825,000 acres of productive forest in the Skeena region.[51] It was the first Tree Farm Licence that the provincial government issued for the large automated pulp and paper mills. Even though promises had been made about establishing a pulp and paper mill in Prince Rupert as early as 1920,[52] it was not until 1952 that Columbia Cellulose finally built the pulp and paper mill on Watson Island (another site earlier used by the US military), which is located 14.2 kilometres outside of Prince Rupert and 750 metres from Port Edward. The pulp and paper mill emerged as the economic heart of the Prince Rupert area.[53] The City of Prince Rupert ambitiously wanted to expand its forestry industry so that it would equal its fishery industry.[54] A local alderman, T. Norton Youngs, compiled an inventory of the forest resources available in the Prince Rupert area in order to encourage investment in the industry.

The Building of Prince Rupert Sawmills

Prince Rupert had been economically depressed since the end of the Second World War, and it thus favoured any economic development that would benefit its citizens, especially since the dream of Prince Rupert becoming a major seaport had not materialized.[55] Building a sawmill at the Old Dry Dock would allow Sohen Gill to take advantage of his timber quota,[56] and the city was supportive of his business venture: "[T]he building of a 'modern' mill would be an important development for the industrialization of Prince Rupert even as it would bring jobs to Prince Rupert residents."[57]

Freighter docked at Prince Rupert Sawmills (1962). Courtesy of the Prince Rupert City & Regional Archives and Museum of Northern BC, Wrathall Collection, WP997-38-12787.

Sohen Gill built his sawmill on Prince Rupert's Old Dry Dock and the surrounding area at Cow Bay. The location of the sawmill was very practical, since the lumber could be conveniently loaded onto freighters at the former shipyard dock for export. Indeed, this was a logistical asset, especially since most of the processed timber and raw logs were shipped to Japan. Moreover, building the sawmill beside moving water was preferred, as it facilitated receiving the logs. A Punjabi man who worked at Prince Rupert Sawmills in the early 1960s commented: "At first [at Prince Rupert Sawmills], I worked as the 'Jack Ladder'; there were two to three switches for manoeuvring the lumber from the water. In those days the logs travelled by water from the bush. The log would be brought in from the water on a moving stretcher and brought into the mill."[58]

In 1958, soon after the terms of the lease were finalized, the company started building the sawmill, at a cost of around $400,000.[59] In the fall of 1960, Prince Rupert Sawmills began its operation; it expanded the sawmill by installing a barker and a chipper to produce wood chips that could be sold to pulp mills.[60] This medium-size sawmill began as a one-shift operation in 1960[61] and became a two-shift operation in 1961.[62] Prince Rupert Sawmills had several sources for its timber, the main source being the company's thirteen logging camps.[63] Sohen Gill had a forester, Barney Johnson, who expanded Sohen Gill's timber stock by purchasing from local logging operators.[64] With the decreasing availability of the high-grade Douglas firs that were logged on

Vancouver Island and the Lower Mainland, lower-grade species like cedar and hemlock began being logged on the north coast. Although some Sitka spruce trees were logged, hemlock and balsam were predominantly used for timber. Sitka spruce logs or large raw pieces of Sitka spruce wood were shipped, while hemlock and balsam timber was processed at Prince Rupert sawmills.[65]

Along with processing lumber, the company arranged in 1962–63 to sell wood chips to the Columbia Cellulose pulp and paper mill on Watson Island. Columbia Cellulose remodelled its mill by adding a Kraft pulp mill for greater pulp production. As a consequence, the company was in greater need of raw material (wood chips) for the mill to process.[66] The shortage of raw material was a common problem faced by many firms as a consequence of the increased consolidation of pulp and paper mill companies in British Columbia.[67]

The Skeena: A New Destination for Punjabis

As centres of the forest industry, the Lower Mainland and Vancouver Island had been places for Punjabis to find employment, especially around False Creek in Vancouver or in the Lake Cowichan district on Vancouver Island. By the 1950s, however, with the decline in the logging of Douglas fir on BC's central coast, many of these sawmills had reached a saturation point with respect to labour or had simply shut down.[68] After 1950, when logging shifted to lower-grade species in the central interior and the sawmill industry was modernized,[69] post-1947 Punjabi immigrants in BC were forced to move outward to more remote areas in order to find work. Thus, the migration trend among Punjabis shifted towards the temporary logging camp settlements or sawmills in BC's central interior (like Quesnel and Williams Lake) and northern interior (like Prince George and Mackenzie). One Punjabi man remembered how he had had to go to the northern interior to find work: "I came in 1967 when I was thirty-three years old. I left in India my wife and three kids. My orientation was that I had to make money to bring my family over. My sister sponsored me. I first went to Vancouver and stayed with her family. There was work available in Mackenzie, so I went there. Mackenzie was not far [for me], I came all the way from the Punjab. I was open to do any type of work where I could make money."[70]

Even when newer immigrants arrived in established Punjabi communities – the communities where the relatives who had sponsored them lived – they still had to leave to find work. Punjabis settled wherever they found employment, even if it was in a remote town on Vancouver Island or, more significantly, in BC's northern interior and coast, especially if there was a Punjabi-owned sawmill. It was inevitable, then, that with Prince Rupert Sawmills being owned and operated by Punjabis, there would begin a gradual, yet steady, migration of Punjabis to the Skeena region.

Employment at Prince Rupert Sawmills

The migration of Punjabis to Prince Rupert began in 1960 – specifically, when Prince Rupert Sawmills Ltd started its operations. During this time, the Punjabi community in the Lower Mainland was relatively small and tight-knit. When Punjabis were searching for work in Vancouver, members of the community would contact Sohen Gill, who resided there, or the management of Sohen Gill's Yukon Lumber Co. with the expectation that they, along with their relatives, might be hired at his Vancouver sawmill. The former general manager of Yukon Lumber Co. recalled hiring Punjabis in the early 1960s: "I hired people because they would be relatives of people in the community. In 1950, there must have been about 1,500 East Indians. We all knew each other. So, one would say, 'Can you give my relative a job?' I would inform them that there was no work for them in Vancouver. However, if they were willing to go work up north to a [remote] town called Prince Rupert, I could employ them. We sent them up to Prince Rupert. They were willing to go because they were in need of a job."[71]

Indeed, Prince Rupert Sawmills made the Skeena region – especially Prince Rupert – the new destination for Punjabis seeking employment. A Punjabi man who arrived to Canada in 1961 explained how he found himself settling in Prince Rupert when he heard there were sawmill jobs there: "Upon arrival on 8 February 1961 I joined my brother in North Vancouver for two to three months. He was working at L&K Sawmill. There were no jobs. A few of my brother's friends were working in Prince Rupert Sawmills. There were no jobs in the Vancouver Lower Mainland in the 1960s, so everyone began to move to other areas ... We had to save money. We had to survive and get established."[72] Punjabi settlement patterns came to reflect the availability of work at the various sawmills throughout British Columbia, and the establishment of a Punjabi-owned sawmill served as a catalyst to draw members of a relatively small immigrant community from the Lower Mainland to northwestern BC.

As in the early twentieth century, most of the Punjabi migrants of the early 1960s arrived as "single" men with the single-minded goal of finding work in order to adapt economically. They came primarily from farming families[73] and more often than not had received a minimal amount of formal education, if any, prior to leaving the Punjab. A Punjabi man who arrived in Canada in 1964 described his background thus: "My father and brother were illiterate like myself; all they knew was how to pull lumber. I attended school, but I could not understand anything because I did not know English ... And that was the end of my studies and the beginning of my career as a lumber worker! My job at the mill was to clean up and to pull lumber from the green chain. We worked from 7 a.m. to 3:30 p.m., and made between $1.25 to $2.25 an hour."[74] Most arrived with limited occupational and language skills, thereby making sawmill labour the predominant type of work available to them.

Very few immigrants with secondary or post-secondary education arrived in British Columbia from the Punjab in the early 1960s. However, there were a few immigrants who were better equipped, at the very least with language skills.[75] Upon arrival, these immigrants engaged in manual labour until they found a job that required literacy skills. A Punjabi man with post-secondary education described the challenge in finding more suitable employment: "I went to Prince Rupert in November 1963 and lived with my distant cousin and her husband. They were living in the Prince Rupert town while he was working in the Prince Rupert Sawmills ... I worked at the sawmill for three months. I mainly did clean-up work but several times pulled lumber on the green chain. I then applied for a post office job ... I eventually became the first turbaned postman in Canada."[76]

Increasingly in the late 1960s and 1970s, better-qualified Punjabi immigrants began to come to Canada. However, those with formal education were not always proficient in English.[77] The lack of English conversational skills was initially a major barrier experienced by many educated Punjabis. Essentially, Prince Rupert Sawmills provided Punjabis with limited literacy and/or language skills the opportunity to adjust economically to British Columbia.

While Prince Rupert Sawmills was a productive operation, it was costly. The sawmill and necessary logging camps became too expensive to maintain. And, according to the general manager of Yukon Lumber Co, "Sohen Singh was very enterprising. But he spread himself a little too thin and had to start selling off his sawmills. Building the house no doubt took away some capital from expanding the business."[78] Soon after building Prince Rupert Sawmills, Sohen Gill bought a new home in the exclusive neighbourhood of Shaughnessy in Vancouver. His ambition to "move up" was a source of some financial burden. As a consequence, Sohen Gill sold Prince Rupert Sawmills in 1966 to Columbia Cellulose, which registered the company as Prince Rupert Forest Products.[79]

Working in the Skeena Region

The founding of Prince Rupert Sawmills Ltd coincided with the tail end of the period when logging peaked in the northern interior region (1946–64).[80]

By the spring of 1964, production at Prince Rupert Sawmills was in decline as a result of limited availability of timber and the consequent reduction of operations to a single shift.[81] Those who lost their jobs began moving eastward towards Terrace, looking for sawmill work. At that time, there were two major sawmills in Terrace – the Skeena and the Pohle sawmills[82] – along with some smaller operations in the area, including Dumont and Sande.[83] The flow of migration to Terrace began in the early 1960s after the slowdown at Prince Rupert Sawmills. A former employee explained: "The Prince Rupert mill shut down one shift. So, I had no job. I moved to Terrace and found a job with Skeena Forests. For one year I worked on the tail saw (lower position to sawyer; feeds log into the saw). After that, I worked as the head sawyer for eight or nine years. When I arrived, there were not many Punjabis in Terrace, about four families. There was no bunkhouse in Terrace. Skeena Forests took Dumont; Pohle took Sande; and then there were smaller operations like LHK, Weber Sawmill and Bell Pole Mill."[84] As soon as Prince Rupert Sawmills revived its second shift in the winter of 1964, most Punjabis returned to Prince Rupert.[85] However, several of the Punjabi men decided to settle in Terrace, since they had found steady work in one of the town's sawmills.[86]

Soon after Columbia Cellulose took over Prince Rupert Sawmills in 1966 (as Prince Rupert Forest Products), the dock was declared unsafe by a Workmen's Compensation Board (WCB) inspector based in Terrace (September 1968). As a result, the loading operations at the dock were cancelled.[87] Despite the unusable dock, the mill's products were used at the Columbia Cellulose pulp and paper mill on Watson Island. The sawmill in Prince Rupert experienced another setback between 1968 and 1969 when it temporarily closed. This closure forced a small out-migration of Punjabi workers, who either settled in Terrace or returned to the Lower Mainland in the hope of eventually finding permanent work. A former charge-hand at Prince Rupert Sawmills described the rehiring of Punjabi men to work at the Vancouver sawmill: "I worked there [Prince Rupert Sawmills] until Sohen sold it to Columbia Cellulose in 1966. He sold it when he made good money at that time ... Columbia Cellulose Pulp and Paper Company could not make it function so well and then [eventually] sold it to Norman Manning who ran it for a few years. They [Columbia Cellulose] sold it after I had left but I remember hiring men from Prince Rupert Sawmills to work for Sohen's Yukon Lumber Company in Vancouver in the late 1960s."[88]

Those who shifted to Terrace found similar work at one of the several sawmills in the town. Another Punjabi man described his experience looking for work while Prince Rupert Sawmills was shut down in 1970: "In 1970, the mill [Prince Rupert Sawmills] shut down. I went to Mackenzie and worked in a sawmill for one year pulling lumber in the planer and dry chain. In 1971,

The Terrace Pohle mill workforce (1969). Courtesy of the Heritage Park Museum and the *Terrace Standard*.

I went to Terrace to work in the Pohle sawmill. I worked indoor at the tail saw. There were about twenty Punjabis who worked in the mill."[89] Although some of the migration to Terrace had occurred as a result of reduced operations at Prince Rupert Sawmills in 1964 and temporary closures in 1968 and 1970, other Punjabis began to migrate to Terrace in the mid-1960s and early 1970s from the logging or lumber camps in BC's northern region, such as the District of Mackenzie. The work patterns reflected the unsteady nature of the lumber industry: "I worked there [in Mackenzie] for two and half years in a lumber camp. I saved my money ... Most of the Punjabis came from farming families and were illiterate ... There was another mill with the same company at Fort Nelson. We worked there for two months before I moved to Terrace [and started working] at the Pohle mill (1972). I knew some people in Mackenzie who had worked at Prince Rupert Sawmills. They shifted to Terrace and they helped me get the job."[90]

Punjabi men travelled throughout BC's central and northern interior in search of steady employment. In the 1970s, some of the men would spend periods of time working at sawmills in a variety of locations in BC's interior, like Quesnel and Williams Lake, before settling down with a permanent job: "I migrated to Canada in 1972, thirty-five years ago ... I first arrived at Vancouver Island [Victoria]. I then found work in Williams Lake. I lived there for a year and then left to find a better job. I did not like the atmosphere in Williams Lake ... I tried working in Prince George, and ended up in Terrace [working at the Pohle mill] in 1974. Terrace was a better place for my wife and children."[91]

It was a common pattern for Punjabi men to move from one place to another over a period of several years prior to settling in Terrace after they had found permanent work there. Another Punjabi man described seeking steady work: "I came to Paldi in 1972. I applied for immigration from Nanaimo. I went to Vancouver to get my papers and then back to Nanaimo. I then went to Quesnel to find work ... I then left and went to Mission to work in a shingle mill. I then went to Kitimat and left after one week of work. I came to Terrace. I got a job at the Pohle mill in 1973."[92]

Punjabi men could afford to be transient, since for the most part they lived as single men. In the case of married men, the wife was often still in India waiting to migrate when the "primary breadwinner" had settled economically. Once a man was joined by his spouse or family, he was less likely to move, especially after the birth of a child. In cases where families had already settled in the Skeena region, some Punjabis preferred to stay in the region and turn to other available labour jobs. For example, some decided to find work in another industry (like the railway) so that their families could stay in the region after Prince Rupert Sawmills shut down.[93]

Columbia Cellulose eventually sold Prince Rupert Forest Products to Norman Manning. After temporary closures while the Canadian Fishing Company began blasting a nearby block at the intersection of George Hills Way and Dry Dock Road,[94] the mill restarted in the spring of 1973. However, both the sawmill and bunkhouse were permanently shut down in 1975 as a result of a Workers Compensation Board intervention. In the early 1970s, local residents complained to city hall about the air pollution generated by the burner moving in the direction of Prince Rupert's residential area.[95] A former Punjabi mill worker explained the events leading to the mill's permanent shutdown in 1975: "I went to Prince Rupert in November or December of 1973. I worked at 'Prince Rupert Sawmills' and lived in the bunkhouse ... It had been shut down for several years (1970–73). And, then WCB [permanently] shut it down in 1975. Someone bought the land and cleaned it up. It was a good manoeuvre to build a big fish plant. We got a notice one month in advance that the sawmill was going to shut down. We had to apply for a pulp and paper mill job on Watson Island."[96] While this particular worker viewed the transformation of the waterfront property surrounding the Old Dry Dock into the New Oceanside fish plant as a good business plan, others saw the WCB incident as a ploy on the part of the city to make more room for the New Oceanside fish plant.[97] Today, the New Oceanside BC Packers fish plant – now called by its original name, the Canadian Fishing Company, under the ownership of Jim Pattison since 1999 – is located right beside the Old Dry Dock where Prince Rupert Sawmills and the bunkhouse once stood.[98]

The Pulp and Paper Mill on Watson Island

The Columbia Cellulose pulp and paper mill on Watson Island began operating in 1952. Even though many loggers initially objected to a large corporate pulp and paper mill in the area, many independent loggers soon began urging Columbia Cellulose to build a sawmill for chipping timber.[99] The company, however, requested instead an expansion of the area designated in its No. 1 Tree Farming Licence in order to increase its timber resources for a proposed Kraft pulp mill at a cost of $70 million.[100] By 1964, the company had been allowed to expand its timber area by 60 per cent, and the new Kraft mill began operating in 1967.[101]

It was not until 1969 that the first Punjabi, Rajinder Athwal, began working at Columbia Cellulose.[102] The second Punjabi to work at the pulp and paper mill described his experience in obtaining a job at the mill: "One of my landlord's friends encouraged me to apply at the pulp and paper mill. At that time there was only one East Indian. I got a job and was working at both jobs. After three weeks, the pulp and paper mill found out and requested me to quit the Prince Rupert Forest Products Sawmill. I was so happy [laughs] with the change. The work was so much less strenuous and it was more money too. When the sawmill shut down [1970], many East Indians shifted to the pulp and paper mill, and some moved to Terrace."[103]

Punjabi workers were encouraged to apply for jobs in the "woodroom" – with a second one under construction in 1970 – because the work was similar to that at Prince Rupert Forest Products.[104] All of the workers who came from Prince Rupert Forest Products initially landed jobs in the woodroom because the work did not require special skills or command of the English language. The woodroom consisted of two rooms: one room contained a chipper for bark, while the second operated a chipper for logs. Unlike the skilled labour required in operating a pulp mill, the Columbia Cellulose woodrooms merely produced wood chips for the pulp and paper mill. It was familiar work, and no trade training was required of the workers. Moreover, workers did not require literacy skills and needed only minimal English. An Italian-Canadian labourer commented: "There were quite a few who had English problems. They were the older workers. But we put them all in one area, like the machine room, so that they could help each other. That was management's strategy. In the machine room, one does not require as much literacy skills. We had them work more in groups because of the language barrier."[105]

Punjabis were glad to transfer to the pulp and paper mill because the wages were higher and the work was not as physically demanding.[106] That said, there was still a wage gap between the labour in the woodroom and the skilled trade labour in the pulp and paper mill in general. While the former was similar to the work of the sawmill, albeit with more up-to-date machinery, the latter required more skill in trades. Even though Punjabis started out by working in the woodroom, those with technical training and/or high school education could move into more skilled labour positions, since they were able to improve their conversational skills quickly and take advantage of the training programs offered by their employer or local community college.

In the early 1970s, increasing numbers of Punjabi men arrived with some high school education and some proficiency in the English language. This change was a result of Canada's decision to accept independent immigrants with skills.[107] Although many Punjabis migrated through the family reunification program, a cohort of the Punjabis who arrived in Prince Rupert and Canada in general in the 1970s came better equipped with educational and language skills and were therefore able to find skilled labour jobs. Note the following account of the recruitment process at a pulp and paper mill: "Since I had relatives there and had a chance to work in the pulp and paper mill, I decided to move out there. The job required education. They needed to train people. There was a questionnaire to fill out which they timed. It took me forty-five minutes. Then they interviewed you. They tested you before you were hired (unlike many other sawmill jobs). I passed the test and medical exam."[108]

Some of the immigrants, in fact, arrived fully intended to work as a skilled labourer in workplaces like the pulp and paper mill. Since Punjabis had become more proficient in the English language, they could also take advantage of the skilled-labour training offered at the mill in order to acquire the necessary trade "ticket" to perform work other than in the woodroom or yard:

I applied to go to the woodroom December 24th, 1974, when we learnt about the woodroom mill. I first started in the shipping department. I first did the clean-up job and then went to the operator job. We had the pulp and had to bundle it up with steel straps. I got paid about five to six dollars an hour. Then, in 1978, I went to the pulp machine. They gave training on the job. I worked in the B machine room. I was first a line man (watching the pulp on line) then I was the scale man (watching the weight). I then did the grading job of the pulp. Then I was the assistant backtender (slow machine for the wet pulp) [the fast machine backtender is for the dry pulp].[109]

In this manner, some Punjabis had the opportunity to upgrade their skills,[110] especially since there was a greater demand for skilled labour.

Not only was Canada in need of skilled labour, but the general impulse of illiterate Punjabi men doing manual labour was to seize the opportunity to move away from this type of work, at the very least for the next generation. One Punjabi man explained how his arranged marriage and subsequent sponsorship had depended on his potential to work as a skilled labourer: "My father-in-law, who was illiterate and worked at Prince Rupert Sawmills, selected me to marry his daughter because I was a machinist in India. This meant I could get a better skilled job in Canada. I first worked at Prince Rupert Sawmills and then at the Pohle mill in Terrace. I took the welding fabrication program at Northwest Community College in Terrace and found work as a welder."[111] This account reflects the efforts Punjabis made to help family members obtain skilled-labour jobs. Indeed, given the language and occupational barriers, illiterate Punjabi men had the "industrial orientation" for upward occupational mobility even if through arranged marriages.

The Industrial Immigrant

In the 1950s and 1960s, the equation identifying Punjabis with lumber labour in British Columbia did not change much. Despite that, in part as a result of changes in Canada's immigration policy (especially in 1967 and 1977), there was a gradual shift in this equation because visible minority immigrants increasingly began arriving in Canada equipped with some secondary or higher education in order to fill Canada's need for skilled labour and professionals.[112] Even though the sponsorship system continued to be the primary means by which Punjabis were able to immigrate to the Skeena region, some changes took place. Some of the Punjabis who migrated to the region in the 1970s and onwards, for example, arrived after acquiring a trade or profession, while others proved more enterprising by upgrading their skills or venturing into business.

The Educated in Search of Professional Work

During the first half of the twentieth century, many members of the Punjabi community did not view education as an important means to establish themselves in the labour market. Given the socio-political climate of the time, educated Punjabis had to work in low-wage labour jobs. The prevailing sentiment in the community was that, even with an education, a Punjabi would still end up pulling lumber on the green chain.[113] The better-skilled or managerial jobs were not accessible to Punjabis, except when Punjabis were the actual owners or operators of the sawmill.[114] It was extremely difficult for Punjabis to break into a profession even with a Canadian education and proficiency in the English language. The restrictive labour market therefore compelled most Punjabis to prefer employment over education. However, by the 1960s, a small group of Canadian-born Punjabis became university-educated professionals; moreover, some students and educated professionals were being allowed to migrate to Canada from India to meet Canada's need for professionals.[115]

With the institution of the point system in immigration policy in 1967, Canada began to favour immigrants with occupational skills and some command of the English language. Punjabi immigrants, therefore, began to arrive with educational qualifications that they had acquired in the Punjab prior to their coming to Canada. However, as argued by Ravi Pendakur, even though the changes in immigration policy in the 1960s lowered barriers for non-Europeans, "the barriers faced by different groups vary depending upon level and area of education and the length of stay."[116] This was confirmed in the course of research for the present study: while several Hindu Punjabi and some Sikh Punjabi immigrants living in the Skeena region had received professional training in India, their employment income did not reflect this fact. Punjabi immigrants who had obtained diplomas or degrees in education or other similar professions in India had to reconcile themselves to working in manual or semi-skilled labour jobs. Indeed, educational credentials acquired in India were not recognized in Canada, as noted by one Punjabi: "I migrated here in Canada in 1972, thirty-five years ago. I came from an educated family in India. I was trained to be a teacher but I could not be a teacher here ... I first arrived in Victoria on Vancouver Island. I then found work in Williams Lake. I lived there for a year and then left to find a better job because I was a teacher in India ... I finally found a job at the Pohle mill in Terrace."[117]

Professionally trained educators began working in manual labour jobs typically associated with Punjabis in British Columbia.[118] An India-trained educator shared his employment history in Canada:

The white guys were less educated than I was ... There were about fifty to sixty Punjabi people working in both mills in Terrace [Skeena and Pohle] in 1972 ... When I came to Canada, I thought I didn't have to work hard in Canada. We didn't work physically hard in India. I was a tutor in India and then a teacher. Many came from the farm. When I first started working in Mackenzie, I was a tally man after the first week. Then, I started grading. I bought a book for one dollar and learned it on my own to move up in the job. I knew English so I was able to do that. I watched the grader do his job. I started correcting him and then he got his ticket. Grading was a fast job and lots of responsibility.[119]

Though some had to settle for manual labour, other Punjabis were able to find work requiring higher skills, albeit not in their chosen profession. Here is an example of a Punjabi man who persisted in trying to escape lumber labour and to find, at the very least, clerical work: "I worked at the sawmill for three months. I mainly did clean-up work but several times pulled lumber on the green chain. I then applied for a post office job. I had been an educator back home. I was the first turban-wearing employee. When I was hired I was put in the back room to sort the mail because I was wearing a turban. I said I would get a lawyer. I knew the local MP and MLA. I told them about the matter. I got a letter within a week from Ottawa stating that I was allowed to be in the front if neatly dressed."[120]

While such immigrants could not work in their chosen field, their proficiency in English enabled them to move out of the labour sector typically associated with Punjabis. Similarly, with their command of the English language, they had the option of attending post-secondary institutions to acquire the necessary credentials. For most, however, this was not feasible because of the cost and the pressure to earn money.[121] Punjabis sponsored by a parent or an older sibling were often disappointed upon their arrival because they found themselves under pressure to find work and were unable to fulfil their dream of acquiring professional training.[122]

There were a few cases where Indian-trained educators found teaching jobs. However, the jobs were of a kind not sought after by non-immigrant Canadians. Ravinder Gill taught and lived ninety-seven kilometres northwest of Terrace on the Nisga'a reservation, Gitlaxt'aamiks (New Aiyansh),[123] for twenty-seven years. He shared his experience of being an educated and unemployed sawmill worker in Terrace who managed to find a teaching position on an Indian reservation:

Based on my qualifications and experience, getting the Professional Teaching Certificate from the Ministry of Education, British Columbia (Canada), was no problem. I had a good interview and I was certified to teach in BC. I sent 500 applications. Nobody said no, but nobody gave me a job. This is the first time in my life when I was a useless unemployed person ... I could not get a teaching job until January 12, 1976 ... Someone was on leave of absence for one month. I accepted the job, and by sheer chance, I landed in the elementary school at New Aiyansh, in the Nass Valley, as a grade seven teacher, teaching all courses. My term was extended for two more months and then for three more months, up to June 30, 1976, the end of the school year. The new secondary school was under construction at that time, in New Aiyansh. It was scheduled to start in September 1976. I was the first teacher to be hired, to teach English and social studies, in this school.[124]

Interestingly, Ravinder Gill's personal experience of the partition of India and teaching in Kenya enabled him to empathize with the Nisga'a struggle for self-government and control over their traditional territory.[125]

In contrast to the India-trained professionals who had to settle for manual labour or entry-level positions, the India-trained tradesmen had greater opportunity to work in their trade. The shift to skilled labour was in part the result of the demand for immigrants with trade or technological skills in an increasingly automated work environment. India-trained skilled labourers were thus able to find work in their specialized trade, such as electrical engineering, metal fabrication, or power mechanics. Indeed, British Columbia was short of skilled labourers, and such immigrants were welcomed, since they could fill this need. A Punjabi man who arrived with engineering credentials remembered how he had to nonetheless upgrade his skills to find work in his trade:

> I left India in 1971. I had no family in Canada, nor did I have any friends. It was pretty scary to come. I came to Canada as a visitor and applied for my immigration papers within a month. I started studies at Vancouver Vocational Institute on Burrard Street to upgrade my engineering credentials. An engineer came from Masset looking for someone to care for the plant at Masset in his absence ... He talked to my instructor, who recommended me. I wanted the work but I did not yet have my immigration papers to work, I only had an immigration interview pending. He asked me, "When and where was my interview to be?" and then stated, "Okay, I will be there." He showed up at my interview and talked to the immigration officer. The officer just simply asked him, "Do you want this man [to work for you]?" That was it. The officer then shook my hand, saying, "Welcome to Canada."[126]

A noteworthy aspect of this story is that the Punjabi man upgraded his credentials in Vancouver before he found employment as an electrical engineer. This aspect confirms Pendakur's position that finding a job in a chosen field becomes easier if the highest level of schooling is received after entry to Canada.[127] With a "Canadian" education, the Punjabis were able to meet the demand for specialized skills in the 1970s, especially given the expansion of pulp and paper production in the forestry industry that required more skill.[128] Moreover, the Punjabi man was willing to go to a remote location where there were no qualified people available.

While most Punjabi men worked in the forestry industry, others – with training in a trade – found jobs in the fishery industry, another major industry in the Skeena region. One Punjabi man easily found employment because of his educational background (BSC in math and physics) and twenty-one years' work experience in electrical engineering: "With all my work experience in Punjab and Delhi, I became an industrial maintenance electrician. Upon coming to Canada, I went to BC Packers in Steveston, Richmond, where their headquarters were. I was hired in a temporary position in Richmond. I filled a permanent position which was vacated in Prince Rupert February 28th, 1973. I worked for BC Packers [Seal Cove]."[129]

Many Punjabi immigrants found jobs as skilled labourers at the pulp and paper mill on Watson Island, the fish plants in Prince Rupert or the Alcan aluminum plant in Kitimat.[130] Since there was such a shortage of tradespeople, companies like Columbia Cellulose provided its workers on-the-job training. For immigrants with a secondary education and some fluency in English, there were opportunities to upgrade their skills.

Upgrading to Skilled Labour

As noted above, the Punjabis who arrived in Canada in the 1970s increasingly came equipped with some educational and language skills. Many had a secondary education, which included learning English. Even though a fair number of Punjabi immigrants were not trained in a trade, they had the opportunity to upgrade by learning new skills in Canada. While India-trained professionals were not able to practise their chosen profession, they had the advantage of having some command of the English language, which enabled them to move to a "higher" or more skilled job. With motivation and persistence, one India-trained educator managed to acquire a grading ticket that enabled him to work in quality control – the highest skilled-labour job in the sawmill – at the Pohle mill: "I have an AA grade ticket and was in quality control. That is a good job. I scored the highest grading scores at the mill with 97.6 per cent. In 1994 I received my AA grading from the Canadian Mill Source Association. Most of the guys were less educated than me. I made three dollars more per hour."[131]

The goal of increasing one's skills to move up in the job was pursued by many immigrants, particularly when the company paid for the training. Since companies like Columbia Cellulose were in need of certain trades, they supported workers who sought training in specific trades. Punjabis working at the pulp and paper mill in Prince Rupert, for example, enrolled at Northwest Community College in Terrace or the British Columbia Institute of Technology (BCIT) in Burnaby to obtain their certification or "ticket" in a skill, such as metal fabrication, power mechanics, and electrical, power or steam engineering.[132] Others found jobs in the fish plants in Prince Rupert or the Alcan aluminum plant in Kitimat.[133] Punjabis eagerly took advantage of training programs as a means to move out of the typical manual labour jobs historically associated with them in British Columbia. While many Punjabis moved into skilled labour jobs, others with an entrepreneurial spirit ventured out of manual labour and into business.

Branching Out into Business

Agriculture and transportation are familiar industries to those from the Punjab. It is, therefore, understandable that, during the pioneer period, Punjabis took to trucking as a business when the opportunity arose for them, even as others purchased farms in the Fraser Valley.[134] In addition to the Mayo-Kapoor enterprise, several other Punjabis, such as Sohen Gill, began operating sawmills, shingle mills, or logging camps during the first half of the twentieth century. The forestry industry also generated other types of entrepreneurship, including small-scale labour contracting, trucking, the wood-fuel business, and the renting out of housing to Punjabi workers. By the end of the Second World War, there had emerged an elite group of Punjabi mill owners and labour contractors, but the majority of Punjabis continued to work as lumber and agricultural labourers. Punjabis were often blocked from the merchandise business, as licences were extremely difficult to obtain for manufacturing or retail businesses.[135] Moreover, since the Punjabi-Canadian population was small and dispersed, it did not have a large Punjabi commercial establishment, aside, perhaps, from a couple of grocery stores.

As in the pioneer period, the employment of Punjabis in the Skeena region was not widely distributed across the various occupational sectors (i.e., business, social services, public administration). In the 1960s and 1970s, Prince Rupert had a very tight-knit retail and construction business community,[136] one that Punjabi immigrants found difficult to penetrate. Moreover, the Skeena Punjabi community was not large enough to sustain Punjabi specialty businesses.[137] Despite the lack of business options for Skeena Punjabis, some of them manifested an enterprising spirit even in such a protectionist environment. Mohinder Singh Takhar shared his story of building a sawmill business in the Skeena region: "We wanted to go further, so some of us started our own businesses. [You] have to take a chance [or settle for] a labour job. [After living in Victoria for two and a half years], I went to Prince Rupert for work. I worked at Prince Rupert Sawmills. I bought a gravel truck and ran a trucking company, delivering wood chips to Columbia Cellulose. I moved to Terrace in 1969. The trucking work slowed down by 1984, so I built Terrace Precut (a sawmill operation) in Terrace. The sawmill is 80 per cent custom work and 20 per cent supply."[138]

Indeed, following the pattern of Punjabi pioneer entrepreneurs in the Lower Mainland and on Vancouver Island in the first half of the twentieth century, Mohinder Singh Takhar began a trucking business that specialized in delivering wood products. There is, however, one main difference: while in the pioneer days the wood products that were delivered were used as fuel, Mohinder Singh Takhar's wood products were used to make pulp.[139] Eventually, Takhar, too, built a sawmill (Terrace Precut) in 1985, a successful small-scale operation that used fibre from local Terrace sawmills for its lumber re manufacturing business.

To be successful in the business environment in the Skeena region, Punjabis needed to have a solid command of the English language, something more easily attained by educated immigrants. Proficiency in English also allowed Punjabis to connect with the larger mainstream community by participating in networking clubs, such as the Rotary, Lions, and Free Masons. Even when Punjabis were not proficient in the English language, they found ways to learn conversational English. One Punjabi immigrant explained how he had been motivated to learn English so that he might start and run a business:

I realized that if I was going to stay in Canada, I have to learn English. I decided to move out of the bunkhouse and rented a room from a Norwegian family ... I didn't want to work in the sawmill all my life – I wanted to learn English and change jobs. In a couple of years, I picked up English. One of their friends encouraged me to apply at the pulp and paper mill. I worked in the yard as a labourer for four to five months ... I did dry work in the sulphide mill for ten years ... I then worked in the yard driving trucks and bulldozers [1978]. I started a construction company in 1979. I worked both jobs for about six months. In the middle of 1979, I took a leave of absence and did full-time construction and then eventually quit working at the mill. I made more money in construction and I was my own boss with my own schedule.[140]

Some Punjabi men kept their labour job while venturing into business; that is, they did not let go of their labour job until they had firmly established themselves in a particular venture. A Punjabi man shared his experience of shifting from manual labour to business: "I temporarily worked the day shift full-time at Oceanside. I drove a cab at night. I was the only Indian cab driver

… I drove a cab for six months. I then quit my job at the fish plant. I put my own car up as a taxi. I was the only Indian shareholder for a taxi. After two years, I became general manager of Skeena Taxi Company … I started a print shop in 1991 and I opened one in Terrace in 2000."[141]

Even though the unskilled mill worker element continued in the Punjabi population of the Skeena region, the Punjabis found ways to move from traditional manual or semi-skilled labour jobs to higher-skilled labour jobs and beyond. By the mid-1980s, many of them had become entrepreneurs, owning and managing small-scale businesses – restaurants, convenience stores, gas stations, as well as furniture and clothing stores. And, more significantly, some of them became landlords – a topic explored in the next chapter. No longer were Punjabis working only in manual labour jobs that did not require interaction with the public. In the 1980s and thereafter, they engaged in successful small-scale businesses in the mainstream Skeena community.

Lumber Decline and Life Disorientation

During the mid-1980s, a weakening in the forestry industry was apparent in the Skeena region, and in the late 1990s, the weakening became a bust. The resulting drastic decline of BC's forestry industry undoubtedly had a devastating impact on the Punjabi community as it did on the Skeena region in general. The decline forced the Punjabi community, in a sense, to readjust as an immigrant group through re-migration to urban locations. While the Punjabi community has experienced and continues to experience emotional and economic disorientation as a result of job losses, the Punjabis have, for the most part, proved to be resilient in the face of economic upset.

Mill Closures

Production at the Columbia Cellulose pulp and paper mill began wavering in the mid-1980s, during which time there were intermittent closures of the "B" mill built in 1978 (after the sulphide mill closed). The "B" mill was eventually shut down, on 30 April 1998.[142] Since tradesmen had transferable skills, some of them left Prince Rupert – as early as the mid-1980s – and found stable employment, primarily in the Lower Mainland, Calgary, and Toronto. Meanwhile, many remained in the Skeena region, particularly those who had limited occupational skills and/or high seniority. It was extremely difficult for many manual or semi-skilled labourers to leave their jobs, as it was the only work they had known. Despite the slowdown in the forestry industry, Punjabi relatives of those already living in the region continued to come to the area in search of work, since employment was also difficult to find in the Lower

Mainland: "In the 1990s, people still came looking for work because it was difficult finding work in the BC Lower Mainland. People started to leave in 1995–96 because of decline in work at the mills. In the last five years [2001–06] there has been a big exodus because the mills have shut down. Most Punjabis in Terrace work in the sawmills; some Punjabis own a business."[143]

By 1997, the forestry industry was hit province-wide with falling production and rising international competition associated with globalization and technological advance. The provincial NDP government led by Premier Glen Clark injected money into Columbia Cellulose, which included Terrace's Pohle mill and the pulp and paper mill on Watson Island, in an attempt to bail out the ailing company. Simultaneously, with the risk of declining wages and job losses, tension grew between the Pulp and Paper Workers of Canada (PPWC) and management.[144] The pulp and paper mill on Watson Island eventually stopped operating in 2002, and it was officially shut down in 2003.[145] A former president of the PPWC Local 4 provided an account of the consequences of the mill shutdown: "There were around 700 people working when the mill stopped operating in 2002. This had a huge impact on the community. Only 30 per cent of the workers qualified for a pension. People who were fifty-five years or older could apply for early pension. Seventy per cent were without a job or were ineligible for a pension. Some stayed around and found local jobs, such as working in security, grocery stores, and taxis. Some found jobs in the coal port or grain elevator on Ridley Island; others hoped to find a job at the new container port."[146]

The decline of the forestry industry was undeniably difficult for workers and their families, but mill closures affected entire communities because of their spinoff effects. Local businesses suffered, since they depended heavily on the workers ability to purchase their goods and services. The trickle-down effect of the mill closure impacted Prince Rupert's entire economy: "Even the old businesses are shutting down, like furniture and clothing stores. It is hard to rent the home. We managed by putting the rent quite low (it was not enough to pay off the expenses and mortgage). I sold it during the 'little boom' [after the announcement about the container port expansion] and managed to break even."[147] Meanwhile, other mills in BC's north also had difficulty sustaining themselves, especially after the provincial Liberals came into power in 2001; the government terminated the NDP initiatives and removed the regulation on processing timber in close vicinity to where the timber had been harvested. In effect, by 2009 four sawmills had shut down in the Northwest, and today only two are operating in the area, in the towns of Kitwanga and Smithers.[148]

The Pohle mill in Terrace was one of those mills that had trouble maintaining its economic viability. After the unsuccessful efforts of the provincial

NDP government in 1997,[149] the mill was closed in 2001. A local Terrace Punjabi businessman, Mohinder Singh Takhar (owner of Terrace Precut), along with other local businessmen, attempted to save the Pohle mill from permanently shutting down in 2005. The local group of businessmen bought shares in order to revive the mill as the Terrace Lumber Company,[150] and Mohinder Singh Takhar became CEO of the mill. This manoeuvre brought some temporary hope to the citizens of Terrace, as the mill began running in August 2005.[151] Unfortunately, by the summer of 2006, it was clear that these efforts had failed as a result of a soft American lumber market, weak financing, and a decline in log supply.[152] The Pohle mill was dismantled in January 2007, and later that year the last mill in Terrace, West Fraser, was shut down.[153] While a new mine was under development in the region, giving hope to forest workers of a potential sector for them to enter,[154] the new manual labour jobs would generally be more available to younger men; that is, older mill workers who lost their jobs faced the physical-age barrier when they sought manual labour jobs in a new industry. The job losses that resulted from the "lumber bust" have, undeniably, been a source of immense economic stress and emotional disorientation.

Emotional and Economic Disorientation

Many mill workers from the mid-1990s through to the first decade of the 2000s experienced a decline in their working hours and faced temporary mill closures, with the accompanying uncertainty over whether their mills would even reopen. Unsteady work and insecure employment are known sources of emotional and economic distress, not only for workers but also for their families.[155] For Punjabis, emotional distress and disorientation have been related both to loss of employment and to a questioning of their identity as Canadians. For better or worse, Punjabis have been identified with BC's forestry industry over the last one hundred years, and in turn they have built their identity as Canadians on this relationship.[156] Moreover, many of the Punjabis who arrived as "single" men not only worked at sawmills but also lived in mill bunkhouses. In effect, the sawmill became a substitute home for these men while they were away from their homeland and separated from their families. Indeed, the Punjabi male immigrant identity became intimately connected with sawmill culture. One Punjabi man recalled watching the dismantling of the mill equipment at the Pohle mill in Terrace: "I worked at the sawmill since I was a teenager. When the cranes came to dismantle the sawmill for the auction, it was like plucking parts of me away. I felt empty inside. It was as if they were taking parts of my life away. The mill was all I really knew."[157]

Along with the emotional disorientation, there were also the hard economic realities that accompany job loss. The Punjabi men traditionally took pride in not relying on social assistance or welfare, but because they saw the Employment Insurance (EI) program as an insurance plan that they had paid into, their attitude toward EI was different, and during the periods of mill closure in the Skeena region, they readily collected EI while also looking for work. However, there were also certain aspects of Punjabi culture that served to mitigate their difficult situation. Traditionally, having primarily migrated from an agricultural society, Punjabi immigrants were well accustomed to the insecurities of farm life. The predominant Punjabi orientation has been to quickly pay off one's mortgage and save money for times of economic uncertainty. Therefore, Punjabis have rarely had to face home foreclosures. Moreover, they have customarily pooled their resources among family members when confronted by financial constraints. This practice has not only helped Punjabis in their initial settling in Canada, but has also provided a buffer during the difficult period of job loss. One Punjab man observed: "The closure of the mill was very bad. Many lost their jobs. Some Caucasians lost their wives and houses. Punjabis do not spend as much money. We tend to save our money to pay off the house and look after the family for sponsoring. The impact compelled many Punjabis to look for jobs elsewhere. A lot went to the Lower Mainland or Alberta. The older generation had rental properties. Now, new waves are oriented towards business, etc."[158] While most of the Punjabis moved to urban centres like the Lower Mainland or Calgary, others remained in northwestern BC, the men either looking for similar work or managing the home while their wives entered the hospitality and food services sector (discussed in chapter 4).

Re-establishing Oneself

While the economic challenges came in many forms, the greatest challenge was finding a job. For mill workers, searching for a new job or obtaining training in a new skill was directly related to the individual's level of education and proficiency in the English language. There were two main cohorts in the Punjabi mill community: (1) Punjabis with limited occupational and language skills and (2) Punjabis with training in the trades. As noted earlier, those trained in a trade had transferable skills and more readily left the Skeena region in search of other permanent employment. Some of them left Prince Rupert as early as the mid-1980s to find stable employment primarily in the Lower Mainland or in Alberta. Some found work in Alberta's booming energy sector, while other Punjabis trained more generally in the trades could often find work in different but related sectors, such as truck, tractor, and trailer repair; farm machinery repair; sheet metal fabrication; and housing development.

In the case of cohort 1 (Punjabi immigrant men with limited occupational and other skills), it was very challenging to find a job equivalent to their previous unionized mill job. A Punjabi man who had trades training commented on the impact of the pulp and paper mill closure on cohort 1: "The government offered training for the workers to change their career. Some did well with it; but it was the educated ones who benefited from the training program. It was very difficult for those who were not very educated, for that was all they knew. It was their only means to their bread and butter. It was morally a big blow to the whole community. The pulp and paper mill was the hub of the city. It employed most of the people and provided business to the other businesses in the town (i.e., taxi, restaurants, building materials, etc.)."[159] This group of Punjabi men continued to live in the Skeena region, particularly those who had been working at the mill for a long period of time. Indeed, most Punjabi immigrant men had arrived with limited education and were therefore trapped in low-skill jobs even though they may have had the potential to do more but had lacked the opportunity to upgrade their skills or education.[160] In effect, just as in the 1960s and 1970s when Punjabi men had been transient and had looked for steady employment in the forestry industry throughout BC's interior, during the mill closures in the late 1990s and first decade of the 2000s, Punjabis who had been accustomed to steady employment in the mills once again had to search for work.

Many Punjabis familiar only with manual lumber labour travelled throughout British Columbia looking for similar work. A mill worker provided an account of his predicament: "I went back to Williams Lake during slowdown. I have returned [to Terrace] because our mill reopened. Although emotionally attached to the mill, I am saddened that it may close. [The mill permanently shut down in 2007.]"[161] Another such worker found similar work at a non-unionized sawmill in the Lower Mainland; however, the wages were much lower than those he had earned previously: "When my mill closed, I went to the Vancouver Lower Mainland. I found some sawmill work there but the wages were not the same. I liked being there because my daughter lives there."[162]

Several Punjabi families have remained in the Skeena region, regardless of the economic situation there. These families have decided to stay, in part, because the men have limited occupational skills and they are still raising young children. The sentiment is that the small towns in the Skeena region are a good place to raise children, but once their children graduate from secondary school, they will move southward to the Lower Mainland. One Punjabi man explained his reasons for staying in Prince Rupert: "I hurt my knee running the machines at work in 1999. I was put on disability until 2000. Since the pulp and paper mill shut down, I have been working at a grocery store now for over five years. I run the freezer and bulk inventory. It is unionized, so it is a good job ... One of my brothers went to Calgary to work in a meat factory; the other one moved to Surrey. [100] While the man cited above was fortunate to have found unionized work, many had to settle for minimum-wage jobs, such as security guard or taxi driver, whether in the Lower Mainland or in the Skeena region.

Punjabis who have been working in Canada since the 1960s and early 1970s are able to collect EI benefits and then take early or regular retirement. The following observation was made by a Punjabi man living in Terrace: "I am a machinist at Alcan. Many East Indians work at Alcan but live in Terrace. In the next couple of years there will be a wave of East Indians retiring. Upon retirement I will move to Burnaby where my son is presently living. I have a house there; my son is living in the house now."[164] However, Punjabis who have worked in Canada since the early 1980s face a greater challenge, as they are not at retirement age. At the same time, these men are at an age when finding a new job or occupation can be challenging, regardless of their ethnic background. Job loss after many years of employment often leads to the experience of a "broken contract of trust," since one's hard work has not translated into job security or protection.[165] What's more, the Punjabi male immigrant's sense of "broken trust" with the forestry industry and the unions also extends to his sense of belonging in Canada, as the Skeena Punjabi male identity is very much connected with BC's lumber industry.

All the same, the orientation of many immigrants is to work very hard in order to provide a solid education for their children and thereby enable them to move up the socio-economic ladder. Skeena Punjabis fit this orientation, and it is noteworthy that many Punjabis had already begun to invest in property in the Lower Mainland even prior to the mill closures, with the goal of providing their children with a place to live while attending post-secondary education. A Punjabi man who worked in the pulp and paper mill explained his situation thus: "I bought investment property in Langley when my son was going to college in Surrey. My son studied and took care of the property. Now I have a good asset there. I have a place to live in Langley."[166]

In a way, the Punjabi custom of providing for their children with the eventual goal of joining them upon retirement has in fact provided a buffer for many Punjabis. The cultural practice among Punjabis has been to follow their children once the latter had their own jobs and had started a family. A Punjabi described his plans of moving to Toronto: "I have lost my job ... but [am] satisfied that my son is a teacher in Toronto. I love Terrace but my wife wants to follow the kids upon retirement in three years."[167] While the economic and social challenges resulting from the decline in the forestry industry are obvious, the inevitable cultural consequences of moving from a small-town BC environment to the Punjabi-concentrated areas in the Lower Mainland are also worthy of study and are further explored in chapter 8.

Summary

Punjabis have had a long and intimate association with the forestry industry over the last one hundred years. This is evident in the Punjabi settlement in the Skeena region. Their arrival in the region was directly related to the establishment of the Punjabi-owned sawmill in Prince Rupert. Sohen Gill's Prince Rupert Sawmills began operations in 1960, serving as a catalyst for the initial migration of Punjabis to the area. When the mill faced a slowdown in 1964 and Prince Rupert Forest Products – under the ownership of Columbia Cellulose – temporarily closed in 1968 and again in the early 1970s, the loss of work led to the Punjabi migration to and settlement in Terrace and the larger Skeena region in general. What is more, even with only unsteady work available in the late 1960s, the sawmill under the ownership of Columbia Cellulose still proved beneficial to the Punjabi workers. While Sohen Gill's Prince Rupert Sawmills served as a catalyst for the initial wave of Punjabi migration to Prince Rupert and the Skeena region in general, by the 1970s many Punjabis had found jobs in the "woodroom" at Columbia Cellulose's pulp and paper mill on Watson Island.

Unfortunately, Punjabi immigrants with little or no education and limited English-language skills were in a sense trapped in manual or low-skilled labour jobs, being unable to acquire or upgrade their education or skills. On the other hand, by the 1970s, some of the Punjabi immigrants were arriving with a higher level of education and some knowledge of the English language, which gave them the opportunity to work in more skilled labour jobs at the pulp and paper mill even as other Punjabi men ventured into business.

There were two main cohorts among Punjabi male immigrants: cohort 1, which consisted of Punjabi immigrant men with low schooling and skills who had arrived under the sponsorship system from the early 1960s onwards; and cohort 2, which comprised Punjabi immigrant men with secondary or higher education and some proficiency in the English language who had begun arriving in the late 1960s and 1970s. While an Indian education did not remove barriers, as Indian credentials were not recognized in Canada, education and English-language skills nonetheless provided Punjabi men the foundation upon which to upgrade their skills. Those who improved their skills were then able to adapt to other sectors when a major decline occurred in the forestry industry.

Aside from the acquisition of new skills, the adaptive strength of Punjabis and certain other cultural assets enabled Punjabi men to navigate through the structures of a foreign economic environment that was not particularly designed to help the immigrant worker overcome its multiple barriers. Despite the Punjabis' long-standing association with manual labour in the forestry industry, their cultural assets – such as their ability to overcome financial uncertainty and their practice of investing in their children – created a buffer for them during the economically and emotionally challenging times of the forestry bust. Specific Punjabi cultural assets are explored in the next chapter.

CHAPTER 3

The First Journey: From Village Punjab
to a Remote BC Town

The majority of Punjabi immigrants who arrived in the Skeena region in the early 1960s came to the remote town of Prince Rupert to work at the Punjabi-owned sawmill. As discussed in chapter 2, Prince Rupert Sawmills was built by Sohen Singh Gill and served as the catalyst for the initial flow of Punjabi immigration into the Skeena region. Besides constructing a sawmill at the Old Dry Dock and shipyard, Sohen Gill also renovated the existing Second World War military bunkers. On the Dry Dock premises, there had stood a large yellow office building with a military bunkhouse located in its south wing; Sohen Gill transformed the bunkhouse into living quarters for his fellow-Punjabi sawmill workers.[1]

The phenomenon of a sawmill bunkhouse was not new. In fact, it was the common type of housing for Punjabi labourers in Canada during the first half of the twentieth century. Although Punjabis came to Canada to work, they were not particularly welcomed as citizens. Most of them actually lived at their employment sites in colonies on the mill grounds. Every Punjabi man of that generation at some stage in his life in Canada had lived in a bunkhouse and eaten in a cookhouse.[2] It was also common for mill owners – both Punjabi and Anglo-Canadian – to build Sikh temples (*gurdwaras*) right on the site, along with bunker-type housing for their Punjabi-Sikh labourers.[3]

Depending on the size and nature of the sawmill workforce, there could be several bunkhouses on the grounds of one sawmill, especially since different ethnic groups – such as British, Chinese, and Japanese – lived in segregated bunkhouses. The bunkhouses were often wooden structures divided into a dozen rooms, housing two men in each room. A long hallway divided the bunkhouse, with rooms on each side and a sitting room at the end of it. Most

Prince Rupert Sawmills occupied the waterfront next to the Old Dry Dock site. The bunkhouse was located in the L-shaped building in front of the beehive burner (1961). Courtesy of the Prince Rupert City & Regional Archives and Museum of Northern BC, Wrathall Collection, WP997-72-13440.

often, the kitchen area was a separate building, called a cookhouse, where food and cooking supplies were kept and meals were cooked. The cookhouses were often staffed by a couple of elderly men who prepared the food for the workers. In turn, the workers would pool their money to cover the cost of the food and the cooks' wages.[4] Certainly, living in the bunkhouse on the sawmill premises was a practical arrangement for the Punjabi labourers, who for the most part had limited education, poor English-language skills, and little or no family support.

Because the immigration and adaptive experience of Punjabi men has been so intimately connected with working in a sawmill and living in a mill bunkhouse, this chapter seeks to shed light on this lifestyle by providing an in-depth narrative of the "first journey" of a single Punjabi male – Nirmal Singh Gill (b. 1944),[5] who, upon migrating to Canada in 1961, worked and lived at Prince Rupert Sawmills. He had left his native village prior to the Punjab's Green Revolution (1966–75), with its technological advances, and therefore was familiar only with manual agricultural labour. When he arrived in the Skeena region, he found himself not only living in a foreign environment, but

Prince Rupert Sawmill worker Atma Singh Kainth (left) and bunkhouse cook Kartar Kainth (right) by the Old Dry Dock (1967). Courtesy of Atma Singh Kainth.

also having to adapt to a mechanized wage-labour economy. Despite that, he brought with him – as did many Punjabi men – a solid work ethic, a strong orientation towards family kinship, and the deep-rooted Punjabi value of landownership, all of which proved to be enormous assets in the adaptation process.

A narrative about the experience of a young, single Punjabi male who worked and lived at Prince Rupert Sawmills sheds light on two important aspects of Punjabi life in Canada: (1) the male experience of leaving Punjabi farm life and migrating to a small remote town in northwestern BC and (2) the many challenges Punjabi immigrants faced in adapting to Canada both economically and socially at a time when the Canadian value of multiculturalism was only in its infancy. The first part of this chapter explores farm life in village Punjab prior to the Green Revolution in order to provide the pre-immigration background of the first journey experience of migrating to Canada. The second part of the chapter tells the story of a Punjabi male immigrant who arrived in the remote town of Prince Rupert in the early 1960s. Significantly, this part reveals the learning process in the male immigrant experience and, more specifically, his socio-economic adaptation to a remote BC town in the early 1960s and 1970s. It provides insights into the initial period of his adjustment to manual sawmill labour while – for economic survival – living in a bunkhouse.

Lastly, the third part of the chapter analyses the challenges and barriers that many Punjabi male immigrants experienced when they initially confronted the difficult reality of having been uprooted from their home and having to make the transition to settling in Prince Rupert at a time when the small Punjabi community lived apart from mainstream Canada. Punjabi men brought with them, however, their Punjabi cultural assets. In effect, this narrative, as well as other interviews with men who had worked and lived at Prince Rupert Sawmills, demonstrates how – despite the challenges – the Punjabi values of hard work, strong kinship ties, and landownership fostered the resiliency and strength these men would need as they settled in Canada.

The research methodology employed here consists of two main components: (1) a textual analysis of traditional cultural mores surrounding Punjabi family and village life and (2) fieldwork. The first component relies on an examination of anthropological studies of socio-economic conditions in village Punjab from the 1950s onwards in order to establish "external validity" for the cultural generalizations offered about Punjabi family and village life.[6] The second component comprises ethnographic field research for the narrative; it involves an analysis of five main types of data:[7] (i) face-to-face semi-structured interviews, conducted in English (and some Punjabi) with the narrator in May 2006, August 2008, November 2008, and June 2009; (ii) four semi-structured interviews, conducted with other family members of the narrator, about their collective experience of migration to Canada;[8] (iii) ten semi-structured interviews, conducted with other Punjabi men who also lived in the bunkhouse (five Punjabi males in the 1960s and five Punjabi males in the early 1970s); (iv) archival data on Prince Rupert Sawmills Ltd, the Columbia Cellulose pulp and paper mill, the International Woodworkers of America, and the Pulp and Paper Workers of Canada as corroborative material; and (v) a survey of the local Prince Rupert newspaper files (*The Prince Rupert Daily News*) and secondary literature on the history of Prince Rupert as corroborative documentation.[9]

Before we turn to the case study narrative on the migration from village Punjab to rural British Columbia during the 1960s, it is important to gain an understanding of farm life in village Punjab during the 1950s.

Farm Life in Village Punjab

The extended family is regarded as the most important social unit in traditional Punjabi society. Kinship forms the basis of an individual's identity, while the extended family provides economic and emotional security. Interdependence within the family is highly valued because the traditional orientation is towards the collective – the family – rather than towards the individual. The extended family (*parivar*) is patriarchal: the father is the head of the family, and the home includes his family and his sons' families. The traditional Punjabi family pattern has been that of the joint family, though the household may or may not include the father's brothers and brothers' families.[10]

The governing principles of social behaviour in the family are duty (*dharam*) and honour or respect (*izzat*). Members are traditionally expected to fulfil their personal duty, based on their particular stage in life,[11] in order to maintain family and community *izzat*. Duty is performed and respect accorded to meet prescribed gender-role expectations. Therefore, a male is reared so that he can fulfil his role as a son, husband, and father.[12] Traditionally, most Punjabi males in rural areas received only limited schooling, even though by the twentieth century the government was gradually increasing the provision of primary and secondary education in rural Punjab.[13] Customarily, the male child learned the trade of his father so that he would be able to support the family in his adulthood.

While there is a wide variety of specialized trades (e.g., carpentry, pottery, masonry) and services (e.g., weavers, barbers, tailors) in rural Punjab, the dominant occupation is farming. During British colonial rule, administrators classified castes into two groups – "agricultural" and "non-agricultural" – as a means of protecting the former and preventing the latter from purchasing the former's land.[14] While members of various caste groups may have engaged in farming, it is the Jat (farmer) caste group that has been predominantly associated with agriculture in the Punjab. In fact, colonial officials were known to give preferential treatment to Jat farmers, as was evident in their allocation of land in the British-developed canal colonies.[15] Whether it was colonial favouritism or political strategy,[16] the British viewed the Jat farmer as the "soul" of farming in the Punjab.[17] And, indeed, landownership has been profoundly valued by Punjabis, especially those belonging to – but not exclusively – the Jat caste.

Subsequent to the partition of India in 1947, land was reallocated to Sikh and Hindu refugees, which allowed not only for the redesign but also for the redistribution of housing settlements.[18] As in the canal colonies, the earlier typical nucleated or dispersed layout of villages[19] was replaced by more modern systematic layouts that allowed for wider access roads and service lanes with open spaces; moreover, village landowners were given an acre of land for their residence along broad streets. While many British colonial initiatives were implemented to sustain farming in the Punjab, colonial policy had a negative impact when it came to the protection of tenants and small landholders. With the growing commercialization of agriculture, together with the fixed land revenue system, land became more marketable and transferable.[20] Instead of the traditional practice of treating land as an inheritable asset, land could now be sold or mortgaged, which resulted in the exploitation of the peasant by money lenders.[21]

Landownership varied. To address the disparity between landowners and cultivators, land and tenancy reform legislation was implemented.[22] The reform process was aimed at eradicating the problem of absentee landowners in order to provide tenants with legal protection. The reform legislation ensured that cultivators became the landowners; however, some landowners in the regions of Ferozepur and Faridkot evaded the land ceiling by acquiring possession of land beyond the limit imposed by the government.

The ownership of property, especially ancestral land (*jaddi*), is without doubt connected to the kinship system. Landownership has been the basis of familial and social organization among Punjabi farmers, just as it has been the main determinant of one's social status and economic and emotional security. Prior to the enactment of the Canadian sponsorship system, Punjabi immigrants came primarily from landowning families, since it was with their farm revenue that families could afford the cost of travel to Canada. Punjabis rarely sold their land in order to finance the migration of family members.[23] A family would be extremely reluctant to risk the loss of their property, as such loss of property would also mean loss of status. At the same time, when family members emigrated, there was little concern over the loss of their labour, since family size did not define the limits of production.[24] For instance, during the peak seasons of harvesting and tilling the land, the entire family worked on the farm and, when necessary, additional casual labourers were hired. The higher the production on a farm, the more hired help were required.

Punjabis often emigrated for the purpose of raising funds to expand landownership. Certainly, it was advantageous to have family members migrate to the West so that they could send back remittances. It is a common practice among Punjabis in the diaspora to send remittances to expand the family's landholdings and to improve the conditions of one's village,[25] an aspect made evident in the following ethnographic narrative.

Life in the Prince Rupert Sawmills' Bunkhouse:
An Ethnographic Narrative by Nirmal Singh Gill

Our family village is Dhudike,[26] which is located in the Faridkot District, Punjab. We are Jat-Sikh[27] and still have our land in the Punjab today. I was born on 12 February 1944 in my mother's natal village of Bhujarika, also in the Faridkot District.[28] When I was a child, life was simple: the ladies took care of the home and children; the men worked in the fields; and the children were groomed for adulthood. It was rare to see people with cash in their pockets because the farmers got paid only after every six months. We used the barter system to buy supplies for the home and farm. The barter system was good because my parents were illiterate. They simply looked at the condition of the goods and negotiated a fair trade.

My parents initially sent me to the village school to learn how to read and write in Punjabi. I left school after grade four because my parents needed my help on the farm.[29] I was the eldest of six children: three brothers and three sisters. My father said I had to fulfil my duty as the eldest son, especially since we had three girls to marry off. I learnt to work hard at a young age and was responsible for operating the bullock-pulled well, delivering food and tea to the workers, tilling the land with a bullock and plough, and harvesting the crop with sickles.[30] We had a *ramdasia*[31] farmer who was employed by our family to help manage our three-acre farm.[32]

When I was twelve years old, my father was sponsored by his cousin-brother to migrate to Canada in 1957. I was responsible for helping my mother take care of my five younger siblings and the family farm. I got good guidance from my *dadaji* (paternal grandfather), who also lived in our home. The work became more demanding, and we did not have any machinery to help plough the field or to harvest the crop. We filled the sacks with grain manually and loaded them onto a bullock- or camel-drawn cart. There was only one tractor in our village and it belonged to a wealthy family. All we had were two buffalos for milk, two bullocks for tilling and drawing well water,[33] and one camel for transporting goods. We had a hand pump for drinking water in the courtyard and a wood-burning clay stove close to the house. We knew things were changing in India and would hear information about new farm machinery on the radio. My family wanted me to make money in Canada so that I could buy a tractor. I was sixteen years of age when I migrated to Canada in the spring of 1961 through the family-sponsorship system.

We knew that Englishmen wore suits and had short hair. We did the same by putting away my head scarf and *pajama*[34] and getting myself a black suit and a Dev Anand–style haircut.[35] I arrived in Vancouver on 26 July 1961.[36] When I got off the plane, the passengers quickly rushed into the airport. I did not know where to go, so I followed the passengers in the hope that I will be welcomed by my father's cousin-brother. I found myself by the luggage claim carousel. I began looking for my uncle whom I could identify based on a family picture we have in our Dhudike home. I was relieved to see my uncle and he kindly helped me get my baggage. As we were leaving

Nirmal Singh Gill prior to immigrating to Canada (1961). Courtesy of Nirmal Singh Gill.

the airport, my uncle informed me that my airfare cost $635 and that my father did not repay him. This was my welcome to Canada – that is, I was already in debt and I had to quickly find a job.

I first lived in Langley with the family of my uncle, Joginder Darbara Singh Gill, who owned and operated a trucking company. He came to Canada in 1930 with not a penny in his pocket. He first worked on farms and then sold firewood door-to-door by horse and buggy. He saved his money to buy a truck, and in 1945 he started Cloverdale Fuels Ltd.[37] Over time, he bought heavy-duty trucks for hauling forest by-products. I helped my uncle by emptying and cleaning the trucks that transported sawdust and bark mulch. I enjoyed working with my uncle. The outdoors in Langley reminded me of the Punjab with its large parcels of farmland. Although we visited some distant relatives and I had the company of my Canadian-born cousins, I still missed my friends and paternal grandfather back in Dhudike.

In June 1962, I travelled by Greyhound bus to Prince Rupert to join my father at the sawmill bunkhouse. My father, who couldn't find steady work in the Lower Mainland, began working at Prince Rupert Sawmills in 1960.[38] It was discouraging to see my father, since he had taken to drinking alcohol and was gambling his money away. I felt hurt that my father, whom we were depending on to bring good fortune to our family and to guide me in Canada, was actually a liability. I approached the sawmill manager, Jack Mann, and asked him if I could get a job working at the sawmill. He said, "You are too young for work. You should go to school!" I replied, "I have no backup for school. I have to work, so give me work." I desperately wanted to work, especially since I could not depend on my father to repay my uncle for the airfare. Jack Mann gave me a job working on the green chain.

Working at Prince Rupert Sawmills was hard compared to the Punjab because we had to pull lumber in cold wet weather conditions. In the Punjab, we were landowners and felt a sense of pride when working on our land and ordering the hired help. In Prince Rupert, we were the ones taking orders and had to work on the gruelling green chain, pulling lumber measuring six by eight inches, six by ten inches, six by twelve inches, and six by fourteen inches. I wore rubber gloves, work clothes, and steel-toed boots that the company gave ten dollars towards.

After working a long and strenuous day on the green chain, we would return to the sawmill bunkhouse. There were about seventy-five Punjabi men ranging from the ages of sixteen to sixty living at the bunkhouse. One Punjabi sawmill worker, along with his wife and daughter, rented a basement suite in the town. The men at the bunkhouse were single, engaged, or married to women still living in the Punjab. Each bunkhouse room had four military-style cots with steel frames and two-inch-thick cotton mattresses. I shared a room with my father and two other men. I hung a colour poster of Guru Nanak Dev Ji in the room that I had brought from the Punjab and had got framed for five dollars in Prince Rupert.[39] When I felt lonely in my room, I would light incense in front of the picture and pray to Guru and ask, "Why am I in this situation? Why did I get this?" The picture of Guru Nanak Dev Ji provided me with comfort while living away from my village. I still have that picture today.

One of the benefits of living at the bunkhouse was the food. All the Punjabi sawmill workers would pitch in fifty dollars a month to pay for groceries and ten dollars a month to pay the two cooks, who were both ex-Indian military servicemen. One of the workers, who had a grade ten education and could speak English, was responsible for ordering the food from a local supply store. We ate fried unleavened bread (*parantha*) in the morning with a Punjabi power drink, which was either hot milk with two spoons of butter or cold milk with three raw eggs. During lunch and supper, we ate unleavened bread (*roti*) with curried vegetables or meat. Salmon curry with rice was a treat, since we didn't eat much fish in the Punjab. The cooks used HP Sauce as the secret ingredient in their tasty curries. The smell of fresh cooked curries at the sawmill grounds made the workers' mouths water. Sometimes I would invite the friendly Italian and Native Indian workers to share a meal at the bunkhouse.[40]

Even after a year of working and living at Prince Rupert Sawmills, I still felt really homesick and would sometimes increase the water pressure of my shower so that the other workers won't hear me crying. Working on the green chain was taking a toll on me, and I felt I was in a dead-end situation. I asked my father to send me back to the Punjab, but he insisted that it was better for me to work here in Canada and help our family back home. My father had no money to pay for my air ticket. I could go back if I paid my own ticket. But I didn't have enough money to pay for the airfare and I still owed my uncle for my trip to come here. I was earning around $125 bi-weekly. Over time I got used to getting paid bi-weekly, which was much better than having to wait six months as in the Punjab. I slowly became used to my life in Canada.

I became more content with my life in Canada, but there were two things that still bothered me – racism and not being able to speak English too much. Some of the Native Indian sawmill workers would often shout, "Hey Hindoo, go back to your country and get out of ours." Sometimes we would get into fights at work. The racism also occurred in the town, but it was the white guys who would call us "Hindoo" or "blacky." One night, while a bunch of us were at the Capitol Theatre on 3rd Avenue, some of the white guys swore at us and became physically aggressive. We left the theatre only to return with baseball bats and chased them away. We never heard from them again.

Not all white people were bad to the Punjabis in the town. When I used to take my laundry to the Koin Laundry on 2nd Avenue, I would walk by the Universal Clothing Store on 3rd Avenue. One day, a white lady working at the store asked me, "Why do you always go to the laundry with only one set of work clothes?" In my broken English and hand gestures I managed to tell her that I only had one set of work clothes. She suggested that I buy more work clothes. I tried to find another Punjabi man to explain that I had no money, but the English-speaking Punjabi was not around in the town. So, I showed her that I only had one dollar in my wallet. She told me to wait and returned with four sets of work clothes and a handwritten note. I took the clothes and note back to the bunkhouse and asked the English-speaking Punjabi sawmill worker to translate it. The note stated that the lady sold me four pants at two dollars each, four shirts at one and half dollars each, and four undershirts at fifty cents each, and that I could repay the lady when I had the money. Every month I returned to the Universal Clothing Store and paid back the lady bit by bit.

I knew I had to learn English to survive in this country, and I learnt it by going to the Capitol Theatre on the weekends.[41] I would buy popcorn for five cents and a bottle of cola for ten cents. I would pay twenty-five cents to watch the seven o'clock evening show and stay afterwards to watch the other movies until one o'clock in the morning. I watched many cowboy movies and managed to learn small sentences to help me communicate.[42] When I had to say something like "I have to go," I would say, "Hey Johnny, I got to get 'em up, pack 'em up!" People sometimes think I speak funny because I sound like a cowboy.

At the bunkhouse, the Punjabi sawmill workers entertained themselves by reminiscing about life in the Punjab. Some men would drink alcohol together and gamble to pass the time. There would often be different card games being played in the different rooms, ranging from three to ten men per room. One worker bought a black and white television set and another worker purchased a radio. We were all surprised to hear the radio pick up a frequency from India, and later learnt that there was an active military communications tower in the area. Prince Rupert still had warning sirens mounted on long metal posts around the town.

The workers also entertained themselves by playing shooting ball and soccer.[43] We built a shooting ball net from an old fishing net and installed it in the Old Dry Dock building. The Punjabis played the Italian and white guys. Sometimes we won, sometimes we lost. The Punjabi men also played *kabaddi* wrestling on the sawmill grounds.[44] These matches would sometimes become very competitive because we wanted to see who was the strongest. Some of the Italian workers would watch and laugh in good humour.

Sohen Gill would sometimes visit Prince Rupert to check on his sawmill. He would often meet with the workers and tell us to save our money to get settled in this country and not to waste it on booze and gambling. In the summer of 1963, I bought a blue Ford car for one hundred dollars. The lights and signals didn't work. My father was angry at me for wasting my money because I lived and worked at the same place. People in the village back home mostly commuted by foot or bicycle and, for longer distances, by bullock-pulled carts. But the car was not a waste of money because I knew I could one day operate heavy-duty machines if I could just first learn to drive a car. I was the only Punjabi worker to have a car and I taught myself to drive on the sawmill grounds. I never took the car to town because the car lights and wipers did not work.

In the spring of 1964, Prince Rupert Sawmills reduced its production to one shift, which made me be out of work while my father continued to work day shift. I went to Terrace and first found work at Dumont Sawmills, then at the Skeena Forest Sawmill, and then at the Pohle mill.[45] I initially rented a room with a Punjabi friend from white people. It was difficult to rent from white people, so I decided to buy a house for twelve thousand dollars on Agar Avenue. I put down two thousand dollars and was able to afford the mortgage payments by renting out rooms to other Punjabi workers who needed accommodation. After six months in Terrace, I returned to work at Prince Rupert Sawmills and still kept the house in Terrace as a rental property.

In the winter of 1964, with my limited English skills, I helped my middle brother migrate to Canada. He lived with us at the bunkhouse and attended the "New Canadian Class" at Conrad Elementary School.[46] After a year in Canada, he dropped out of school and began working at the sawmill. During the time period between 1964 and 1966, the workplace at Prince Rupert Sawmills became tense due to the workers being treated unfairly. We had many grievances against the supervisors; a major grievance was the taking of gifts, like liquor, in exchange for overtime work. I, too, made a complaint against the supervisors and was threatened that I would be fired. The supervisor didn't fire me because I threatened to tell Sohen Gill how his sawmill was being mismanaged.

In 1965, the president of the local IWA, a white guy named Fred, who was a millwright at the mill, met with me and my co-workers. He encouraged us to join the union to help ensure that we were being treated fairly. Sohen Gill tried to persuade us not to join the union by promising the workers the same wages and benefits as unionized sawmills. Fred met with the workers daily, and we eventually had enough signatures to become a unionized shop in 1966. Sohen Gill did not penalize the workers, and the conditions improved because now we had a procedure for making a grievance. If there wasn't a resolution, we would start a picket line right away and put a sign on the gatehouse to notify the next shift that there was no work until a solution was agreed upon. We had the power back then because the freighter would be waiting to be loaded. Time was money.

In December 1966, I got my licence; it was not a straightforward task. I couldn't fill out the application and requested the officer – a white guy – to read me the questions and write down my responses. He agreed but was surprised that I scored 97 per cent on the test without taking any driving lessons. I still have my original driver's licence certificate stored away. That was my first certificate.[47]

In 1967, my parents got me engaged to my wife, who was still living in the Punjab. My parents took care of all the arrangements. I didn't even know what she looked like prior to getting married. I sponsored her in 1968 and got married at the Khalsa Diwan Sikh Temple in Abbotsford.[48] We had to marry down south because there was no Sikh temple in Prince Rupert at that time, nor was there a Sikh priest who could marry us.[49] Before marriage, I bought a house on 11th Avenue East in Prince Rupert for eighteen thousand dollars. The bunkhouse was not a place to bring a bride to. I became friends with my Italian neighbour, who to my surprise had actually built my house. He taught me how to make homemade wine, something I still do to this day. My eldest son was born in 1969, my daughter was born in 1970, and my youngest son was born in 1974.

When I first moved into my house, my father and middle brother lived with me for three years and then moved to Terrace. My eldest and middle sisters, along with their husbands, migrated to Canada in 1969 and lived with me for two and four years, respectively. In 1972, my mother and little sister and brother migrated to Canada, and lived with me for two years and then moved to Terrace. My sisters, along with my wife, worked at the salmon cannery in Port Edward, and their husbands worked at Prince Rupert Sawmills. I sold my house in Terrace in 1970 to my parents at below market value to help them get settled. We still sent money back to the Punjab to expand our family farm.[50]

In the winter of 1969, our manager at Prince Rupert Sawmills told us to apply for work at the pulp and paper mill because the sawmill might be shutting down. The pulp and paper mill was building a second woodroom. Several of us got jobs working in the woodroom at the pulp and paper mill. I started on 16 March 1970. The work was similar to what we did at the sawmill. The workers at the pulp and paper mill were Canadians, Italians, Portuguese, and Punjabi. My co-workers used to call me "Gilligan," because my last name is Gill and I also wore a hat like the white guy from the TV show *Gilligan's Island*.

My Spanish supervisor encouraged me to apply for better jobs in the pulp and paper mill. I was hesitant to apply because a grade ten education was the minimum requirement. They said, "You're educated, go apply." I got promoted to other jobs and finally worked as a Peco crane and clamp operator in the shipping department. I would go to work one hour early to make sure my machine was ready, to find out who my supervisor was, and to write simple Punjabi notes about the shipping orders. The work was easier and better paying. In 1976, I asked my Italian neighbour to make me a new house on a lot I bought for nineteen thousand dollars on Sloan Avenue. I still kept the other house as rental property.

In 1984, there was a strike at the pulp and paper mill which lasted four to five months. I stood two hours a day on the picket line and received ninety dollars bi-weekly from the PPWC. There was a lot of uncertainty in the pulp and paper mill during the 1980s and 1990s. We always had the fear that the mill was going to close. Because my seniority was high, I managed to keep working even though the mill decreased its production. In 2003, the pulp and paper mill officially closed and I took early retirement at age fifty-nine. My children had already left Prince Rupert after they graduated from high school and made their homes in other parts of British Columbia. I continue to live in Prince Rupert and visit my village back in the Punjab every second year during the winter season. When I'm in Dhudike, I tend to the family farm, support local charitable causes, and visit historic Sikh temples. I know one day I will have to join my sons in the Lower Mainland because we are getting old and would like to spend time with our grandchildren. But for now, I think I'm doing well in this little town and in my village back home.

The First Journey: Creating a Home in the New Country

Despite the Punjabis having come to Canada in search of greater economic opportunity in terms of both a higher standard of living and a prosperous future, they faced the risks and challenges that immigrants often do on their arrival in a new country.[51] In seeking a better future, Punjabi immigrants of the Skeena region proceeded through four general phases: (1) confronting the new reality, (2) grieving over the new life situation, (3) coping with the new life, and (4) adapting to the new life.[52] While one can delineate these four phases in the narrative above and among Punjabi immigrants in general, the process of adjustment among immigrants should not be viewed as if immigrants are simply passive recipients of change.[53] Rather, immigrants are themselves, in essence, "social actors" during the course of their social and cultural transformation as minority groups, and their ethnicity can also be viewed as a source of adaptive strength.[54]

Confronting the New Reality

Upon their arrival in the new country, the Punjabi immigrants' initial experience of Canada was often contrary to what they had heard about the country in the Punjab. There was a considerable disparity between Punjabi pre-emigration expectations and the actual post-migration experience. For example, in the narrative above, the initial goal of the young man migrating to Canada was to earn enough money to afford a tractor for the family farm in the Punjab. However, once he arrived in Canada, he had to deal with both (1) the fact that he was already in debt and (2) his disappointment to discover that his father had taken to alcohol and gambling.

Punjabi men often came to Canada with the impression that they could easily prosper in a straightforward manner without having to work as hard as is necessary in a developing country like India. Instead, they discovered very quickly that they had to work harder in Canada. A common initial reaction among Punjabi men migrating in the 1960s was to contemplate returning home,[55] since the work most often available to them in Canada was extremely strenuous. Note the comment of a Punjabi male who arrived in Canada in the 1960s: "At that time, everybody dreams about going to Canada, a rich country. When I arrived, nothing I had heard about Canada was true. I learnt that no matter how rich a country is, you have to work very hard. After two to three weeks I wanted to go back home."[56] While much attention has been given to the loss in professional status experienced by South Asian immigrants to Canada,[57] Punjabi men who came from a farming society with limited education also had to contend with a new and difficult life situation.

On entering the Canadian labour market, Punjabis often faced many barriers and challenges, as they came predominantly from an agricultural society, had limited occupational skills, and lacked competency in Canada's official languages of English and French. Moreover, it was quite common that upon arrival, new immigrants – as in the case of the present narrator – found themselves already in debt and often under pressure to reimburse relatives for their travel expenses. This state of financial debt impelled early migrants to find jobs quickly, as is evident in the experience of the narrator, despite his not being old enough to work. The Canadian-educated Punjabi manager of Prince Rupert Sawmills told him that he was too young and should instead be attending high school.

Even when young immigrants wanted to upgrade their education, language, or employment skills, they often lacked the time or money to afford it.[58] A Punjabi man described the disappointment he felt when he arrived in the Skeena region in 1970: "I wanted to go to university but my brother found me a job in the sawmill where he was working. My idea of support was to go to university, but my brother's idea was to go to work to earn money. The focus was on earning money in order to build one's home. I was forced to quit school and got a job on the green chain."[59] The lack of education does not necessarily reflect a lack of appreciation of the value of education. In fact, to this date, the narrator has kept his original driver's licence certificate – his first certificate and first symbol of formal education. Given the lack of education among Punjabi immigrants, the job opportunities open to them were limited to manual labour, even as many of them managed to learn English on the job.

Grieving the Sawmill Life

When Punjabis could not find work in the Lower Mainland, they simply left the city and searched for work up north. Their willingness to travel to remote places under arduous conditions in the hope of finding better employment reflects the determination and resilience in the Punjabi character. Survival was the driving force for socio-economic adaptation to Canada, and the transition entailed the change from manual labour within the context of an agricultural society to manual labour within the context of an industrialized one. On entering the Canadian labour force, Punjabi immigrants – like the narrator – found the work to be physically demanding, much more so than back in the mother country.

Punjabi immigrants also had to contend with the harsh weather conditions of northwestern BC, where the work – like pulling lumber on the green chain – was sometimes done outside in the cold wet weather. One Punjabi man described his adjustment to working at Prince Rupert Sawmills:

> The first year [1961] was very hard because I was separated from my family and friends. Punjab was far away and I did not have to work too hard in the Punjab. I worked several months on the farm but we had [hired] help. After a year [working in Canada], you get used to the money. It was harder work but the benefits are in the long run better. In the Punjab, you work and then have to wait for six months to get the reward. If there is bad weather, your work or crop can be destroyed. The reward depended on the weather. Here you get a pay cheque every two weeks regardless of the weather. You still work in the cold weather but you know that you will get money for your work.[60]

The initial reaction of many was to consider returning to the Punjab. They were homesick for the social network and family support they had been accustomed to in the Punjab, and they hadn't had to work as hard on the farm. Many had gone through the experience narrated in the story below told by a Punjabi man who, after being sponsored by his father in 1967, had pulled lumber on the green chain at Prince Rupert Sawmills at the age of twenty:

> Sawmill work was very hard. My first day, I worked for only four hours. They know that you will only be able to tolerate four hours on the green chain. After work my dad gave me a drink (cream and half a pound of butter) to make me strong. I could only drink half of it.
>
> After two to three weeks, I wanted to go back home. I said [to my father], "I will give back every penny that you spent to bring me [here]. I will return it to you; I just want to go back." Dad said, "You are grown up, I'm not going to stop you. Give back my money and earn your own return plane fare." His answer made me question as to how he could really be my dad. In tears, I thought, "What is wrong with this country?"

A couple of months later, I realized that all the older Punjabi men talked this way. Other men in the bunkhouse used the same wording as my dad did. The Punjabi men didn't want to be too soft with you so that you get used to [the new life]. And, by the time you save up the money [to return back to the Punjab], you are used to it.[61]

Being stern with newly arrived immigrants was the typical Punjabi way of "toughening them up" so that they wouldn't be afraid of working hard in an unfamiliar environment. The new immigrants predictably wanted to return home after their first day of work on the green chain, but the older Punjabis told that they could only return once they had saved for their own airfare. Having to raise their own funds for the return airfare meant that recent immigrants would have to put in many days' work. By the time they could afford the airplane ticket, they would have grown accustomed to Canada, not only in terms of hard labour, but also in terms of receiving bi-weekly wages. It was this tactic that the Punjabi elders used to help their younger fellow Punjabis build resiliency (*charhdi kala*) and persevere in the new country.

Charhdi kala is an important Punjabi expression that extols fortitude in the face of fear or pain.[62] While the phrase can be loosely translated as "resilience,"[63] it connotes having or maintaining a positive attitude towards life and the future. That is, one should always be forward looking and evolving. In facing the harsh realities of adjusting to a foreign environment, Punjabis could draw upon their own traditional strategies to build strength and resiliency. That ethos played an important role in fostering resiliency among them. Since Punjabi immigrants carry with them a strong traditional orientation characteristic of agricultural society, they maintain, for the most part, an oral or traditional mode of communication. Their thoughts also express a collectivity orientation, often in a concrete form based on personal life experiences. And this oral tradition has its own method of providing social support.[64] When older or more experienced Punjabi immigrants dramatically act out a situation (such as allowing kin to return to India on the condition that they have saved enough money for the airfare), they are in fact employing a traditional strategy to motivate or empower individuals. Moreover, their communication style involves telling traditional stories of Punjabi warriors, freedom fighters, and martyrs with the goal of empowering kin.

Coping with the Canadian Way

Besides the economic challenges, the Punjabis had to contend with challenges relating to their belonging to a visible non-Christian minority group in both the mainstream society and the workplace. Certainly, an established ethnic community provides some social and emotional comfort to new members. The sawmill bunkhouse was a mechanism that allowed single male immigrants to recreate a Punjab village environment while living outside their birth country with little family support. It also provided difficult yet affordable living arrangements for those who lacked proficiency in English, and it allowed them to save money so that they could establish themselves.

The work set-up at a Punjabi-owned sawmill and the ability to live on its premises at the bunkhouse no doubt reduced some of the acculturation-related stresses frequently faced by new immigrants, such as a language barrier, culture clash, and discrimination. The acculturation stress associated with interactions with the mainstream community often leads to loneliness, social isolation, and alienation; as a result, keeping company with one's ethnic group, or ethnic insularity, emerges as a coping strategy.[65] With little or no family – most often the norm during the initial stage of adaptation – the Punjabi immigrant workers found the bunkhouse to be an asset. The sawmill bunkhouse provided a familiar Punjabi environment for most Punjabi male immigrants; there, they could speak their mother tongue, share memories of the "homeland," and empathize with one another's life situation.

Other adaptive coping strategies were available to Punjabi male immigrants. The Sikh temple (*gurdwara*) was eventually established in 1973 and served as a religious, social, and cultural base for members of the growing Punjabi community. Religion can invest human existence with meaning that finds expression in goals that ease adaptation to challenging circumstances.[66] Sikhism provides a framework through which Sikhs can draw meaning from sorrowful realities. This is made evident in the above narrative; that is, the Punjabi immigrant relied on his religious and cultural practices (such as praying to Guru Nanak) as a source of strength.[67] Moreover, to cope with stress, the narrator played shooting ball and *kabaddi* and watched movies to learn English. Indeed, the narrative well illustrates some of the coping strategies that emerged in the survival and adaptation process.

There were Punjabis, however, who took to maladaptive coping mechanisms in the sawmill bunkhouse. Some of the men hung around at the bunkhouse drinking alcohol and gambling. Indeed, the narrator was disillusioned to see that his own father had taken to drinking and gambling. Alcohol is perceived as a "fortifying drink" among Punjabi males, especially labourers, who believe it makes a man work harder and longer, a view also held among white working-class men.[68] More significantly, acculturation stress can aggravate the Punjabi male's tendency to drink alcohol. In fact, alcohol-related problems in the Punjabi diaspora have largely been attributed to acculturation stress.[69] With migration, there occurs a change from a collectivity orientation to a self-orientation, which often results in a breakdown of traditional forms of social control; that is, rather than the personal autonomy and anonymity that characterize Western communities (as typically found in Canada), Punjabi male immigrants have been accustomed to norms associated with the collective nature of the Punjabi village, where people watch over each other.[70] These traditional norms begin to erode after migration.

While the bunkhouse set-up was for the most part economically and culturally beneficial to Punjabi male immigrants, the workers nonetheless experienced stress in their interactions with their supervisors. The tense relations at work caused many of them to join the IWA. Indeed, the Punjabi manual labourers became involved with the union so that they could speak out for their rights and improve their working conditions. This, too, was a form of coping among Punjabi men, who experienced the language barrier acutely in an unfamiliar environment. The union was a mechanism through which their voices could be heard.

Adapting to a New Life in the Skeena

Despite the many different challenges and the enormous homesickness that the Punjabis of the Skeena region faced during the 1960s following immigration, the Punjabi cultural ethos of a strong work ethic played an important role in fostering resiliency among them. Indeed, as a result, they were able to establish themselves in the remote Skeena towns. The present narrative illustrates how the narrator made personal efforts to improve his English by watching cowboy movies and to learn how to drive a car so that one day he might be able to get a "prestigious" job operating heavy-duty machinery. While learning English was a strategy to improve his life in Canada, learning to drive a car was a specific manoeuvre to help him escape the arduous manual labour of pulling lumber and find work that required higher skill and paid better wages. Interestingly, Punjabis have put certain Canadian practices to good use. Indeed, the regular bi-weekly pay cheque was very different from the six-month pay cycle that came with farm work in India, and the Punjabis used the new system to set personal goals for themselves in Canada in order to improve their own well-being and that of their families.

The majority of Punjabi immigrants who arrived in the Skeena region in the early 1960s were young single men in search of work. Once they found steady employment, Punjabi male immigrants had three main goals: (1) to send money back to family members still in the Punjab; (2) to sponsor family members for immigration to Canada; and (3) to purchase a home and later to invest in rental properties. These goals helped them organize their efforts to build a new life in Canada. It is noteworthy that, as "social actors," many Punjabi immigrants maintained – even after their relatively successful adaptation to the Skeena region or Canada in general – strong ties with their village both by investing in it and by spending long periods of time in it after retirement.[71] So, even though many of these men had adapted to Canada, they remained connected to their Punjabi roots. For instance, the narrator visits his village in the winter season every second year. Indeed, many Punjabi immigrants have created a comfortable situation for themselves, having two places that they consider home – their ancestral village and Canada. This would not have been feasible in an earlier era, but globalization certainly facilitates it.

The narrative above describes one example – among many – of Punjabi male immigrants facing difficulties on migrating but in fact being far from passive. Rather, they have been active social actors, strengthened by their Punjabi cultural ethos of boldness and industriousness.[72] This is evident not only in terms of their going to and settling in remote areas in search of work, but also in terms of the cultural mechanisms that have been used to help Punjabi newcomers become more resilient as they acclimatized themselves to Canada. The Punjabi cultural ethos includes a strong commitment to family – as well as to clan or ethnic group – and a high value placed on landownership.

Sponsoring the Family

The initial migration to Prince Rupert resembled the migration of the Punjabi pioneers of the early 1900s in that it mainly consisted of single Punjabi men in search of employment to earn money and send it back to their families. However, there was a major difference between the two: in contrast to the early pioneers, who for the most part came with the intention of returning to India because of uncertainty over immigration and social policy, the Punjabi immigrants of the 1960s generally came to Prince Rupert with the aim of eventually sponsoring family members and bringing them to Canada through the family reunification program, a program that was instituted by the federal government in 1951 but came into full force only from the 1970s onwards.

The family has been the key mechanism in the migration process of Punjabis, especially Sikhs, since the 1950s up to the present.[73] The early 1950s were marked by increased East Indian immigration to Canada based on the sponsorship system, which worked in favour of Sikh immigrants because most of the earlier East Indian immigrants had been Sikhs.[74] In their study of the Sikh community in Canada over the period 1965–87, Norman Buchignani and Doreen Marie Indra put forward the proposition that Sikh kinship is a principal feature of the Sikhs' informal but intensive community networks and was related to "heavy" Sikh migration.[75] The present study confirms this finding. A Punjabi male immigrant gave the following account of his kinship chain of migration: "I was born in village Punjab in 1940. My father had migrated to Canada in 1906 but returned back to India after injuring his hand on the job in the 1930s. I came from a family of three boys; I was the middle one. My eldest brother came in 1951 or so on the claim that he was the son of a Canadian citizen. His declaration allowed me to migrate. I arrived at Alberni and then shifted to Vancouver in 1959. My elder brother sponsored me to come to Canada. At the time of my immigration to Canada, he was living in North Vancouver working at L&K lumber."[76]

Punjabis have mainly relied on the sponsorship system for their migration to Canada. Not only has this been true with regard to immigration, but it is also evident in terms of their finding work and living in the Skeena region. Punjabi men who arrived in the 1960s and 1970s often came alone to the towns of the Skeena region, hoping to find work, start a new life, and establish a family. They were willing to work hard so that their children could obtain a post-secondary education and move up the socio-economic ladder. Because higher education wasn't available in the Skeena region, many second-generation Punjabis, after graduating from high school, left for the Lower Mainland or Victoria to pursue their education or careers. Upon retirement, parents followed their children and settled in the large urban centres. The immigrants of the 1960s and 1970s made many sacrifices during the time they worked at the manual labour jobs that were available to them, but they had the dream that their children would acquire a better education than they had received. Their basic orientation was to work hard and establish their family's position in their new country by supporting their children through the school system and by paying off the mortgage on their home.

Acquiring Investment Properties

Not only did the sponsorship system make possible the gradual establishment of one's own family, but it also fostered the development of the Punjabi community in the Skeena region, especially through the acquisition of property. Just as the early pioneer Punjabi men had banded together to purchase sawmills, members of extended families in the Skeena region and elsewhere banded together and pooled resources to purchase real estate. Once Punjabi immigrants realized that they were going to stay in Canada, their ultimate goal became to acquire land in the new country. For the Punjabis – as for the Chinese and Italians – home ownership is not just related to socio-economic factors like social status and economic security, it is a value in itself.[77]

At first, when finances were strained, Punjabis often networked creatively with family members in order to purchase a home. Having only limited funds, they might rent a room to extended-family members, charging a modest amount, or to people from their village. They used the rental income to help pay off the mortgage, while their tenants benefited financially from lower rents that allowed them to save for a down payment on a future home. Crowding propensities are often understood in terms of economic constraints, but cultural differences are apparent in residential crowding even when there are no economic constraints. Michael Haan has noted that East Indians have a higher tendency to residential crowding when they rent than when they own.[78] This held true for the Skeena region in the 1970s and 1980s, as many families avoided residential clustering once they owned their house. In fact, in the 1980s, many Punjabis moved to the new development area on the west side of the town, where they could build larger homes. However, Skeena Punjabis were inclined to rent out rooms or basement suites, especially during the salmon canning season, in order to earn money to pay off their house. Once the house was paid off, the Punjabis tended to expand their landholdings by acquiring new investment properties. One Punjabi man made this observation about the Punjabi tendency to acquire investment properties: "Punjabis do not spend as much money. We tend to save our money to pay off the house and look after the family by sponsoring. The impact [of the shutdown of the pulp and paper mill] made many Punjabis leave [the area] looking for other jobs. Many left for the Lower Mainland or Alberta. The older generation had rental properties."[79]

The wish to acquire investment properties was not only about survival; it was also about the deep Punjabi cultural desire for landownership. Although many immigrants have continued to invest in their respective Punjab villages, the inclination to expand landownership has been carried over into the Skeena region. Even though the unskilled mill worker element in the Punjabi population remained large in rural British Columbia during the late 1960s, many Punjabis typically acquired rental properties as a way to build up their financial assets. Thus, while many Punjabi men still earned a wage through manual or semi-skilled and skilled labour, they also tended to acquire investment properties. Note the comment of one Punjabi man who had migrated in the early 1960s:

Families worked together, saved money by living together, and made bigger houses. In the late '70s and into the '80s, people started buying rental properties and built houses on the weekend as well. Our value of the land came from the Punjab. We say, "You buy property, you will never lose." Punjabis have a good habit. We pay off the house first, and then rent the basement to help pay bills. As compared to white people, Punjabis were better off when the pulp mill closed. We had less financial pressure, no problem at home. A lot of the white people lost their homes and had marriage problems when the mill closed.[80]

During the 1960s and 1970s, the Skeena Punjabi immigrants were establishing themselves and their families. By the 1980s, many Punjabi manual labourers had become landlords, and some of these families started to branch out, acquiring investment properties in other areas, especially in the Lower Mainland.

With their orientation towards working hard so that their children might pursue a profession or business, some Punjabis had the foresight to plan for their children's move to the Lower Mainland for post-secondary education. They therefore acquired investment properties in the Lower Mainland before or at the time of their children's departure to that area. The property would be fully rented out until their children were in need of living arrangements. Their prudence in building assets in the Lower Mainland paid off, for the properties not only provided living arrangements for their children while they studied at a post-secondary institution, but in some ways also served as a buffer for Punjabi mill workers when they faced economic difficulty following BC's lumber bust.

The "first journey" of Punjabi immigrants, from village Punjab to the Skeena region, was often the consequence of the informal but strong kinship networks. Interestingly, the "second journey," from remote towns to urban centres in Canada, of the older "retired" generation has also been the result of kinship networks. There is one major difference, however, between these two journeys: while the first journey consisted primarily of single men who sponsored, and then were followed by, their family members, the second often started with the children, who were then followed by their parents. While the cultural orientation towards landowning proved to be a great asset in the socio-economic adaptation of Punjabis in Canada, the acquisition of land in the new country, along with the sponsorship of families, sometimes became a source of contention and resentment among some First Nations people and Anglo-Canadians, a subject examined in chapters 6 and 7.

Summary

The narrative in this chapter by one Punjabi immigrant provides insights into the Punjabi male immigrant experience in Canada. It sheds light on how such immigrants, with limited schooling and skills, navigated through the social system in Canada as they adapted, socially and economically, to a remote BC town in the early 1960s. While many Punjabi immigrant men eventually availed themselves of better economic opportunities, they experienced economic and social challenges along the way. In overcoming the various challenges, Punjabi male immigrants found the Punjabi cultural ethos to be a source of enormous adaptive strength. That ethos played an important role in fostering resilience (*charhdi kala*) among them.

Punjabi immigrant men – despite their language and educational shortcomings – were quite able, because of their cultural ethos, to steer through the structures of a foreign environment. The narrative presented above delineates very well the cultural ethos of the Punjabis. Their hard work, strong kinship ties, and landownership proved to be great cultural assets to Punjabi families and the community at large in getting established in Canada. On their arrival in Canada and during their initial period of settlement, Punjabi immigrant men set for themselves the goals of sponsoring other family members and acquiring investment properties. Although many had to settle for manual or semi-skilled labour jobs, they endeavoured to build their financial assets so as to support their children in proceeding up the social ladder. Many acquired investment properties in the large urban centres that could be useful when their children were ready to pursue post-secondary education. This practice also proved to serve as an economic buffer upon the decline of the forestry and fishery industries.

CHAPTER 4

Women, Household Labour, and Paid Work

While considerable attention has been given to the Punjabi male immigrant story, especially in regard to the forestry industry,[1] the Punjabi female immigrant experience has often been overlooked. Punjabi women began settling in the Skeena region of British Columbia in the early 1960s. Their migration to the region was consequential, since it served as a catalyst for their venturing out of the private sphere to participate in paid labour in the public economy of Canada. Though many were reared with the traditional understanding that a woman's work is within the home, Punjabi immigrant women gradually entered the paid workforce in order to improve the family's economic situation. In due course, it became the norm for Punjabi women to work in the fishery industry, the same type of paid labour that First Nations women had been doing since the late 1800s.

Punjabi women's entry into the workforce had a significant impact on their previous traditional social patterns of behaviour. While Punjabi women were initially propelled into the paid workforce for the sake of the economic welfare of the family, their entry into the public sphere proved to have more than monetary consequences. After their arrival in the Skeena region, Punjabi women experienced tremendous social isolation, since there was no Punjabi community as such that could provide – at the very least – a sense of belonging. Over time, a subculture emerged among the Punjabi women who worked in the salmon canneries of the Skeena region. The transformative impact that working in the public sphere had on their lives becomes clear when one notes the effect that the later decline of the fisheries, beginning in the mid-1990s onwards, had on them. Punjabi women experienced considerable economic and psychological distress as a result of reduced work hours or job loss. Interestingly, they have continued to participate in the workforce even if the work differs from their initial women-dominated cannery experience.

The focus of this chapter is twofold: (1) it investigates the specific immigrant experience of Punjabi women in the Skeena region in the light of their traditional gender orientation and their entry into the paid Canadian workforce, and (2) it analyses the economic and emotional impact that the decline of the fishery industry has had on them, as well as the ability of these women to cope with adversity and maintain their economic and social autonomy.

This chapter has three parts. The first provides the background of Punjabi immigrant women, looking at the traditional gender-role expectations that came with them in their 1960s and 1970s migration, along with a critical look at their adaptation process while living in the remote towns of the Skeena region before a consolidated Punjabi community had developed there. The second part examines the entry of Punjabi women into the salmon canning industry. The third part analyses the impact that the decline of the fisheries has had on Punjabi women. The chapter as a whole goes beyond demonstrating that the women's participation in the workforce had a significant impact on traditional social patterns of behaviour; it further demonstrates that much of the transformation resulting from working in the salmon canneries occurred because of the women's need, not only for economic, but also for social and psychological survival in the course of their adaptation to the remote towns in the Skeena region.

Unpaid Labour and Immigrant Homes

Since women are often regarded as the essential medium through which traditional culture is transmitted, traditional gender roles tend to be viewed as constraining a woman's autonomy.[2] However, new cultural transformations can occur as a result of their migration and adaptation to a new and, especially, an industrial environment.[3] Most Punjabi women immigrated to Prince Rupert – and to the Skeena region in general – through arranged marriages with men who were already working in the area. Coming straight from the home country, they brought with them the Punjabi customs characteristic of traditional agricultural society and thus arrived with the orientation of fulfilling their traditional role of unpaid labour within the home. While primed to fulfil their gender role as wife and mother, Punjabi women were, upon settling in the Skeena region, unprepared for the social isolation that came with living in a remote Canadian town that lacked a Punjabi community. Along with social isolation, Punjabi women missed the Punjabi way of life that they had been accustomed to back home.

The governing and gender-based principles of social behaviour in traditional Indian society include duty (*dharam*) and respect (*izzat*); these are applied according to one's particular stage of life in order to maintain the integrity of the family. Since the members of the household constitute an economically interdependent unit, the woman has a crucial role in it, one that is essentially home-based, oriented towards the smooth functioning of the household as well as towards child-bearing and rearing.[4] A female is therefore raised to fulfil her role as wife, mother, and daughter-in-law: "In childhood let her remain under the protection of her father; under the protection of her husband in youth; and under the protection of her son after the demise of her husband in old age."[5] Since a woman is dependent on men – such as her father or husband – she has to assume a cooperative attitude or role. Note the comment made by a Punjabi woman who migrated to Prince Rupert in 1972 at the age of seventeen: "I was a young shy village girl from Punjab. While growing up, I was raised in a traditional home where the father is the boss. Girls help their mother in childhood, serve their husband and raise children in adulthood, and take care of grandchildren in old age. In the Punjab, there was no need for women to leave the home. Women stayed at home, and the men went out to work on the farm. When I migrated to Canada, my life changed."[6]

As she is growing up, the female is primarily trained for married life within the household. As she approaches adolescence, the girl increasingly becomes responsible for fulfilling some household duties and is expected to look after the younger children. Social status is mainly ascribed on the basis of the family or caste the girl is born into. Traditionally, a Punjabi married woman also acquires status and respect from the wealth she possesses through material possessions like gold jewellery, most often received as a dowry at the time of marriage, as well as from the son(s) she bears. There is social pressure on a woman to produce a son, not only for the family at large, but also for her own sake, as he will function as her social security in old age.[7]

Respect is not only related to social status; it is also established by a person's seniority in the family system. Indeed, elders traditionally command authority and respect. Take the case of the wife. When she first enters into her new family as a wife, she is subordinate to her mother-in-law and is expected to be very respectful towards her. When she bears a son, she acquires greater respect and status. And when she becomes a mother-in-law herself, it is her turn to enjoy respect and decision-making power within the household. Still later, she moves into a more solid position of power and authority within the household and assumes a more powerful position in the internal economy of the village.[8] Female elders play important roles within the extended family, such as guiding the young, arranging their marriages, and helping to raise the grandchildren. A woman is wholly dependent on her sons later in life. Traditionally, women have had no property rights, and land was passed down from father to son.[9]

Marriage and Migration

Women are entitled to immigrate to Canada under one of three categories: (1) family, (2) independent, and (3) refugee. While women can qualify under any one of the three categories, they predominantly immigrate under the family class. In fact, since the 1950s, 50 per cent of female immigrants have come under the family class.[10] This has held true for Punjabi women who usually immigrated to Prince Rupert, and to the Skeena region in general, through arranged marriages with men already working in the area.

For centuries in the Indian subcontinent, marriages have customarily been arranged by parents and other trusted family members, since matrimony is conceived as uniting two families. The suitable match is usually based on factors such as age, physical appearance (e.g., height, skin colour), personality, family background (e.g., education level, social standing, wealth), and caste affiliation. In fact, in the past, marriages were arranged without the prospective bride and groom ever meeting each other. The two may have had the opportunity to view a photo of the other, but of course, that has only been made possible with the fairly recent availability of cameras. Once the parents of both the bride and the groom agree with the match, all relatives and acquaintances from both sides are invited to witness and bless the agreement.

In line with the traditional Punjabi custom of arranged marriages, two main patterns emerged among Punjabis in the Skeena region. In one pattern, a single male immigrant with limited education and skill married – following arrangements made by family and clan networks – a woman of a similar background from India. This pattern was common in the 1960s and continued into the 1970s. In the second pattern, a married male immigrant with secondary or higher education either arrived accompanied by his wife and children or sponsored his wife and children once he became settled in Canada. This pattern emerged in the late-1960s as a result of Canada's institution of the immigration point system (1967). Along with the two main marriage patterns, a third marriage pattern surfaced among some Punjabis in the Skeena region in the mid-1970s and 1980s; it involved an uneducated yet established man marrying and sponsoring an educated woman. This pattern was made possible by the fact that some families back in the Punjab, although not well educated, acquired over time higher status through the financial support they received from their relatives in Canada. Moreover, once male family members – fathers or brothers – became established in the Skeena region, their sponsored daughters or sisters had their marriages arranged with grooms in India in the 1970s and 1980s.[11]

During the 1960s and 1970s, parents arranged – according to tradition – the engagement or marriage of their daughters, most often back in the Punjab, and these women then followed their fiancés or husbands to Canada. In his study of the Vancouver Sikh community in the early 1970s, James Chadney found continuity in the custom of arranged marriages where spouses were "recruited from India so that at least one of the parties was born in India."[12] The practice of recruiting Indian spouses for members of the Punjabi community living in the Skeena region in the 1960s and 1970s, however, was not a strategy to prevent assimilation into Canadian society. In contrast to Chadney's observations, the majority of Punjabi men in the Skeena region were recent Indian-born immigrants who, in order to follow the Punjabi custom of arranged marriage, simply had no choice but to marry spouses born in India. Since most of the members of the relatively small Punjabi community in British Columbia of that period had migrated through the family sponsorship system, the number of "suitable matches" available locally in Canada was limited. According to Punjabi custom, marriage cannot take place between two people from the same village; likewise, one is also forbidden to marry someone with the same surname. Therefore, at that time, there was not a large enough pool of suitable matches from one's district or region in Canada.

While some Punjabi immigrant men returned to India for their engagement or marriage, others waited for their fiancées to arrive in Canada without ever having seen them previously. In the 1960s and early 1970s, once the marriage arrangements were made in the Punjab and one's fiancée received her immigration documents, she would travel to Vancouver. Upon the fiancée's arrival in British Columbia, the Sikh marriage ceremony was commonly conducted at the Khalsa Diwan Society Gurdwara, either in Vancouver or Abbotsford, and followed by a civil marriage if a registered priest was not available. The ceremony took place in the Lower Mainland because no Sikh temple (*gurdwara*) existed in the Skeena region until 1973 and no registered priest was available until the 1980s.[13] Since no Hindu temple was ever established in the Skeena region, Hindus had to marry in Vancouver or settle for a civil marriage.[14]

According to tradition, the woman joins her husband's family after marriage. Therefore, in the Punjab, marriage entails the wife moving to another village. However, with migration to the Skeena region (or Canada in general), a woman had to move a lot farther away from her natal family and village than she would have had to do if she had not left India. Her initial migration experience was thus often shaped by whether any of her own family members were already living in the Skeena region or Canada. The experience of migration was more intimidating and overwhelming for those women who had no relatives in Canada. The lack of a family presence led to emotional distress and loneliness. When a Punjabi woman was the first in her family to migrate, the predominant description of her experience was that she was "nervous to come" and that she was extremely "lonely" after her arrival and during her adjustment period in Canada.[15] A Punjabi woman who arrived in the Skeena region in 1971 described her immigration experience thus: "When I came, I only had one sister-in-law. I left India via Hong Kong. We lived in Prince Rupert because my husband worked at the pulp and paper mill in Port Edward. I was crying all the time because I missed my family ... Initially, I was very homesick, since I had no family or friends in Prince Rupert. For the first year, I had no friends and felt so lonely."[16]

Some of the women who migrated to Canada in the late 1960s and 1970s had stayed behind in India on their own for a time while their husbands were settling in Canada. In these cases, coming to Canada was an ambivalent experience: women were sad to leave their natal country, yet glad to reunite with their husbands. A Punjabi woman explained how, after two years of separation, her immigration experience was a mixed one: "When I arrived in Canada in 1974, I was happy to see my husband. But I was sad because it was hard for me to leave my family and friends. I was now more relaxed because I had help with the children. After my husband had gone to Canada, I was left behind with all the responsibility. My husband came from Prince Rupert to the Vancouver airport to pick me up. We stayed with my sister-in-law in Vancouver for two weeks. Then we went to Prince Rupert. Having come from Delhi, Prince Rupert seemed small."[17] Punjabi men who arrived in the Skeena region with their wives or whose wives followed them later were often more educated than the single men who married later and sponsored their wives.

A woman can be sponsored for immigration by a relative on her side of the family or by someone from her husband's side. A woman who is sponsored by a sibling or a cousin from her family, or by a member of her spouse's family, might not have necessarily wished or planned to settle in Canada. Many women, however, have come to Canada through the family sponsorship system as a consequence of marriages arranged by their parents. The marriage was ultimately the decision of the parents, and it was the parents who believed that their daughters would have a "better future" in Canada. From the perspective of the bride's family, an arranged marriage to someone living in, or moving to, Canada was a great opportunity, not only for the daughter but also for other family members. In keeping with the economic factors in the selection of the spouse,[18] the migration of a daughter gave parents the hope that other family members, including themselves, might be sponsored in the future.

Marriages were also arranged with the notion that education would make for better job prospects in Canada. Therefore, families began to seek more educated spouses for their children, spouses who could work in, or at least be familiar with, the English language. As a result, greater numbers of women migrating to Canada in the late 1970s and 1980s had received a secondary and/or post-secondary education in the Punjab. While this practice had a pragmatic motive, by the 1980s it had become a source of tension, since it created an imbalance in an otherwise patriarchal system, with the women now being better educated than their husbands, who worked as manual or skilled labourers.[19]

Disconnected from the Punjab and Its Culture

When Punjabi women began migrating to the Skeena region in the early 1960s, their numbers were small. Gurmail Kaur Walia, whose husband worked at Prince Rupert Sawmills, was the first Punjabi woman to migrate to the region, in 1960. The couple soon had a daughter, the first Punjabi to be born in Prince Rupert.[20] The second woman to migrate to the region, Bunt Kaur Sidhu, arrived in 1961; her husband also worked at Prince Rupert Sawmills. Since the bunkhouse was not a suitable place for women or married couples, the two women initially lived with their husbands in rental suites in houses located in the town. By 1966, six Punjabi families were living in Prince Rupert, while about seventy-five Punjabi men lived at the Prince Rupert Sawmills bunkhouse. Though small in number, this was the beginning of the Punjabi community in Prince Rupert.[21]

The first few female arrivals in Prince Rupert were recent immigrants to Canada. Therefore, not only did Punjabi women have to adapt to the life of a married woman in Canada and to the language and cultural barriers that came with immigration, but they also had to contend with the social isolation that came with settling in a remote town in the Skeena region.

Like the pioneer Punjabi immigrant women in Canada in the first half of the twentieth century, Punjabi women in the Skeena region later in the century fulfilled their traditional gender roles as wife and mother within the home.[22] However, there was one major difference: while a woman's social life in Vancouver and on Vancouver Island in the pioneer period centred on the home and the local *gurdwara*, a woman's social life in the Skeena region initially centred only on the home because there was no meeting place for female members of the community. The only place for Punjabis to get together was the bunkhouse, an environment unsuitable for women.

In due course, women increasingly immigrated to the Skeena region as a result of arranged marriages and family sponsorships; yet they still found themselves isolated and disconnected from their Punjabi culture. According to Ames and Inglis, women were becoming less satisfied in the home because – unlike in the Punjab – it offered only limited links with the outside world; meanwhile, the men continued to behave in a traditional manner in the home even while developing links with the larger community through their jobs.[23] This observation finds confirmation in the present study. Note the comment made by a Punjabi woman who arrived in 1972 when the Punjabi community was small compared to her Punjab village: "I came when I was twenty-two years old ... From 1972 to 1976 there were six of us – my family, brothers-in-law, and aunties – and we lived on three hundred dollars per month. I was lonely because India is crowded ... here the town was scary because there were very few people. There were only four to six Punjabi families to provide support emotionally and socially."[24]

Even during the late 1970s, by which time the Punjabi community was more consolidated, women continued to experience loneliness in their separation from their extended family, friends, and familiar surroundings: "I was born in a village in the Punjab. I received up to grade twelve education. A lot of people talked about Canada as being a rich country, but when I came, I thought India was a much better place. I had my friends. In a different country one gets lonely ... My son was born in 1977. I had a daughter in 1981. The first year was very hard. I was crying all the time. I was missing my parents. I knew a little English but was not able to speak much."[25]

For Punjabi women, raising their families in the new environment – as opposed to in a Punjabi village – was very isolating. While the primary role of a Punjabi woman is to bear children, it is customary that this role be fulfilled in the context of an extended family, kin group, and village community. In the Skeena region, however, women were isolated in their role of bearing and rearing children, since they lacked the established family and social network that they were accustomed to in village Punjab. Moreover, the Skeena region – in contrast to village Punjab – lacked the sounds of activity (*raunuk*), especially during the long winter months when the cold rainy weather forced people to stay indoors: "I came [to Terrace] when I was seventeen years old [1975]. My husband worked in the Pohle mill. I stayed home to raise the children ... It was intimidating to be living in Canada. I felt isolated with the cold weather and language barrier."[26]

Over and above the feelings of disconnection from family and familiar social life, the experience of isolation was amplified by the language barrier. Many of the women came with limited language skills, making it difficult for them to communicate with non-Punjabis. The major acculturation stress for women upon migration to Canada is associated with their interactions with the mainstream population (out-group stress), the sources of which include language barrier, cultural incongruence, and discrimination. Such stress can and often does result in loneliness, social isolation, and alienation.[27] The common Punjabi coping strategy for out-group stress is to rely on people from their own family, village or region, and caste.[28]

Even with an education, many of the women lacked experience in conversational English, which aggravated their social isolation and alienation: "I attended Punjabi school in the Punjab up to grade eight. I received a little of English but I could not speak the language. We didn't talk in English in my country ... It was scary to come to Canada because I did not know the language. I did not know how to speak with the people."[29] Even though some women understood English, there was still the issue of being able to converse in the language comfortably with other members of the larger Skeena community. Gradually, however, the women managed to "pick it up."[30]

Unlike the majority of Punjabi women, a few arrived in the Skeena already proficient in the English language. This reduced their out-group stress, but they too, living in a remote town, felt disconnected from their native country and its social culture. One interviewee illustrates this pattern: "I knew English from back home. I studied in English medium in the Punjab. I could talk to everybody [when I came to Canada], including Punjabis, Caucasians, and Natives. I felt comfortable speaking English. I was not too shy to speak to others. Even so, I missed an Indian atmosphere. I felt cut off from India and my culture. There were very few Indian families with whom I could socialize. I could not purchase any Indian cooking items or clothes. Then there was also at that time no Indian TV shows or channels."[31]

Indian products like clothing and spices were not readily available in the Skeena region. Therefore, in the 1960s and 1970s, women found it difficult to dress and cook according to Punjabi custom. Punjabi women purchased their clothing and spices when on trips, either to India or Vancouver. A Punjabi woman described acquiring Indian products: "There are no stores here to buy Indian things. There are only stores in the Vancouver Lower Mainland. [In the late 1970s], I used to buy from a Fiji man named Patel in Vancouver in the early days. We would also bring food and clothing from India. We made our own clothes and cooked our own food ... In Prince Rupert, ladies would get together and make our own sweets and samosas; we could not buy these anywhere."[32] By the early 1980s, Punjabi women would stock up on spices, clothing, dried lentils, and the like on shopping expeditions in Vancouver (Main Street and 49th, an area which has since been designated as the "Vancouver Punjabi bazaar").[33] Still, the non-availability of Indian food items and clothing in the Skeena region heightened the women's sense of disconnectedness from their Punjabi culture. Contributing to the sense of isolation, television was limited to local regional stations at this time, and long-distance phone calls to the Punjab were very expensive. Moreover, the towns in the Skeena region were far from the activity of big urban centres, and the road between Prince Rupert and Terrace was hazardous in the winter and early spring.

Employment Patterns and the Fishery Industry

When Punjabi women first arrived in the Skeena region in the 1960s, they assumed the traditional role of the dutiful (*dharmic*) wife who did not participate in the paid workforce. Though reared in the traditional understanding that a woman's work is in the home, over time Punjabi women increasingly came to participate in paid labour. This meant that as well as raising their children, they became secondary wage-earners by working as seasonal labourers in the salmon canneries, regardless of their educational background.

Punjabi Women in the Canneries

While only a handful of Punjabi women participated in the workforce in the 1960s, there gradually emerged by the early 1970s a significant group of Punjabi women who worked in the salmon canneries. The second Punjabi woman to have settled in Prince Rupert in 1961, Bunt Kaur Sidhu, became the first Punjabi immigrant woman to work in the fishery industry in the Skeena region in 1966.[34] Although she found permanent work at Prince Rupert Fishermen's Co-operative,[35] the Co-op was not the main place Punjabis worked; in the 1970s, the central place of employment for Punjabi women was BC Packers at Port Edward.[36] BC Packers was convenient for many Punjabi women because the work was seasonal and their husbands often worked nearby at the pulp and paper mill on Watson Island.[37] In 1970, three Punjabi women were employed by BC Packers at Port Edward (see table 4.1).[38] Over time, more and more women – whether residing in Prince Rupert, Terrace, or even Kitimat – worked in the salmon canning industry (see map 2.2). For instance, in 1972, two Punjabi women were hired; in 1973, an additional ten women were recruited. Meanwhile, in 1974, twenty-three Punjabi women began working at BC Packers in Port Edward.[39]

Although BC Packers at Port Edward was the most popular place for Punjabi women to find work, the Canadian Fishing Company (CANFISCO) at Oceanside in Prince Rupert also hired a few Punjabis beginning in 1976 (see table 4.2).[40] BC Packers bought the New Oceanside plant in 1980 and centralized their operations in that plant in 1982. The Port Edward seniority list merged with the New Oceanside seniority list, which resulted in a large pres-

Table 4.1 | Punjabi females hired by BC Packers
(cannery) at Port Edward (1969–1978)

Year	Number	Year	Number
1969	0	1974	23
1970	3	1975	24
1971	2	1976	1
1972	2	1977	8
1973	10	1978	19

Note: Only one Punjabi male worked at Port Edward in the 1970s. He was a welder and thus had a year-round position.

Source: Based on "Seniority List, B.C. Packers Limited, Women, Nov. 1/78," Fisherman's Hall (UFAWU, Local 88), Prince Rupert, BC.

Table 4.2 | Punjabi females hired by BC Packers
(cannery) at Oceanside (1975–1978)

Year	Number
1975	0
1976	5
1977	2
1978	4

Source: Based on "Seniority List, Cannery (Oceanside) Women as of June 01, 1979," Fisherman's Hall (UFAWU, local 88), Prince Rupert, BC.

ence of Punjabis at the New Oceanside plant.[41] Rupert Cold Storage[42] and BC Packers, both at Seal Cove,[43] hired Punjabis starting in 1976 (see tables 4.3 and 4.4). On the other hand, Babcock Fisheries (later J.S. McMillan)[44] hired only four English-speaking Punjabis in 1976, and by 1983, there were no Punjabis employed there.[45] However, when J.S. McMillan bought out Prince Rupert Fishermen's Co-operative in 1997, the seniority lists were merged, resulting in a Punjabi presence in the workforce. Meanwhile, there were fish plants that

Table 4.3 | Punjabi females hired by Rupert Cold Storage
(fresh fish) at Seal Cove (1976–1979)

Year	Number
1976	1
1977	4
1978	5
1979	19
1980	4
1981	0

Source: Based on "British Columbia Packers Ltd., Rupert
Cold Storage, Women's Seniority List as of May 5, 1980," Fisherman's Hall (UFAWU, Local 88), Prince Rupert, BC.

Table 4.4 | Punjabi males hired by BC Packers (shed) at
Seal Cove (1976–1979)

Year	Number
1976	2
1977	0
1978	1
1979	4
1980	3
1981	0

Note: None of the Punjabi men worked in engineering. Their
primary work was driver or clean-up.

Source: Based on "British Columbia Packers Ltd. – Seal
Cove, Shed Seniority List as of 4 July 1980," Fisherman's Hall
(UFAWU, Local 88), Prince Rupert, BC.

rarely had any Punjabis in their workforce, such as Atlin Fisheries (Canadian
Fresh Fish) and Royal Fisheries.

Processing salmon was the major fishery industry in the Skeena region.
Importantly, it was the only work that was available to First Nations or immigrant women regardless of their educational background or skill. Punjabi
women – like women from other ethnic backgrounds – were tagged as "sea-

Table 4.5 | Punjabis hired by BC Packers (cannery) at New Oceanside (1985–1996)

1985	m=0	1988	m=8	1991	m=0	1994	m=3
	f=10		f=39		f=3		f=2
1986	m=2	1989	m=3	1992	m=2	1995	m=4
	f=4		f=9		f=5		f=8
1987	m=0	1990	m=0	1993	m=3	1996	m=11
	f=0		f=3		f=9		f=17

Note: One Punjabi male worked as an electrician at the Seal Cove plant all year round from 1973 to 1980; he then worked at the New Oceanside plant from 1980 to 1992, when he retired.

Source: Based on "British Columbia Packers Limited, Prince Rupert Plant, Master List" of 1990, 1996, and 1998, Fisherman's Hall (UFAWU, local 88), Prince Rupert, BC.

sonal workers."[46] Cannery work involved the least amount of skill in the fisheries. A child of a Punjabi cannery labourer describes the work environment at one of the cannery plants in Prince Rupert thus:

The odours of fish and stagnant salt water permeate the air. The fish plant is a large two-level, wood-framed structure situated at the water's edge, to one side of the town. I am first bombarded by the strong smell of fish as I enter the plant and then deafened by the din of machines – the harsh clanging of the trays of fish as they are stacked and unstacked and as the fish are unloaded onto collecting trays, the revving and braking of forklifts as they shuttle back and forth transporting trays to various locales inside the plant, the incessant swishing and grinding of the mazes of conveyor belts as they move fish and cans to their various destinations, the clinking and crunching of cleaning machines where the fish are decapitated, slit, and gutted and then passed on to the women that stand on the lines to inspect and clean any residual blood and guts, the slamming of monstrous freezer doors as they are opened and closed, and the clinking and clanking of the cans as they jerkily move along in a continuous stream, being filled with salmon and then inspected and sealed.

The environment is cold and wet from the constant cold running water washing away waste from cleaned fish and the lines. The water from the hoses is kept ready to wash floors at regular intervals. The opening and closing of the freezers and the melting ice as the fish are packed onto and unpacked from four-by-four-foot aluminum trays contribute to the bleak atmosphere.[47]

Since education was not required for work at the cannery, Punjabi women easily found employment. A few Punjabi women, however, were overqualified. While many had received some secondary education and were therefore regarded as *pari-likhi* (literate),[48] several Punjabi women had also acquired higher education in the Punjab before migrating, though their Indian education was not recognized in Canada.[49] One Punjabi man referred to his wife's predicament in searching for work: "My wife was also trained to be a teacher, but she could not teach here. She was a housewife."[50] Note, too, the comment made by a Punjabi woman who had received a master's in education prior to immigrating to the Skeena region: "After passing grade eleven, I attended a small college [Dev Samaj College]. I received my MEd. I did not want to come to Canada. I wanted to become a lecturer in India. My dream was to become a professor ... In 1972, I started working at the Port Edward cannery. I felt demoralized working there, given my education. A job is a job. I had to settle where my husband worked. I earned around two dollars per hour cleaning fish. It was a labour job. I took the bus from Prince Rupert to Port Edward."[51]

A number of the Punjabi women who had graduated from an Indian secondary school or university intended to pursue careers in their field of study prior to migrating to Canada. However, because they were obliged to marry according to their parents' wishes, they could not attain their career goals. Upon migrating to Canada, their first responsibility was to bear children. There was not much opportunity to pursue a career, especially in a small remote town like Prince Rupert or Terrace. Indeed, they had to settle for the manual labour jobs that were available to them. A Punjabi woman described how immigrating interfered with her career goals: "Many of the Punjabi women had their graduation [from high school] in India. Upon coming to Canada, they were dissatisfied. When I was in grade ten, I decided to be a nurse. I got admission in nursing college but my father did not like it. My father was a farmer. In 1972, I came to Canada and applied for my immigration papers. I had no trouble getting my papers because I had a BA in political science and economics and I knew English. I was able to speak with Canadians. In 1973, I worked at the Port Edward cannery for two dollars per hour. Then, in 1976, I started working at Prince Rupert Fishermen's Co-operative."[52]

Some women had the desire to pursue a career in their new country, but living in a remote location and having to fulfil their familial duties of having children made it difficult. A Punjabi woman who was not only well educated but also had relevant work experience explained how immigration and motherhood essentially made it impossible for her to upgrade her credentials in order to teach: "I completed a BA and MA in economics and was working in a government office in the Punjab. I was married in 1973 and migrated to Canada in 1974. After my first child was born [November 1974], I started working in March 1975. I could only do cannery work. I wanted to do education. I sent my certificate to get a teaching licence. I was required to do a year at UBC. How could I do that with kids in Prince Rupert? I also did not know anyone to care for the kids."[53]

Since credentials acquired in India were not recognized as equivalent to Canadian credentials, these women had to settle for manual labour. A Punjabi woman described her difficulties in adjusting to manual labour: "I migrated to Prince Rupert because of an arranged marriage. I had received a BA in English, but my conversation skills were not good ... It was a big change to come from India to Prince Rupert. It was hard to adjust to labour work because I was educated. It was so humiliating for me to do labour work. It took me years to adjust. There are a lot of educated women in the cannery. We worked there because it was the only place where we could find a job."[54] For the educated Punjabi women, it was demoralizing to work in the salmon canneries. The challenge was twofold: (1) instead of using their educational training, they had to do the demeaning work of washing fish; and (2) the work was physically demanding. In sum, educated women found it difficult to work in the canneries, since they were not used to manual labour and they could not use the skills they had acquired through education.[55] Note the comment made by a former First Nations floor supervisor:

I began working as a floor supervisor at Co-op in 1971. I was questioned by the Chinese, East Indian, and white workers about favouring my own people. The Chinese and East Indians were reliable workers, but they couldn't do the heavy work. The East Indian ladies did not seem to know much about fish, and they had trouble coping with the cold working conditions and fish odours. I asked an East Indian co-worker, "Why don't you upgrade your education and do a better job?" At that time [the 1970s and 1980s], there were a lot of job opportunities in places like the schools and hospital. I could tell she was not suited for the job. But I guess it was quick money. She did not say.[56]

By the late 1970s, several educated Punjabi women who were proficient in English managed to leave the salmon canneries and branch into other areas of work. For instance, one of the first women to work in BC Packers at Port Edward later found a child-care job at a Prince Rupert daycare centre in the late 1970s, while others managed to find work at a bank or at the post office, even though these were not their initial career choices. Although the work was not demeaning or physically demanding, these women still felt that they were not fulfilling their professional potential.

A few Punjabi women had received a Western education prior to migrating to the Skeena and were therefore more successful in finding skilled or professional work. In contrast to women who had received only an Indian education, they could transfer credentials obtained in countries like the United Kingdom as Canadian equivalent.[57] One woman recounted how she found work relevant to the clerical training she had received in the UK before migrating to Canada in 1977: "I was born in Punjab, India, and moved to the UK with my family at the age of eleven years. I lived with my family there, so I went through the school system and received clerical training. I was married there ... We shifted to Prince Rupert ... I worked at the front office as a receptionist. At that time, the Punjabis thought I was Italian because I never spoke Punjabi on the job. I was accustomed to speaking in English."[58] The place they received their education prior to immigration has been an ongoing issue for Punjabis in Canada. While Punjabi women who had been educated in Western countries were able to enter the appropriate occupations, this was definitely not the case for those educated in India. The salmon cannery labour force therefore consisted of a fair number of overqualified women.

Another barrier, and perhaps the most important one for the women, was the lack of proficiency in the English language. While many women had attended primary and secondary school in the Punjab, they often lacked command over spoken English. Although education was not a requirement for employment in the salmon canneries, the canneries differed from one another in the language skills they required of their workforce. For some canneries, like BC Packers at Port Edward and Seal Cove, it did not matter whether or not a worker could speak English. It is for this reason that, in the 1970s and 1980s, many Punjabi women in the Skeena region began working in those canneries. Many from Prince Rupert, Terrace, and Kitimat were also employed by BC Packers because "the company did not mind if the workers could not speak, read, or write English."[59] While some canneries hired a person regardless of his or her proficiency in English, others – such as Prince Rupert Fishermen's Co-operative or J.S. McMillan – only hired workers who had a command of the English language.[60]

Some Punjabi women who had studied English in the Punjab could understand the language but lacked oral fluency; however, they quickly learned to speak English and found employment, such as at Prince Rupert Fishermen's Co-operative: "When I started at the Co-op [in 1974], there were not many Punjabis working there at that time ... I wanted to work in the cannery like the other Punjabi ladies. The company started to hire more Punjabi ladies when they saw that they are hardworking ... They had the condition that they would only hire if you could speak English. This was not the case at BC Packers."[61] Even though proficiency in English was a requirement of some of the canneries, cannery work was nonetheless the most available job for Punjabi immigrant women.

The type of cannery work one was required to do was extremely important to the labourers, even if there was only a slight difference in wages. There are two basic types of work at the cannery: (1) "dry" work, during which one remains dry and warm, which includes canning, labelling, warehousing, quality control (one has to be able to read and write), and first aid (one has to receive first aid training); and (2) "wet" work, during which one is wet and cold, which includes cutting fish heads and tails, fish washing, and pulling or packing eggs. The pay for a dry job is not much higher than for a wet job, but it is regarded as more prestigious, whereas the wet job is seen as lowly work.

Fish washing was viewed as the lowest of all jobs in the cannery and thus as the demeaning work. It was especially hard to clean fish during the 1960s and 1970s, when it was all done by hand. Washing fish was the first job manual labourers had to do when they were hired. In fact, Punjabi women predominantly washed fish all through the 1970s. It is noteworthy that they were kept at this job regardless of their seniority, an implicit form of discrimination that was brought to the union's attention (this is further explored in chapter 6).

Secondary Wage Earners

When Punjabi women migrated to the Skeena region, their role changed from the traditional one of being solely a homemaker to also being a secondary wage-earner. This finding is in direct contrast to what was observed about the Punjabi female behavioural pattern in Vancouver during the same period. Specifically, most Punjabi women living in Vancouver in the 1970s remained homemakers alone,[62] whereas most Punjabi women living in the Skeena region began entering the fishery industry.

By the late 1970s, most Skeena Punjabi women worked to earn extra money to improve the financial health of their families. The purchase of a house and the sponsoring of relatives were the two major economic goals that Punjabis held to be of primary importance. When Punjabi women arrived in the Skeena region to settle, many came with the impression that Canada was a country of great luxury. They had not anticipated the financial burden of a mortgage, since most of them had lived on ancestral farming property, either at their natal home or at their husband's home after marriage. A Punjabi woman described her surprise upon finding out that everyone had to work in Canada: "After migrating to Canada, I realized that everyone in the family had to work to make ends meet. My brothers attended school in Canada, but they had to drop out to work in the lumber mills and help the family. Like everyone else, I had to work. With a grade ten education, my job was to wash fish. My job at the fish cannery was manageable because I had the skills to clean fish."[63]

Many Punjabi immigrant families also carried the responsibility of providing for family members in the Punjab. For instance, when a member of the family was ill in the Punjab, family members (especially the sons) living abroad were seen as a source of financial aid. More significantly, there was also the familial expectation that Punjabi migrants would sponsor relatives or assist in sponsoring their spouse's relatives still living in the Punjab. Some Punjabi women carried the burden of supporting their husband's family either by giving their wages to their husband or mother-in-law or by sharing their wages to support their husband's family back in India. This financial responsibility was hard for them,[64] but for many women, it served as the catalyst that prompted them to assert themselves and save their wages to support their own family.

In addition to working for the well-being of their nuclear family and their husband's extended family, Punjabi women were also motivated to earn wages to sponsor their own natal family members in immigrating to Canada, especially if they themselves had no other relatives living in Canada. Participation in the paid workforce allowed Punjabi women to go against traditional norms about helping their own family. Customarily, a bride would take on a new name at the time of marriage, signifying the embedding of her new personhood in her husband's household and her no longer being a contributing member of her natal family. Moreover, after marrying off their daughter, parents would traditionally not take anything from their daughter's new household. However, with both husband and wife earning wages and with the family sponsorship system, women often set their own goals and saved their money to sponsor their own relatives, particularly their parents and siblings.[65] Sponsoring relatives involved not only the cost of the immigration procedure and travel, but also the responsibility of assisting them after their arrival in Canada.

The appeal of working at the salmon cannery in Port Edward was for many women related in part to the fact that the husbands were employed at the Columbia Cellulose pulp and paper mill on Watson Island, which was situated close to BC Packers at Port Edward (see map 2.2). Many women would schedule their work time to complement their husband's work hours in order to ensure that one parent would be at home with the children. A Punjabi woman described how she balanced mothering and working: "In 1973, I worked at the

Port Edward cannery for two dollars an hour. Then in 1976, I started working at the Co-op in Prince Rupert. We bought a house and I wanted to be near my children during my breaks at work. I did the opposite shift my husband did at the pulp and paper mill in Port Edward. I did seasonal work."[66] Another Punjabi working mother gave a similar account: "The seasonal work at Port Edward was good. I worked in the season and then collected EI the remainder of the year. I took a morning shift and then my husband did an evening shift. He worked at the pulp and paper mill. If he did a night shift; he would take a ride and then I would show up for a morning shift with my child. Then he would take the kid and go home in the car."[67] While some women managed to do a shift opposite to that of their husband, other women had to find hired help. During the early 1970s, when the community was relatively small, it was difficult to find help to care for the children within the Punjabi community. If extended family members were living in the area, they were often depended upon for help when mothers went to work.[68]

The most critical lifestyle change for Punjabi women related to mothering. No doubt, balancing home and work life was emerging as a source of stress among woman living in the West, regardless of background. For Punjabi women without relatives in Canada, it was difficult to adjust to the idea of leaving their children with non-relatives when working in the salmon cannery. To leave one's children with non-relatives had been unheard of in village Punjab. While some Punjabi women managed to complement their schedule with their husband's or to leave their children with extended-family members, others had no choice but to leave their children with family friends. As a last resort, some women left their children with non-Punjabi childcare providers. However, it was difficult for immigrant families to afford daycare when they were in the process of establishing themselves in a new country.

The issue of having to find someone to care for their children was more challenging for women who worked year-round in a fresh fish plant. By the 1980s, a few Punjabi children attended daycare when both parents worked full-time; some Punjabi mothers accepted this arrangement when several educated Punjabi women, fluent in both Punjabi and English, were working at daycare centres in Prince Rupert. The majority of Punjabi women, however, preferred seasonal work, since it allowed them to balance work and motherhood.

Seasonal Work and Employment Insurance

The majority of Punjabi women worked on a seasonal basis in the fishery industry. There are two main canning periods for the seasonal fishing period: (1) roe herring in the spring (March and April), and (2) salmon during the summer (mid-June to the end of August). The Punjabi women tended to work long hours during the herring and salmon seasons, and then collected Employment Insurance (EI) benefits during the remaining non-working months of the year. They preferred seasonal work and accumulating a large number of hours so that they could benefit from the EI program once the herring and salmon seasons ended. While Punjabis have traditionally not relied on social assistance or welfare, their attitude differed towards EI because they viewed it as an insurance plan to which they had contributed.

Since the traditional role of motherhood remained strong for many Punjabi women, working during the canning seasons and then collecting EI out of season actually proved to be a suitable employment strategy for them, especially when their children were young. Mothers remained at home for most of the autumn and winter, which fit with their children's school schedule, and then worked during the spring and summer months. Some mothers chose to work only during the salmon season, when their children were on summer holidays.[69]

Along with doing seasonal work for the salmon canneries, Punjabi women readily took to overtime work. The majority of Punjabi women were very concerned about their seniority, as it was a factor in the overtime system. One Punjabi woman commented on the importance of seniority thus: "When I started in 1971, I washed the fish for two to three years, and sometimes only for four to six hours. I was paid $1.88 an hour. My first pay cheque was for $65.00. It was seasonal work. By the third or fourth year (1974–75), I had more seniority. My work hours increased to twelve hour shifts because of my seniority. I also got a lot of overtime work."[70] Many Punjabi women worked overtime, when eligible, to earn more and higher wages. If called upon to work beyond an eight-hour shift or on Saturdays, labourers earned time-and-a-half wages; if called in to work on a Sunday, they made double wages.[71] While overtime work was an opportunity to earn more wages, it was also a way to bank EI hours. For many working women, the goal was to bank hours through overtime work during the peak season so that they could maximize their EI benefits during the non-working portion of the year. A Punjabi woman described the seasonal work cycle as follows: "At one time, there were eight hundred people for two shifts. Anyone who would go for work would get a job. It increased for everyone and it increased for Punjabis. I would work 1,100 hours during a season, and with overtime work it would be around 1,400 hours. I would start in March to May for herring and in June to September for salmon. We did seasonal work for four months. If there was a lot of work, we would perhaps work for six months. Then we would collect EI for the remaining part of the year."[72]

While the majority of Punjabis saw EI as an earned entitlement, not everyone took that approach, especially once their children were no longer young. In fact, over time some women opted to work full-time when their children were old enough to attend high school or pursue post-secondary education. For them, it was more enjoyable to work than to stay at home alone. There were also a few Punjabi women who preferred to work year-round rather than seasonally during the canning season. Year-round work was available at fresh fish plants, for example.[73] Prince Rupert Fishermen's Co-operative processed both seasonal fish (herring and salmon) and fresh fish (sole, perch, cod, turbot). Workers were eligible to work full-time in the fresh fish plant through the seniority that they had accumulated working in the salmon cannery.[74] While seniority played an important part in getting overtime work during the cannery season and in obtaining a year-round position in a fresh fish plant, it became an even greater issue when the fishery industry began its decline and workers simply wanted to have some work.

Working and Networking in the Fish Canneries

Following the work pattern of First Nations women, who have customarily worked in the salmon canneries, Punjabi women, too, in due time, entered the public sphere doing the same type of paid labour. Indeed, migration to the Skeena region proved to be a catalyst in motivating Punjabi women to work outside the home in the public sphere, even if in the relatively low-paid and low-skilled work of the salmon cannery. Cannery work was not only a means to economic gain, but, paradoxically, also served as a basis for social life among Punjabi women in the Skeena region.

Cannery as a Social Base

When only a few Punjabi women were working in the cannery, they often found themselves working alongside women from other ethnic backgrounds, especially First Nations women. It was not until the late 1970s and early 1980s that there developed a large cohort of Punjabi women employed in the fish canneries.[75] Once the fish-canning industry became known as a potential workplace for Punjabi women, it in effect became a major "social base" for them.

As the Punjabi cohort grew in the late 1970s and early 1980s, Punjabi women began working alongside one another rather than with other ethnic women. Later, in the 1990s, some Punjabi women were promoted to the position of charge-hand, supervising and taking primary responsibility for the Punjabi-speaking workforce. This arrangement served the managers well, since the charge-hands could speak to the workers in Punjabi on the managers' behalf. For instance, in the early 1990s, both BC Packers and Prince Rupert Fishermen's Co-operative employed a couple of Punjabi women as charge-hands to help overcome the language barrier.[76] In a sense, the charge-hands had a function similar to the "straw-bosses" in the lumber mills, whose role was not one of decision-making, but rather of monitoring workers who could not speak English, thus facilitating the work of the managers in handling a multi-ethnic workforce. Indeed, managers encouraged the ethnic work-based networks and used them to their own benefit as a means to maintain control over their diverse workforce.

Punjabi immigrant women continued to identify with their kin group or clan, in which primary importance was placed on social interactions with people from one's family, village, and community. They maintained this collectivity orientation well after their entry into the workforce at the cannery, especially since the in-group provided immigrants with support and guidance during their process of adapting to a new or foreign environment.[77] Just as the Punjabi chain of immigration was linked through kinship networks, Punjabi women found employment through the same mechanism. Once Punjabi women had begun to work in the fish canneries, they made it much easier for the more recent immigrants to adapt; the latter could learn about cannery work, find out when the companies were hiring,[78] and acquire knowledge on the job by word of mouth.

As discussed above in this chapter, Punjabi women experienced a great deal of social isolation upon their arrival to, and settlement in, the Skeena region. In reaction to this isolation, they chose to follow the example of their family and friends and find work in the salmon cannery, since it also catered to their own social needs. A Punjabi woman recalled how others had encouraged her to enter the workforce: "In 1980, I started working because all my friends were working. They said come on. Punjabi ladies liked to work because it brought money but also because it kept them busy. They liked it because they could speak Punjabi on their breaks with other ladies, gossip, socialize with other people. There were eight to ten Punjabi ladies when I started working. The other ladies were Italians, Portuguese, Natives, and Chinese. I worked seasonal, and then collected EI. It was good to work overtime."[79]

While entry into the Canadian paid labour force was primarily a means of earning money in order to help establish the family in the new country, the cannery emerged as a social base for Punjabi women. A Punjabi woman explained: "I felt lonely sitting at home by myself. I applied to work at two canneries. I found out about them from a Punjabi woman. Another lady took me there. I saw how the ladies were working. It was so smelly. I couldn't breathe. In India we lived like kings, but now I am working in a smelly place ... But we were glad to go to work, too."[80] Indeed, the cannery became a place for alleviating social isolation and loneliness. In fact, the cannery, ironically, became a "substitute" for village life.

A secondary benefit of the cannery's function as a social base was that it made the demanding work more bearable. A Punjabi woman described how the cannery was a source of social support in her experience of acculturation stress: "In this suffering of having to work, there was a small support network. I was not alone at the cannery. There were also other Punjabi immigrant women working at the cannery. They all worked alongside each other, and they brought Indian food to eat during lunch breaks. Lunch breaks provided an opportunity for us to disclose our pain and also to reminisce about the good old days in village Punjab."[81] The salmon cannery thus became a place for Punjabi women not only to network with other Punjabi women, but also to socialize during coffee and lunch breaks.[82]

Many Punjabi women would gather together in the lunchroom and talk in their mother tongue. With such activity, the lunchroom served as a social forum. The women were able to network with one another without the presence of male family members.[83] In a sense, work time was also their female time. A child of a Punjabi worker remembered accidently catching a glimpse of how Punjabi women socialized in the lunchroom: "I was surprised to see how different the aunties behaved at the cannery. They didn't walk around playing the parental role like they did at the temple. One auntie joked with her friends that she had to go home quickly because her husband had to have 'his carrot pealed.' Thank God they didn't notice me using the pop machine outside their lunchroom."[84]

The cannery not only alleviated the women's sense of social isolation and, later, boredom within the home, but also provided them with an opportunity to reconnect with their Punjabi culture and adapt to living in a remote town.[85] The fishery industry became a major economic and social base for Punjabi women. Women often looked forward to the "season of networking" at the cannery plant.

Cannery Networking Culture

Cannery work not only fostered work-based networks within the fish plant, but also helped Punjabi women build work-related relationships throughout the Skeena region. Transportation played a large role in enabling Punjabi women to build social networks, bringing them together at the canneries from their homes in Kitimat, Terrace, or Prince Rupert during the summer season. Before BC Packers consolidated its Port Edward operations at New Oceanside in 1982, the company bussed its workers living in Prince Rupert to the salmon cannery in Port Edward (the seventeen-kilometre commute takes around twenty minutes). A Punjabi female worker shared her seasonal work experience during the 1970s: "Companies needed more workers in the 1970s.

We heard this on the radio. People started coming from Terrace, Kitimat. The women would stay at family friends' houses. The women would pay for room and board. They came for the salmon and herring season. Work depended on the seniority list. The company would give us a ride [from Prince Rupert]."[86]

Punjabi women travelled daily to work along with other workers of various ethnic backgrounds. The daily commute to the salmon cannery reinforced the emerging subculture among Punjabi women, as they were at greater liberty to socialize with one another. A Punjabi woman provided an account of the commute to the salmon cannery: "We lived in Prince Rupert but a bus would pick up the lady workers at the Henry B-Y Store on the East side. I would walk or get a lift by my husband to the stop. The bus would pick us up at 7:30 a.m. and then [we would] start our shift at 8 a.m. to 4:30 p.m. Sometimes it took three to four buses to pick us all up. There were a lot of Native Indians, Chinese, and Italians working at the cannery. Many Natives lived in the Port Edward area. People came to work from Prince Rupert, Terrace, Prince George, and Kitimat to work at Port Edward."[87]

The commute provided Punjabi women with a social base not only for networking among themselves, but also for interacting with other women living in the Skeena. However, just as rivalry existed over the type of work the members of different groups were required to do in the salmon cannery, intercultural tensions emerged on the bus, especially between First Nations and Punjabi women. In the late 1970s, by which time there was a substantial number of Punjabi women in the workforce, a dispute emerged over language. A Punjabi woman remembered the intercultural dynamic on the bus: "When I started work in Port Edward, there were mostly First Nations people working there. Not all but some were very bitter and did not like East Indians. There was a lot of tension because of the language and cultural differences. They wanted us to speak in English, but we spoke Punjabi."[88]

In fact, over the period from 1979 to 1981, some First Nations women circulated a petition against Punjabi women for speaking Punjabi on the bus and took it to the union.[89] Undoubtedly, Punjabi women who could not speak English experienced more difficulty in their interactions with other ethnic groups. One Punjabi woman shared her experience of this sort of discrimination: "I was raised with the manners not to talk back to anyone, so at work I kept my head down and cleaned the fish as fast as I could to show Native Indians that their 'tricks' did not affect me. At times, I felt very frustrated because I did not have the English language skills."[90] English-speaking Punjabi women, in contrast, did not encounter as much tension when they spoke in English; it made a tremendous difference when a Punjabi woman was able to speak comfortably in English with other members of the broader Skeena community.[91]

While BC Packers arranged for a bus between Prince Rupert and Port Edward, Punjabi women living either in Terrace or Kitimat would car pool with other Punjabi women and rent a basement suite or room in Prince Rupert.[92] When BC Packers relocated to New Oceanside in 1981, many Punjabi women continued to work in Prince Rupert.[93] Interestingly, a whole culture of networking with fellow female workers emerged during the salmon season as a result of being transported to, and being accommodated in, Prince Rupert. Note the comment of a Punjabi woman who worked in the cannery: "When the cannery was shifted to Prince Rupert, then women continued to come from Terrace and Kitimat, but they would rent a room and go home on the weekends when not working. We rented our basement to eight women. Four of the women would work day shift and the other four women would work night shift. They would go to Terrace on the weekend or after fifteen days or so. When they returned home, they would cook a lot of food and bring it to Prince Rupert. A lot of Punjabis rented their basements to family or friends."[94]

It was initially difficult for the Punjabi women to coordinate their transportation to and from Prince Rupert, as well as their living arrangements. However, over time they managed to get to know women from all three towns and to build social networks in the Skeena region. After a couple of seasons, Punjabi networks crystallized for transportation and living arrangements.[95]

Women enjoyed travelling together and living with one another. It gave them the time to catch up on gossip, news, and family events. In effect, working in the cannery led to the establishment of friendships throughout the Skeena region. Meanwhile, residents of Prince Rupert found the BC Packers' takeover of the New Oceanside plant a very advantageous change, since the plant had up-to-date machinery and was close to their homes.[96]

Punjabi Cannery Lifestyle

While working in the salmon canneries certainly led Punjabi women to network among themselves, it also gradually connected them to the larger Prince Rupert community and the Skeena fishery industry. Punjabi women now had something in common to talk about or share with people outside their own community. In addition, some Punjabi women actively engaged in the union-management and intercultural politics of the workplace.[97]

Another significant trend that emerged in the Skeena Punjabi community was that the Canadian-born or -raised children began to work alongside their mothers and "aunties"[98] at the salmon canneries. While some joined the workforce in the late 1970s, many entered in the late 1980s or later (see table 4.5). Most of the children began working seasonally at the salmon cannery once they reached the age of sixteen.[99] These children were often expected to help support their family financially and help fund their own post-secondary education. It was much more common for children to take up their mother's line of work in the salmon cannery than their father's in the forestry industry, because cannery work by nature was seasonal and thus corresponded with the secondary school calendar.

The cannery was a well-paying summer job for high school–age children, providing them with the opportunity to earn and save money for post-secondary education. When studying at a post-secondary institution away from home, many children would still return to the Skeena region to work in the salmon cannery during the summer months; this allowed them to return home to their families and to earn money. Not only was working in the salmon cannery a Punjabi woman's "thing to do," but seasonal cannery work became the pattern for second-generation Punjabis as well. A Canadian-born Punjabi described her immigrant parents' expectations thus: "My mother's attitude was that every Punjabi kid is doing it, it is good money, and the kids do it while growing up. The family would get what they could afford. Kids had to help out. Parents started off with very little. I started working in the cannery when I was in high school. It was a job that paid well. I got seventeen dollars an hour. I started in grade eleven and did it for four years; two years while I was in high school; and for two years while I was attending university. For working two months solidly, I would earn about six thousand dollars."[100]

While Punjabi-Canadian children were encouraged to work at the salmon cannery, it was seldom intended to be a career choice; rather, working at the salmon cannery was a means to pursue post-secondary education, thus allowing the children of Punjabi immigrants to have greater upward social mobility.

We're Still Going to Work

The fisheries in the Skeena region have experienced a gradual decline since the late 1980s. What is more, from the summer of 1997 onward, the decline in the industry has accelerated drastically as a result of conservation and globalization-driven competition. And today the fishery industry is weaker than Punjabi women have ever seen. One Punjabi woman described the changes in the salmon canning industry: "During the salmon season [2008], there are only one to two lines running. We used to have thirteen lines before. In the last few years there have been only about six to seven lines. Last year, I only worked for twenty to twenty-five days. It was okay ... The cannery now looks empty. There used to be a lineup for lunch break with two lunch rooms. Now there are only about four people in one of the lunchrooms."[101]

The decline has undoubtedly been a source of economic and emotional stress, and some have experienced physical ailments as a result of the stress that comes with job loss. Despite the economic and emotional disorientation, Punjabi women have demonstrated resiliency in coping with the transition. They have been resourceful in their attempts to look for jobs elsewhere and maintain that, regardless of the fisheries, "we're still going to work." No doubt the decline in the fishery industry has threatened jobs and necessitated some painful readjustments, but these women have nevertheless undertaken various measures in order to keep their economic and psycho-social independence.

Decline in Cannery Work

The negotiations and eventual signing of the 1985 United States–Canada Pacific Salmon Treaty were, in part, a means to curtail the growing tension between Alaskan and Canadian fishermen.[102] However, the Alaskan fishermen continued overfishing while Canada was implementing its conservation policies to prevent depletion of fish resources. Canadian fishermen were angered by the fact that while they were fishing according to a quota system, their American counterparts were reaping the benefits of Canadian conservation practices. In July 1997, protesting the lack of progress on a new fishing rights treaty, fishermen in the Skeena area barricaded the Alaskan Marine Highway ferry, the M/V *Malasapina*, preventing it from leaving the Prince Rupert ferry terminal.[103] While these actions received the attention of the White House (under the presidency of Bill Clinton), rather than the United States responding by negotiating a new treaty with Canada, the Alaskan government sued Canadian fishermen.[104]

Along with the unresolved Alaskan-Canadian fishing dispute, there was fierce – and growing – competition with Chilean salmon farmers as well as ongoing tension among commercial, sports, and First Nations fishermen. There was a drastic reduction in profitable fish like sockeye salmon but growth in cheap, not-in-demand fish like pink salmon. Labour work at the canneries began waning as salmon prices fell. Moreover, unionized cannery wages had increased over the previous couple of decades, making it more profitable for companies to ship the fish elsewhere for processing at non-unionized plants in the Lower Mainland or in other countries where workers were paid less. For instance, the Cloverleaf brand – a symbol of Canadian canned salmon – was sold to the American company International Home Foods Limited, which outsourced the salmon to be processed by lower-paid workers in Korea.[105] Prince Rupert could then no longer rely on sockeye and other profitable species of fish as its staple processing industry.

Just as the decline in the forestry industry was hard for Punjabi men, the decline in the fisheries has been challenging for Punjabi women.[106] Indeed, since the fish plant had become a place where Punjabi women built their identity, not only as Canadians living in the Skeena region, but also as women, there was much at stake in losing one's economic and emotional autonomy. Yet unlike the attachment Punjabi men had with lumber industry or the attachment First Nations had with fishing, salmon cannery work for Punjabi women was more about finding their autonomy than about an actual attachment to the canneries. A Punjabi woman described how working and then losing her job had affected her life:

When we were younger, we had energy and excitement to go to work. We have a chance to work with other ladies to make money. It gives a social life, talk with others. Punjabi women get more independence when they make their own money. It helps women! Instead of asking their husband for money to spend, they can buy whatever they want. I think it gives women more power in the house. When husband-wife both working, it gives equal opportunity rights in the house. When parents, children, and friends were leaving, I got depressed. I had to take pills. There was no one here ... work was getting less. I got bored at home.[107]

While loneliness was the most-voiced issue that Punjabi women had to contend with when they initially arrived in the Skeena region, boredom was their general experience after they had grown accustomed to the work and social life of the salmon cannery. Indeed, it became an even larger problem when the canning season ended and, from the late 1990s onwards, when the availability of work declined as the fishery industry weakened.

Many women began to leave the Skeena region with their families because their husbands had to look for work elsewhere when the forestry industry either slowed or shut down for extensive periods and they could no longer sustain themselves. The majority of Punjabi women have been secondary wage earners, and many of them have relocated to other places because their husbands lost their jobs at the pulp and paper mill on Watson Island or at the sawmills in Terrace. However, some Punjabi women with high seniority have continued to work at the salmon canneries even if they have relocated elsewhere. Note the comment made by a Punjabi woman who works seasonally: "I worked two months in a year and then collected EI for four to five months. Herring comes in the spring [March] but I never worked the herring season. In the 1980s there were ten to eleven lines. By the mid-1990s, it started to slow down. By 2002, people started to move down south especially because the pulp and paper mill shut down. Even so, some ladies would come during the fish season to work and then return to Vancouver Lower Mainland."[108]

The Punjabi women who left the Skeena region as a result of the decline of the forestry industry nevertheless maintained the connections they had made through salmon cannery work. As a consequence, the earlier Punjabi work-related social network among working women throughout the Skeena (Prince Rupert, Terrace, and Kitimat) had by the mid-2000s become further extended into large urban centres, including the Lower Mainland (the most popular location), Calgary, and Edmonton.

Not Enough EI Hours

While those with high seniority managed to continue working during the salmon season,[109] their work hours have declined to the point that they no longer qualify for EI benefits during the non-work season. Consequently, they have contemplated not returning to the region. For example, one Punjabi woman who had been working since 1983 was considering not returning to Prince Rupert during the salmon season, as she could no longer accumulate enough hours to qualify for EI: "I am working at the CANFISCO plant since 1983. I have been working with BC Packers for twenty-five years. My husband worked in the pulp and paper mill at Port Edward. We moved to Calgary three years ago after the mill shut down ... I work during the season and then collect EI for five months or so. I rent a room from another Punjabi lady, my friend, when I work in Prince Rupert ... There are very few hours this summer [2008]. Not enough to collect EI ... Perhaps I will stop coming here."[110]

The incentive to return during the summer months has thus been gradually decreasing: "Since 2005, there have been problems surrounding workers not able to get enough hours in order to collect EI. It started three or four years ago. In 2007, I was able to work a decent number of hours (about 400 hours) but it was not enough to qualify for EI. In 2008, I have been able to work only fifty to sixty hours. I get now seventeen or eighteen dollars an hour. I forget how much I was earning before ... I would like to work in a hotel/motel. You feel bored at home; there is nothing to do at home."[111]

While some of the Punjabi women have managed to keep year-round jobs in the fresh fish business, the majority have faced job loss or have not had enough work hours to make work economically worth while. While some Punjabi women are approaching early or regular retirement, many others still have some work years ahead of them. These women voice the sentiment that they do not want to lose their economic and psycho-social autonomy. Thus, many of them have found other sectors in which they can work. In a sense, they have been more versatile than their male counterparts in re-establishing themselves in the workforce. A former cannery worker offered this comment on the actions of Punjabis:

Punjabis are survivors, we don't like to go on welfare. Even if they have to work as a dishwasher, chambermaid, or at McDonald's, they will. Last year I was not able to collect enough hours at the cannery for EI, I worked at a corner store for cleanup and delivery of groceries. We are trying to make extra money. If I didn't have this job, I would have to go somewhere else. Every year, cannery work is going down, ever since Jim Pattison took over the plant. Instead of eighteen dollars he is paying nine dollars per hour in Vancouver. Women are not as attached to the cannery as the men to the mill. Men work in the mill all year round. Women are more attached to family and kids and housework. Work is just seasonal.[112]

The cannery provided Punjabi women with the opportunity to experience both economic autonomy and a social base while living in the Skeena region. However, unlike the importance of the pulp and paper or lumber mill in the lives of Punjabi men, the salmon cannery did not define them as women workers. Rather, women still gave primary importance to their role as mother and simultaneously exercised their autonomy by working as paid labour. Thus, many Punjabi women have been determined to continue working elsewhere, regardless of the decline in the fishery industry.

Finding Other Work

Punjabi women who have had to face the challenges of job loss fall into three main categories: (1) women with high seniority who have either retired or are approaching retirement and who may still work a few hours a week at the cannery if they are still residing in the Skeena region; (2) women with limited education who have started working in other sectors, most often for lower wages; and (3) women who have upgraded their training or education to do more skilled work.

The largest cohort of Punjabi women consists of those who are not near retirement and who prefer to work for both economic and social reasons (cohorts 2 and 3). Some of them have managed to find similar cannery work in other places, such as the BC Lower Mainland, albeit earning non-unionized wages. While the women in cohort 2 have limited occupational skills, they still have managed to venture out into other sectors, especially the hospitality and food services. Significantly, those Punjabi women who relocated to a large urban centre have found themselves searching for jobs in an environment in which they are "triply disadvantaged" as immigrant, visible minority, and female.[113] In effect, their job prospects have largely been in minimum- or low-wage jobs, including housekeeping, dishwashing, and food services.

Punjabi women who have remained in the Skeena presently face economic challenges, since the region itself is economically depressed; however, they have settled, for the most part, for minimum- or low-wage jobs. A Punjabi woman described her role in the food service industry: "I got employment in the restaurant for the last twelve years. A friend got me the job. Punjabi women find employment in the service industry, like at a hotel or restaurant. It is an easy job because this is what we did at home. We know it. I have survival English in the workplace. When the mill shut down, this job helped us because it enabled me to bring an income to maintain the household. Our house was paid off long ago but we feel the pressure in terms of helping our children receive an education in Vancouver. Our girls are encouraged to get a part-time job."[114]

Some Punjabi women have, as a consequence of the lumber bust, become primary wage earners, supporting the smooth functioning of the household. They have managed to find full-time employment during the downturn in BC's forestry industry, which in fact has been an empowering experience for them. A Punjabi woman who had worked for many years in the fishery industry described her trials in finding new work with Canada Post: "My friend was working at the post office and told me to give an application. I was called for an interview. I worked for about six or eight weeks … The post office needed me to fill in a sick leave. So I quit McMillan. I have been working there since then. At times there is no work. But I have been there for eleven years. I was casual at the post office. I have been getting enough hours for the last five years."[115]

Interestingly, the more educated among Punjabi women who are fluent in English have returned to school to upgrade their occupational skills. Indeed, a number of women belonging to cohort 3 were propelled by the decline of the fishery to move into an area akin to their original career goals at the time of their immigration to Canada. One Canadian-born health professional living in the Skeena region observed: "There are some older East Indians who have trained to be care aides since the cannery work slowed down."[116] Similarly, a first-generation Punjabi woman assessed how some Punjabi women reacted to losing their work in the cannery: "Some said, in a way it was good that there became less work in the cannery because we would have been stuck in the job. It motivated some ladies to get a better job. They did training for it."[117] Moreover, note the account provided by a Punjabi woman who became a care aide after having worked in the cannery since 1973:

I got the opportunity to do the care aide certificate in 1997. I collected EI, and then the employment centre helped. I got my training in Northwest Community College. The first six months I struggled because I had to do grade ten math to get in the program. Then I did a six month home-care support worker certificate. I learnt CPR, WHMIS, and Food Safe level 1. Earlier I had worked as a cook for minimum wage [$8/hr] for five to six months. I found it difficult to have such a drop in my salary. My boss said I was too old to go to college. I quit because I felt I could not work as a cook forever. After my training, I worked in a woman's transition house for four years [1999–2003]. I then got a job in the hospital in 2000. I did casual work while still working at the transition house. When the hospital job became secure, I quit the transition job. It was good at the transition house but I always wanted to be a nurse. The transition house paid seventeen dollars an hour and the hospital paid nineteen dollars and now twenty-two dollars an hour.[118]

Fluency in English, along with prior education, played a major role in the ability of Punjabi women to upgrade their skills and find other unionized jobs in the Canadian workforce.

While three groups have been differentiated among the Punjabi women in the workforce who grappled with the decline of the fishery industry, what is noteworthy is that many of those who had not reached retirement age have demonstrated a determination to continue participating in the workforce. Their attachment has not been to the demanding work of the fishery industry as such; rather it has been to earning money for the economic welfare of the family. While the motivation to help the family financially propelled them into the workforce, the reasons for their continuing to work are twofold: (1) to help their family readjust economically, since many of them have a husband who lost his job in the forestry industry; and (2) to maintain their own economic and social autonomy.

Summary

Traditional gender roles may be viewed as constraining a woman's autonomy. However, cultural transformations occurred among Punjabi women in the Skeena region as a result of their employment in the fishery industry. Punjabi women had been initially propelled into the paid workforce for the sake of the economic welfare of the family from the 1960s onwards. However, while the cannery was primarily a place where these women could earn money, it also served as a social base for them in overcoming the tremendous social isolation they experienced because of the lack of a Punjabi community. Such a community could have provided – at the very least – a sense of belonging during the early period of Punjabi settlement.

The transformative impact that working in the public sphere had on their lives is further underscored by their experience after the fisheries began to decline from the mid-1990s onwards. Punjabi women at the time of the decline of the fishery industry belonged to one of three cohort groups. Cohort 1 includes Punjabi women who had reached or were approaching retirement age but continued to participate in the workforce even when the work differed from their initial women-dominated cannery experience. Among those who lost their fishery jobs, cohort 2 consists of women who found work in other sectors, albeit in minimum- or low-paying jobs, while cohort 3 pertains to Punjabi women who upgraded their skills in order to qualify for higher-wage jobs. Regardless of the cohort group, Punjabi women have continued to earn wages or are collecting a retirement pension in order to maintain their autonomy.

It is important to recognize that it does not do Punjabi women justice to characterize them as a homogeneous group, even if the majority of them may have worked as manual labourers in the fishery industry. Rather, heterogeneity prevails among the Punjabi women who settled in the Skeena region; this is evident in their different marriage patterns, educational levels, and the strategies they used in coping with the decline in the fishery industry. Punjabi women had to navigate through the social structures that came with female immigration to the Skeena region; they had to overcome structural barriers in the job market that pertained not only to their belonging to a visible ethnic minority group, but also to their gender. By the time of their arrival in the Skeena region, seasonal cannery work had already been tagged as suitable employment for First Nations and immigrant women. Punjabi women experienced economic and social autonomy through their work in the salmon cannery, and they each have their own stories to tell about having to adjust both to their work in the fishery industry and to life in general in the Skeena region. These stories are, significantly, most often voiced within the framework of their Punjabi ethos, which served as a "cultural asset" in their struggle to adapt to a new and foreign environment, the subject of the next chapter.

CHAPTER 5

A Woman's Journey: From *Pardah* to the Paid Workforce

When Punjabi women initially arrived in the Skeena region in the 1960s, they were oriented towards fulfilling their traditional gender role of wife and mother, doing unpaid work within the home. Over time, however, these women increasingly engaged in paid labour, primarily as secondary wage earners on a seasonal basis in the salmon canneries. For them, leaving village Punjab undoubtedly also resulted in a major shift away from the practice of *pardah* – the custom of placing a headscarf (*chunni*) low over the forehead so that eye contact in public is minimal, if possible at all.

Married women in the Punjab have traditionally been required to conform to *pardah*, and the practice has definitely been characteristic of a female's upbringing and life in village Punjab. Even though it has been more widely practised in northern India, *pardah* can be considered a pan-Indian custom.[1] As a consequence of the practice of *pardah*, even by the turn of the twentieth century, girls were, by and large, not attending public school in India;[2] had they attended, they would have to have been in the company of the opposite sex, both in terms of the student body and the teachers, the latter primarily being men belonging to the Brahmin caste.[3] Accessibility of public education to women, notwithstanding the culturally ingrained practice of *pardah*, was one of the main goals in the effort to raise the social status of women and increase the roles open to them during the Indian women reform movements in the late 1800s and early 1900s. To overcome this barrier, women – most often young widows[4] – opened schools exclusively for girls.[5] However, rural areas remained largely unaffected by such reform efforts.

Migration from village Punjab to Prince Rupert meant a departure from the custom of *pardah*, as the immigrants settled in a remote area that lacked a Punjabi community. Newly arrived Punjabi women were generally not accustomed to moving about freely in public areas where they would have contact with the opposite sex. Furthermore, the women's entry into the Canadian workforce, which was initially done solely to achieve economic security, entailed a major shift from observing the *pardah* cultural practice of keeping a low profile in the company of strangers to working with people from various ethnic backgrounds and the opposite gender in the public sphere.

The main part of this chapter comprises an ethnographic narrative of the journey of one Punjabi woman – Bunt Kaur Sidhu (b. 1935), who, after settling in Prince Rupert in 1961, became the first Punjabi immigrant woman to work in the fishery industry in northwestern British Columbia in 1966. In effect, her arrival in the Skeena marked a major change in her life, from practising *pardah* to wearing the "pants" as an employee in a fish plant. This single ethnographic narrative on the experience of one Punjabi woman who, a few years after coming to Prince Rupert, entered the paid workforce in order to assist her family sheds light on two important areas: (1) the experience of a Punjabi female who gave up the traditional practice of *pardah* when she migrated to and settled in northwestern BC, especially at a time when there was no Punjabi community in the area that could give her guidance or support; and (2) the specific barriers, challenges, and responses experienced by Punjabi women in adapting to the Canadian labour force.

The chapter consists of three parts. The first investigates traditional views about female dignity (*izzat*) in village Punjab. The second is devoted to the ethnographic narrative of one Punjabi woman's experiences in the public sphere from the mid-1960s onwards in Prince Rupert[6] – a narrative based on her personal experiences both in terms of her being the second Punjabi woman to reside in Prince Rupert and in terms of her being the first Punjabi immigrant woman to enter the paid labour force in the Skeena region. It offers in-depth insights into the specific Punjabi female experience in adapting to a new country with its own distinctive social norms and institutions, especially after she began working in the public sphere. The third part of the chapter analyses the social challenges and barriers that the early Punjabi immigrant women often experienced after they settled in Prince Rupert. The narrative bears importantly on this analysis in that it demonstrates that while the Punjabi cultural value of *izzat* proved to be a source of strength and resiliency for Punjabi women, entry into the Canadian labour force had a significant impact on the traditional practice of *pardah* in that, by working outside the home, women discovered a new kind of "respect."

Female Dignity in Village Punjab

The governing principles of social behaviour in the Punjabi villages include duty (*dharam*) and respect (*izzat*). People are traditionally expected to fulfil their personal duty, based on their particular stage in life, class, and gender, in order to maintain family dignity or honour. A girl is reared to fulfil her role as wife, mother, and daughter-in-law. Along with household training, it is imperative for a maturing young girl to maintain her virginity so as to be marriageable and, in turn, maintain family respect and integrity (*izzat*). The loss of respect results in the collective experience of disgrace and shame (*sharam*). While one's specific duty is determined by several personal factors, the value of *izzat* is rooted in a collectivity orientation.

The traditional Indian custom has generally been that females – especially after the onset of puberty – should not interact with males, except with certain family members, such as their father and brothers. Hence, when females are in public places, they are either segregated from their male counterparts (e.g., in a place of worship) or in the company of other women in small groups of three or more (e.g., at the local market or the public village well). The crop field is viewed as a particularly vulnerable place for a woman, as it carries the potential for rape or an illicit love affair, both of which would damage the female's dignity and marriageability as well as her family's sense of integrity and respect.

Women are typically protected from unknown men before marriage. As a maturing girl approaches the marriageable age of about sixteen years or so, her parents make great attempts not only to prevent their daughter from engaging in a local romance, with its potential pregnancy, but also to find a suitable match for her.[7] A bride traditionally takes on a new name at the time of marriage, signifying her new personhood within the husband's household. As a wife and mother, her activities include cooking, cleaning, washing clothes, sewing clothes, buying food in the market, and child bearing and rearing.

Along with performing household activities, a woman might or might not help her family members on the farm. If she does participate in farm work, it is almost always in the company of other women so as to protect and maintain family integrity. Even after marriage, women are protected from unknown men so that they do not damage the family's *izzat*. Punjabi rural women after marriage have traditionally been required – especially in the presence of older and senior men – to conform to *pardah*. Women generally remain secluded in the home (*ghar*).[8] In fact, the layout of a traditional home in village Punjab is designed according to the practice of *pardah*.[9]

Izzat is a pan-Indian value, but it is more important among people belonging to the higher classes, including the Brahmin and Kshatriya classes. While the Brahmin class emphasizes religious and social purity, the Kshatriya "warrior" class typically places greater importance on fighting to protect one's integrity as a value at both the personal level and the community level. Consequently, *izzat* is very highly valued among Punjabis.[10]

It is important to note here that the differentiation made in this study between women's practice of *pardah* and their working in the public sphere is not intended to parallel the difference between India and Canada, respectively. In various ways, gender segregation was also practised in the West during the nineteenth century and earlier. Moreover, while in India in the twentieth century the custom of *pardah* weakened more quickly in large urban centres like Mumbai, New Delhi, and Kolkata, it remained strong among women raised in the rural areas.

As Punjabi women left village Punjab and migrated to the Skeena region of British Columbia, many of them in due time found themselves entering the paid labour force. And, for many, their entry into the Canadian workforce had a significant impact on their previous traditional social and cultural patterns of behaviour. Especially important in this regard was the discovery by many of a new kind of respect, one made evident in the narrative below.

Wearing the "Pants" in a Fish Plant: An Ethnographic Narrative by Bunt Kaur Sidhu

My mother gave birth to me at my paternal village called Bassian, which is located in the Ludhiana district of the Punjab. The birth date on my passport reads 1 April 1935; however, we are not sure about the true date when my mother gave birth to me.[11] Our village was larger than the neighbouring villages because we had three schools, a Sikh temple, and many stores. The girls went to school too, but I attended an all Sikh girls' school. Boys and girls were kept separate, and we would wear a headscarf (*chunni*). There was also a third school which was for Hindu and Muslim girls which only went up to grade five.[12] Since my school went up to grade eight, the Hindu and Muslim girls had to transfer to it for grades six to eight. I studied until grade eight and also learnt the English alphabet. I did not know how to speak, read or write in English. I was raised in a traditional Punjabi Sikh family.

My father's friend from our village sponsored my second brother to migrate to Canada in 1952. Our "uncle" lived in Lake Cowichan on Vancouver Island. My maternal uncle residing in Vancouver – with my parents' permission – got me engaged to a Canadian-born Punjabi boy. My husband's parents wanted him to marry a traditional girl from the Punjab. [When I was] age twenty-one, my family sent me off to Canada on 18 August 1956 to get married. Because my husband was Canadian-born, I was given landed-immigrant status. We got married at the Khalsa Diwan Society Sikh Temple on Second Avenue in Vancouver.

It was hard living in Lake Cowichan. The Punjabi community was small and I really didn't know anyone. I befriended a Punjabi woman, with whom I

Bunt Kaur Sidhu at the time of her marriage, Vancouver (1956). Courtesy of Bunt Kaur Sidhu.

would go shopping. We had a hard time doing the simplest things like shopping, something that we were trained for in the Punjab. We couldn't make sense of the pricing at the store because we didn't know English numbers nor could we sort our money to pay for the goods. My friend emptied her purse in front of the cashier and used hand gestures for her to take the amount we owed. The cashier took how much was needed and my friend took the leftover change. I felt helpless not being able to shop for food, and I insisted that my brother-in-law teach me how to count in English. I learned how to count up to one hundred and was able to shop at the store without being dependent on another person.

My sister-in-law filled out my application for Canadian citizenship. I was called in for an interview because she wrote "Punjabi" as my spoken language. I had to demonstrate that I knew survival English. I passed the interview and received my Canadian citizenship in Canada. I knew I had to learn English to survive in Canada and also to sponsor my brother who was still living in the Punjab. When [I was] applying for my brother, some of the Punjabi ladies recommended that I write "English" as my spoken language on the application form so I wouldn't have to do the interview. However, I wrote "Punjabi" as my spoken language and was called in for an interview with the immigration officer. I prepared some responses to questions that I thought the immigration officer might ask. He didn't ask any of the questions I had prepared for prior to the interview. I was so nervous during the interview, but to my surprise the interview was successful and I was able to sponsor my brother. I continued to learn English, and by 1960, I was able to read and say simple sentences.

I gave birth to my first child, a son, in 1961. Like the other Punjabi ladies in the town, we went to the public health clinic to learn how to care for my newborn baby. I felt uncomfortable at the clinic because everything I saw and learnt about child care in the Punjab was being discouraged by the nurses. In the Punjab, we breastfed all our babies and the men would take pride that their children got their strength from having drunk their mother's milk. We also didn't use cribs and slept with our babies at night. We were taught to be devoted mothers. We were often told stories about how mothers would sleep on a soiled sheet so that their baby could sleep on a dry sheet. But in Canada, we were told that formula milk was superior and that breastfeeding was not needed. We wanted to be Canadian and took their advice in good faith. Giving formula milk was difficult because the instructions were in English and it was hard to give the recommended amount. When people saw us unable to read and speak English, some of them made sarcastic comments about how we should learn English. I also felt shy to breastfeed, since no one did it openly like they did in the Punjab.

All this occurred while my husband was working at Prince Rupert Sawmills. He began working at the sawmill in May 1961. He lived at the bunkhouse for five months before my son and I joined him in Prince Rupert. I cried every day before I left for Prince Rupert because I had no idea where it was on the map and I didn't know what to pack. My father-in-law asked, "What's the matter? What's the big deal? Take enough clothes for two people. You don't need a lot because if the mill shuts down you will have to come back." I didn't want to go to Prince Rupert because I would have no one to talk to. There was only one Punjabi lady in the town, whose husband also worked at the sawmill. Her name was Gurmail Kaur Walia and she had one daughter who was born in Prince Rupert. They lived in a rented basement suite. I travelled to Prince Rupert with my son and joined my husband in a one-bedroom suite with a shared bathroom he had rented from the same German family that had rented to the Walias. I got Indian spices and lentils from either my brother, who would visit us in Prince Rupert, or when we would visit Vancouver.

In 1963, all three of us went to India to visit my parents in the Punjab. During this time I was expecting my second child. When we returned to Vancouver, my husband returned to work at Prince Rupert Sawmills and lived at the bunkhouse, while my son and I stayed with my brother. My husband tried to find a suitable place for a family of four; however, it was hard because the basement suites were for single workers or couples. The advertisements in the paper usually said "no children." I called Gurmail Kaur, who was now renting a two-bedroom suite from a Portuguese family on Taylor Street, and asked her if my son and I could stay with them until my husband could find a suitable place for us. Gurmail Kaur kindly let us stay with her.

My husband had no luck finding a place. I wrote a letter to my father-in-law and asked him, "Where are your grandchildren going to live?" My second child, a daughter, was born in 1963. My husband came to visit me at the hospital, and to my surprise he was accompanied by his father, who was also staying at Prince Rupert Sawmills' bunkhouse. My father-in-law said he came to Prince Rupert to help us buy a house; he put a down payment of three thousand dollars for a house valued at nine thousand dollars. We moved into the house when my daughter was just two weeks old. The house was located on Alfred Street. We were one of the first Punjabi families to buy a house in Prince Rupert. Two years later, we had a second daughter in 1965.

During my first five years in Prince Rupert, I did not work. I fulfilled my duty as mother, wife, and daughter-in-law. Soon I was under pressure to find a job because we needed extra income to pay off the house and our trip to India. I looked for work but was unsuccessful. I had a hard time trying to find out what type of work was available because not a single Punjabi woman had a job. I got my first job at the Rupert Hotel on First Avenue. I heard about the job at the Employment Office. A clerk called the hotel to check if they still needed a dishwasher, which they did. I went to work on the same day and started my shift at five o'clock in the evening and earned $1.25 per hour. My family objected to me working at a hotel because it would bring shame to the family. It was not honourable for a Punjabi woman to be out late, especially at a place where alcohol was being consumed. I still went to work that day because I wanted to earn money for the family; there's nothing more honourable than making honest earnings. During my first shift of work, I was supposed to work from 5 p.m. to 12 a.m., but I told my boss that I did not want to be left alone in the kitchen. She took me home that night at 10 p.m. I quit the next day after working three hours because I had to walk home alone at night. I felt scared. In the Punjab, women never went out after dark, and when we went out during the day, we either walked in a group or under the supervision of a mature relative or neighbour.

Soon after, I found another dishwasher job at the La Gondola Restaurant, which was at that time located on 3rd Avenue. The wage was $1.35 per hour. Again, I had to work late at night by myself. The dishes were often broken and the ashtrays were filled with cigarette butts. The work was dangerous because there were a lot of broken glasses and I could cut my hand. I quit after my first eight-hour shift because if I cut my hand on a glass, I wouldn't be able to cook and clean for my family. Later – through the assistance of an educated East Indian lady – I got a job as a housekeeper with BC Ferries. I cleaned the *Queen of Prince Rupert* ferry, which would dock in Prince Rupert after sailing from Vancouver Island once or twice a week. I was paid $7.00 for a four-hour shift. The work was better because I cleaned the ferry while no one was on it and the company paid for our taxi to and from work.

One day, while waiting for a taxi, I spotted a lady wearing a blue kerchief on her head. I asked her, "Where are you coming from?" She replied that she worked at the Royal Fisheries.[13] I asked her who her supervisor was and she replied that it was "Betty." While going home, I was uncertain if Betty was a man or woman. The thought of having to talk to a male supervisor was intimidating because in the Punjab the girls were separated from the men. Even though the idea of having to talk to a white man was unsettling, I still built up the courage to visit Royal Fisheries and asked for Betty. I was relieved that Betty was a woman and not a man. She took down my name and phone number and told me they would call if they needed any extra help.

I later got a call from Royal Fisheries in July 1966 and they offered me a temporary job packing salmon eggs. I was not a regular employee and was contracted to help pack salmon eggs for $1.89 per hour. I didn't enjoy the work because of the foul smell and felt uncomfortable working alongside Japanese men, who also smoked cigarettes. In the Punjab we did not work alongside men and the men never smoked cigarettes in the presence of women. I initially wore dresses to work because I felt wearing pants would be disrespectful to my husband and father-in-law; however, I later wore pants to work and found them to be more practical and comfortable. I worked a twelve-hour shift from 7:30 a.m. to 7:30 p.m., and had to walk home afterwards. I was scared to walk home alone, especially since I would encounter Native men who asked if I wanted to go out drinking with them. I often felt overwhelmed by the fear that my dignity could be taken away from me. I warded off the men by standing bravely and telling them that I would call the police.

The work at Royal Fisheries was not steady. I was called in only if they needed me to pack salmon eggs. After a month, I began applying at some canneries but was not successful. One day, on my way home from Royal Fisheries, I spotted a white lady with a white kerchief. I asked her where she worked. She worked at the Prince Rupert Fishermen's Co-operative and told me to contact her supervisor at the Co-op fish plant. I looked up the supervisor's name [Mrs Anderson] in the phone directory and found her number and address. I walked to her home and asked if there was any available work. She said there was no work. Soon after, I bumped into the same lady at the Henry B-Y grocery store and she kindly informed me that they would be needing workers soon. She took down my name and number. A few days later, my father-in-law told me the Co-op fish plant had called for work.

The Co-op fish plant was expanding their production plant located at the waterfront Fairview area. I began working at the fish plant on 30 August 1966 as a regular employee and was the first Punjabi immigrant woman to be employed in the fishery industry in Prince Rupert. Working at the fish plant was challenging because I still had to fulfil my household responsibilities. My father-in-law went to India in January 1967. I had no one to look after the children and missed some days of work. A white lady from work helped me find a babysitter. I felt uncomfortable leaving my children with a babysitter because in the Punjab we never left our children with non-relatives. My youngest child was only twenty months old, and I felt guilty that she was not getting the motherly love that all children yearn for. I prepared the children's food myself and paid the babysitter two dollars a day for looking after my three kids. I could afford it because I was making sixteen to seventeen dollars a day. My husband did not mind that a white lady was taking care of the children because he was born in Canada. He would take care of the children after his day shift at Prince Rupert Sawmills. He fed them canned spaghetti.

I knew my children were going to be Canadianized, but I still wanted them to grow up with good values. There was no Sikh temple back then, so I took my children to the Evangelical Free Church near our home and they also attended Sunday school. I went to church and prayed to the "One God" which is everyone's God. The Sikh gurus taught that there is one god and that God dwells in all places of worship.[14] The Bible was difficult to understand, but I enjoyed singing hymns like "Amazing Grace." The church was the only place I could find in Prince Rupert where my children could learn good values like we learned in the Punjab. All religions teach the values of honesty, compassion, and hard work.[15]

By 1969, there were a few more Punjabi families and we began getting together in a rented hall on Sundays to have our own Sikh service. We would listen to a tape recording of Sikh hymns, and a local Sikh gentleman would explain the meaning of a hymn selected from a Sikh prayer book. We also signed up for different cooking duties, such as making *roti*, lentil and vegetable curries, yogurt, salad, and rice pudding. We all cooked the food at home and brought it to the Sunday service. Everyone worked together like we did in the Punjab. In 1973, the community purchased an old church and converted it into a *gurdwara*. The Sikh temple not only fulfilled my spiritual needs, but also gave me a sense of belonging that I had missed since I arrived in Canada.

As the Punjabi community began to grow in the early 1970s, Indians from outside the Punjab had also come to learn about our small community. It was not uncommon for Indian sailors, docked at the grain and coal terminals, to look up Punjabi names in the phone directory and contact us. We would prepare a home-cooked Indian meal and take it to them on the ship. The children loved visiting the ship because the sailors would give them a tour. During this time, Punjabi women from Sikh and Hindu backgrounds would get together in their homes for tea and talk about cooking and clothing, and reminisce about life in the Punjab. They also had a lottery, where each person would put twenty dollars into a pot and a name would be drawn to determine the lottery winner. Ladies did this in the Punjab, too. It allowed them to buy things that they usually couldn't afford, like nice shoes or a fancy lady's watch.

My husband continued to work at Prince Rupert Sawmills as a carrier driver. Even though the sawmill shut down between 1970 and 1973, my husband was rehired to help repair machinery prior to its reopening in April 1973. My husband did not see the sawmill reopen because he unexpectedly died on 24 March 1973. He was thirty-five years old and died of an aneurism. I was a widow at thirty-seven years and had to raise three children and pay the mortgage on my own. I was grateful for the support I received from my third brother whom I had sponsored and who had arrived in Prince Rupert with his wife and children in 1962.

I travelled to Vancouver where my aunt told me that I should learn to drive. After getting my learner's licence, I took driving lessons from a male driving instructor. He was too rigid and kept saying, "You have to take control of the car." He didn't understand that I had limited English, little familiarity with motorized equipment, and I was still grieving from the loss of my husband. I found another driving instructor who was a white lady. She was gentler and explained how to drive in a very simple and kind manner. I passed my road test on my second try and got my licence in Prince Rupert in 1975. Although I got my licence and wore pants to work, I still retained the cultural custom of wearing simple light-coloured suits that widows typically wore in the Punjab. A friend of mine in Vancouver would purchase cloth from an Indian clothing store on Fraser Street and have it sewn by a local Punjabi woman.

In 1978, I was encouraged to apply for the assistant floor lady position at the Co-op fish plant. I first refused the position because I would have to be assertive with the other workers. A white lady [Blanche Adams], whom I respected at work, persisted that I apply for the position. When I read the job posting, it stated that a handwritten application would have to be filled out by the applicant. That same white lady told me not to worry and helped me complete the application form. I got the position and became the first Punjabi woman to get a supervisory position at the Co-op fish plant. Some of my co-workers opposed my getting the position because they had more seniority than me. I was selected because of my work ethic. I supervised up to fifty women during a shift and had to train new workers. Things sometimes got tense with management because they would comment that our day-shift crew was less productive than the night-shift crew. I told management the night-shift crew was only more productive because they did not clean the fish properly and they left a lot of bones in the fish. When supervising the day-shift crew, I would send the dirty fish back to the washers and reject fish that had too many bones. I valued quality over quantity and wanted to keep my integrity as an assistant floor lady.

I got help from an Italian lady who would laugh in good humour that she was my secretary because I would ask her how to spell words. There were ladies from many different countries, like Italy, Portugal, Philippines, and India. Canadian white ladies and Native Indian ladies also worked at the Co-op fish plant. All the ladies stayed in their own cultural group during the shift and would sit together during the breaks. It was easier for them to work alongside their own nationality because the experienced ladies could explain the job to the inexperienced ladies. There were always a couple of ladies who could speak English fluently and would translate to the rest of the group. During breaks, the ladies brought and shared meals from their own country on special occasions. They would sit, talk, laugh, and eat together like they would have in their home country. Tension would sometimes arise when some of the Native ladies would say, "You are taking our jobs, go back to your country!" Some Native ladies tried to prevent the Punjabi women from moving into better jobs by insisting that the Punjabi women should do the dirty jobs, like cutting the heads off and washing the fish as opposed to dry jobs like making boxes. I tried to give all the ladies the opportunity to learn new jobs that they would be good at.

In 1997, the Co-op fish plant went into receivership because its profits began to shrink. J.S. McMillan, another local cannery, which was profitable and needed more equipment, bought out the Co-op fish plant. I thought I wouldn't be affected by the takeover because the two seniority lists were going to be merged together and, besides, the Co-op fish plant was older than J.S. McMillan and I was number two on the list. During this time, I also began having chronic leg pain because of having had to stand on cold wet concrete for the past thirty-one years at the Co-op fish plant. To my surprise, I was not contacted by J.S. McMillan and they called whoever they wanted to on the seniority list. My union, the Prince Rupert Amalgamated Shoreworkers and Clerks Union (PRASCU), was not able to help me get my job back. However, they helped me receive my disability benefits for three years, until I qualified for retirement at age sixty-five. Some of my close friends and family have passed away and others have moved to the Lower Mainland. I spend some time in Prince Rupert and most of the time in Langley looking after my grandchildren. Although I lived most of my life in Canada, I am fulfilling my role as a maternal grandmother like I would have in the Punjab.

A Woman's Journey: Discovering a New Kind of Respect

Cannery labour was the work available to immigrant women at a time when Anglo-Canadian women were challenging the 1950s image of the blissful stay-at-home mother as portrayed in iconic television shows like *Leave It to Beaver* and *Father Knows Best*.[16] Although women had often worked in the paid workforce prior to marriage, the general attitude of the growing middle class was that a "good" married woman's place was in the home.[17] Following the Second World War, however, much debate erupted over wage-earning wives and mothers in English Canada, and a growing cohort of women found they had to choose between working both at home and at a job, on the one hand, and staying at home, with a lower standard of living, on the other. The new-found economic stability, even if only with part-time work, allowed women to improve their lives.[18] Subsequently, by the 1960s, feminists' discontent with middle-class suburban culture led to much social upheaval.[19]

Just as the wave of feminism of the 1960s brought change to the lives of women in English Canada, becoming part of the Canadian paid labour force brought a socio-cultural transformation to the lives of Punjabi immigrant women. Bunt Kaur Sidhu's participation in the fisheries had provided an entry point for other Punjabi immigrant women in the Skeena region. Entry into the workforce entailed a major shift for such women, as it entailed turning from the traditional Punjabi practice of *pardah* to actively working in the public sphere in Canada.

Izzat *in the New Country*

Women in India have traditionally been required to conform to *pardah*, and that practice was certainly characteristic of the narrator's upbringing in village Punjab. Leaving village Punjab undoubtedly resulted in a drastic shift from conforming with *pardah* as a means to maintain a sense of respect both for oneself and for other members of the collectivity. Punjabi women experience both inner and external pressures to uphold the Punjabi value of *izzat*, which for them is intimately connected with *pardah*. The narrator's traditional values of *izzat* and the practice of *pardah* at times came into conflict with her new lifestyle in the Skeena region, especially when she first entered the workforce. Entry into the workforce itself runs counter to the practice of *pardah*, a custom that requires women to remain separate from men. While the workforce at the cannery primarily consisted of First Nations and immigrant women, there were also men at the cannery, working as fishermen, machinists, and shed workers.

In her initial attempts to find employment, the narrator experienced the inner and external pressures to maintain the norm of *izzat*. Her sense of relief upon realizing that her job interview was with a woman – "Betty" – instead of a man reflects her comfort level with respect to contact with members of the opposite gender. The narrator also found it challenging to hold jobs that were not deemed respectable, in some cases because she had to face the dangers of returning home alone late at night. Moreover, her family objected to her working at the Rupert Hotel for fear that other people would think she was drinking alcohol, which would bring disgrace and shame (*sharam*) to the family. While the narrator alluded to her fear of rape when working late hours, she never used the actual word "rape," regarding it as a word of abuse that no respectable woman would utter.

Punjabi women often experience acculturation stress arising from the misunderstandings common to the meeting of disparate cultures. The narrator initially experienced alienation and loneliness as a result of cultural gaps regarding the respect one should show towards others in the public sphere. For instance, it was disconcerting for her to work alongside Japanese men, especially when they smoked cigarettes in her presence. This gave her an unsettling feeling of disgrace and shame. In the Punjab, women rarely worked alongside men, and men never smoked cigarettes in the presence of women, children, or elders, regarding it as disrespectful; men traditionally smoked only among themselves. The narrator felt alienated and socially isolated in an environment so different from her life in the Punjab. While the practice of *pardah* and the value of *izzat* are incongruent with working in the public sphere, the concept of *izzat* nonetheless proved, for the narrator and other Punjabi women, to be a source of adaptive strength.

Izzat *as a Source of Strength*

In the face of acculturation stress, one's own cultural resources can prove to be beneficial in the adaptation process. The value system of *dharam* (duty) and *izzat* (respect) has been effective in helping Punjabis cope with the changes that occur with immigration and thus has helped Punjabis adjust to their new life in the Skeena region. The Lake Cowichan area, where the narrator initially lived, already had an established Punjabi community. While the community provided her with some support and guidance during her

i to her new country, she still found it difficult to adjust because
⌐as unable to speak or read the English language. Fulfilling her duty as
⌐oth a wife and a mother was made more difficult for her in Canada especially because of the language barrier. While the language barrier was a
major source of acculturation stress, her persistence in learning English was
an issue of *izzat* not only for her family but also for herself. For instance, once
the narrator had learned "survival" English, she felt confident shopping for
food for her family. In turn, this allowed her to fulfil her duty as a Punjabi
wife and mother.

Likewise, in order to maintain *izzat*, the narrator asked her father-in-law
for assistance in buying a house. For the narrator, the acquisition of a home
signified emotional and economic security for the family even as it provided
social status reminiscent of landownership in the Punjab. Similarly, she felt
pressured to work in order to pay off the mortgage. There were only a few
other Punjabi women living in Prince Rupert at that time, and they did not
work, and thus the narrator was unable to acquire information in the traditional way, through word of mouth, about how to enter the paid workforce.
In contrast to her experience on Vancouver Island, she had very little opportunity to interact with fellow Punjabis in the remote town of Prince Rupert
in the mid-1960s, when the town lacked a Punjabi community. The narrator
thus had to rely on her own resources to find a job. She undertook all these
actions for the welfare and dignity of her family.

Despite her limited English skills, the narrator eventually managed to find
out about work available to women. Interestingly, while she did not know any
women who worked in the fish canneries, she heard about such work from
women of other ethnic backgrounds (such as Italian-Canadian, Portuguese-
Canadian, and Anglo-Canadian) who – with low education and skills – perhaps all shared the same goal of being a working wife and mother. Punjabi
immigrant women largely engaged in relatively low-paid work, but even so,
it gave them an entry into the paid workforce and introduced them to the
camaraderie that existed among working-class women in the Skeena during
the 1960s. While the narrator's main link to the working world was certainly
through her gender, her ability to pursue what she saw as necessary for the
welfare of her family came from her understanding of respect and her collectivity orientation, something that women in English Canada were also grappling at the time.

Contrary to the Western tendency to view Indian women as servile and to
think that Indian culture has no doctrine of gender equality and empowerment, there exist traditional Indian or Punjabi resources that inspire women
in challenging times. For example, the imagery and mythology of the Hindu
warrior goddess, Durga, describe a female deity of full independence with
the ability to challenge and defeat evil forces while embracing the entirety

of life (from birth to death). This powerful image of the feminine was used by the tenth Sikh guru, Guru Gobind Singh, in his literary works. His use of Durga was for the purpose of evoking a martial mood to inspire confidence and courage so that people would succeed in rising up against oppression.[20] Similarly, Sikh scriptural teachings emphasize equality and universality. The daily prayer composed by Guru Nanak, *Asa di Var*, in a sense uplifted the position of women at the time when Guru Nanak composed it:

> From the woman is our birth, in the womb we are shaped.
> To the woman we are engaged, to the woman we are married.
> The woman is our friend and from the woman is the family.
> If one woman dies, we seek another;
> Through the woman are the bonds of the world.
> Why call a woman evil?
> She gives birth to kings!
> From the woman comes the woman;
> Without the woman there is none.
>
> (*Guru Granth Sahib*, p. 47)

Religion and spirituality can function as a lens or framework through which one can make sense of one's existential situation.[21] The various traditional Indian cultural and religious resources can be a source of strength and serve as an instrument for empowering women to navigate the prescribed traditional gender roles as well as the economic independence that comes with work in the public sphere. The narrator's story exemplifies the enormous strength that can be gained from religion, even when – as in the Skeena region – there is no institutional set-up whereby Sikhism can be practised as a community.[22] While the Punjabi value of *izzat* and Punjabi religious teachings helped Punjabi women adapt to their new lives as members of the paid workforce, the women's new role also had a significant impact on their previous traditional social patterns of behaviour. In the process, the Punjabi value of *izzat* became modified.

Izzat *Redefined*

The traditional value of respect in the context of a collectivity orientation is comparable to the Western notion of self-respect in the context of a self-orientation. Punjabi immigrant women in the Skeena initially experienced both inner and external pressures to maintain the traditional norms of *dharam* and *izzat* while simultaneously contributing – primarily as secondary wage earners – to the economic health of the family. While becoming a working wife and mother was for the most part an act of helping the family economically, it also became a transformative experience for many Punjabi women, especially in terms of their economic and psycho-social adaptation to the Skeena region.

Economic Independence

Many Punjabi immigrant wives and mothers entered the paid workforce, even if only on a seasonal basis. Punjabi women who arrived in the 1960s and early 1970s did not initially envision an explicit role for themselves in the economic adaptation of their families to Canada. However, the financial pressures to pay off the mortgage for their home and to sponsor other family members propelled women to enter the workforce. Once Punjabi families are certain about settling in Canada, their orientation is to earn money quickly in order to establish the family through the acquisition of a home and property. In effect, Punjabi women found themselves entering the Canadian workforce out of economic necessity.

Joining the workforce emerged as a *dharam* for Punjabi women. Working for pay was the fulfilment of one's duty as wife and mother, since it was understood to have been done out of necessity for the welfare of the family – the collectivity. Paradoxically, however, Punjabi women who entered the paid labour force began to experience, as a consequence, a sense of economic independence or greater autonomy. While the traditional orientation had been towards the collectivity, economic independence was a very important step towards realizing one's own autonomy. Furthermore, over time as families have settled in Canada, the family has often shrunk to a nuclear size, which may or may not have included grandparents, even as family dynamics have undergone change within the household. This shift in the power dynamic within the family may have occurred as a direct result of the economic independence that many immigrant women gained through participation in the paid labour force.[23] When women achieve economic autonomy, social and cultural transformation inevitably follows.

Reinterpretation of Values

As the traditional governing principle of social behaviour, *izzat* continues to be based on seniority. However, the notion of respect has been modified as a result of migration to Canada; that is, *izzat* is now taken to be deserved by immigrant parents who have worked hard to survive and establish the family in a foreign and often harsh environment.[24] The inclusion in the understanding of *izzat* of an individual's efforts to establish his or her family reflects a gradual shift towards a self-orientation. Naidoo and Davis assert that South Asian women have successfully adapted to modernity through differentiating the economic sphere from the social and local sphere, treating the former as modern and the latter as Western.[25] However, it has been noted that in the Sikh community in Vancouver, the values that come with or follow economic independence – like self-orientation – can become a source of personal tension, engendering conflict as women become torn between fulfilling the traditional role expectations of wife and daughter-in-law and desiring to exercise personal choice.[26]

The consequence of this tension is likely to be a sense of alienation with respect to role playing – a reluctance on the part of women to play the role of the "obedient" wife and/or "dutiful" daughter-in-law, even if they have not fully developed a self-orientation. While this alienation from role playing was evident in the Sikh community in the Lower Mainland,[27] it was generally not a feature that emerged during the interviews conducted with Punjabi women from the Skeena region. Rather, the experience of economic independence among the Skeena Punjabis seems to have resulted in the expansion of personal choice and self-orientation. Participation in the larger Skeena cannery culture apparently provided an environment in which Punjabi women began to generate change or, at the very least, to modify Punjabi customs associated with religious values.[28] Moreover, the cannery world provided an important link to the larger Canadian community, where working-class women from various ethnic backgrounds were grappling with the same socio-cultural changes while engaging in the paid labour available to women. The socio-cultural transformation that occurred among Punjabi immigrant women became evident and was reinforced when the forestry industry drastically declined in the region and a fair number of Punjabi women had to, in a sense, "wear the pants."

The narrator was not only one of the first Punjabi ladies to enter the workforce in Prince Rupert in 1966, but also the first Punjabi immigrant woman to work at a cannery in the Skeena region. In that capacity, she introduced the canning industry to Punjabi women as potential workers. In effect, she provided an entry point for the emerging subculture of Punjabi female fishery workers. There is an ironic reversal in community identification here: the narrator, who for the most part had grown up practising *pardah*, now became the one to initiate the cultivation of a new sense of community for Punjabi women in the Canadian public sphere. And for the narrator, the transition occurred when she shifted from wearing the headscarf to wearing the "pants," both at work and within the home.

Along with experiencing economic self-reliance, Punjabi women continued to place great importance on rearing their children. They generally preferred seasonal work in order to fulfil their role as mother. While most of the women preferred to stay at home with their children, such care was often based on how they remembered children being reared back in the Punjab.

For many, as discussed in chapter 4, leaving children with non-family members (such as a babysitter or at a daycare) was very unsettling. They expected that children, in turn, would be respectful of, and dutiful towards, the welfare of the collectivity.

The collectivity remained important in the women's sense of connectedness – especially in relation to children and grandchildren – and in their sense of the smooth functioning of the household and community at large. Despite their economic independence, Punjabi immigrant women still had a strong traditional orientation and a psycho-social need to live in close proximity to the extended family. While the family continued to be central to Punjabi women, their social circle at the cannery became important as well. In contrast to Sikh women living in Vancouver in the first decade of the twenty-first century,[29] Punjabi women living in the Skeena had, in fact, acquired skills that allowed them to move outside the comfort of a Punjabi milieu and build a social network beyond it. Over time, the newly acquired social, work, and language skills gave Punjabi women the confidence to enjoy engaging with "their" larger Skeena community.

By the mid-1970s, working in the cannery had become popular among Punjabi women. There was steady growth in the Punjabi community during the 1970s and 1980s, and, in fact, Punjabi women migrating to Canada from the late-1970s onwards came with the expectation that they would be required to work. This expectation became normal in the Skeena Punjabi community. Ironically, many Punjabi women wanted to enter the workforce precisely because it brought with it socio-cultural benefits. For example, over time the narrator discovered a new kind of respect, a respect she earned through self-reliance, integrity, and the work ethic, which enabled her to support her family under the ill-fated circumstance of widowhood. As well, she became the first Punjabi floor supervisor at her cannery. That development was a step towards experiencing *izzat* with a self-orientation – self-respect. Women's entry into the Canadian labour force for the sake of survival – economic, but also social and psychological – and their adaptation to remote towns in Canada therefore had a profound impact on their previous traditional social and cultural patterns of behaviour. Note the comment of an educated Punjabi woman who came to Canada in the 1970s: "When you leave the house you have a good time, a good social life. Naturally women will want to work because it makes you have friends, a good time. Once you work you can't stay at home; you want to go outside of the home to have experiences. It is not easy to let it go. It is not a life to just make *rotis* [unleavened bread], eat it, and then go to sleep. Everybody should work ... My view is that ladies should be smart enough to work outside the home, socialize, and make money at the same time. If both men and women work, then the family can settle more quickly."[30]

Punjabi cannery worker Jaspreet Kaur Uppal cleaning herring (1983). Courtesy of Nancy Robertson.

While working in the cannery proved to be beneficial for Punjabi women, it could also lead to hostility between Punjabis and some First Nations women (e.g., in the period of initial contact, in the 1960s and 1970s). The presence of the Punjabi women in the cannery stirred up resentment among some First Nations women, who saw the fisheries as their territory. One Punjabi woman gave an account of hostility in her work environment: "When I started in Port Edward there were mostly First Nations working there. When I started working at the cannery, First Nations had a problem with us because we were not speaking in English. One day a First Nations lady threw water on my sister-in-law because she could not speak in English. I took her place. They threw water on me. I threw water on them. They complained to the foremen but nothing ever came of it."[31]

Intercultural tension is undeniably a source of acculturation stress, and it is compounded when there is also a language barrier. While Punjabi women who had a command of the English language could stand up for themselves in the preservation of their dignity according to the norms of *izzat*, doing so was much more challenging for those who spoke very little English. For the Punjabi woman cited above, the workplace was a hostile environment. However, as she learned to speak English over time, she was able to assert herself; this was a matter of *izzat* not only for herself (self-respect) but also for her people and community (community respect).

It is noteworthy that while the literature on race relations tends to focus on interactions between a particular ethnic minority group and the Anglo-mainstream, the intercultural dynamic in the work environment at the salmon canneries and within the Skeena community at large was much more complex, encompassing relations among the Punjabis, the people belonging to the First Nations, the Anglo-mainstream, and the many other ethnic communities in the region. In particular, the occasional derogatory remarks against Punjabis were voiced by First Nations women who had traditionally held most of the jobs in the salmon canning industry. Paradoxically, while the union sought support from the "ethnic" community, it also found itself inadvertently playing the role of "intercultural mediator" in the mid-1970s and well into the 1980s. This is the subject of the following chapter.

Summary

As Punjabi women arrived in Canada, and even more when they entered and adapted to low-wage work at the salmon canneries, their traditional Punjabi value of *izzat* and their practice of *pardah* conflicted with the norms of an industrialized setting. However, the value of *izzat* proved to be a source of adaptive strength for Punjabi women, even as the understanding of it was modified by the influence of economic independence. Drawing upon traditional cultural resources, the Punjabi value of *izzat* turned out to be a source of adaptive strength in Punjabi women's social acclimatization to the Skeena workforce.

Izzat means a sense of dignity in relation to one's family and people. For Punjabi immigrant women it served as a source of strength in the face of acculturation stress, existential crisis, and inequitable circumstances. While the traditional value of *izzat* was manifested within the context of a collectivity orientation, it was extended somewhat in Canada to include the notion of self-respect in the context of a self-orientation. In turn, Punjabi women's entry into the Canadian labour force had a significant impact on their traditional social and cultural patterns of behaviour as they struggled for economic as well as social and psychological survival and adapted to life in the small remote towns of the Skeena region. In other words, entry into the Canadian workforce offered Punjabi immigrant women the opportunity, over time, to discover a new kind of respect. It made them more self-confident.

CHAPTER 6

Occupational Segregation, Intercultural Conflict, and Mediation

As the Punjabis settled in the Skeena region, they found work in the natural resource–based industries: the men in forestry and the women in fisheries. While the Punjabi immigrant experience is undoubtedly gender-specific, there is convergence on issues surrounding rights relating to working conditions and intercultural matters at the workplace. It was inevitable that, as an immigrant group working in the Skeena region's resource industries, the Punjabi community would face multiple barriers in the workforce and would therefore support and participate in the labour movement to improve their situation.

The Punjabi migration to the Skeena region began after the Second World War, when the mass-production model – which was based on a social contract – provided a stable and structured system for resource extraction. Along with rapid growth in production came the strengthening of the labour unions in their efforts to secure higher wages and better physical working conditions through collective bargaining.[1] Upon entering the Skeena region's multi-ethnic workforce, Punjabis also turned to their unions for help with intercultural-labour issues. While labour unions are recognized for bargaining for better working conditions, they also had to mediate conflicts over discrimination that Punjabi workers experienced in the workplace. In effect, the union – through its efforts in addressing Punjabi grievances – came to play the role of intercultural mediator.

As Punjabis entered unionized workplaces, the unions began to serve as a platform from which their voices could be heard. Notwithstanding the significant role that the unions played in the lives of Punjabi manual labourers from the mid-1960s up to the 1980s, the labour politics associated with the globalization-driven decline in the forestry and fishery industries led to disillusionment with their respective unions. During the 1990s, BC's labour supported the provincial New Democratic Party (NDP) government; however, even after government intervention, the forestry and fishery industries continued to decline. The consequential bust in both industries not only had an economic and social impact on the Punjabi community, but also caused disenchantment with the labour movement – that is, with both the unions and the labour-supported NDP.

The focus of this chapter is twofold. First, it investigates the Punjabis' personal and collective use of, and involvement with, labour unions, particularly with regard to the intercultural tensions that emerged within the workplace. Second, the chapter looks at the decline in Punjabi support for the labour movement. While the unions played a supportive role for Punjabis during the 1970s and 1980s, serving as a platform for the Punjabi immigrant voice, that role began to decline in the early 1990s, especially when the unions were struggling for their own relevancy in a changing, competitive globalized economy.

This chapter has three parts. The first part provides a critical look at the social and cultural aspects of the Skeena region's multi-ethnic workforce, particularly with respect to the First Nations. It also investigates the work-related discrimination that Punjabis experienced upon entering the Skeena region's workforce during the 1960s and 1970s. The second part examines the role of labour unions in relation to the Punjabi community, notably their initial role in voicing the Punjabi immigrants' concerns as members of the workforce. The third part discusses how the unions' decision to narrow their focus to labour-management issues alone alienated the Punjabi workers from the movement. In treating these issues, the chapter makes evident that while the union movement depended on immigrant support to strengthen itself politically, it unintentionally also played the role of intercultural mediator within labour.

The Skeena Region's Multi-ethnic Workforce

The Skeena region comprises the area surrounding the Skeena River, which is the second-longest river in British Columbia (560 kilometres), draining a 54,390-square-kilometre area of northwestern BC. The Skeena River flows into the Hectate Strait at Eleanor Passage between Port Edward and Port Essington, which is south of Prince Rupert (see map 2.2). Based on archaeological evidence and oral histories, the Prince Rupert area was occupied by the Tsimshian, "the people at the mouth of 'Kshian [Skeena]."[2] The Tsimshian people depended on cedar and salmon, benefiting from the fact that the greatest run of fish was up the Skeena River. The Tsimshian often acted as middlemen in the bartering of goods between the further inland First Nations (including Nisga'a, Gitxan, and Haisla) and the Hudson's Bay Company.[3] It was in the late 1800s that William Duncan of the Church of England established a mission among the Tsimshian at Metlakatla (1862) and Rev. Thomas Crosby of the Methodist Church established another at Port Simpson (1874). The two denominations were rivals in their efforts to convert and "save" First Nations people from their "savage way of life."[4] According to James Miller, these missions were in part the result of First Nations initiatives, since they apparently had their own social, political, and economic motives for bringing in missionaries.[5] Besides the Skeena region has seen a lot of tension over land claims and fishing rights.

First Nations and BC's Resource Industries

It was during the last quarter of the eighteenth century that Europeans first came into contact with the First Nations in the coastal regions of BC through approaches by sea. Subsequently, in the early nineteenth century, Europeans came into contact with the First Nations through the land-based fur trade.[6] It was, however, not until the gold rush in the Fraser (1858–60) and Cariboo (1860–63) regions of central interior BC that competition between the two groups erupted over the region's resources. The mining operations disrupted the livelihood of the First Nations – for example, their fishing on the Fraser River – and the First Nations resented the gold miners for exploiting their land and its resources.[7] The ensuing conflict led to violent clashes between the two groups.[8]

When British Columbia joined Confederation in 1871, the First Nations people were hopeful that the federal government would address their concerns. Despite their initial expectations, Canada adopted policies that addressed only the needs of the new frontier Anglo-Canadian settlers. Policies on private ownership and claims over the land and its resources were consolidated in the Indian Act of 1876.[9] These policies (e.g., the government's right to relocate the First Nations and expropriate their lands) were backed by armed force. Of course, with their superior weaponry, Anglo-Canadians were at an advantage in facing the First Nations people militarily and in enforcing the Canadian policies of "civilization" and assimilation.[10] By the 1880s, Anglo-Canadian settlement in British Columbia had become firmly established.

Thereafter, British Columbia began to emerge as an industrialized power within Canada, accomplishing this at the cost of the devastation of the First Nations. Divided among many factional clans,[11] the First Nations were primarily tribal, with their livelihood based on small-scale hunting, fishing, and food gathering.[12] No doubt, their subsistence economy was seen by Anglo-

Canadians as inefficient in contrast to the industrialization taking place in the province, and First Nations' interests were not a big factor in the decision-making of governments and industrialists. In fact, as one of its initiatives for the modernization of the Native economy, the Canadian government in 1885 made the northwest coast Aboriginal practice of bartering wealth through the offering of gifts (the potlatch) a crime. While the ban had largely been urged by government officials and missionaries because they saw the potlatch as an "unproductive" and "uncivilized" custom, it could also be seen as a manoeuvre to dismantle the indigenous tribal societies in order to facilitate the Anglo-Canadian industrialization of British Columbia.[13] The government also enforced conservation laws and regulations whose purpose was not only to allow the government to acquire control over the land and its resources, but also to create a body of people to perform labour jobs. The First Nations later mobilized for their rights over the land and waters, but to no avail. Eventually, in 1927, the Canadian government amended the Indian Act to make the pursuit of land claims illegal, thereby driving the First Nations' land movement underground.[14]

Industrialization involved the assembly-line mode of mass production, and the First Nations people were an essential part of this type of production, as they were a marginal group, employable only for manual or semi-skilled jobs.[15] The growth of the lumber industry, with its logging and depletion of trees, had a devastating impact on the First Nations, disrupting hunting as the basis of their livelihood. In the northern interior, where the primary means of livelihood had been hunting with traplines, First Nations people had to increasingly turn to other means, such as fishing, to survive.[16] The peak years in logging operations in the north-central region (1946–64) also marked the high point in the employment of First Nations men in the forestry sector, even though their participation was never as high as in the fisheries.[17]

Traditionally, the First Nations did not make extensive use of BC's lush forests;[18] however, the indigenous people, especially from the coastal areas, depended heavily on the fisheries. During the 1870s, when the fish-canning industry was established in BC, people of the First Nations had to adjust to the newly imposed Anglo-Canadian capitalist economy.[19] The First Nations fishermen lost their direct ownership of, or control over, their means of production; that is, the dominion set aside a small portion of fisheries for the First Nations while opening up the resource to the enterprising Anglo-Canadians.[20] There was now a drastic shift to large-scale production and an increasingly complex distribution system. The First Nations had to face competition from fishermen more experienced in commercial fishing and with a technology more sophisticated than their traditional tools, basically a hand-made spear for salmon fishing. Previously, salmon had been caught – and cured by the salting or smoking process – mainly for the local community's own use; some salmon may have been bartered for other products from other clans. Anglo-Canadians, however, began canning fish in large quantities for export to the United Kingdom and elsewhere.

With the establishment of commercial fishing, the First Nations found it necessary to move to the central fishing and canning locations in the Nass, Skeena, Fraser, and river inlet areas.[21] Their leaders, whose positions were hereditary, were now replaced by contractors who could hire and fire First Nations fishermen and cannery workers. Still, at the very least, they were able to find wage employment in the fisheries, an occupation in which they already had cultural knowledge and skills.[22] From the late 1880s, many First Nations participated in the fishery industry both to make use of their traditional skills and to earn wages. A woman belonging to the Nisga'a Nation spoke of her family's strong ties with BC's north coast fishery industry:

> I came from a fishing family. During the season, my family came down from the village and worked in the cannery. The family worked at the Arrandale Cannery [located] right across from our village Kincolith [Gingolx] in the Nass Valley [near the mouth of the Nass River].[23] My mother worked in the cannery, while my grandmother mostly made the fishing nets. My father was a fisherman. He went to residential school. When we were kids, my father permanently moved the family to Port Edward so that we did not have to go to residential school. The family lived in the bunkhouse for First Nations. In Port Edward, my family worked for BC Packers.[24]

A large majority of workers in the fishing industry and canneries came from the First Nations. Their numbers decline, however, after the 1920s as a result of technological change. The introduction of gasoline-powered boats in the 1920s meant canneries could be further apart; similarly, refrigeration – introduced in the 1930s – meant that fish could be transported long distances before being processed. As a result, the work done in the small, dispersed canneries was consolidated in canneries in Vancouver and Prince Rupert.[25] The Great Depression of the 1930s had a dreadful impact on the First Nations and their paid-wage labour, forcing them to return to their traditional subsistence economy but now with restrictive rules on extracting resources from land and water. The First Nations were forced to rely on relief payments that were dramatically lower than those for non-Aboriginals. Indeed, there existed a two-tiered welfare system that favoured the latter.[26] During the Second World War, most of the First Nations were brought back into wage-paid work, mainly in the forestry and fishery industries.

In response to discrimination in the workplace, First Nations workers mobilized for their rights as workers through the Native Brotherhood, which had Native rights as its primary interest.[27] It was not until 1956 that an agreement was reached to extend equal treatment to First Nations and allow them into the labour union.[28] Furthermore, the ban against soliciting funds for First Nations' land claims was lifted in 1951. Consequently, there gradually developed a movement for self-determination among the First Nations, and since the 1960s, First Nations groups, including the Nisga'a of the Nass Valley, have mobilized for land claims and self-governance.[29]

Cheap Wage Labour

With only a limited Anglo-Canadian labour force in BC's resource industries at the turn of the twentieth century, employers – out of necessity – sought out First Nations men, but also many Chinese[30] and Japanese[31] men to work for them. By 1885, there was a dramatic increase in Chinese and Japanese immigration and presence in both the forestry and fisheries workforce. Industrialists sought cheap labour in order to maximize their profits. Sawmill and cannery managers hired from these groups because they were sources of "inexpensive labour" and were also considered to be hardworking.[32] First Nations' participation in the forestry industry was not as high as it was in the fisheries, since the latter industry was their traditional livelihood.

By the first decade of the twentieth century, labour in the sawmills was structured along lines of ethnicity or "race." This process of "racialization" was deemed necessary both to compete economically and to legitimize differential wages.[33] At this time, Punjabi men began to enter BC's forestry industry. The Punjabi pioneers of the early decades of the twentieth century migrated to Canada when the dominion was not receptive to "non-whites," but tolerated them only insofar as they filled the labour needs of the country. As a part of the "cheap" labour force, Punjabis were known for their hard work at a time when British Columbia was undergoing industrialization, with an emphasis on property rights and "negative freedom" (i.e., the state should not interfere with freedom).[34]

Industrialists benefited from a non-white workforce. In the early 1900s, wages differed according to racial and skill-level divisions. A Punjabi pioneer spoke of the racial and skill divide in the forestry industry: "The jobs that were offered to these ethnic communities were somewhat different. The labouring groups were the Chinese and the Punjabis. The Japanese managed to get better jobs that involved more technical training. The best jobs, the engineers and people who were the bosses at the mill, went to the Europeans."[35] During the first decade of the twentieth century, the better- or higher-paid jobs in sawmills, like head sawyer (a job that paid four to five dollars per day), were in fact not available to First Nations and Asian workers. Meanwhile, for the same low-wage unskilled labour, Asian workers were given lower wages than Anglo-Canadians. For example, an Anglo-Canadian unskilled labourer earned $1.75 to $2.00 per day, whereas Japanese workers received $1.00 to $1.60 and Chinese labourers $0.90 to $1.30.[36] A Punjabi-Sikh pioneer who joined his father in 1925 to live and work at Fraser Mills in Burquitlam explained the disparity in wages thus: "There were between two and three hundred Sikhs. They had four or five cookhouses and different-sized bunkhouses; some had thirty, forty, or fifty people living in them. That's how they lived then. We had our own temple, a small one built by the mill at their own expense. It was a very good company, but for wages there was a five-cent difference between us and white people. We got twenty-five cents an hour and the whites got thirty cents for the same job."[37]

Since Asian workers were given lower wages, companies could keep operations at the mill going during economically difficult times, even while maintaining the high-skill wages of the Anglo-Canadian workforce.[38] Along with receiving lower wages, East Indian, Chinese, and Japanese workers were often expected to give a percentage of their wages to their foreman or manager. While this system of handing over a percentage of one's salary was an unwritten norm, it was widely practised and was expected by both managers and Asian workers.[39]

Similar to the forestry industry, industrialists in the fisheries sought cheap labour. Women were, in fact, thought to be the ideal labour force for the low skill and low wages of salmon cannery work during the late nineteenth century.[40] However, it was hard to find women workers, since they were in charge of the nuclear home. Industrialists, therefore, turned to other categories of labourers for cheap labour, including First Nations people and immigrants from China and Japan. As with the forestry industry, wages were lower for First Nations women as well as for Chinese and Japanese workers. A man from the Nisga'a Nation described First Nations' role as cheap labour in the fishery industry: "The fisheries were at the heart of our life, our culture. My mom has been working since she was thirteen years old (now she is eighty-four years). She said in those days there was a lot of discrimination against the First Nations. She was paid only about twenty-five cents an hour. In the early 1900s, the canneries were mostly filled with First Nations workers, some Chinese and Japanese. The Chinese had more guaranteed work than the First Nations because they got hired by Chinese contractors. We felt they were taking our jobs."[41]

It was not until after the Great Depression and the Second World War that the Chinese contractor system was eliminated from the cannery industry.[42]

A woman from the Nisga'a nation shared her observations on the changes that have occurred in the cannery workforce:

> My mom used to get her pay cheque from a Chinese contractor. Up to the 1960s, we [First Nations] were paid for the piece. I never did "piece work." When I started working at Port Edward in the early 1960s, we were paid by the hour. We had to make the cans by our hands; now they come ready made. In those days, we had to do a lot with our hands. That is why there were so many jobs in those days. We had to work hard and fast. But the bosses were more respectful then than they are now. The machines do a lot of the work now. We were segregated, so we worked only with the First Nations. The Chinese worked together. When the wages got better, then more white people started working there as well.[43]

While First Nations women served throughout the history of BC's salmon canning industry, immigrant women from various ethnic backgrounds would later follow this work pattern, especially during the post–Second World War boom in the resource industries and when non-Anglo immigration increased.[44] Then, as wages rose, other non-traditional cannery workers began seeking employment in the industry. With the industrialization of the province, much of the manual cheap labour was performed by immigrants from eastern Europe (Ukraine), southern Europe (Italy, Portugal), and Asia (China, Japan, India), while skilled and managerial positions were primarily filled by Anglo-Canadians.[45]

A Segregated Workforce

Occupational segregation patterns emerged and persisted in many industries, especially those with low wages that required little skill.[46] Scholars have come up with various theories to explain why women and members of ethnic or immigrant groups have been concentrated in particular sectors or jobs within a single industry. Some theorists attribute occupational segregation to the competitive labour market and exogenous factors such as discriminatory practices on the part of employers and schools (neo-classical theory). Other theorists argue that the structures of the labour market discriminate against minority groups and that employers encourage intercultural or gender rivalry (labour-market segmentation theory). Regardless of the cause of occupational segregation, labour was racialized in both the forestry and fishery industries.

With industrialization in the late 1800s, BC's forestry and fishery industries were no exceptions to the patterns of occupational segregation. Workers of different ethnic backgrounds were assigned to different tasks and segregated from one another. The First Nations men were most often fishermen, while the women worked in the canning plants. The First Nations in the Skeena region were heavily dependent on fishing, and despite the challenges they faced in regard to fishing and land claims, they participated in the fishery industry.[47] While many First Nations people continued to pursue their traditional livelihood, albeit within the overall context of a capitalist economy, other ethnic groups, too, performed tasks directly related to what they had done in their place of origin prior to migrating to Canada. For instance, in the early 1900s, immigrants from Scandinavia, Iceland, and the British Isles earned their living by fishing, since they had been fishermen in their native country. Some of these fishermen settlers built villages along the coast; the Norwegians, for instance, established their own village in Oona River.[48]

At the turn of the twentieth century, the migration of Japanese and Chinese displaced some of the First Nations fishermen. This displacement created apprehension among the First Nations, who felt that fishing was their traditional livelihood and that immigrants were taking it away from them. Generally, First Nations fishermen felt threatened by the Japanese fishermen.[49] The cannery hired Japanese and Chinese workers because they were a cheap labour pool and were considered hardworking.[50] A man from the Nisga'a Nation described the workplace environment: "First Nations people mostly worked at the North Pacific Cannery.[51] There were some Japanese and Chinese but they were working in separate areas. They did towing and worked in the boiler room. We mostly did not interact with them … We had a problem with other people who came here. The bosses [management] were white, telling us what to do. The manager of the North Pacific Cannery was German. The workers spoke in their own language."[52]

Chinese men were often employed through contractors as shore workers in the canning of salmon – particularly for the "butcher work."[53] A union representative noted how the Chinese were segregated according to race and skill: "Chinese men came from the Vancouver Lower Mainland and held a lot of seniority in the canneries. The Chinese worked as the butchers; they were known as the 'Butcher Crew Gangs' … and they all came from Vancouver. In fact, because the Chinese were known for their role as the butcher, when machinery was acquired for cutting the fish heads and guts, it was referred to as the 'Iron Chink' until 1982, when the company realized it was discriminatory to do so."[54]

The Japanese began to arrive in Canada in the early 1900s. While the Japanese men commonly worked as fishermen, their wives worked as shore workers in the canning plants or as net menders. However, with the internment of the Japanese during the Second World War, they were forced to leave the Skeena region and most did not return to the area.

With the centralization of canneries in Prince Rupert in the 1930s, the Skeena region evolved to become the home of a unique multi-ethnic workforce, albeit with the members of the various minority groups working and living in informal segregation. The companies benefited from this segregated pool of workers, not only because they could pay First Nations and Asian labourers lower wages, but also because they could rationalize the cheaper living arrangements for these workers on the grounds that they did not require a living space like that of the "white man."

As with the bunkhouses at the lumber mill sites in the Lower Mainland and on Vancouver Island during the first half of the twentieth century, the living arrangements at the cannery sites were segregated according to ethnicity. A woman from the Tsimshian Nation described her entry into the paid labour force:

> I was born in Port Simpson [Lax'Kw'alaams] in 1930 but really was of the woods. My family hunted and fished. In the mid-1940s, my parents decided to meet up with an aunt in Port Edward. There was so much work then. I ended up working at Nelson Brothers at the age of fifteen. In those days there was no age limit. It was like working in a new country. The people working there were mostly from the Nass [Nisga'a], Haida, and Tsimshian Nations. My parents, cousins, and I lived in row housing. There was no electricity or plumbing. Our toilet was outside over the water. The company supplied us with wood for heating. The Chinese, Japanese, and white man lived separate from us. By the 1960s, the Chinese men slowly came with their families.[55]

The cannery companies applied a double standard with regard to the living arrangements: the First Nations people lived among themselves in tents or bunkhouses near the plant (termed the "Native village"), the "whites" were housed in bungalows (labelled the "White village"), and the visible minority immigrants resided in the very tight quarters of a bunkhouse allotted to their particular ethnic group (referred to as the "Chinese village" and the "Japanese village").[56] Note the comment made by an Anglo-Canadian woman, born in 1928, who began working in the canneries in 1942: "I started working at the North Pacific Cannery in Port Edward when I was fourteen years old. I lived in a waterfront bungalow home with my family. I also worked in other canneries, like Sunnyside, Cassiar, and Inverness."[57] In contrast, note the account of a woman from the Nisga'a Nation who has been working in the fisheries since 1961: "Our living quarters then were not that good in Port Edward. We had a metal bath to fill up with water. We would reuse the water that was used by one of the other kids, but during the winter we would keep adding hot water to it so that we would not get cold ... There were rows of bunk-houses for the workers. The First Nations had to go to the outhouse to go to the bathroom. The First Nations were the last ones to get a bathroom in their bunkhouse. The white people had a better set-up. They had their own family bungalow–style homes."[58] While the hiring of First Nations people as work-ers in the labour force, especially within the fisheries, was considered a man-oeuvre to remove them from their "savage" lifestyle and assimilate them into the "white man's" culture,[59] Asians were viewed as an "oriental menace"[60] and thus a threat to the British-Canadian culture of the province.[61]

By the 1960s, it was primarily First Nations women who worked in the salmon canneries, but, increasingly, the canneries hired women of Anglo, Japanese, Italian, and Portuguese origins. When the Portuguese came to the Skeena region in the 1960s, they – both men and women – found work at the canneries, although some of the men fished as well. Most of the Italian men were shore workers, while the Italian women and some of the men worked in the canneries. The workers were segregated in the fish plants according to their ethnicity, with the members of each ethnic group working together on their own fish-washing or fish-canning line. The segregated set-up both in the living quarters and at work continued up to the second half of the twentieth century. Interestingly, a local politician in the Skeena region explained that the segregation within the cannery was a carryover from the first settlement:

> Segregation is a carryover from the first settlement. There were melt-ing pots for the fur trade. There were settlements for fishing. Then the fishing canneries were set up. Native men and their sons did the fish-ing. Wives and daughters did the net loft and cannery work. There were some Chinese and English as fishermen, but they were mostly Natives and some Japanese and other white people (such as Norwegian). Can-neries had some English and Japanese; the Chinese crew tended to work in the cannery and cut off the fish heads. There were foremen from different nations, including English, Natives, and Chinese people, but the bosses were always white. Then, the many different groups lived separately in their quarters. There were some mixed marriages like Native-English or Native-Chinese. When people from other ethnic backgrounds began entering the canneries, the segregation continued. The intercultural dynamic is similar to the set-up of the initial fish canneries.[62]

While today the companies no longer provide living arrangements for their workforce, the initial occupational segregation has continued in the salmon canneries.

The Ethnic Intruder

The resource industries of the Skeena region relied on a pool of "cheap labour" that worked and lived in a segregated set-up. Most importantly, the workplaces were deeply embedded in the traditional territory of the First Nations of northwestern BC. Since the industrialists needed immigrants for their workforce, the Skeena region grew to be a very distinct multi-ethnic community. As a consequence, the Punjabis who settled in the Skeena encountered a triadic dynamic among (1) the First Nations (primarily, but not exclusively, those belonging to the Tsimshian, Haida, and Nisga'a Nations); (2) Anglo-Canadians; and (3) other ethnic immigrants (such as Chinese, Italian, Portuguese, and Ukrainian) within the labour force.

While this intercultural dynamic, especially with respect to the First Nations, existed at the workplace in both the forestry and fishery industries, tensions erupted more frequently in the salmon canneries, since historically the First Nations had a greater presence in that industry. Punjabi immigrant men experienced less tension in the sawmills than the women did in the salmon canneries, because forestry was less sought after by the First Nations in the Skeena region. Although Punjabis would be hired because they were generally considered to be hardworking, First Nations people blamed them for stealing their jobs when Anglo-Canadian management chose Punjabis to fill the manual labour jobs in the Skeena region's resource industries.

"Hardworking People"

Punjabi men worked in the lumber industry throughout the twentieth century. While they were thought of as cheap labour during the pioneer period, they were also recognized for their hard work and reliability. During the Great Depression of the 1930s, for example, when the Hillcrest Lumber Company was close to bankruptcy, the Punjabis continued to work, without pay, in order to keep the mill in operation. When the industry picked up, the owner, Carleton Stone, was so grateful to the Punjabi workers for their hard effort that he began to favour Punjabis when hiring.[63] In due course, Punjabis gained the reputation as hardworking labour in the forestry industry. It was precisely for that reason that Sohen Singh Gill preferred to hire Punjabis to work at his lumber mills, including Prince Rupert Sawmills. Two of Sohen Singh Gill's former workers explained: "Sohen Gill preferred hiring Punjabi men because they were hardworking even though now (in the 2000s) our reputation may have changed with us drinking. But, at that time, the First Nations and white people were considered as less reliable.[64] The First Nations people were not that reliable because after working a couple of weeks they would disappear once they received their pay cheques."[65]

Punjabi men were perceived as reliable in terms both of showing up for work and of being willing to do overtime work. During the 1960s, when Punjabis began to settle in the Skeena region, non–First Nations people were commonly referred to as hardworking, the underlying implication being that the Punjabis were both hardworking and reliable, unlike, or in contrast to, their First Nations counterparts. There were, no doubt, hardworking First Nations people, but during the 1960s and the 1970s, the prevalent opinion was that the First Nations possessed a transient orientation.[66] A man from the Haida Nation, however, provided a more rational explanation for the short-lived work pattern of First Nations in sawmills:

> I worked at Prince Rupert Sawmills from 1966 to 1967. I was twenty-one years old at the time. I worked on the green chain. My uncle and cousin were working there as well. There may have been about twenty First Nations working there out of about a hundred people ... During the summer, lumber mills slow down because of forest fires. Many First Nations would work in the mill during the winter and then go back to their main line of work in the fisheries during the summer. First Nations were transient with the lumber mills. It was subsidiary work. First Nations people really worked in the fisheries: our women worked in the canneries, while the men graded or caught the fish.[67]

The First Nations people's occasional failure to show up for work was thus not related to a lack of work ethic, but rather to their giving priority to their traditional livelihood of fishing. A non–First Nations counsellor pointed out that the concept of "Indian time" has to do with priorities – that is, with what is the most important thing to do. Whereas the stereotype of the First Nations as "lacking a work ethic" might be true of anyone with an addiction problem, in the present case the explanation might sometimes lie in an inter-generational transmission of the trauma inflicted on First Nations people by the residential school program.[68]

The reputation of First Nations as unreliable has nonetheless persisted. A former shop steward at the Columbia Cellulose pulp and paper mill on Watson Island raised the issue in the 1970s when he questioned why First Nations men did not transfer to the woodroom when many of the former manual labourers at Prince Rupert Forest Products were encouraged to do so. His account of the situation is of some interest: "My personal view, which challenged upper management, was that there should be First Nations people working in the pulp and paper mill. I asked, 'Why so few Natives are working at the mill?' ... At the time when Columbia Cellulose was running Prince Rupert Forest Products, there was about 65 per cent of First Nations working there. But this didn't transfer over to the pulp and paper mill. There may have been only 10 per cent of the workforce who were Native."[69]

On the other hand, many Punjabis successfully transferred to or later acquired jobs at the pulp and paper mill; that is, they managed to differentiate themselves from their First Nations counterparts and built a reputation for themselves as hardworking. Even when Punjabis had limited English skills, they were still hired for their labour.[70] Their reputation for being hardworking, however, contributed to an underlying source of tension between them and other members of the Skeena community.

Unlike in the forestry industry, First Nations had an overwhelmingly large presence in the salmon canneries; this was because fishing had been their traditional livelihood and the management of the fisheries relied on the First Nations' hard work and traditional skills once the fishery was established as an industry. Prior to labour unions becoming a factor in the industry, working conditions and wages were very poor. By the time the Punjabis began working in Skeena salmon canneries in the late 1960s, the working conditions and wages had improved. While the First Nations constituted a large majority of those working in the canneries, women from other ethnic backgrounds, such as Italian and Portuguese, were also represented.

Issues surrounding the Punjabis' reputation for being hardworking and reliable were played out in the cannery workplace as well. For example, when Punjabis first entered the salmon cannery workforce, they complained that their Anglo-Canadian supervisors often attributed the same negative stereotypes to them that they attributed to the First Nations. Both ethnic groups were described as brown-skinned and were officially recognized as "Indians" – the Punjabis categorized as "East Indians" and the First Nations as "Native Indians." The Punjabi women felt they had to demonstrate to their supervisors that they were different, especially in regard to their work ethic and willingness to do overtime work: "When I started at the Co-op, there were not many East Indians working there. The Natives had the most seniority. There were some English, many French people from Quebec, Italian, Greek, and Portuguese. There must have been 5 per cent or even less of Punjabis. I wanted to work in the cannery like the other East Indian ladies. They started to hire more East Indian ladies when they saw that they are hard workers."[71]

Once the Punjabis were recognized as hardworking, many more were hired at the canneries and tensions started to emerge in the workplace.[72] Anti-immigrant attitudes were experienced thus: "Some of my Native co-workers

Salmon-cleaning lines at BC Packers, New Oceanside plant (1981). Courtesy of the Prince Rupert City & Regional Archives, The Daily News Collection, P2003-093-3424.

often made racist remarks to me. They called me Hindoo in a derogatory manner and criticized me for coming to Canada. It was common to hear in the lunchroom: 'We don't want these f—k'n Hindoos in our country.' They also made my work difficult and stressful, because they would dump a lot of fish on my table."[73] Another Punjabi woman shared her experience working with First Nations women: "Native Indian people were okay but they did not always show up for work. They would get mad if I was called in to do overtime work, because the Natives had higher seniority. But when they would be called by the supervisor, they did not answer the phone call. With less seniority, I would then be contacted. They would say, 'You are taking other people's jobs.' Management did not get after the Natives for not doing their job. They just left them alone."[74]

Punjabi women told many stories about the intercultural eruptions that took place while they worked alongside First Nations women in the salmon canneries during the 1970s and 1980s. One of them explained the causes of the intercultural tension: "We were only a few. There were only a small number of Punjabi ladies working at Port Edward. Some of us knew English, and some did not know how to speak English … We [Punjabi women] did a lot of overtime work. We always said 'yes' to overtime work … Once a Native worker pushed fish to our side to make it look like we were slow and that they were fast. Their area looked clean and they showed it to their supervisor. We would then get into trouble because we were going too slowly, while they had already finished."[75] On the other hand, the First Nations people had their own insecurities to contend with. In particular, they resented foreigners coming into what had been their territory and seemingly taking away their jobs.

"Stealing Our Jobs"

Upon joining the Skeena region's workforce, the Punjabis encountered anti-immigrant hostility, which was primarily expressed as the Punjabis "stealing our jobs." A significant number of First Nations people resented Punjabis when they first arrived in the Skeena region to work in the forestry industry in the 1960s, but an even larger proportion felt this way when Punjabis began participating in the fishery industry. The Punjabis experienced anti-immigrant sentiment in the form of explicit verbal, and sometimes physical, aggression from some of the First Nations people in the sawmills and salmon canneries. They were not, however, the first to experience such reactions. Rather, First Nations have long held the notion that other people – foreigners and "newcomers" – had come to "steal" their jobs, an understandable sentiment given the rivalry between the First Nations and the "white man" over land and resources. A woman of the Tsimshian Nation explained this long-standing fear that people would come and take away their livelihood: "When there are newcomers, we [First Nations] see them as 'strangers.' We feared they were coming to take our jobs. When the Chinese came to build the railways, there was tension. When the Japanese came to fish, there was tension. When the Portuguese came to work in the canneries, we didn't like it. [First Nations] women feared the Punjabis [would take] their jobs and overtime work, especially when they saw how they brought in their relatives to work."[76]

When Punjabi men initially arrived in the Skeena region, they worked at the Punjabi-owned and -managed Prince Rupert Sawmills. It was natural that the majority of the mill's workforce would be Punjabi. A former charge-hand at the mill commented on the ethnic makeup of the workforce: "During that time [in the early 1960s], there were about seventy-five men working at the mill. Most of the men were Punjabi, but there were also about fifteen Euro- and Anglo-Canadians and a few Natives."[77] Even though only a few First Nations men were working at the sawmills, the Punjabis experienced anti-immigrant sentiment. A Punjabi man explained the intercultural dynamic in the Skeena region:

There were not many Native Indians working in sawmills. They were mainly in the canning and fisheries. There was a lot of bitterness. There was also bitterness toward East Indians, Italians, and Portuguese. Now these people are coming to our land. They saw these people as coming to our land and taking our jobs. But, at the same time, they did not have the same work ethic as found among immigrants. There was a chronic problem of them being sick or not showing up because they would go fishing, etc. The mill owners knew this and they then preferred to hire East Indian, Italian or Portuguese, who were known as hardworking and wanting to establish their family ... Only about 1 per cent of the mill labour consisted of Natives but many were in the fisheries. Punjabis worked really hard and saved their money in order to build a house and raise their kids.[78]

Since there were few First Nations workers in the sawmills, it was more common for Punjabi men to encounter hostility about "stealing our jobs" from the First Nations in the towns. An Anglo-Canadian editor of a local paper in northern British Columbia gave her opinion on the dynamic that led to the street fights between First Nations and Punjabis in the early 1970s: "The East Indian ... is an exceptionally reliable worker. He minds his own business, does his job to the best of his ability, lays off the juice and shows up for work every day – on time. It's only a common-sense tactic that would find an employer showing preference to the reliable worker over the unreliable worker. But – somewhere along the line, the preference for reliability has been misconstrued as racial preference and the Canadian Indian is quick to harp on it."[79] While the editor's interpretation of the tensions between First Nations and Punjabis may be biased, her comments nonetheless bear witness to the framing of intercultural tensions in such rhetoric as "lazy Natives" that was going on in northern BC at the time the Punjabis were establishing themselves in the Skeena region.

Some First Nations people expressed hostility towards newcomers in general. However, the hostility baffled many Punjabis. A Punjabi man reflected on the reaction of some First Nations people to the presence of the Punjabis: "In Prince Rupert, we experienced a lot of trouble with the Natives ... They would say, 'This is our land.' They thought we wanted to take their jobs, but we thought they didn't want to work. I couldn't understand this. Why the victims [Natives] were victimizing another victim [Punjabi]? They should have been able to empathize with our pain."[80] Punjabis were perplexed by the

First Nations' reactions. In fact, many of them could not comprehend why First Nations would target another visible minority group that had also been colonized by the British Empire. A Punjabi man recalled raising this issue with a First Nations man: "I went to a beer parlour with two other Punjabis. A Native Indian man wanted to fight us. I told him, 'Why don't you fight the white people? It was the white man who took your land.' He didn't say anything. He did not know how to answer the question. He just took off."[81]

Just as the early Punjabi pioneers of British Columbia (who emigrated from British India) felt indebted to some British industrialists for having employed them, regardless of the fact that the latter used Punjabi cheap labour for profit, the First Nations viewed Anglo-Canadians as having provided them with jobs, despite the harm that these settlers had inflicted on them, their land, and their culture. Paid-wage jobs were preferable to no jobs within the overall context of colonial relations, even though First Nations people were mistreated as second- or even third-class citizens. A Nisga'a woman described the harm done and the gains brought by the first British settlers:

> I worked in the cannery because it was good money. The white man brought jobs for us. We could make good money. There was lots of overtime work back in those days. The white man also brought alcohol. That hurts our people. Italians, Portuguese brought wine. East Indians drink too. My people would tell them to go back to their own country. They were coming and taking our jobs from us[82] ... We were not treated well by the white man but we got good jobs. We did not really interact with the Chinese or Japanese. We worked separately. There was a Native village and Japanese village and a white village. East Indians weren't working there when I started in 1961. They came later. They had to wash the fish. We did not want these people to take our jobs. What else were these people going to take?[83]

The First Nations were familiar with outsiders arriving and working, especially in their traditional industry. As the Punjabis entered the fisheries, their notable presence by the 1970s became problematic for the First Nations. Moreover, the timing of the arrival of Punjabis coincided with higher wages, better working conditions, and technological advancement. With improvements in canning technology, the First Nations' traditional skills were in less demand, and consequently the First Nations found that they were becoming more dispensable. A man from the Haida Nation shared his observations: "In 1968, I started at Prince Rupert Fishermen's Co-op. My grandmother, mother, uncles, and cousins worked there. If management liked some workers, they were happy to hire other members of their family. So you see networks of families. My family was respected for their hard work. In the 1960s and 1970s, people were respected for their hard work and knowledge. Since the mid-1980s, management has changed. They do not value our tradition of fishing."[84]

The Punjabis were arriving at a time that some First Nations felt that Anglo-Canadians were increasingly entering the fisheries to reap the benefit of improved wages. A man from the Nisga'a Nation explained the reasons why First Nations people resented others entering the canneries:

> In the 1970s, First Nations had tension with people coming and taking the jobs. The First Nations did not know who these people were. When the Punjabis came, we were just beginning to get better wages [1967] in the cannery. Back in the day of segregation at the canneries like North Pacific or Nelson Brothers, we were treated like second- or even third-class citizens. The quarters for white workers were the best; the Chinese and Japanese had tight quarters; the First Nations were the last to get a bathroom in their bunkhouse. We were starting to get better treatment and recognition ... But even now, we don't like the companies setting up fishing nets higher up in the stream for sport fishing. The companies are hiring Vietnamese. Why not hire First Nations people? In Alaska, they are hiring Mexicans. A similar sentiment existed when Punjabis were coming. It is to protect what is yours.[85]

The sentiments that some First Nations people voiced about the Punjabi workers at canneries sometimes related to the kind of work the Punjabis were assigned or to the work the First Nations wanted the Punjabis to do. According to a First Nations woman who worked in the cannery, "They [Punjabis] brought problems to the cannery; they would fight our own people and were picky about the work they had to do."[86] In contrast, a Punjabi female cannery worker described the environment in which she worked: "The cannery was very segregated, where each ethnic group would work in the same row, wash their hands together, and have their lunch breaks at the same table. There was little communication between the ethnic groups. There were sometimes racial tensions at the workplace. Some people would want Punjabis to cut the heads instead of washing the fish. They wanted the Punjabi workers to do the 'lowest' job."[87]

The tension did not only revolve around foreigners taking jobs that First Nations people felt were rightfully theirs, but also related to how First Nations perceived the conduct of Punjabis in the cannery workplace. Many saw it as problematic. A woman from the Tsimshian Nation explained what some First Nations thought of the Punjabis in the workforce: "Women feared the

Punjabis taking their jobs and overtime, especially when they saw how they brought in their relatives to work ... [Also,] Punjabis like to speak in their own language even when they know English. They stick together. So if you are talking and laughing, others are not sure if they are laughing at them."[88] Likewise, a Punjabi woman astutely recognized that hearing Punjabis speak their own language may have bothered some First Nations people: "Not all but some were very bitter and did not like East Indians. There was tension because of the language, cultural differences. They wanted to speak their language; we spoke Punjabi. Perhaps they were also uncomfortable thinking we were talking about them."[89]

The issue most commonly voiced by the First Nations concerned the Punjabis' tendency to speak in their own language among themselves, even in the company of non-Punjabi workers. This was an alienating experience for many First Nations.[90] Immigrants speaking in their own language not only evoked in First Nations people feelings of insecurity about being mocked, but also reminded them of their experiences of cultural devastation (i.e., when they were forbidden to speak their traditional language in the Indian residential schools). Indeed, the right to speak or "keep" their traditional language has been a long-standing sensitive issue for the First Nations. Moreover, First Nations people experienced the federal government's double standard with respect to speaking one's native language: on the one hand, Trudeau put forward a white paper on Indian policy in order both to eliminate special status for Canada's Aboriginals and to push for cultural assimilation (1969), and on the other, the Liberal government – again under the leadership of Trudeau – promoted ethnic diversity through its multiculturalism policy (1971) in order to accommodate immigrants.

First Nations people took pride in their territory and their culture. It was therefore natural for them to try to protect both. The protection of their traditional livelihood was also demonstrated in the way some First Nations female supervisors made decisions in the workplace. According to many Punjabi female workers, they helped members of their own group secure the better "dry" jobs and obtain overtime work. A Punjabi woman recalled her experience working with a First Nations charge-hand: "One day the Native charge-hand complained that we had not started work. She began shouting, 'Go to your work.' I asked her to show us how to work hard. I took it to the supervisor. The charge-hand had to say sorry that we had to listen to this every day. After that day, she never spoke to me. Before being a charge-hand, she used to work with us. We knew she was not fast, she was very slow. When I asked her to show us how to work hard, she took me to the supervisor [and said] that I talked back to her."[91] Punjabi women believed that intercultural relations often worsened when a First Nations charge-hand was supervising

Punjabi workers. In most cases, the "prestigious" job of charge-hand had been obtained through family connections, since hiring practices then were more informal. In effect, many First Nations charge-hands had acquired their positions through clan loyalties rather than seniority.[92]

Ethnic-based work networks in the salmon canneries perpetuated the occupational segregation of the workforce. Just as Zavella observed in her analysis on the Chicano workers in the canneries of Santa Clara Valley, California,[93] the ethnic cohesiveness found in informal work networks amplified occupational segregation and proved to be a source of antagonism. This dynamic was evident in relations between the First Nations and other ethnic communities in the salmon canneries. Given their historical third-class treatment – for example, their previous discriminatory living arrangements – First Nations people were particularly sensitive to others entering their traditional line of work at the canneries.

Workplace segregation across racial lines suited management, since it allowed workers not proficient in English to work more efficiently. It was a practical tactic for businesses that relied on what was seen as a pool of cheap and low-skilled labour, and it allowed management to seize control over their "cheap labour." Workplace segregation perhaps served as a divider, since it encouraged immigrants to self-segregate rather than intermingle among people of other backgrounds. However, segregation also provided an arrangement that immigrants would initially find more comfortable, especially if the workers had limited English language skills. Although remaining in the company of one's own people is an acculturation coping strategy often used by immigrants, it can nonetheless prevent them from moving up in the workforce. Specifically, workplace segregation can hinder workers from acquiring the necessary skills that would enable them to advance.

"Not Meant to Be Skilled"

While the Punjabis spoke of experiencing substantial anti-immigrant hostility in the workplace from the First Nations people, they remembered enduring prejudice of another sort from Anglo-Canadians – that is, Punjabis working in a trade or business were often treated as if they were "not meant to be skilled." Punjabi men had come to be equated with the manual labour of the forestry industry, and deviation from that norm was not welcomed by some Anglo-Canadians. Punjabi men who came to the Skeena region in search of work in high-skilled and high-wage jobs, whether in a unionized or private operation, encountered discrimination, especially from the 1960s through to the 1980s. When Punjabis advanced in the labour force or established their own businesses, many Anglo-Canadians who had low expectations of Punjabis were dismayed to find their earlier attitudes undermined. One Italian-Canadian labourer commented: "When East Indians got laid off from the Prince Rupert Sawmill, they came to the pulp and paper mill. They were called 'lazy f—kers,' but people were jealous that they were doing something. They were working hard. They first came into the town driving cabs and then over time they owned the cabs. Others were lazy, not them. In the pulp and paper mill, the East Indians were doing more and more, and moving up. They did not stay behind, they kept moving up. People did not like this."[94]

Many of the Punjabis who held skilled labour jobs believed that they experienced double standards on the job; that is, job output expectations differed along ethnic lines. The Punjabis felt that Anglo-Canadians received preferential treatment on the job, whereas they were put under close scrutiny, especially those of Sikh background who kept their hair and wore a turban.[95] The Punjabis often simply "sucked in" the discrimination, since they felt their jobs were at stake.[96] A Punjabi man shared his work experience in the trades: "You can be successful here [in Canada] if you are determined, not scared, and take on Canadian culture. But if you do something wrong, then you are in trouble because it will go against you and your people. 'This guy with the turban and beard is getting our jobs. How can he be more qualified than us?' they would say. Some unqualified Anglo-Canadians were working in jobs because there were not enough qualified people."[97] The Punjabis felt that double standards were practised by some managers and owners.

A few Punjabi men who ventured into non-traditional businesses experienced similar negative reactions from Anglo-Canadians. In fact, Punjabi immigrants trained in a profession found it a challenge to contend with the stereotype of a Punjabi as only a mill labourer. Note the comment of a Punjabi immigrant who arrived in Canada in 1974 after receiving chartered accountant training in England: "I applied for jobs in Canada. I arrived in 1974. They would ask, 'Which mill do you work at?' The reaction I got was 'Oh, you are not like one of them.' People had a stereotype or image of East Indians through the media. In Winnipeg, the image is 'Are you a lawyer or a doctor?' In British Columbia, people think all we do is labour."[98]

In the case of Punjabi women, even though the large majority were seasonal workers, a few worked in higher-skilled or professional jobs. They, too, voiced their feelings about double standards in the professional arena.[99] Take, for instance, the experience of a Punjabi woman who had received clerical training in the United Kingdom, but felt that she was put through a much more rigorous hiring process than others:

I applied to work as a clerk at Prince Rupert Fishermen's Co-op. I had to proceed through three interviews before I was given the job. It was for a regular office job. After the first interview, they thanked me and said they will call back but that there were a lot of applicants for the job. I was then called in for a second one. There was a Caucasian lady who was testing my ability. She seemed to have the belief that I could do the job. They could tell by my name that I was East Indian. I knew the different skills and was very comfortable with the tasks. A man stated, it is OK, he will call back. I then had a third interview. I found it strange to have three interviews for the job. They asked me, 'What else can you do?' The man said, 'We will let you know in a few days.' They called me the next day. There were different people (three at a time) during each interview. A mixed bag of people: I was well dressed, perhaps they thought I was just posing as a clerk. I also had an East Indian name ... the people perhaps had the attitude that Punjabis did labour jobs.[100]

While Punjabi women primarily worked as secondary wage earners in order to help the family financially, it is interesting to note that, even up to the present time, the attitude continued to be that cannery work was a cozy situation for Punjabi and First Nations women. A female cannery manager made this comment: "Women loved to come to work; it was social networking for them. Native Indians came from different villages and communities. Punjabis would come from Terrace, Kitimat, and Prince Rupert to do seasonal work. It was a time for the ladies to get together and meet with their friends and families. Many women wanted to get out of the house due to feeling lonely, isolation, and unfriendly terms. Working for the money was secondary."[101]

The management's perceptions were simply an exaggerated version of what both Punjabi and First Nations women themselves voiced about the cannery workplace. It is true that there were psycho-social benefits associated with women's entry into the workforce. However, in reality, their entry was fundamentally propelled by economic necessity. The work was hard and demeaning, especially in the 1970s and 1980s when these women experienced ethnic and gender-based discrimination on the job and there was less machinery to do the "dirty work." Even if camaraderie among Punjabi women was highly valued, they had to endure the demeaning, foul-smelling, cold, wet, and dirty work, in addition to the discrimination and the close and strict supervision. It would nonetheless be fair to say that the social benefits made the job more tolerable.

While some non-Punjabis may have the attitude that Western culture has the potential to save "subservient women" from their traditional patriarchal culture, Punjabi women in fact drew upon (as demonstrated in chapters 4 and 5) their own cultural assets for strength and resiliency. The above comment on the social benefits of cannery work seems to be an attempt on the part of management to rationalize low wages for a hardworking labour force. What Punjabi – as well as other – women needed was not to be saved from their patriarchal culture, but rather to be treated fairly on the job, something that the unions were able to provide to a certain extent.

Union as the Intercultural Mediator

While unions at the turn of the twentieth century had excluded non-white workers, by the 1940s major labour organizations, like the International Woodworkers of America (IWA) and the United Fishermen Allied Workers' Union (UFAWU), had come to the realization that they needed immigrant and ethnic support in order to strengthen their bargaining power.[102] Beginning in the 1940s, some Punjabi pioneers became actively involved in the unionization of the workplace. By the 1960s, the labour unions had gained momentum and won greater collective bargaining power in the struggle to protect labour and achieve safer workplace conditions.[103] It was into this environment that the Punjabis came when they settled in the Skeena region. And it was through the union that the Punjabis would find fair, or at least better, treatment at the workplace. Yet, while unions were oriented towards equality and fair treatment for the workforce, some shop stewards did not always practise equality in spirit.

Seeking Fair Treatment

In the 1930s and 1940s, a number of Punjabi pioneers were actively involved in helping Punjabis gain the right to vote and improve their working conditions through the unionization of the workplace.[104] For example, after having received two years of post-secondary education at a Canadian university, Darshan Singh (referred to by Punjabis as "Darshan Singh Canadian") served as the recording secretary of the Victoria IWA local. In 1942–43, he began translating IWA leaflets into Punjabi so that Punjabi workers could get information about the labour union movement.[105] There was, however, great resistance to unionizing the mills. A Punjabi pioneer recalled his experience in joining the union: "I made a mistake going along with the union in the early 1940s. My brother and I wore union buttons. We were then fired by a manager at Kapoor Singh's mill for siding with the unions. The unions were good for the Punjabi community, since they fought for equal pay, opportunity, and paid attention to seniority."[106] In fact, since both Punjabi and non-Punjabi mill owners opposed unionization and had influence with Sikh temple management committees, union organizers could not garner support in the Sikh temples, which were historically the political base of the early Punjabi community.[107]

By the 1960s, labour unions were gaining greater collective-bargaining strength in at least some of the mills. As Punjabis increasingly entered unionized workplaces, they regarded the jobs as "good," since they provided higher wages and better working conditions than non-unionized workplaces did. The labour unions were also acquiring an important role, certainly from the perspective of Punjabis, in mediating the intercultural tensions that were emerging in the workplace.

Unionization of the workplace did not occur all of a sudden, however. During the initial period of Punjabi settlement in the Skeena region, the IWA gradually began to sign up sawmill workers. This was indeed the case for Prince Rupert Sawmills and the Pohle Lumber Company in Terrace. The Punjabis were at the forefront of the struggle to unionize the workplace. As described in the first narrative in chapter 3, IWA organizers approached the workers with the assurance that they were concerned about the treatment of workers. And many workers had grievances, especially regarding workers who bribed lower management for overtime work: "The Punjabis were doing what is done in the Punjab, and they give a tip to have more overtime work. The workers would give a bottle of liquor to the foreman so that they would be given good OT [overtime]. Bribing is an old custom in India and they brought it here."[108]

In contrast to this comment that bribery was a carryover from the Punjab, a Punjabi pioneer explained that the practice in Canada was the result of what Anglo-Canadians had expected of them in the first half of the century: "There was not really a practice of undercutting the East Indian worker; they simply had cheaper wages in the early 1900s. Punjabis were viewed as hardworking and reliable. East Indians were also willing to work overtime, unlike the Anglo-Canadians and First Nations. In the 1900s, East Indians, Chinese, and Japanese were expected to give a percentage of their wages to the foreman, manager. This was an unwritten norm. East Indians, once they got into these kinds of positions, then followed the pattern."[109] Whatever the case, the workers were disenchanted with their rights as workers, and they unionized with the IWA in 1966 against the will of their Punjabi owner at Prince Rupert Sawmills.

Interestingly, the unionization of the Poehle mill in Terrace was initiated by a Punjabi man who had first worked at a unionized mill in Mackenzie. Other Punjabi workers followed suit. In contrast to Prince Rupert Sawmills, however, the management of the Pohle mill actively fought the union. One of the Punjabi men who had been involved in the unionization campaign explained:

The Mackenzie mill was unionized with IWA. When I went to Terrace, the mill was not unionized. There was an "artificial union." It was called the Christian Labour Union but I think they made it to stop IWA. The Christian union was set up by company people. I got involved with the IWA. I gave IWA a call and met with them in the Terrace Hotel. There were some Punjabi men and some "white" men there. We drank beer and made the deal. The IWA came over for two weeks. Punjabis were at first hesitant to get involved with the IWA because they thought they would lose their jobs. The company tried to bribe me with a better job or a promise to hire people I knew. I began collecting names for the union in 1973. We first lost by six votes. The next year in 1974 we won a majority. We were unionized. Some Punjabi men said we should have a Punjabi union leader. I disagreed, we should support the white guy and we will have influence and get the job done for us. The goal is to get the job done.[110]

While several of the sawmills in the Skeena region became unionized under the IWA, the Columbia Cellulose pulp and paper mill on Watson Island was unionized under the Pulp, Paper and Woodworkers of Canada (PPWC) before Punjabis began working there.

Punjabi women began entering the workforce in 1966, but the fresh fish plants and salmon canneries had already been unionized. In 1967, a major labour dispute broke out between the fishermen, who were represented by the Prince Rupert Vessel Owners Association (PRVOA), and the shore workers, who were represented by the United Fishermen Allied Workers' Union. The BC Packers and Prince Rupert Fishermen's Co-operative were under the UFAWU; however, after the 1967 strike, the workers at the Co-op cannery created a new union, the Prince Rupert Amalgamated Shoreworkers and Clerks Union (PRASCU). Meanwhile, the UFAWU remained the main labour organization for the fisheries, representing both the fishermen and the salmon cannery workers. Despite all this union activity, there was little awareness among Punjabi female workers of what union membership entailed; a Punjabi woman described going to work during the labour dispute:

I recall coming to work and noticing that many of the ladies had their aprons folded under their arms and were not working. When I came to the table, the ladies said the "fish was hot," I responded by saying, "When I touch the fish it is cold, not hot." I did not understand what they meant by that saying. Many of us decided to keep working because we felt the union president was unfair to the fishermen, and I was also afraid that I would lose my job. When we crossed the picket line, it was somewhat scary because the pro-union members would say bad words to us. Some even said some racial comments towards me, like "these Hindoos are taking our jobs." Those who decided to work got support from outside the cannery; the city councillors and police would call us at our homes and give their support. After this dispute, the workers decided to get a new union.[111]

When this Punjabi woman entered the Skeena fishery industry, she was unfamiliar with union politics and the bargaining process. A language barrier is evident, since she could not understand the labour term "hot fish," which refers to "illegal" fish that a company had purchased during a strike. Moreover, she feared losing her job. Despite this first experience, however, she later became involved with union affairs. While Punjabi men were familiar with politics in the Punjab, Punjabi women were primarily accustomed to the private sphere. Once they grew more familiar with labour culture and union politics, they came to recognize their role as union members, although they did not participate in the union to the extent their Punjabi male counterparts did.

Punjabi Workers Fight for Their Rights

As sawmills became unionized and as Punjabis entered unionized workplaces, such as the pulp and paper mills and salmon canneries, the Punjabis began to have a platform from which their voices as immigrants facing various barriers could be heard by the mainstream. Although Punjabis welcomed collective bargaining in pursuit of higher wages and better working conditions, their involvement with the unions was gender-specific. Punjabi male immigrants working in sawmills were often involved with the unionization of their workplace. The unions initially served a springboard to help Punjabis get involved in grassroots politics and derive economic benefits while remaining in a familiar milieu. Unlike in the Lower Mainland, where Sikh temples were valuable political centres for the Punjabi community,[112] in the Skeena region, the political voice of Punjabis emerged through their involvement with the unions. Indeed, labour became the link between the Punjabi community and the larger Skeena community. A former Punjabi labour representative explained the significance of unions in the region: "The union was critical during the 1970s and 1980s; it was the peak of our [Punjabi] employment in the forestry industry. At that time, sawmills were mostly unionized under the IWA. The Punjabi community had tremendous influence on the IWA because of the large numbers of Punjabi sawmill workers. They got involved. Punjabis were politicized through the unions. It was a place for them to gain a voice. IWA encouraged them to get involved since an 'informed member is a strong member.'"[113]

Punjabi immigrants in general strongly embrace the democratic process while also standing up for their rights. A Punjabi man who worked in the trades explained: "The union was good for fighting for the workers' rights, for better pay and seniority ... In 1973, I made $4.83 an hour as an electrician. This was the same wage for a lot of the trades. When I stopped working in 1992, I was paid $16.00 to $17.00 an hour. I also had a lot of OT and double-pay work. The union helped us work in fair conditions."[114]

The unions provided the Punjabi male immigrant the means by which he could voice his workplace and political concerns. And, in line with Punjabi political culture, the Punjabis also enjoyed the political opportunity that came with union membership. A Punjabi man assessed the role of the union at Prince Rupert Sawmills: "With union, working conditions changed fast. If a company did not respond to grievances, we would have a picket line right away. Picket line would last around half an hour. Morning shift would tell afternoon shift not to work. The sign on the gatehouse would tell the workers that there is a union dispute and that there is no work. 'Time is money.' Every two weeks a ship would come, they had to have the lumber ready for the load. Power was on our side."[115]

Punjabi workers at the pulp and paper mill on Watson Island also took part in the labour movement. Their orientation was that the union helped those in labour jobs. Punjabi men were involved both collectively through strike action for better wages and working conditions and personally through grievances when they felt they were not being treated fairly at the workplace. A Punjabi man shared his views on participation in the union:

I was in the union when I was working at the pulp and paper mill. Working there without the union would have been very hard. The union is good for everyone working in labour jobs. You need someone to help you. I would say that 80 per cent of the time grievances were legitimate. You need the union for the right wages and good conditions. I participated in strikes. There was one about every three years when the contract was being renewed. The strike could last for two to three months. I made grievances about seniority and getting promoted to higher jobs. A company does what helps them. You need back up.[116]

Like Punjabi men, the women, too, saw the union as "a good voice for the worker, especially immigrant worker."[117] However, in contrast to Punjabi men, many Punjabi women were less interested in partaking in union action and politics. While they valued union efforts, respected the picket line, and were grateful for higher wages and improvements in their working conditions, their loyalties were still more centred on the home. By the 1970s, many Punjabi women were voting for their union representatives (shop stewards)[118] but were not themselves involved in strategic planning or mobilizing members, because their priority was their responsibility for their children and the smooth functioning of the household. A Punjabi woman explained: "UFAWU gave us the feeling of security with the job. If we had a problem, we would go to the union representative. I was a member of the union but not involved. We were busy with our families. We had no time. When the union was on strike, I followed the union rules. We liked their protection."[119]

Women belonging to other immigrant groups were also less involved in union affairs. A Punjabi woman noted: "I signed for grievance petitions. Usually they were about seniority, leaving some behind. There were strikes about every three to four years over the renewal of the collective agreement. We would go on the picket line. The union would pay us. We would go for every four hours. There would be six to eight people at a time. A few Punjabi ladies would get involved with the union but not too many. We were mostly busy with the kids. There were a few Italians, Portuguese, but whites were mostly involved with the union."[120] Punjabi women were thus not as involved as their Anglo-Canadian counterparts. Acculturation stress played a role in their reluctance to participate more actively. One Punjabi woman suggested that the language barrier was a factor: "There was also a problem with speaking and discussing the issues. It is one thing to go to the store to ask for a loaf of bread, but for the union you have to be able to speak about things deeply. You need good English skills. The Punjabi ladies did not have this."[121]

Noteworthy as well is the factor of gender. In the traditional Punjabi culture, Punjabi men were involved in political matters, whereas women exercised their power within the home. These traditional forms of behaviour continued in the Skeena region. The men arrived with the benefit of their previous involvement in politics, while the Punjabi women arrived without any experience in representing others on a public political platform. A Punjabi woman explained the cultural gap: "I would vote for the union representative. We would discuss as a group [Punjabis] as to who we should vote for. Punjabis never stood up because they did not have enough English, education, or time. You need guts to stand up as a union representative. East Indian women had a tendency not to want to play the role. There is also the fear one may have trouble with management or company. There is the fear of losing one's job."[122]

Despite Punjabi women's inexperience in politics, by the 1990s, two Punjabi women had become shop stewards for the UFAWU; their duties were mainly to translate and interpret union information for their fellow Punjabi workers who had limited English skills.[123] The first Punjabi shop steward at BC Packers described her role: "I was a member. I was the first Punjabi shop stew-

Punjabi women take job action along with their First Nations co-workers, at BC Packers, New Oceanside plant (ca. 1982). Courtesy of the Prince Rupert City & Regional Archives, The Daily News Collection, P2003-093-3397.

ard. I did that for ten years. When I was the shop steward, I helped Punjabis understand the issues. I became the shop steward because they needed more stewards and they needed one East Indian who could explain the items in Punjabi. The issues were mostly related to seniority and OT as well as fights or arguments between the ladies. Sometimes the supervisor may not be careful in abiding by the rules for overtime; they may not remember who has higher seniority and give it to another with less. Now they do not discriminate."[124]

The unions fought on behalf of their workers, including Punjabi workers. Although Punjabi women began working in the late 1960s, it was only in 1979 that a Punjabi filed an official complaint to the union. The first Punjabi grievance centred on the right to work in two different plants; a woman had complained because a company had refused to hire her because she had a job elsewhere. Since the collective agreement stated that the employer had to give preference to union members when hiring, she managed to get the second job.[125]

The unions fought with management on many issues, including the right of women to perform jobs that had traditionally been done by men, like unloading fish, warehousing, and cleaning up.[126] Most of the grievances that Punjabi women brought to the union, however, involved the right to overtime work as per seniority.[127] A breach in seniority would almost certainly result in a grievance. Punjabi women took the seniority system very seriously, especially in respect to fair treatment at the workplace. During the period of their initial entry into the salmon cannery, Punjabi women were not always assigned work according to their seniority. This treatment became an intercultural-labour issue, in which the union played the role of mediator.

Intercultural-Labour Mediation

The antagonisms within the Skeena region's multi-ethnic workforce propelled Punjabis to bring their intercultural-labour issues to the attention of their union. In effect, the union – through its efforts in addressing Punjabi grievances – played the role of an intercultural mediator. A former Punjabi sawmill worker shared his experience of discrimination that led him to participate in union politics:

In the 1970s, there was big turnover of workers so they were beginning to hire East Indians. There were arguments on the green chain. There would be graffiti in the lunchrooms and washrooms. Most Indo-Canadian workers had lunch in the No. 2 lunchroom. One day, nine or ten of us went to the room for lunch and found "White man's lunchroom, Hindoo curry stinks, Hindoos stay out" written on the wall. This left a big mark on me. So we called the union. There was a meeting between the manager and union officials. Union officials asked, "What were they going to do?" The manager stated that he did not know what could be done unless they found the person. The union official agreed that if they found the person, they would suspend him and then only go through arbitration. The union never found the person. The union encouraged East Indian workers to get involved.[128]

While racial slurs are difficult to prove, concrete discriminatory practices on the job that breached contract rules were more easily handled. Given the basic union premise of equality, the union had to attend to any breach of seniority and to other issues related to the labour contract. Indeed, the unions thus not only performed the role of bargaining for higher wages and better working conditions, but also mediated intercultural-labour issues in the workplace that Punjabi workers brought up, especially from the late 1960s through to the 1980s.

Since the economy of the Skeena region revolved around several natural resources, immigrants were tolerated so long as they filled the manual labour needs of its industries. On the other hand, Punjabi men with skills found it a challenge to work for Anglo-Canadians because of the prevailing view that Punjabis were "not meant to be skilled." While Punjabis worked in a variety of areas – as graders, electricians, and machinists – Punjabi tradesmen at the pulp and paper mills and the fish plants often reported experiencing discrimination on the part of their Anglo-Canadian charge-hands or supervisors. They found it difficult to bring such grievances to their union, because shop stewards sometimes shared the same opinion as the supervisors about Punjabis. A former union representative of Italian descent commented on how Punjabis were treated on the job by both management and shop stewards: "It must have been difficult for Punjabis because at the end of the day they had the 'ticket' for trades. It was hard for them because they were visible and able to get engineering tickets. Punjabis were smart and it pissed others off. If Punjabis did not have the skills, they got the training."[129]

While the union was founded on the principle of equality, not all union representatives applied this principle in true spirit. A Punjabi tradesman passionately recounted his experience with the union: "I had both credentials and experience. I was able to move up because of the union rules. Union people were jealous, too, because I was bumping everybody. I must have bumped about thirty people. I felt that the white people had a problem with me moving up ... The PPWC bylaws supported me, but not the PPWC people. I was a union member but I never got involved. I was disgusted by the union representatives. My fault was that I was bumping others. I am a family man; I work and like to sit with my family."[130]

Moreover, Punjabi men were also the recipients of various forms of hostility aimed at non-Europeans by Anglo-Canadians in the sawmills. As a consequence, realizing that they could not expect to be treated like the "whites," many Punjabis tried to differentiate themselves from the First Nations, since the latter were viewed as "lazy." They wanted instead to be viewed as hardworking immigrants. Therefore, in cases of a breach of the seniority principle with respect to overtime work or promotion, Punjabis turned to the union shop stewards or to union bylaws for support.

In the 1970s and early 1980s, Punjabi women experienced unfair intercultural-labour treatment in the salmon canneries. As with the Punjabi male situation, racial slurs or workplace harassment were difficult to prove and penalize. A Punjabi woman explained how the union could only listen to such complaints:

When I started in Port Edward, there were mostly Natives working
there. They saw that we would not tolerate their behaviour. For those
who could not speak English well, we spoke on their behalf. When
we stood up for ourselves, the Natives complained to the foremen but

nothing ever came of it. The union representative spoke with the supervisor. Nothing came of it for us either ... We complained to the union about the way in which the Natives treated the Punjabis. The union would listen to us but they ultimately could not fire them. Some of the supervisors were Natives, too.[131]

The union limited its role to that of "listener" until there was concrete evidence to warrant union intervention. Over time, the Punjabi women found themselves having to contend with three concrete intercultural-labour issues: (1) a petition against Punjabis speaking in their mother tongue on the Prince Rupert–Port Edward bus as well as in the lunchrooms; (2) Punjabi women not being promoted to better types of cannery work as per seniority; and (3) the lack of Punjabi representation at the level of floor supervision. The union managed to mediate these three issues.

As mentioned in chapter 4, during the period from 1979 to 1981, some First Nations women circulated a petition against Punjabi women for speaking in "East Indian" on the bus. They took the petition to the union. A UFAWU representative explained how the union mediated the situation: "In the late 1970s, there was a petition against Punjabis on the Prince Rupert to Port Edward bus. First Nations had started a petition that no one on the bus should be allowed to speak in 'East Indian.' In order to mediate the situation, the UFAWU local stated that the petition could pass so long as it stated that workers can only speak in English on the bus and lunchrooms. In order to be fair, the union asserted that no one then can speak in their mother tongue, including First Nations language. The petition was dropped by the First Nations."[132] Starting from the premise that all workers should be treated fairly and equally, the union mediated in the situation by accepting the rule that the First Nations wanted to impose on the Punjabis as long as it is was applicable to everyone. By succeeding in this effort at mediation, the union unintentionally defined for itself the role as intercultural mediator.

The second intercultural-labour issue faced by Punjabi women had to do with seniority and the type of work they were assigned in the salmon canneries. Punjabi women predominantly washed fish all through the 1970s. Many of them complained that they were kept at this job regardless of their seniority. They later brought this issue to the union's attention as a form of discrimination. Since such discrimination fit well within the framework of labour-management relations, the union could assess the informal work-based networks that were responsible for hiring, job assignment, and promotion.

The issue was also brought to the forefront by an Anglo-Canadian shop steward. When the Port Edward plant closed in 1981 and the seniority list was merged with the one at BC Packers at Oceanside in Prince Rupert, an astute shop steward noticed that the work assignments given to Punjabi women were unfair. A labour representative provided an account of the shop steward's discovery: "A shop steward with BC Packers at Oceanside brought forth that our East Indian workers should be placed by seniority. Port Edward women then bumped the Oceanside ladies. In 1983 there was a big push on the seniority list. High seniority should be moved around to more prestigious jobs (7–15 cents per hour pay difference). East Indians only washed the fish – the hardest job."[133] The union ensured that seniority was honoured or enforced for both overtime and for the type of work or job assignment within the salmon cannery. It is for this reason that Punjabis were happy with the consolidation of the Port Edward plant with BC Packers at New Oceanside; they were pleased that the union had lobbied that they keep their seniority and were placed in better jobs based on their seniority.[134]

In due course, some Punjabi women were promoted to the job of charge-hand or floor supervisor – considered "prestigious" even though it only paid twenty-five cents more per hour. Floor supervision required the charge-hand to plan and allocate the different jobs among the labourers. A manager commented on the changes that occurred among Punjabis: "Previously, during the 1970s and early 1980s, there were prejudices. Punjabis mostly were the 'fish washers' or 'popping herring,' the harder and less-paying jobs. It was very hard physical labour. The Punjabis did not have much mobility within the cannery to do the more sophisticated labour jobs. Now over the years workers have begun to move around a lot. I started to have a couple of Punjabi charge-hand ladies in the early 1990s to help with the language barrier."[135] Having ethnic representation on the job – for example, having Punjabi charge-hands – was helpful to management, especially since Punjabis sometimes experienced difficulties with their First Nations charge-hands.

While Punjabi women supported having charge-hands from their own ethnic group, some of them were afraid to raise the issue with management; this reluctance reflected both the cultural difference between ethnic groups when it came to asserting themselves with management and the Punjabis' sense of insecurity in a foreign environment, which was compounded by their lacking the confidence to converse in English. Lack of English proficiency prevented many Punjabi women from pursuing their cause. There was also the underlying fear that they would be accused of having a Punjabi clan mentality if they sought to have good jobs assigned to relatives. At one salmon cannery, the issue of having Punjabi representation in the category of charge-hand was, in fact, raised by a Punjabi female worker:

In 1992, it came to my mind: "Why is there not a Punjabi charge-hand since there are so many East Indian workers?" I spoke with —— who was a charge-hand and close to retirement. She said, "You are not together. If you want, you need to go to management." I went to Punjabi friends and they agreed: "Yes, there should be." I said, "We should all talk to our plant supervisor." I went by myself to —— and asked, "How come there is no Punjabi charge-hand?" She asked, "Do you want to be?" I said "Okay." She said, "I will let you know tomorrow" ... The same season I began training for it.[136]

While Punjabis began working as charge-hands, many did not want such a position. Since a charge-hand is responsible for solving minor problems that emerge among workers, even those women who took on the role were concerned that they would be "accused of favouring their own people."[137]

In accord with the union's unintended role as intercultural mediator, some union members made a special difference in the workplace. When intercultural tension arose between First Nations and Punjabi workers, for example, these individuals transcended cultural boundaries and made concerted efforts to create an environment of equality in the workplace. Note the comment of a cannery worker from the Tsimshian Nation: "My first experience of racism was when I was a kid. It was a surprise for me. I have had to live with people looking at me as 'inferior.' I was taught to treat everyone equally. When there are newcomers, First Nations saw them as 'strangers' and feared they were coming to 'take our jobs' ... Union was good to make sure things were equal or fair. At work, it should not matter who you are so long as you do the job."[138]

Some First Nations people treated other workers with respect, even at the cost of being beleaguered for it by their First Nations co-workers. A woman from the Nisga'a Nation explained: "My parents taught me to treat everyone with respect. I never threw water at anyone ... When workers sign up to work, we are to give a uniform to them. One lady would give aprons with holes to the East Indian workers. We had the supplies, so I always gave them new ones. I got along with all of the Punjabis. I never put them down. Because of that, some First Nations people called me the 'East Indian Lover.'"[139]

In return for their respectful treatment, Punjabi women thanked these progressive individuals with gifts of appreciation, including bracelets and trinkets brought back from India, *samosas*, *gulab jamuns* ("sweet brown balls"), and *laddoos* ("sweet balls for weddings").[140] A man belonging to the Nisga'a Nation who had received gifts of *samosas* and *gulab jamuns* from Punjabi workers explained his work attitude: "As a charge-hand, I had a good reputation for being fair. I did not give overtime work to my 'own people' because they were my own people. I gave the overtime work to those who were reliable. In fact, I gave overtime work to a lot of students – regardless of their background – because they were serious in working and saving money. They were not rushing out to spend it. And, education is a good thing to support. When I was seriously sick, East Indians made me food. They even told me that they prayed for me. This meant a lot to me. I have their respect because I was fair."[141] Not only was this individual progressive in transcending cultural. boundaries, but he also had the insight to support "reliable" student workers who were saving money for their education.

By the 1990s, one-third of the Punjabi community were working in the salmon canneries. The Punjabi community worked with many First Nations people, and gradually relations between the two groups improved. First Nations people became accustomed to working alongside Punjabis, and Punjabi women became more familiar with First Nations people, a process that is further examined in chapter 7. Meanwhile, as the fisheries began to decline, the realization grew that they were all in it together.

We're All in It Together

By the 1970s, a strong organized labour movement had emerged, providing the New Democratic Party (NDP) with a large support base. British Columbia's NDP was elected to govern in 1972, staying in power until 1975, and served again from 1991 to 2001. While the unions had won better wages for the then predominantly First Nations, immigrant, and female labour force, the reforms implemented by labour and social democratic parties came into question during the stagflation crisis of the 1970s. The energy crisis of 1976, induced by OPEC (Organization of the Petroleum Exporting Countries), together with long-term problems with the Fordist production model, resulted in falling productivity. The strengthening trend towards globalization and technological advances heightened international competition. With the rise of neo-liberalism following the stagflation crisis, the NDP failed to promote its socialist vision and found itself serving instead as a mediator between the many interest groups, including corporations, unions, environmentalists, and First Nations.[142]

The globalization-driven decline in the forestry and fishery industries became a major source of tension between labour unions and management. Unlike the 1970s, when labour unions had considerable bargaining power, the period from the mid-1990s onwards saw a loss of union power. The decline in the forestry and fishery industries affected everyone, and as a consequence, labourers – regardless of ethnic origin – became disillusioned with the bargaining process. Workers felt let down by both their labour unions and the provincial NDP.

The Disillusioned Labourer

Consistent with Punjabi political culture, Punjabis value the right to vote, and they exercised this right once they won the BC franchise and became

Canadian citizens. In the Skeena region from the 1960s through to the 1990s, Punjabis as well as many other Skeena citizens supported parties that heeded the needs of labour. Therefore, provincially, they primarily voted for the labour-supported NDP. The labourers of the Skeena multi-ethnic workforce were bound together by the strong thread of common interests. At the time, all politicians sought the labour vote: "In those days, all parties catered to the labour force, because labour was a big force in those days."[143]

During the 1970s and 1980s, when the employment of Punjabis was at its peak in the forest industry, most Punjabi workers were represented by the IWA. In turn, the Punjabi workers were able to influence the IWA because of their large numbers in the union.[144] However, by the late 1980s and early 1990s, both the forestry and fishery industries were in decline. The initial round of layoffs impelled some Punjabis to enter other occupations or to move to an urban centre. Other Punjabi workers, dismayed by the layoffs, were disgruntled and disillusioned with the labour movement; they criticized the unions for pursuing their narrow interests ("union militancy") and for ignoring or not articulating the viewpoints of workers. "Union militancy" was the most common phrase used by workers against the unions: "[T]he unions can be just as bad as the business management as they too became militant; that is, not thinking of the workers but what fits with their agenda. They need to realize the change in times."[145] A Punjabi female cannery worker described the "militancy" problem within the UFAWU: "The union should represent all the voices of the workers. If we elect them, it does not mean their voice is everyone's voice. It is only one voice and not necessarily the only right one. If you do not watch time, you lose. The union spoke for us when we needed help with a problem. But now they are too militant about wages. You have to go with the waves; the waves are changing. They did not want to. Now we lose."[146]

Although many Punjabis acknowledged the support the unions provided in the 1970s and 1980s for higher wages and better working conditions, they felt the unions failed to recognize how global issues affected local industries in the mid-1990s. A Punjabi man explained the downfall of the PPWC as representative of the workers at the Columbia Cellulose pulp and paper mill on Watson Island:

> The union was good to the Punjabi community. But they did a lot of
> fighting with the management. They had the mentality "us" versus
> "them." It was like that from when I started in 1978 clear up to the time
> I ended my job in 1998. The union is good but then after some time they
> get more power and then get corrupt. It becomes ego games with man-
> agement at the cost of the worker. They get out of touch with reality and
> the way things are changing. The mill was always making good money

but management was taking money out of it and selling it to the private sector. The mill has a big timber licence attached to it. The last owner took loans on the mill and invested back in eastern Canada and left it to the government as a bankrupt company. It was then taken over by the NDP. You want to have a good contract but have to make sure the business is making money. The union thought the mill was theirs. A lot of supervisors of the mill were ex-union presidents at one time; that is, it is politics on the back of the worker. People like the package and cross over to management.[147]

A Punjabi tradesman referred to the misuse of power by the union players: "The heads of the union make a lot of money from the common fund that all workers have to give. The funds are misused. So the misuse of power and funds can be done by both management and union. The union was good for the Punjabi community but some people have more say in management or union than others."[148]

Many Punjabis felt that they had, in fact, been "burnt" by both management and the labour unions. A former Punjabi millworker candidly shared his dismay: "I was not impressed with it. The way they were working or dealing with management. They would tell us different stories. In 1998, they cut our salaries 10 per cent, while management [supervisors] had an increase of 10 per cent. I was not happy with PPWC tactics. They could have done more. The union president was bought out by the management, making deals … Management was building their own books, etc."[149] The workers' disillusionment with their union led to a sense of common interests among the different ethnic groups.

The Blur in Ethnic Boundaries

The immigrant Punjabi voice in the unions had undeniably begun to diminish by the late 1990s and 2000s, when the unions were struggling over their own relevancy in a changing competitive globalized economy. For instance, in order to stay afloat, the UFAWU merged with Canadian Auto Workers (CAW) in 1996 and the IWA merged with United Steelworkers in 2004. The impact of the bust in the forestry industry on union politics was so strong that politicians who traditionally appealed for the labour vote stayed away from forestry-related issues in their speeches at the local Sikh temples.[150] Indeed, labour-based politicians could no longer rely on the traditional labour issues they had once used in their campaigns. On the positive side, the decline in the forestry and fishery industries inadvertently improved intercultural relations because the various ethnic groups perceived their existential situation as a shared one, one that affected everyone, regardless of their ethnicity. In a sense, the larger Skeena community developed the feeling that they were all in it together. Note the comment made by a man from the Nisga'a Nation: "The First Nations and the ethnic people do not get the management jobs. I train a lot of people who move up but you never see the colour going into management. We were here first and lost our culture in our country. The history is very bad, including residential schools and the prejudices of being First Nations. White people at work say, 'We built this country.' I say, 'No, it was the First Nations, Chinese, Japanese, Italians, East Indians, and so forth.' We did the work. The white man came and built businesses to make money and did a lot of damage."[151]

As the labour vote shrank to an insignificant level in the Skeena region and as out-migration took place among the migrant groups in the region, political parties began to appeal for the vote of the First Nations, since they now comprised the region's majority. The First Nations are thus beginning to receive the recognition that they have been demanding over the last century and a half. However, greater attention to northwestern BC's First Nations has, ironically, coincided with the decline in the Skeena region's resource industries. While intercultural antagonisms have been subsiding since the 1990s onwards, this is not solely because of the shared experience of the decline of the resource industries. Rather, it is related to others – including the Punjabis – acquiring an understanding of, and giving recognition to, the First Nations people, a topic further explored in the following chapter.

Summary

Occupational segregation existed in the resource industries of the Skeena region. Even though the workplace has traditionally been segregated along gender and ethnic lines, the Skeena region as a whole emerged as a unique multi-ethnic area. With the arrival of Punjabis in the region, a triadic intercultural dynamic developed among First Nations, Anglo-Canadians, and more recent immigrant groups. The Punjabis stood on a continuum somewhere between Anglo-Canadians and First Nations; they were neither "white" nor "Native Indians." While the Punjabis initially made a concerted effort to distance themselves from the First Nations by trying to prove that they were hardworking and reliable immigrants, the First Nations people saw them as new immigrants who were "stealing our jobs." At the same time, some Punjabis experienced discrimination at the hands of Anglo-Canadians when they worked in non-traditional manual labour jobs that required more education and skills.

With the rise of the unions, the Punjabis obtained a platform from which to voice their grievances. All workers embraced the union agenda to bargain for better working conditions and higher wages. The Punjabis, however, were also distressed by the intercultural-labour issues that erupted in the Skeena region's multi-ethnic workforce. Interestingly, they used the union as a mechanism to establish their place in the Skeena region's "ethnic hierarchy." While Punjabis were not treated as the whites were in the workplace, they nonetheless attempted to strengthen the ethnic boundaries that separated them from First Nations people. They did this both by actions at the personal level as well as through the unions, which were built on the premise of equality and fair treatment of all workers. The unions in the 1970s and 1980s acted as intercultural mediators in Punjabi–First Nations disputes in the workforce.

Punjabis recognized the important role played by unions. However, their active participation in union politics was gender based. Punjabi men involved themselves in union politics, since doing so allowed them to raise sociopolitical issues that were important to them. Punjabi women, on the other hand, kept their traditional orientation and continued to view their power as being based in the home. However, they began giving attention to the union once it demonstrated its ability at intercultural mediation. Still, although many Punjabi women picketed during labour disputes and voted for union representation, most of them were not active members.

The disillusionment that workers felt with the loss of labour power, together with their sense of having been let down by both the unions and the provincial NDP government, resulted in a common experience of alienation among all workers. Ironically, while the unions had served as intercultural mediators in the late 1970s and 1980s, the bust in the forestry and fishery industries and the consequent weakening of labour power coincided with some blurring of ethnic divisions in the late 1990s and early 2000s. The decline in the forestry and fishery industries affected everyone; it led to a widespread sentiment that labourers were all in it together. No longer could local politicians rely on the labour vote; as the region experienced an out-migration of the earlier immigrant families, they turned instead to the First Nations vote. The out-migration of the Punjabi community from the Skeena region and its resettlement in large urban centres demonstrate sharp differences in the way immigrants have experienced Canada's practice of multiculturalism, the topic of the next two chapters.

CHAPTER 7

Cultural Synergy, Ethnic Insularity, and the Public Sphere I

The local experience of Punjabi immigrants in the Skeena region has certainly been a dynamic one, during the course of which they – carrying the social and cultural norms of their native country – faced pressures to interact with their new social environment in northwestern British Columbia. The ethnic composition of the Skeena region is diverse, and therefore the intercultural dynamic has been complex. While perceptions about the adaptation of immigrant communities to their new environment have tended to focus on relations between a particular immigrant community and the Anglo-mainstream, Punjabi migration to the Skeena region has involved a range of multifaceted intercultural interactions with people belonging to various other immigrant communities and – more significantly – with people belonging to the First Nations. This intercultural interaction, perhaps also prevalent in other small and remote towns like those in the Skeena region, reveals both the complexity of ethnic pluralism and the process through which immigrant communities become collaborative members of Canadian society.

When Punjabis began arriving in the Skeena region in the 1960s and 1970s, they were, for the most part, unknown to the general community even though various other ethnic groups had already settled in the region. These early Punjabi settlers experienced intercultural tension, and for this reason, they felt the need to assert themselves and create their own place in the community. Thus, they set about establishing social, cultural, and religious space for themselves. Meanwhile, they also had to adjust to the existing social and political structures. They first migrated to the Skeena region when Canada's practice of multiculturalism was still in its infancy; Canadian society itself was changing from the models of assimilation (1950s) and integration (1960s) to the model of multiculturalism (1970s onwards).

After its members had achieved socio-economic security, the Punjabi community had consolidated itself by the mid-1980s. Subsequently, by the late 1980s and early 1990s, the Punjabis had become collaborative members of the larger Skeena community. This adaptation process reveals the distinctive manner in which multiculturalism was practised in the Skeena region. The distinctiveness of the practice of multiculturalism in the Skeena region was underscored when the Punjabis of the region relocated to large Canadian urban centres in the wake of the decline of the region's resource industries. This relocation has involved readjustment on the part of the Punjabi immigrant community, a process that brings to light the different ways in which immigrants have experienced Canada's practice of multiculturalism. These differences in the immigrant experience seem to be a function of whether the experience took place in small remote towns or in large urban settings. Interestingly, the Punjabis who have relocated to the Lower Mainland are now confronted with the incongruent experience of, on the one hand, having greater contact with their earlier religious and cultural heritage and yet, on the other, being discomforted by the manner in which the broader Punjabi community and mainstream Canadian society interact with each other.

The present chapter and the next (chapters 7 and 8) examine the immigrant experience of Punjabis and the process of their becoming collaborative citizens in the Skeena region and then readapting to large Canadian urban centres following out-migration from the Skeena. This chapter has three parts. The first takes a critical look at the process by which Punjabis sought religious and cultural space for themselves in the Skeena region's multi-ethnic environment. The second part analyses how members of the Punjabi community, after successfully achieving socio-economic security, created social space for themselves – space that allowed for greater interaction with other ethnic groups in the community. The third part delineates the process in which increased Punjabi participation in the larger Skeena community resulted in "cultural synergy," which can be defined as the meeting of different ethnic groups of the society in such a manner as to productively and fruitfully combine their particular cultural assets on the foundation of acceptance of a set of shared values.[1]

Following this examination, chapter 8 investigates the contrasting Punjabi experience following the subsequent relocation of many members of the community to a large urban centre. This examination demonstrates the drastic shift from the cultural synergy apparent in the small remote towns of northwestern British Columbia to the considerable ethnic insularity present in the large urban centres. The summary for the two chapters appears at the end of chapter 8.

Seeking Space in the Skeena

The word Skeena is derived from the Tsimshian word 'Kshian, which means "water out of the clouds" or "the river of mists." Interestingly, Punjabi immigrants commonly pronounce Skeena as "Sakeena," which is a common name for (Punjabi) Muslim women; Sakeena means "deep and inner peace of mind and heart."[2] Apart from the indigenous First Nations peoples of the Skeena region (such as the Tsimshian and Nisga'a Nations), the region received many waves of ethnic migration during the nineteenth and twentieth centuries. The early migrants to the Skeena region were primarily British, arriving either directly from the United Kingdom or from eastern Canada, southern British Columbia, or the United States.[3] With Charles Hays's plans to build Prince Rupert as a world-class seaport, the Skeena region also drew people from other parts of the world, including northern Europe (Norway), Eastern Europe (Poland, Ukraine, the old Yugoslavia), southern Europe (Italy), and Asia (China, Japan).

The local historiography of the Skeena region focuses on the First Nations people as the original inhabitants of the region and on the initial waves of immigration settlement that occurred in the early 1900s up to the Second World War. Subsequently, interest shifted to the return of the Japanese from the internment camps; while some Japanese did return to the Skeena region after the Second World War, the Japanese population never returned to its original numbers. When the waves of post-war immigrants (like the Italians and Portuguese) began to arrive, however, little interest was shown in the multi-ethnic nature of the region's population. Therefore, the Punjabis, who primarily migrated from the 1960s onwards, are hardly mentioned in the local history.[4] Surprisingly, even after the institution of multiculturalism in Canada, the later wave of Filipino immigration in the mid-1970s and the most recent wave of Vietnamese immigration are also scarcely mentioned in the local history.[5]

The ethnic composition of the Skeena region has been diverse since well before Canada's introduction of the Multiculturalism Policy (1971). However, contrary to the way some of today's journalists may write about BC's "multicultural history,"[6] the social environment in the province was not always friendly or sensitive towards its multi-ethnic communities. Immigrants, especially – but not exclusively – those from visible minority or "racialized" groups, were tolerated only for their cheap labour and were kept divided on an ethnic basis. As observed in the previous chapter, the various groups were segregated along ethnic lines in the workforce and in the workplace living arrangements. This long-standing multi-ethnic social environment did not celebrate ethnic diversity. Rather, the concern was simply about the labour required for the Skeena region's resource industries. A Punjabi pioneer of Vancouver explained: "Punjabis going to Prince Rupert in the 1960s were similar to the pioneer days, mainly because of transiency. Punjabis went there to work. They had to build the community from nothing. In the 1960s, it would have been more difficult for Punjabis to settle in Prince Rupert than in Vancouver, where families were established with homes and religious centres."[7]

Despite the many challenges they had to face, the Punjabis who began arriving in the Skeena region in the 1960s sought and gradually established "Punjabi space" in the region. This process of establishing group space started when the Punjabi community consisted primarily of Punjabi men living in the sawmill bunkhouse, informally segregated from the multi-ethnic milieu of the region's small towns.

Informal Segregation and the Bunkhouse

Like the first wave of Punjabi pioneers to the Lower Mainland in the early 1900s, the initial migration of Punjabis to Prince Rupert consisted primarily of single Punjabi men in search of employment so that they could support their families in the Punjab. It was Sohen Singh Gill's Prince Rupert Sawmills that initially brought Punjabis to the remote town of Prince Rupert. The mill's bunkhouse provided Punjabi labourers with accommodation on the mill site. As mentioned above, like other post–Second World War immigrants, "East Indians" or Punjabis are rarely mentioned in the local archival history of Prince Rupert. In fact, members of the general community of Prince Rupert would be aware of the sawmill and bunkhouse only if they had spent their adult years living in Prince Rupert when the sawmill and bunkhouse were in operation.[8] An Italian-Canadian who attended high school during the peak period of the sawmill's operation commented: "I had no idea of the bunkhouse. I never saw a Punjabi until I came back from a welding course. In 1972, I started working at the pulp and paper mill. As time went on, I socialized and intermingled with the other co-workers. There were East Indians when I started at the pulp and paper mill. I worked as a welder for a couple of years at the mill."[9] The history of and stories about the Prince Rupert sawmill bunkhouse have been gradually fading away since Prince Rupert Sawmills was completely demolished in 1977.[10]

In the initial period of Punjabi settlement in the Skeena region, the first Punjabi cohort lived in the sawmill bunkhouse at the worksite, apart from the Prince Rupert community. With only a handful of families living in rented basement suites by the mid-1960s, there was still no established Punjabi community at the time. In fact, one can consider the bunkhouse as having been the centre of the Punjabi community in the 1960s. The number of men housed in the bunkhouse depended on the volume of lumber produced at the sawmill, but it could accommodate over seventy men. About seventy-five men lived there when the sawmill had two shifts, but the number declined when production was low or as the men gradually moved to the town to establish their families. By 1973, there were only about ten recently arrived Punjabi immigrant men living in the bunkhouse; at that time, they were responsible for cooking their own food.[11]

Since the bunkhouse was informally segregated from the town – northeast of the town centre – people living in the Skeena region in the 1960s were generally not aware that Punjabis were living there. For instance, when Punjabis were encountered, they were sometimes mistaken for Italians.[12] This is understandable since the majority of post–Second World War Italian immigrants came from southern Italy or Sicily,[13] and the Italians and Punjabis shared similar physical characteristics, including dark brown eyes, dark brown hair, and light brown skin. Along with these physical traits, the Italians and Punjabis shared other similarities; for example, both groups primarily came from agricultural societies and both had a strong kinship orientation and a machismo culture.

Punjabis were also sometimes mistaken to be members of the First Nations. A Nisga'a man recalled that a Punjabi man working in a fish plant was misidentified as an indigenous man from Hawai'i: "The North Pacific Cannery was mostly First Nations people working there. There were some Japanese and Chinese but they were working in separate areas. They did towing and worked in the boiler room. We did not really interact with them. I worked with an East Indian man. He was a very tall man, over six feet tall. People would ask him if he came from Hawaii. He would bring a lot of sweets."[14]

While the Punjabi presence was not known to many of the citizens in Prince Rupert, certainly the non-Punjabi workers – both the First Nations and other Canadian immigrants – at the Prince Rupert Sawmills were familiar with the fact that the mill was initially owned by a Punjabi businessman who housed his fellow Punjabi workers in the bunkhouse. Since most Punjabi workers remained on the sawmill grounds, intercultural interactions were primarily with other labourers. A man from the Haida Nation recalled his interactions with Punjabi men: "I worked in Prince Rupert Sawmills from 1966 to 1967. I worked on the green chain. I was twenty-one years old at the time ... There may have been about twenty First Nations working there out of a hundred people. I remember being invited by a Punjabi man to the bunkhouse to eat lunch on several occasions. I enjoyed eating the 'beans' (*dal*). Maybe they invited me because I look Punjabi."[15]

As described in chapter 3, the men had their work routine and entertainment activities. The majority of them spent most of their time at the mill site, working or socializing with their Punjabi co-workers. Therefore, there was minimal interaction with the larger Prince Rupert or Skeena community. A Punjabi man who had worked at Prince Rupert Sawmills observed: "I was friendly with the mayor [Peter Lester], who came and socialized with the men at the bunkhouse. The ones who lived in the bunkhouse stayed and drank. About fifteen guys went into the town to dine and see movies. We would go to the coffee shop. Most of the workers did not go into the town. It was the younger guys that would go into the town. They were not the drinking type. They had different interests. Our volleyball team once beat a high school team in a match. We played soccer and volleyball. We mixed well with the Italians."[16] Drinking alcohol, gambling, and reminiscing about the Punjab were common pastimes in the bunkhouse. A small group of sawmill workers also engaged in promiscuous behaviour with vulnerable First Nations women. This atmosphere was considered undesirable for the Punjabi immigrant teenagers, since it exposed them to activities that were usually discouraged at their age.[17]

The sawmill grounds had their own intercultural dynamic, given the multi-ethnic workforce. For instance, the different ethnic groups played sports, primarily soccer but also volleyball, together. Significantly, the names of the teams signified the different nations that the workers came from, and the workers played for their respective nations. A Nisga'a man remembered playing soccer with Punjabi men at Prince Rupert Sawmills: "I used to play soccer with the guys at the Prince Rupert Sawmills. There used to be a Prince Rupert Sawmills. It stood where the New Oceanside plant is today. We used to play soccer there. It was First Nations against the East Indians. We always won. [He laughs.] The East Indians used to tease us. 'We are the real Indians. You are the Native Indians!' [He laughs.] There was some understanding but not too much. We just wanted respect."[18]

The few Punjabi men who chose to explore the town were able to have more than work-based interactions with non-Punjabis; these men had the opportunity to engage with Prince Rupert's citizens and slowly connect with Skeena culture through activities like eating local food, shopping at clothing stores, socializing at a beer parlour, or being entertained at the local movie cinema.

The sawmill bunkhouse served as the centre for Punjabi men in the early 1960s. However, the men who moved to Terrace when Prince Rupert Sawmills reduced its production (from 1964 onwards) did not have the benefit of a bunkhouse at their sawmill. Instead, most of them, along with other workers, rented cabins and had to make their own food. A Punjabi man described the living situation in Terrace: "There was no bunkhouse in Terrace. I rented a cabin and lived there by myself. It cost about $100 to $120 a month. I had to cook for myself. My eldest brother taught me how to cook when I was staying in Vancouver. We worked hard and lived simply to save money for a house."[19]

The narrator who told his story in chapter 3 purchased a house in Terrace and rented out rooms to fellow Punjabi workers who found it difficult to find a place to live. Anglo-Canadians did not like renting to East Indians because of their "ghetto-like habits," with many people living in one house, and also because of the strong residual odours from cooking with spices.[20] When Punjabis rented from non-Punjabis during the initial period of settlement whether in Prince Rupert or Terrace – the landlords were mostly Euro-Canadians, such as Germans, Portuguese, or Italians. It was economically, as well as socially, more challenging for the workers to live in Terrace than in Prince Rupert. Regardless, Punjabis living in either town experienced an ethnically diverse environment, one that included a First Nations presence.

First Nations and "Their Land"

The British categorized people from India as "East Indians" in order to distinguish them from "Native Indians." However, during the first half of the twentieth century, "Hindoo" was the popular term used by Anglo-Canadians to refer to all Hindus, Sikhs, and Muslims. Even though the label "Hindoo" was mainly used in a derogatory manner, Punjabis preferred it to "Indians," which at that time was the term used to refer to the First Nations. Indeed, Punjabis did not want to be mistaken for First Nations because of the negative perceptions that Anglo-Canadians had of the latter.[21] This sentiment existed even when Punjabis migrated to the Skeena region during the 1960s and 1970s. A Punjabi man who settled in Prince Rupert in 1963 explained: "The Punjabi-Sikhs mobilized themselves to function as a distinct community because they were often misidentified as First Nations. The *gurdwara* committee would encourage its members to wear their turbans on election day to show their presence as a significant community."[22]

Unlike during the Punjabi pioneer period in Vancouver in the early 1900s, when interactions with the First Nations were limited by their small numbers, the Skeena region's population in the 1960s largely consisted of First Nations, making interactions inevitable and unavoidable. While Anglo-Canadians and Euro-Canadians referred to the First Nations as "Native Indians," Punjabis, interestingly, began referring to them as *taike*. The Punjabi word *taike* means "[family] from my father's eldest brother (*taia*)." Within the Punjabi family system, the word is an expression of respect for an elder and was therefore an appropriate term to use, given the history of the First Nations in Canada. However, from the 1960s through to the early 1990s, Punjabis began to attach the negative stereotypes of First Nations people to the word *taike* and used it in a derogatory manner when communicating among themselves.

The contemporaneous framing of the intercultural tension that existed between the two groups – Punjabis and First Nations – is often done through a retrospective lens. The earlier Punjabi immigrants in the Skeena region have much to say about their experiences of both workplace and group discrimination. However, all of the Punjabi male immigrants and a majority of the female immigrants interviewed for this study initially minimized the intercultural tension between the two groups. The most common response was that "the relations are good." As the interview would progress, however, the interviewees would typically begin to offer their personal accounts of workplace and group discrimination in the larger Skeena community. It then became apparent that many of the interviewees considered it very important to differentiate present intercultural relations from the relations "back in the earlier days," when Punjabis had just begun arriving and were establishing themselves in the Skeena region. For some Punjabis, conjuring up memories of intercultural tension threatened their present sense of cultural synergy or their sense of camaraderie with the Skeena people; however, these memories also contributed to a greater awareness of the social history and contemporary situation of the First Nations.

During the 1960s and 1970s, Punjabi men mainly reacted to the First Nations' verbal and physical aggression by fighting back; to them, it was important to "stand up for oneself and one's people." The more hostile encounters involved alcohol, perhaps because drinking lowered one's inhibitions. One Punjabi man explained: "I was surprised that First Nations men would speak nice to you. But then at the beer parlour they would shout 'Hey you f—k'n Hindoo! Get out of our country!' to your face. I mean it was the same guys who speak nicely to you at work."[23] It is important to note that this dynamic was also experienced by Italians and Portuguese prior to the arrival of, and during the initial settlement of, Punjabis.[24] Note the comment made by an Italian-Canadian:

We played soccer with the different nations: Italians, Portuguese, Czech, and Natives. There was bullying in public. Italians did most of the construction in Prince Rupert, building homes. They made a lot of money that way when the economy was good ... When we would go around town, people were not always treating us well. There would be physical fights with Natives. We had fights with English, too. You would group with more Italians to protect yourself if something developed. It was not intentional what the Natives were doing; they were threatened by our lifestyle. People came and worked hard for the fruits of it, building houses, car.[25]

While both Punjabis and First Nations acknowledged that there was tension between the East Indians and the Native Indians, an Anglo-Canadian editor gave sharp expression to the situation in a letter she wrote from Fort St

James about the brawls that occurred in the early 1970s in northern BC: "The Canadian Indians, when half drunk, are great to sense fear in others and they certainly sensed it in the groups of East Indians. Using whatever excuse for a fight they could find, they would set upon the East Indian men ... The East Indian men, I suppose had finally reached the breaking point, and for a change, they retaliated."[26] While her account is perhaps biased, it interestingly points to a dynamic that was prevalent in the 1960s and 1970s. However, her explanation does not shed light on the underlying tension that existed between the two groups for over two decades.

As discussed in chapter 6, the industrialization of British Columbia was accomplished in part through government initiatives that devastated the First Nations' traditional way of life – for example, criminalizing the potlatch, enforcing conservation laws and regulations aimed at acquiring control over land and water, and enforcing the Canadian policy of "civilization and assimilation." Since it was not until 1951 that the federal government lifted the prohibition against the soliciting of funds for First Nations legal land claims, it was only from that time onwards that First Nations groups could legally mobilize to achieve self-determination through self-governance and land claims. In addition to fearing that immigrants took away their jobs, the First Nations, in response to the perceived threat posed by waves of immigrants who were seemingly coming in significant numbers, also feared that immigrants might perhaps take away "their land." A Punjabi man described his experience in the Skeena region: "There was a problem with the Natives. In those days, there were a lot of physical fights with the Natives. They would come to fight with wood pieces ... There was a division between the Natives and the whites. Although Natives were permitted to go to the places whites went, there still remained a lot of tension. The whites took over their land. There was a lot of bitterness. There was also bitterness with the East Indians, Italians, and Portuguese. Now these people are coming on their land."[27]

The discrimination experienced by the Punjabi community was undoubtedly a complex affair, since the First Nations were grappling with their own cultural and geographical losses, which had come with the colonization of British Columbia. The tension between the two groups, however, was initially puzzling to Punjabis, since they actually seemed to have a lot in common with one another, albeit without truly knowing each other's histories. With the passage of time, the Punjabis attempted to make sense of the intercultural dynamic that existed between them and the First Nations. Despite their many similarities, such as physical features, collective cultural values, and a history of colonization by the British, there existed a major difference between them. The Punjabis had fought against British rule and in 1947 had succeeded in gaining independence (even though the state of Punjab was divided into two), whereas the First Nations still had to contend with the ongoing issue of cultural devastation and unresolved land claims. A perceptive Punjabi observer explained:

> There are many things East Indians share in common with the Natives. There is a closed-knit family, importance of spirituality and co-existence. A connection was there, but over the years after the invasion of the white man, the Natives were all uprooted from their system. The white man completely destroyed them with alcohol. The roots were cut off and the value system shifted. The Natives did not know what to do. Now it is alcohol and junk food. The difference is that the Natives did not have anything established like the East Indians. Nothing of their civilization was written down. The British came to India and Indians were not allowed to read their scripture, but there was an already-established civilization which could not be destroyed.[28]

When the Punjabis arrived in the Skeena region or in Canada in general, for the most part they knew very little about the history of the First Nations in Canada, if anything at all. Upon meeting First Nations people, the Punjabis thought of them as tribal (*jungalee*). Notwithstanding what they had in common, Punjabis did not know the exact nature of what had happened to the First Nations people: "I knew nothing about Native Indians in the Punjab. We learned about Columbus in India and thought that Natives were tribal people behind the times. That's all. We knew nothing about the residential schools and all the abuse."[29] Similarly, many Canadians were unaware of the abuses suffered by the First Nations people while in the "care" of residential schools.

Residential schools were first established by the government in the nineteenth century, with the purpose of assimilating First Nations children into Anglo-Canadian society.[30] Beginning in the 1980s, there has been growing awareness of the detrimental impact of these schools on generations of First Nations children. That impact was a major grievance of the First Nations against the government. It was not until 11 June 2008 that the Canadian government made a public apology in the House of Commons and provided compensation in the form of payouts to former residents of these schools. Tragically, the residential school survivors "just got payouts, and since many of them had poor coping strategies, compensation led to a number of them taking their lives. They need[ed] proper holistic counselling."[31]

The impact of the residential schools has been pervasive. In fact, out of the ten First Nations people interviewed (who were recruited through different networks) for the present project, three participants had attended residential schools (Alberni, Lytton), six had a parent or in-law who had a attended residential school (Alberni, Alberta, Alert Bay), and, in the case of the one remaining participant, the topic did not come up during the interview. A man of the Tsimshian Nation generously shared his experience:

I did not want to go to residential school. They came to get me. I hid in Port Edward. I went to residential school in Port Alberni when I was eleven years old. I went for four years. I was a very angry man for many years. I carried around the anger. I never spoke of it. Then, twenty-five years ago I heard a woman talk about it [in the community]. I reacted to the talk, "Hey, that's my story." I got up and talked about my experience. I needed to talk about it to get it out of my system. Now I want to bury it. I don't want to talk too much about it. It was very bad. I started to drink at the age of seventeen because of the residential school. Everything was me, me, me. It [residential school] made me a very angry man.[32]

While the abuses of the residential school program have entered the contemporary public discourse, people in Canada, only a few decades ago, were generally ignorant of, or simply turned a blind eye to, the tragic impact of the program. This lack of awareness and acknowledgment of the consequences of the residential schools is another aspect of First Nations history that has had a damaging effect on the psychology of the First Nations people. An Anglo-Canadian social worker explained:

The residential schools were devastating to the various First Nations communities. The raising of awareness occurred only during the 1980s and 1990s. There has been a minimizing of the [impact of the] schools. The mainstream feels the First Nations are lazy and ungrateful, whereas the First Nations feel shame. The First Nations don't want to admit the trauma. With trauma there is always fear, the fear of rejection by family, community. So, they turn to drugs and alcohol for coping ... I have heard accounts in detail of what it was like in the residential schools. They were one cause of the break in the structure within the villages, nations, and families. It was quite profound. Parents were punished if they did not place their kids in the residential schools. The military or police got them and dropped the children off at the schools. There has been a sense of isolation, fear, and trepidation. First Nations are very suspicious of anyone other than their own.[33]

It is apparent that at the time the Punjabis were entering the Skeena region and in the process of creating their own space, the First Nations had their own struggle, one embedded in a long-standing history of oppression and trauma.

In contrast to the Punjabi male's response to fight back when confronted with First Nations' hostility, the Punjabi women responded variously along a continuum from "sucking it in" to "speaking up"; a few even had friendly interactions with some First Nations people. A Punjabi woman fluent in English described the relations that existed between Punjabis and the First Nations:

> If Natives and Punjabis had a problem, it was usually related to a language or communication barrier. Both sides did not approach each other properly. Sometimes Natives mainly came from reservations and our own people mostly came from villages. The Natives also have a complex because they thought the ethnics are taking their place and job. Natives don't like to mix with others because they feel scared. There is a complex. You can tell by their body behaviour; they are reserved, closed, and shy. On the other hand, when I would speak to Natives, the Punjabis and Chinese would ask me, "Why are you talking to the Natives?"[34]

Interestingly, a few Punjabi women who were fluent in conversational English had a different understanding of, or approach towards, the First Nations. In fact, since they were more comfortable in conversing with the First Nations, they could more easily overcome the communication and cultural barriers. At that time, mutual interactions would have been primarily in the context of the salmon cannery plants. A Punjabi woman who worked in the cannery office – not on a fish line – narrated her different experience with the First Nations:

> They are nice people. I had experience with them in dealing with the fishermen on the job. Also, there was one lady in the office with whom I spoke. I thought they were mistreated by the white men. They were hurt and lost in their booze ... I found them to be quite spiritual. The Punjabi community did not have much relation with the Natives. Perhaps because of the way they came across. I was lucky to be in an environment where I could get to know them ... *Taike* is used in a looking-down way. The Punjabis say it because then others will not understand who they are referring to. I never felt the racism of "go back to your country." They would just swear a lot when they were drunk. But in a drunken state they are not picking or choosing.[35]

In addition to the language barrier, there was also a general fear of the unknown, something to which the First Nations people were also susceptible.

Note the comment made by a man belonging to the Haida Nation: "One day my grandmother saw me going to school with a white girl. She insisted that I go out with my own kind. Lack of understanding produced fear. People are fearful when they do not know. My grandmother went to residential school but still managed to keep her language. The kids spoke it among themselves but were really not allowed to speak it. Some were killed or physically beaten because of it."[36]

First Nations people felt insecure, especially given their history of being treated as third-class citizens. A Tsimshian woman remembered her initial encounters and experiences in Prince Rupert: "When I first arrived in Prince Rupert [1957], I felt hurt and confused. To me, we are all humans. White people called us 'dirty Indians.' We could not go to certain hotels. I remember going to Capitol Cinema with my husband. I was escorted to my seat. At first, I thought I had been given special treatment, but I soon learnt that First Nations people were only allowed to sit on one side of the cinema hall. They segregated us! We started on a rough ground with a lot of people who are now our friends. The discrimination is still there, but it is a lot less."[37]

The Punjabi–First Nations dynamic that emerged in the Skeena region is interesting in that it involved intense interactions between two types of "Indians": Native and East. A woman from the Haida Nation explained the intercultural dynamic from the perspective of the First Nations people:

> First Nations with darker skin experienced a lot of racism. If in a store, the storeowners would watch them for stealing. In the Chinese restaurant, they would serve the Chinese people or anyone else before the First Nations. You don't notice too much when you are young; you just take what is there. The darker Indians experienced a lot of racism from the whites … So many years ago Europeans came to take their life, their kids. We were to be made "more human" and our land was taken away. The people who came used up the resources; we did not waste. First Nations were and have been wary of people coming, including the East Indians. First Nations did not know who were the East Indians and did not trust them. We interacted with each other but we did not know each other's history. There was no understanding because we did not know the histories.[38]

The limited awareness and lack of acknowledgment of the "other's" story became a source of intercultural tension. Perhaps the tension between the "third-class Native Indian" and the "second-" or "ethnic-class East Indian" had more to do with their feelings of insecurity in an environment in which both were perceived as inferior by the "white establishment" in the Skeena region.

Punjabis and the Other Canadian Immigrants

Punjabis also had interactions with various other immigrant Canadians, besides the First Nations, at the workplace and in the larger Skeena community. The intercultural dynamic was complex, and discrimination against the Punjabi minority surfaced in the town as well as the workplace.[39] While Prince Rupert is a multi-ethnic town, with people from many different backgrounds living alongside each other, it is not necessarily "racism free," as Anglo-Canadians commonly believe. A Euro-Canadian educator who once lived in Prince Rupert described the intercultural environment of the town prior to the 1990s:

> Prince Rupert is very cosmopolitan. This is striking even in comparison to Terrace, which is more like a cowboy town. Prince Rupert is a port town and one is able to encounter so many different ethnic groups along with a high percentage of First Nations people. It is a small town so there is room for all of us. The town's tolerance, however, was that of ambiguity. People noted the difference. People noticed someone who has a different odour, instead of asking "Can I have some of your food?" I am not sure whether it was race generated or about oppression. There was a "deep-rooted superiority," a sense of what is normal, which was a quick assumption. It was not labour-related because fishermen could be wealthy and own a boat. Everyone supported labour, since it was a resource-dependent town. It was more about the white and the First Nations and the ethnic. There was not really a celebration of cultures as such when I was there until 1990.[40]

According to many Punjabi immigrants, two types of discrimination were directly related to ethnicity and class: overt and covert. The overt kind was in the form of verbal and physical abuse by Anglo-Canadians who belonged to the labour or working class. Among the ethnic groups themselves, overt discrimination was rooted in their ignorance and fear of the "others" who were similarly placed in the labour hierarchy at the workplace. As antagonisms erupted between ethnic groups in the sawmills, the pulp and paper mill, and even more so in the salmon canneries, the management used the ethnic-based networks led by the "straw-boss" and charge-hand to maintain control over its multi-ethnic workforce. Some Anglo-Canadians in the workforce had an attitude of "superiority" based on their ethnicity. This attitude not only cropped up in the workplace but also extended to interactions within the larger Skeena community. Punjabis were of the view that Anglo-Canadians often expressed their sense of racial superiority in an overt manner. While

North Americans usually consider the words "black" or "nigger" to be derogatory terms used for African-Americans, in Canada these terms have sometimes been used to refer to East Indians.[41] In fact, during British colonial rule in India, the word "nigger" was used liberally to refer to Indians. A Canadian-born Punjabi recalled the intercultural tension in the Skeena region during the late 1970s and early 1980s:

> Sometimes some white people would call us nigger. We were treated as the blacks were in southern USA. If I sat on a chair, when I would get up, a white person would say to another kid, "Don't sit there, a Hindoo sat there." It happened at the drinking fountain as well. Poverty played a role in the behaviour. Now when I look back, the ones who were physically aggressive were mainly from broken homes, alcoholic families, and dysfunctional homes. The ones who were more verbal but not aggressive were from more stable homes. This was the case for both the white and First Nations people alike. Ignorance shows itself.[42]

As the above interviewee noted, this overt form of discrimination was practised most often by those from disadvantaged households.

The prejudicial treatment took place along racial lines. The "racialized location"[43] of Punjabis was somewhere between the First Nations and Anglo-Canadians. While Punjabis were successful in demonstrating that they were different from the First Nations, this differentiation – regardless of what they endured as immigrants at the hands of the First Nations – only perpetuated the First Nations' status as third class and reinforced the stereotypical image that the "established elite" had of the First Nations. Clearly, the Punjabi effort would not make Punjabis white. Unlike the Jews, who – especially those with Anglicized names – over time came to be taken as white in the United States,[44] the Punjabis could never completely achieve this end because of their skin colour. Even as the Punjabis made every effort to be accepted by the larger Skeena community as a visible minority, they continued to live with the unspoken pressure and tension that such a visible minority experiences. It was a common belief expressed by both Punjabi immigrant parents and their children that "if a Punjabi would do something wrong at the workplace or within the community, all Punjabis would be under great scrutiny."[45]

Interestingly, the Punjabis' negative relations with the Anglo-Canadians and First Nations in the Skeena region inadvertently created camaraderie among the non-Anglo ethnic Canadians in the manual or skilled labour workforce. The Punjabis most often mentioned the Italians in this context, explaining that the Punjabis and Italians would "help each other out." While these two ethnic groups shared some common goals, more significantly they were neither First Nations nor Anglo-Canadian. This comment by an Italian-Canadian is representative of his group: "There was name calling between whites and East Indians: 'Hindoo' or 'Ragheads.' I felt bad about it because I too was an immigrant and had gone through it. I got along with the different ethnic groups."[46]

Importantly, since the main wave of Italian immigration occurred after the Second World War, the Italians were a visible presence when they settled. Like the Punjabis, they made an effort to be regarded as part of Canadian society. Thus, the two groups shared a common experience as immigrants. A Punjabi woman reflected on her intercultural experiences and underlines the distinctive stance of the Italians (and Portuguese):

> We were not too many, so we wanted to and had to mix with the other Canadians. Some Natives did not like to see us in our Indian clothes. They would shout out "Hindoo" in a rude way. The Portuguese and Italians were not rude to us, we all worked together. Canadian younger [white] generation would throw magazines on the East Indians they hated. Once at a grocery store a young guy around seventeen or eighteen years old said, "Hey Hindoo, go back to India." I said, "You are not from here. This land does not belong to you. You go back to the land you came from." The guy ran away.[47]

As evidenced in the two narratives provided earlier in this study, there was mutual camaraderie among the different non-Anglo-Canadian ethnic groups, all of whom were attempting to build their lives within the structure established by the Anglo-Canadian elite that held political power and tended to exercise covert discrimination.

Besides experiencing overt discrimination at the hands of the working-class Anglo-Canadians, the Punjabi immigrants also encountered discrimination of a covert nature from the Skeena region's established white community, which consisted of professionals, politicians, businessmen, and managers. The Punjabi interviewees found it more difficult to talk about covert discrimination (as opposed to overt discrimination) or to substantiate it, perhaps because of its subtler nature. Their "feeling" that a group of higher-class people (Anglo-Canadians) perceived them (the Punjabis) to be "inferior" was embedded in a power structure characterized by marked differences in educational level, occupation, and monetary worth. The experiences of Punjabis, Italians, and First Nations people demonstrated that attitudes of superiority ranged along ethnic lines.

The Punjabis for the most part responded to the covert form of discrimination by "sucking it in." Not all Punjabis complained about covert discrimination; some earnestly stated that they had never experienced it; others acknowledged that it existed, but were quick to state that it had not happened to them. It is worthy of mention here that according to their testimony, Punjabi men experienced more covert discrimination at the hands of Anglo-Canadians than the women did. This discrepancy reflects a gender difference with respect to efforts to advance in one's job: while Punjabi men pursued upward mobility in the labour force (public sphere), Punjabi women generally saw their work as secondary to their role as homemaker (private sphere) and consequently made less of an effort to move up in the cannery.

Socio-economic Security and Inter-community Relations

The Punjabis' willingness to travel to remote places like Prince Rupert under difficult conditions in the hope of finding employment reflected the determination and resilience of the Punjabi character. Nevertheless, during the initial period of settlement in the 1960s, the Punjabi community lacked a centre for religious or cultural activity. As a consequence, some of its members attended church or sent their children to Sunday school. A Punjabi woman described the initial period of adaptation: "I wanted to pray to God but a Sikh Temple did not exist. So I attended church ... I went to the Sikh temple once it was made in 1973. The congregation would cook food from their homes because the temple did not have a kitchen at that time; each family signed up for a specific item. We all worked together, just like how the Sikh gurus taught us: to repeat God's name, to work honestly, and to share our earnings. We learned this simple teaching while growing up in the village. It helped guide many of us in Canada, too."[48]

While Christianity as the religion of the dominant culture could be a means for some Asians to connect with, or develop a sense of belonging to, the dominant culture, this was generally not the case with the Punjabi-Sikhs and Punjabi-Hindus in the Skeena region.[49] In the face of acculturation stress – and especially in the face of complex intercultural relations – the Punjabis sought to create a religious and cultural space of their own for intra-group support. In fact, Punjabis displayed boldness and resiliency in building Sikh places of worship in the Skeena region. By the late 1970s, they had consolidated themselves as a community in the region by establishing their own religious and cultural institutions. Meanwhile, they purchased homes for themselves and sent their children to public schools. The establishment of social space for Punjabi immigrants signalled that they had achieved socioeconomic security, and it set the stage for enhanced interactions with other people of the Skeena region.

As the Punjabi-Sikh communities grew in British Columbia during the 1970s and 1980s, so did the cultural landscape of Sikh temples (*gurdwaras*) throughout the province. The *gurdwara* has been the primary medium through which Punjabis successfully created religious and cultural space for themselves, even in small remote towns in the Skeena region.[50] Initially, with limited resources, the small community of just five Sikh families in Prince Rupert still managed to congregate and recite prayers.

By the early 1970s, when the Punjabi-Sikh community had grown to fifteen or so families along with around thirty men who lived in the sawmill bunkhouse, the community rented a hall belonging to the Catholic church for religious services. A Punjabi man recalled their monthly gatherings: "Once a month, we had the hall from 10:00 a.m. to 12:00 p.m. We would have a local person come and speak about the Sikh religion. We had *langar* [community dining hall] on the floors with some tables and chairs. The food was brought from home. The ladies wore Punjabi suits and the men usually dressed in Western pants and shirts. They all covered their heads. There were about thirty to fifty people who attended this monthly congregation."[51]

In 1972, the Indo-Canadian Association was formally established as a registered BC society.[52] One of the chief aims of this society was to establish a *gurdwara*, but the Punjabi-Hindu families living in Prince Rupert (there were about seven) preferred to have a cultural hall. As a consequence, there was some disagreement among the factions within the Indian community (consisting of Sikhs and some Hindus). A Sikh man explained the religious factions:

This organization was comprised of mainly Punjabi-Sikh members as well as some Punjabi-Hindu members. This organization held monthly meetings to address the community's needs as well as to keep its members in the loop. In 1972, some of the Sikh executives proposed the idea of creating a Sikh temple to function as a central community centre and to help generate revenue for community projects. However, the Hindu members rejected the idea and stopped attending the monthly meetings. They also convinced some of the Sikh members to join their protest against the Sikh temple project.[53]

The term "Indo-Canadian" was used in the name of the association as a manoeuvre to diffuse the tension over whether to create a cultural centre or a religious place of worship (Skeena Punjabis generally refer to themselves as "Punjabi," while other Skeena citizens refer to them as "East Indian"). The original board of directors proposed that the association should purchase an existing church from a German Christian group and transform it into a *gurdwara*.[54] When they brought this to the members' attention, those against a Sikh temple and in favour of a cultural centre became disenchanted with the association and rejected the proposal. Subsequently, without further consulting the Punjabi community, the board of directors grouped together and bought the church with a bank loan, using their own homes as collateral. After the church was bought, the loan was transferred to the society.[55] The property cost thirty-eight thousand, which the community paid off within six months. The society's name was subsequently changed to Indo-Canadian Sikh Association on 16 June 1974.[56] It is worthy of mention here that the Hindu-Sikh faction that disapproved of the Sikh temple project later attended the *gurdwara* during auspicious occasions that both Hindus and Sikhs alike celebrate.

Once the Punjabi-Sikh community successfully established a religious and cultural space for itself in Prince Rupert, some Anglo-Canadian citizens expressed their disapproval. A founding member recalled: "When we first opened the *gurdwara*, there were incidents of our windows being broken by rocks, hockey sticks, and a pellet gun. This lasted for about six months. The broken glass looked like rocks of the size of a golf ball were thrown. Rocks were found in the kitchen. There was also a pellet found in the side windows."[57] The congregation felt that they were being targeted, especially since the church across the street had no problem with vandalism, and so the Royal Canadian Mounted Police (RCMP) were contacted. An active member of the temple at that time felt that these acts of vandalism were not taken seriously by the RCMP:

According to the RCMP, it was done by young Caucasians during the night. The officer said it must have been coming from the neighbouring house. The RCMP would take a look but it was not a priority for them. It was how they were with the Natives. We did not matter in the eyes of the RCMP. If Natives would make a complaint, they did nothing. It didn't really matter. At that time, the RCMP officers were all *gore* [white]. It was only when I threatened to tell the media in the Lower Mainland that we got immediate attention. We placed grills on the windows. We also changed the windows to Plexiglass. The problem then stopped.[58]

While the temple had been established, there was no priest to provide religious services to the congregation. Harbhajan Singh Bhamrah volunteered to serve: "There were only a handful of families going to the *gurdwara*, and

Indo-Canadian Sikh Temple on Fourth Avenue, Prince Rupert. Courtesy of Prince Rupert City & Regional Archives, The Daily News Collection, 1998-040-102.

they only went once a month. There was no priest in Prince Rupert. In 1973, I offered service as a volunteer to be the *granthi* [the one who reads the scripture and explains it to the congregation]. I served as *granthi* for fourteen years. I worked full-time as an electrician and volunteered as a *granthi* at the *gurdwara*."[59]

The congregation met every Sunday, and it gradually grew over the months. Within three to four years, the congregation grew to about one hundred people. With the volunteer *granthi*, the first marriage, albeit not a registered one, was performed in the Prince Rupert Sikh temple in 1976. Since a *granthi* did not reside in either Terrace or Kitimat, Harbhajan Singh Bhamrah also volunteered to go to those towns three to four times a year to perform religious services. The Terrace Punjabi-Sikh community eventually built its own temple – called the Skeena Valley Guru Nanak Brotherhood Gurdwara – completing it in 1977.[60] Following this, the Kitimat community established the Kitimat Sikh Society, which built a *gurdwara* between 1982 and 1983.[61]

The Sikh temple represented a physical space where Punjabis could be validated socially, psychologically, and culturally. They were able to relive memories of life in the Punjab, find comfort in a familiar social environment, and speak with one another in Punjabi.[62] Punjabis attended the Sikh temple even when they were not of a religious bent, because the temple also served as a way of creating a home for themselves in their new country.[63] A

Punjabi woman offered her insight: "The Prince Rupert community also had regular visits from Sikh preachers (*gianis*) and musicians (*ragis*). Even the non-religious-minded Punjabis would listen to them because it felt like the homeland for many. And for the religious-minded, it was a blessing to have these figures come to our towns. They [the visitors] liked it, too, because they would be invited to different homes every night for dinner and the congregation also gave them money for their services."[64]

From the mid-1980s to the mid-1990s, the Prince Rupert Sikh temple was the last stop that visiting Sikh preachers and musicians would make on their circuit from Vancouver to the BC interior. Along with providing their religious discourse, these travelling Sikh preachers also encouraged the members of the congregation to preserve their religion, culture, and language. Interestingly, this encouragement was often articulated within the framework of "what happened to the First Nations." An orthodox Punjabi-Sikh man explained: "It was planned [by the white Canadians] to ruin their community, they outlawed their culture and sold alcohol to them ... This was all done on purpose in order to break them. Sikh preachers would come to Prince Rupert and would tell us Sikhs to retain our language, religion, and culture or else we would end up like the Natives and lose our culture. If we lose our cultural heritage, we will also lose ourselves."[65]

While intercultural tension did exist between the Punjabis and First Nations, Punjabis gradually learned more about First Nations through contact with them, and this prompted some members of the Punjabi community to make a concerted effort to preserve their own religion, culture, and language. By 1983, the Prince Rupert Sikh temple was offering both Punjabi and scriptural reading (*path*) classes. There was an ironic turn of events here: while the tension between Punjabis and First Nations were partly the result of First Nations people objecting to the Punjabis speaking their own language, Punjabis were taught First Nations history by travelling Punjabi preachers, so that it would not be lost.

According to many Punjabi interviewees, their community was like "one united family." All families participated at every social function. Since only a handful of Hindu families lived in Prince Rupert and Terrace, they did not build a Hindu temple; instead they followed the common Hindu practice of building small shrines in their homes and performing their prayers and rituals there. Moreover, upon invitation, Hindus often attended religious functions at the *gurdwara*. One woman described her experience as a Hindu-Punjabi: "We pray at home. We made a *mandir* in our house. We taught our kids Hindu culture. We used to get together for special holidays like Diwali, Dusshera, Rakhi, Independence Day, etc. We never felt separate from the Sikhs. We were all friends and like a family. We were so few people we were like a big family. We attended the *gurdwara* for some functions when we were invited. In 1984, we never cared about the politics. The politics was not here, because we were friends. There was no resentment. This is a small village, people are friendly."[66]

Even after the events of Operation Bluestar in 1984,[67] Hindu-Sikh relations did not change on the whole. Some members of the Prince Rupert community were baptized (*amritdhari*) after seeing the sacred Sikh shrine desecrated in Amritsar, Punjab. However, the community was generally not politically engaged in the Khalistan movement.[68]

Establishing Social Space

The creation of religious and cultural space provided intra-group support for the Punjabis in a foreign milieu. Yet the achievement of socio-economic security has also been of primary importance, for it allowed the Punjabi immigrants to establish themselves in Canadian society and create social space for themselves in the public sphere. The Punjabis – like most immigrants – arrived in Canada with the primary aim of seeking greater socio-economic security; such security not only involved steady wages and job protection, but also the stability and safety afforded by establishing their families in the larger community. Besides through the workplace, immigrants initially engaged in the public sphere primarily through the purchase of housing and through their children entering the school system. As discussed in chapter 3, Punjabis also created social space for themselves by acquiring rental properties as an investment. This behavioural pattern – further amplified by the Punjabi cultural ethos of landownership – emerged as a source of tension between some First Nations people and Punjabis. Home ownership is no doubt related to socio-economic factors, but it is also a cultural value among such various immigrant groups as the Chinese, Italians, and Punjabis.[69] On the other hand, the First Nations people were less compelled to purchase homes, since they had already owned homes in their traditional villages. A woman from the Tsimshian Nation explained: "There were wartime houses on the way to Seal Cove [right outside Prince Rupert proper] up for sale in the 1950s. A lot of immigrants, like the Italians, Portuguese, and Germans, bought them. We rented from them. We [First Nations] thought that the work and workplace accommodations in Port Edward would never end. We also thought it was not necessary to buy homes in Prince Rupert because we had homes in our villages. My husband and I moved around seven times as renters. After that we realized that we needed to buy our own home."[70] Subsequently, home ownership became an issue for those First Nations who believed that these immigrant groups were buying property on what they saw as their land, just as First Nations were engaged in lobbying for land-claim rights.

By the 1980s, many Punjabis had come to own rental properties in the Skeena region. They often leased their rental properties to non-Punjabis, including Anglo-Canadians and people from the First Nations. One Punjabi residing in Prince Rupert recalled renting a house to First Nations people: "In the 1980s, a Native man lived in our rental house ... I would say, 'Hey brother, how is it going? Look, the blood inside us is the same.' They did not like renting from 'us Hindoos.' They saw it as their land."[71] This tendency of not only buying their own home but also acquiring rental properties, whereby the Punjabi was the landowner and the First Nations people were the tenants, further aggravated the tension between Punjabis and First Nations. Indeed, some First Nations people resented having to pay for living on what they perceived as "their land." One Punjabi man told of a specific incident when he rented out his property to a First Nations man: "Natives want respect. Sometime in the 1980s I learned this the hard way. I drove a Native Indian out of my house. I was renting the main floor to the Natives. He was a middle-aged Native on welfare but not paying the rent and wrecking the house. I asked him to vacate, he did. He put my house on fire. I know, because he agreed with the police that he had set my house on fire. I could not recover any money because he had none. They feel, 'Who are these people coming and taking our land?'"[72] More importantly, the same Punjabi man explained what he learned over time: "If you want respect, you have to respect others. But Punjabis and Natives were talking rudely to each other. Punjabi people were thriving, making money. The Punjabi community was not smart. They came from villages and did not respect the Natives. They confronted them while not knowing Native history. If you give Natives respect, they are fine. But one has to show respect. If you want respect, you have to respect others. The Natives are always friendly if you don't hurt their feelings and give them proper respect."[73]

The above citation bears witness to how Punjabis over time became more aware of the condition of the First Nations people and how this growing understanding played a significant role in Punjabis becoming collaborative members of the larger Skeena community. It is worth mentioning here that while many Punjabis residing in Terrace had acquired rental properties by the 1980s, they really only began renting their property to First Nations people after the Nisga'a Highway, which connects the four Nisga'a villages of the Nass River Valley to Terrace,[74] was constructed (1999–2005). The construction of the highway resulted in the First Nations population increasing to comprise up to 30 per cent of the town's total population.[75]

While some First Nations people did not like to see the Punjabis and other ethnic groups acquire property, other aspects of the East Indian lifestyle may also have had a negative effect on the standing of Punjabis in the general community, such as the odours from Indian cooking ingredients (onions, garlic, and spices) and the brightly coloured Punjabi clothing. A child of Punjabi immigrants commented on prevailing attitudes towards Punjabi products in the late 1970s and early 1980s: "Back then, the white people disliked Indian stuff. Henna was referred to as cow shit; curry was stinky Hindu food; Indian fabric was for the circus; and nose rings were tribal."[76]

Furthermore, Anglo-Canadians generally frowned upon related families living in a single house. Joint-family living, however, was only a temporary situation – that is, a circumstance endured until relatives could afford their own house.[77] In fact, once large numbers of Punjabis became economically established by the mid-1980s, they moved to the new subdivisions on the west side of Prince Rupert, where they could build larger homes in "better" neighbourhoods. Moreover, even though joint families were an important factor in creating resiliency during the socio-economic adaptation period during the 1960s and 1970s, the traditional "extended" family structure has experienced some social and cultural change as a consequence of migration to Canada. As in the case of the Sikh community in Vancouver,[78] the basic pattern has been that of a nuclear family, often supplemented – but not always – by grandparents.

Once Punjabi families began settling in the larger Skeena community, their children started attending school. In the 1960s, the children of most Punjabi immigrants did not enter the school system, opting instead, out of necessity, to work. Even when they did enter, the school experience was not pleasant and this was a deterrent to their continuing with it. A Punjabi male told of his first year at Conrad Elementary School upon arriving in Prince Rupert:

I started going to school after Christmas in 1965. I was in the New Canadian Class. The class had Italian, Portuguese, Greek, and Vietnamese kids in it. I felt very alone because I had no one to relate to or to speak Punjabi with. I only lasted one year in school. It was frustrating, it was not like the ESL [English as a second language] classes they have these days. I couldn't speak English. I couldn't understand anything the teacher was saying. It was a very demoralizing experience. To add to the frustration, I encountered a fair share of racism as well, most of it verbal. There was one kid who would bully kids in the New Canadian Class. I got into a tussle with him; it was daunting because not only was he bigger than me, but everyone else watching was cheering him on while making racial comments towards me ... The administration tried to help, but their approach did not fit well with the situation. I remember punching a kid out and making his nose bleed for calling me a "Hindoo." The principal asked me if "I was ashamed of it." I was Sikh, not Hindu. He did not know the difference. We [South Asians] were all the same to him. I could not defend myself because my English was poor, I just kept quiet.[79]

The "New Canadian Class" was a special class meant to assist children of immigrants who experienced a language barrier in the mid-1960s. At this time, educational and social systems in Canada were not yet oriented towards training professionals to have cultural competency skills, since Canada was only in the initial stages of developing a multiculturalism outlook. Young Punjabi immigrants thus faced multiple barriers when entering the school system and, as a consequence, mainly opted to drop out and work.

The children of Punjabi immigrants who entered the school system in Prince Rupert could be divided into two main cohorts.[80] Cohort 1 consisted of children who started school in the mid-1970s and early 1980s on the east side of the town, while cohort 2 included children who entered elementary school in the new subdivisions of the town from the mid-1980s onwards. The children in cohort 1 belonged to the initial wave of Punjabi immigrant parents. Their period of entry was marked by an inadequate understanding of intercultural relations and poor minority identity formation. In the late 1970s, when the Punjabi community was relatively small, there was a general lack of awareness of Punjabi culture in the wider Skeena area, and overt discrimination in the school system was common. Punjabi males belonging to cohort 1 recalled having endured verbal and physical abuse from both First Nations and white boys. A Punjabi male who entered the school system in the early 1970s described his experiences:

Everyone looked at you differently, especially the Natives and some white guys. It was difficult in the playgrounds, at school. I went to Roosevelt Park School. I had a lot of fights at this school, so I was transferred to Conrad Elementary by the school district. The Natives were always picking fights with us Punjabis in the 1970s. There were also some Italians, perhaps some Portuguese, being picked on by them as well. Booth, a junior high school, was also rough. When I was in grade eight going to my class, a First Nations guy was trying to get someone. He pushed me down. He says he wants to have a fight with me. I said no. I kicked the locker. The teacher came out and I explained the story about having been pushed down, and how he came back to fight. I used to get calls at home threatening me: "Hey you f—k'n Hindoo, come out here in the park, I want to fight."[81]

During the 1970s, when Punjabis were residentially dispersed throughout the east side, the area was considered to be low income and rough, and it had a high proportion of First Nations living there. Moreover, First Nations children from Metlakatla also attended school on the east side.[82] A Punjabi male recalled the situation at Conrad Elementary School:

> I lived on the east side, which was regarded as a rougher place of town. I went to Conrad Elementary and some of the Natives would bully us Punjabis. The kids would come on a bus from the ferry from Metlakatla. There would be one to two buses packed with kids from the reservation. Some would make a lot of trouble with Punjabis. At that time, there were only about four or five Punjabi kids attending Conrad school. The First Nations kids would shout, "Hey Hindoo, you want to fight?" or "Hey Hindoo! Get out of our country." There were quite a few aggressive Natives always trying to pick a fight with us. They would just come up to us and say, "You want to fight?" Most of the First Nations girls were okay so long as they did not feel pressured to support their brothers or cousins.[83]

While Punjabi males were harassed by First Nations males, the intercultural dynamic changed during senior high school in the late 1980s. Students from all areas of the town attended the high school, as there was only one high school in Prince Rupert. The First Nations students who had instigated fights with the Punjabi students were considered "high risk" and did not make it to senior high school; they had either dropped out of school or begun attending remedial school classes.[84]

When Punjabi children began entering the public school system in the mid-1970s, so did the First Nations children from nearby villages. In the 1950s and 1960s, only a small number of First Nations children had attended public school, since some residential schools were still operating. Many of the First Nations children attending the public system were either mixed race or had lost their Indian status.[85] By the 1960s, some children on Indian reserves were participating in the Indian School Boarding Program (boarding in people's homes while attending school away from home), since secondary education was not available on the reserves. It was only in 1969 that a local Indian School Boarding Program was started in Terrace, because the previous program had placed students far away from their village (such as in the Lower Mainland, Edmonton, and on Vancouver Island) with only marginal success.[86]

In the 1970s and 1980s, First Nations children were bussed in from Port Edward or brought in from the reservations (like Metlakatla) to attend school in Prince Rupert. One educator explained the attitudes of these children: "The mentality is Native versus non-Native. There has been a high proportion of special needs children in the First Nations population. There is defensiveness on the part of First Nations. They are defined or categorized as less than adequate. They have learning disabilities, but the system is too rigid, so many First Nations students drop out."[87] Similarly, another educator noted: "Graduation rate is typically 50 per cent. About half of the First Nations children do not complete their schooling. There is a big dropout rate. Many people blame the residential schools. It is passed down intergenerationally that school is not essential and is not good."[88] As mentioned previously, the First Nations people felt they were being treated as third-class citizens and were immersed in their own struggle for autonomy. Most of their children shared the same attitudes.[89]

As already noted, cohort 2 consisted of the children of immigrant Punjabis who entered elementary school in the newer subdivisions from the mid-1980s onwards. The children in this cohort began their education when their families had become economically established and were able to afford homes in the new subdivisions, away from low-income neighbourhoods and housing projects.[90] For these families, the move demonstrated social upward mobility – that is, a shift away from their earlier dwelling places in the east side or "rougher" part of Prince Rupert.[91] Subsequently, many Punjabis attended the then new Pineridge Elementary School, where there was a large Punjabi presence in the classrooms, along with children of other immigrants. A Punjabi male from cohort 2 explained: "School life at Pineridge Elementary was quite enjoyable. There was so much exposure to different ethnic groups like Italians, Portuguese, and Chinese. I did not experience any problem of racism. It was off in its own world. We were protected. As a child, I knew our physical boundaries. We were not allowed to go to the east side of McBride. It was like the other side of the tracks. But in grade eight, when I started to go to junior high school on the east side, I had a culture shock. It was rough. Some Caucasian boys said, 'Hey you Hindoo! Get out of here.'"[92] According to some interviewees, Caucasian boys did not utter racial slurs only to Punjabis or East Indians; rather, they also made fun of children from other visible minority groups, including the Japanese, Chinese, and Koreans.

The Punjabi female experience at Pineridge Elementary was similar to the Punjabi male experience in terms of intercultural relations between Punjabis and people from other ethnic groups. However, Punjabi females did not speak of having experienced as much discrimination as the Punjabi males had endured at Booth Memorial Junior High School on the east side. For example, one Punjabi female recalled: "At school, I had one Punjabi friend and the others were Italian, Portuguese, etc. As girls we were more restricted than the boys. We could not mix with the boys. So our social life was mostly with family and family friends ... I don't remember racism at that time."[93] Indeed, it was in the home that female children of Punjabi immigrants most frequently experienced double standards in relation to their social life. While they had friends from different ethnic backgrounds at school, they were not allowed to socialize with them as much outside school.

Public Participation and Cultural Synergy

The establishment of social space for Punjabi immigrants that came with socio-economic security set the stage for enhanced interaction with, or participation in, the Skeena region. The new stage saw Punjabis gradually become more fully engaged with the public sphere, which resulted in the development of cultural synergy. After the establishment of the first Sikh temple in the Skeena region, its governing committee undertook initiatives to enhance the Skeena community's understanding of Punjabis and the Sikh religion and sought to engage with, and participate in, the mainstream. The committee would regularly release media briefs to the *Daily News* on positive activities in the Sikh community (such as Punjabis donating money to the Salvation Army and books to the Public Library or the announcement of the annual Guru Gobind Singh Archery Award). Moreover, it provided the local newspaper with quarter-page articles about the Sikh religion and Punjabi culture.[94] Interestingly, the local paper also published articles about social challenges faced by the Punjabi community – pertaining, for example, to gender roles and the Canadian-born generation.[95] Some members of the *gurdwara* committee gave presentations on the Sikh religion and the history of Sikhs in British Columbia at the local high school. A Punjabi man described the Sikh Temple's intercultural role: "The *gurdwara* took an active role in local politics by inviting municipal, provincial, and federal politicians during their respective election campaigns and for auspicious Sikh religious festivals. The Punjabi-Sikhs mobilized themselves to function as a distinct community because they were often misidentified as First Nations. The *gurdwara* committee would encourage its members to wear their turbans on election day to show their presence as a significant community. We wanted the turban [symbol of the Sikh faith] to be an asset, not a liability."[96]

The goal of the *gurdwara* was not only to serve as a place of worship for Sikhs, but also to educate mainstream society about the Sikh faith and Punjabi culture. The Sikh temple undertook genuine initiatives on the religious front. However, since these activities were based in the *gurdwara*, the Punjabi-Hindus and non-religious Indian immigrants in the community were not necessarily involved. Upon her arrival in Prince Rupert in 1977, a Punjabi woman observed: "I was surprised that there was no culture outside the Sikh temple. Nothing was there to share with the greater community. No non-Sikhs went to the temple to learn who we are. The other communities

Prince Rupert mayor Peter Lester congratulating Harnek Singh Brar after he completed a 202-kilometre run from Kitimat to Prince Rupert for the Save Our Future, Run for the Children Fund (1989). Courtesy of Harwant Singh Brar.

were participating in folk festivals, having 'Italian Night' or 'Filipino Night.' At the folk festival I saw the Filipinos put up a booth with food and dance. I began to ask myself that we should do the same."[97]

Other Punjabis interested in Punjabi arts and culture mobilized to fill this gap in cultural activities, initiating and participating in an annual local festival, FolkFest. Generally, Punjabi cultural activities were limited to the local Skeena arts scene. The Prince Rupert India Association, however, was formed to reach out to the broader Skeena community in order to educate others about Indian culture in general and Punjabi culture more specifically. At FolkFest, the association showcased traditional dance, cuisine, and fashion. Oddly, the 1977 official FolkFest brochure stated that the East Indian community was providing a film and slide show on "East India." Notwithstanding the slip-up made by the organizers of the event, the association had gone on to display a cultural store-window exhibit, perform a dance, and showcase Punjabi clothing in the fashion show.[98] This celebration of culture was funded by the Secretary of State and the BC Cultural Fund. While it was funded by government and organized by progressive, like-minded citizens regardless of cultural background, many Punjabis still felt that they were looked upon as the "other" in view of the dominant Anglo-Canadian lifestyle outside the arts scene.

Prince Rupert India Association exhibit at FolkFest (1977). Courtesy of Nirmal Singh Gill.

In the early 1980s, the Prince Rupert India Association organized an "East Indian Night" and participated in the Christmas pot luck dinner. During Vaisakhi,[99] the association served food and put on a show for everyone at the civic centre. The audience included many Caucasians, Chinese, Filipinos, Natives, and Italians.[100] It is significant that just as Sikh preachers encouraged members of the congregation not to allow themselves to suffer the same fate as First Nations and lose their language, a Punjabi woman was motivated to showcase her culture after a First Nations woman confided in her about her experience with the dominant Anglo society:

There was a Native teacher I bumped into when talking about Punjabi culture to the students at the various schools. She requested to interview me. During my interview about our culture, she looked very sad as if she was going to break down and cry. I asked her, "Is everything okay? Did I say something to upset you?" She answered, "I am happy and sad. I am happy that you are able to speak your language and dress in your clothes. I am sad because we were not allowed to speak our language. We were not able to do anything. We had to speak English, and if we did not, we were beaten up." The Native lady then said, "They drowned us. Our children were abused." It seemed by her body language that she was abused. It gave me goose bumps. This interaction made me stronger. I walked away thinking that people can't take my culture or language away from us. I realized that I have to go forward with teaching our culture to the other people in the Prince Rupert community.[101]

As a result of this conversation with the First Nations woman, the Punjabi woman began to celebrate her heritage, beyond religion and language. She helped create the Indo-Canadian Arts Club, the main focus of which was Punjabi dance: *gidda* for females and *bhangra* for males. Punjabi children met weekly to learn about their traditional dance, music, and folk songs. In 1985, these children performed for the first time at the Prince Rupert Art Stravaganza.[102] The Punjabi men also took an interest in the Indo-Canadian Arts Club, and they formed a *bhangra* team that practised weekly through the 1980s. In 1986, the club's *bhangra* team auditioned to represent north-western BC at Vancouver's Expo '86. Along with the dancers of All That Jazz, the Kwe Unglis (Haida) dancers, Peter Orgryzlo and Sandy Gilmour, and the Port Simpson Concert Band, the Indo-Canadian Arts Club was chosen to perform at Expo '86.[103] A Punjabi member described how she felt when the club was selected:

We were so surprised but it was so validating to have been chosen. We were so happy to be representing the Skeena region. We did not do it to represent Punjabis, we did it to represent our Prince Rupert commun-ity. We then had a chance to improve. It was announced on radio, it was the main headline. They interviewed us on the radio. We later got support from the Prince Rupert community as well as the Sikh one. All of the *gurdwara* came to support us at the competition. It gave us confi-dence. Then we got support from the Lions Club, and Betty who worked for multiculturalism Canada. We managed to raise the money for us to go. If there wasn't any, we would have still paid for it ourselves. It was an honour. Expo did not pay our way but they gave us free two-day passes after we had performed. The *bhangra* group comprised all men, the female *gidda* group did not go. I was the only female who danced. We flew to Vancouver and stayed there for a week.[104]

The *bhangra* group was proud to represent its community, Prince Rupert, and the Skeena in general. This cultural milestone gave the Punjabi commun-ity confidence to move beyond the arts scene and enter events like the annual Sea Festival, which was meant for the entire community. While Punjabis had previously participated in cultural events organized by those engaged in the Skeena arts scene, once they gained confidence in showcasing Punjabi cul-

Punjabi girls performing
gidda at the Prince Rupert
Arts Stravaganza (1983).
Courtesy of the Prince
Rupert & Regional Archives,
The Daily News Collection,
P2003-115-4154.

ture, they entered events for all citizens. Punjabis did not reject their heritage, but neither did they live separately from other people. Rather, while still keeping their traditions, Punjabis began to engage with the larger community within the public sphere.

By the mid-1980s, when Punjabi families had become more established and the community had grown to a substantial size, a shift occurred, with members now actively seeking to establish relations with the larger Skeena community at the various Prince Rupert multi-ethnic events. The Punjabi float and dance group at the Sea Festival were integral to the event in the 1990s and continue to be to this date. In some years, the float won first prize in the "best ethnic" category, which began in the late 1980s.[105] Moreover, the float included coastal emblems, such as the orca, rather than merely displaying elements of Punjabi culture. The most striking element observed in the 2009 Sea Festival was the nature of the reactions of some First Nations people. They were excited by the way Punjabis showcased their culture. Their comments about the Punjabi float seemed quite different from their stories about inter-

top | Punjabi float at the Prince Rupert Sea Festival (2008). Courtesy of Jean Eiers-Page; above | Punjabi *bhangra* dancers at the Prince Rupert Sea Festival (2008). Courtesy of Jean Eiers-Page.

community relations from the 1960s through to the early 1990s. One woman from the Nisga'a said: "Sea Festival was really great. I really liked the Punjabi float and dance group. They did a good job showing their culture. They have our respect."[106] A man from the Nisga'a Nation described the intercultural relations of the time in the light of cultural validation: "In the 1970s, some First Nations had tensions with people coming and taking the jobs. The First Nations did not know who those people were. Now the interaction is good with other groups of people. There is more attention to the First Nations as a people. Fifteen years ago, there was nothing. But now we see it in education, culture, etc. East Indians understand our cause for the land. Maybe they did not know it earlier."[107] Indeed, there was a disregard for the First Nations' culture of dance, arts, and crafts from the 1970s though to the mid-1990s; for example, children from all backgrounds were instead required to learn square dancing at school.

Completely absent in those years was the cultural validation of the region's indigenous people. Cultural validation involves acknowledging and understanding the historical, religious, and cultural identity of diverse peoples, and this can often result in the breaking down of barriers.[108] Therefore, diverse ethnic communities getting to know and understand each other has been pivotal in towns like Prince Rupert. Cultural validation is also important in minority identity development, as will be discussed in chapter 9 with respect to the children of Punjabi immigrants.

As in Prince Rupert, the Punjabi community of Terrace participated in the activities of the larger Skeena community. In contrast to Prince Rupert's focus on the arts, however, greater attention was given to sports. There were various sporting events, including *kabbadi* and an East Indian sports day. Besides sports, Punjabi language classes were offered at school and Punjabis participated in the town's celebration of Canada Day. A former temple committee member explained: "I was on the Sikh temple committee. On Canada Day, the Punjabi community got involved with the parade. Starting around 1979, mill workers made a float. Some wanted to put Sikh flags on the float. I said no, because it is Canada's birthday, not India's. People don't know us. They have to get to know us."[109]

Punjabis also began the practice of raising the Sikh flag at the Terrace city hall for the Vaisakhi Parade. However, in 2002, in an attempt to prevent some Terrace citizens from raising a rainbow flag (representative of the gay community in Terrace), the municipal government banned proclamations by or for any ethnic, religious, or social group.[110] Nevertheless, a gay organization – Queer Youth Alliance – has been permitted to participate in the annual Prince Rupert Sea Festival Parade with its own float.

Much discrimination had been experienced in the Skeena region throughout the 1970s and 1980s; the Punjabis nonetheless made a concerted effort in showcasing their religion and culture as a part of the local community. As Punjabis gradually succeeded in establishing religious, cultural, and social space for themselves, they began to feel, in turn, that they were members of the larger Skeena community. Their participation in various cultural events was primarily intended to inform and connect with the whole community; the Punjabis were oriented towards educating others about their Punjabi heritage. As a consequence, there was an experience of connectedness between the Punjabis and the other people of the region. Various groups could meet as equals and share their heritage.

CHAPTER 8

Cultural Synergy, Ethnic Insularity, and the Public Sphere II

From the 1960s up to the 1990s, most Punjabi immigrants to Canada, having left village Punjab, sought to establish a new space for themselves as Canadians in the Skeena region. Whether they lived in Prince Rupert or Terrace, Punjabis viewed these towns as Canadian "villages." Indeed, the towns seemed similar to what they had been accustomed to back in the Punjab. A Punjabi man explained: "I came from a small Punjabi village with a strong community base. You want to have that again. We were able to develop that in the small town. I did not want to leave Terrace, but I shifted to Surrey because our family is here now ... I miss Terrace but now all the mills are shut down, the logging is shut down. Now in a big city we really feel out of place. We did not have Punjabi radio or TV shows. In Terrace, we would get together with family and friends on the weekend. In Surrey, no one knows anybody, everyone is too busy."[1]

Punjabis in the Skeena prefer the small towns of the region because everyone knows everyone else, the cost of living is lower, there is a stronger social network than in the cities, and goods and services are close by. The decline of British Columbia's forestry and fishery industries, however, forced many Punjabis to move from their initial settlements in the Skeena region, where they had been able both to recreate a village atmosphere and to connect with the larger Skeena community.

Ethnic Insularity in the Multicultural Vancouver Metropolis

Relocation to large urban centres has resulted in Punjabis having to readjust to a different Canadian lifestyle. This relocation process has not only involved socio-economic re-adaptation, but also has required socio-cultural readjust ment, during the course of which differences in the workings of the country's multicultural policies in small remote towns as compared to in large urban settings may stand revealed. Upon moving to an urban location, the Punjabi community experienced a kind of "culture shock," especially with regard to the shift from the cultural synergy they had experienced with the mainstream in the remote towns of the Skeena region to the ethnic insularity they experience in Canada's large urban centres.

Cultural Disorientation in the Punjabi Enclave

Many of the early Punjabi migrants to the Skeena region had faced a language barrier. Since many initially had difficulty speaking English, they tended to band together, or "self-segregate," both in terms of where they resided and in terms of their participation in public activities. Not only did Punjabis socialize mainly among themselves in Punjabi homes, but they did the things they had been accustomed to doing in village Punjab. Humans generally gravitate towards the familiar. Keeping to one's own group for intra-group support has been used by Punjabis as a coping strategy to overcome language and acculturation barriers while economically adapting to Canadian society. However, over time Punjabi families learned English and became active participants in the larger Skeena community. One Punjabi man explained: "Punjabis congregate with each other because of the language barrier. When Punjabis speak English, there is no problem with other people like Italians and Portuguese. You have to make the first move with your neighbour. They have to get to know you and then everything is fine."[2]

Language is an asset in the adaptation process. Even though Punjabis initially experienced intercultural tensions, the gradual acquisition of English-language skills empowered them to establish a space for themselves and create a Punjabi presence in the larger Skeena community. In turn, they also developed a sense of belonging both to the region specifically and to the country of Canada in general. Indeed, Punjabis grew to enjoy their new space as Canadians in the Skeena region. Economic security was key to their adaptation to their new country of residence, but it also enhanced their self-confidence, allowing them to connect with the larger community. The result was cultural synergy: the combination of different cultural assets of the various ethnic groups on a basis of shared values yielded a civic fruit that was greater than the sum of its parts.

Upon relocating from the Skeena region to large urban centres, the Skeena Punjabis have experienced some cultural disorientation. Having to adjust to living in a Punjabi enclave in a Canadian metropolis is the daunting challenge frequently identified by the relocating Punjabis. In retrospect, they have been surprised that the space they had created for themselves in the Skeena region could not be found in their new locations, especially given the large concentrations of Punjabis in areas like Vancouver, Surrey, and Abbotsford.[3] At the same time, the kinship chain of migration has served to reinforce clustered residential patterns, especially in areas where housing is very expensive.

As in the initial settlement of the Skeena Punjabis, new immigrants arriving in BC's Lower Mainland have preferred to live among members of their clan, village, or region, since they share a culture, language, and religion. Most of all, however, clustered residential patterns are directly related to the socio-economic factors often faced by newer Punjabi immigrants as they adapt to a new society and economy. This is especially true in the large urban centres where major swings in the housing market have sometimes reduced the availability of affordable housing to new entrants in the market.[4] New immigrants often choose to live in ethnic enclaves out of economic necessity.[5] With minimum-wage work and high real estate prices, many Punjabi immigrants can only afford houses if – to meet the conditions for a mortgage – various extended-family members hold shares in the house and secondary suites are rented out. Similarly, those Skeena Punjabis who had not entered the housing market in the Lower Mainland prior to the economic bust find it a challenge to relocate to the large urban centres, since their housing assets in the Skeena region are of lower financial value than comparable housing in the Lower Mainland.

Besides overcoming the language barrier and becoming economically secure in the Skeena region, Punjabis developed cultural synergy in their multicultural environment by relying on the general values of their culture and religion, such as universality and social equality. They did not focus on the specifics of cultural or religious practices to differentiate themselves from other communities. Despite their initial reliance on intra-group support on arriving in the Skeena region, Punjabis eventually ventured out in the public sphere and developed inter-group relations with other Skeena citizens. It is for this reason that the Skeena Punjabis, upon their relocation to urban centres, have found it odd to see people living as if they were still in India – going about town wearing casual village clothing, speaking mainly in Punjabi, and, especially, remaining and socializing within their own extended-family network. One Punjabi man compared life in Prince Rupert with that in the Lower Mainland thus:

Prince Rupert is friendly because everyone knows each other. A small town is connected and peaceful. We liked Prince Rupert because at that time we were coming from the village. The small town is like the village. My children live in Surrey, but it is busy, you need a car, and everybody keeps to themselves. Multiculturalism is a good system because it brings many people together. If you are now coming from India, you would like Surrey because it is like the Punjab, with all the stores and businesses. Any Punjabi house in Surrey never really watch the news, they just watch dramas as if living in the Punjab. The people now work twelve to fifteen hours seven days per week. They do not know much beyond Surrey. They don't know English. It is a bad thing. They should learn something about here, the language, the news. If you always watch only Punjabi shows, how will you know what is going on? We are paid in Canada, so we should learn the language and customs in Canada. Canada is our country, so I have to think about it. I became Canadian in 1977. I vote. It is my right.[6]

Along with the belief that one ought to take to the "Canadian way of life" – which Skeena Punjabis articulate as offering the opportunity to retain one's heritage while focusing on shared values – the most frequent issue raised by the former Skeena Punjabis revolves around their limited interactions with non-Punjabis or non–South Asians in the large urban centres. Indeed, ethnic enclaves not only result in, but also perpetuate, social fragmentation. The Skeena Punjabis see Punjabis' limited interactions with people of other ethnic groups as a weakness, especially in terms of building a sense of belonging to, and having influence in, the greater community. Note the comments made by a Skeena Punjabi man who resettled in the Lower Mainland: "I wish the Punjabis here in the Lower Mainland were more concerned with the present rather than fixed on the past. I like Prince Rupert better than the Lower Mainland. It was a smaller community and a better set-up. There, you formed attachments. I was involved with many things, the Rotary Club, Chamber of Commerce, Library Board. You felt part of the community."[7]

A young woman of Punjabi immigrant parents described her surprise at the lack of inter-group interactions in the Lower Mainland:

I thought it will be diverse and that I will see different cultures [as in Terrace]. When I worked at Metrotown, I encountered a lot of people from many different backgrounds. I had never heard of Persians, Afghans. In a way, I was culturally handicapped in Terrace. But, after going to school, everyone just sticks together, to their own ethnic group. You rarely see a diverse group of friends. They don't branch out of their own. They don't step out of their comfort zone. I think that is because it is safe to remain with your own group. People have a strong ethnic identity. Everything is ethnic or culture based.[8]

Prince Rupert Sea Cadets (1982). Punjabi cadet bottom row, far right. Courtesy of Jesse Sandhu.

The difference between the Skeena area and urban centres does not rest in lifestyle alone, but also has a great deal to do with "mentality." For some, this recognition of a difference in mentality emerged when they realized that they could not expect to recreate in the Lower Mainland the social environment or cultural synergy that they had developed in the Skeena region. One Punjabi woman described the difference in mentality:

> When we moved to the Lower Mainland, I started a Prince Rupert Night in Vancouver. There were enough people who came from Prince Rupert then living in the Lower Mainland. We held it at the Taj Restaurant on Main Street. We did this for five years or so [1989–93]. Our desire was to promote our Punjabi culture to other people, but [non-Skeena] Punjabis just wanted to keep to themselves. I stopped because I did not like it. In Prince Rupert, the audience was mixed with *gore* [whites], Chinese, Italians, etc. We liked to be mixed, to show people who we are. We did not do the cultural shows for ourselves, we did it to show our ways. If there was anything Canadian, I jumped to the occasion. In Prince Rupert, people respected who we were because of our intercultural effort. It made a difference. Here the audience and mental-

ity is different. There is a lot of talent here, but Punjabis are caught up with themselves. The shows are for them to stick together, not to mix.[9]

While the Skeena Punjabis have been oriented towards showcasing their culture to others and connecting with the larger community on equal terms without rejecting their own heritage, most of the Punjabis living in the ethnic-enclave context of the large urban centres have seemed to prefer to maintain and celebrate their culture for and among themselves. Notwithstanding the tendency to stay among themselves, some progressive Punjabi professionals raised in the Lower Mainland have recently made significant strides in reviving the Punjabi efforts of the 1960s and 1970s – prior to the consolidation of South Asian enclaves – to promote *bhangra* in the mainstream.[10] However, it is worthy to note that unlike the Skeena *bhangra* group – which represented and was supported by the broader Skeena community when it showcased the North Coast at Expo '86[11] – the present Punjabi dance, music, and cinema culture offered in the public sphere of large urban centres is often sponsored by the corporate sector (such as financial institutions and communications companies), which views the now large South Asian or Punjabi communities as viable markets. Interestingly, controversy erupted during the Vancouver 2010 Winter Olympics when East Asian and South Asian Canadians were dismayed not to see their respective communities showcased in the opening or closing ceremonies,[12] an omission that reflected the lack of cultural synergy in the broader Canadian community.

Punjabis from the Skeena region generally dislike the ethnic insularity that can be described as a "Punjabi bubble." The Punjabi bubble has three basic dimensions:[13] (1) the Punjabi community is physically segregated from the mainstream; (2) differences relating to geographic regions in the Punjab (e.g., Doaba, Majha, and Malwa) cause divisions within the Punjabi community; and (3) Punjabis have limited interactions with people from other ethnic backgrounds. For instance, a Punjabi female described her surprise at the concern in the urban centres over "homeland" regional differences: "My Punjabi friends at college would want to know which village (*pind*) I was from and which side of the river I was from. I had no clue."[14] Besides an orientation towards regional differences in the Punjabi bubble (e.g., whether the family came from the Doaba, Majha, or Malwa region), there are other points of reference for contextualizing or framing a person's place in the group, including caste, physical traits, spending habits (conspicuous consumption), and religious and political affiliations. Significantly, in contrast to Punjabis in large urban centres, the Punjabis living in the Skeena region gave greater attention and importance to occupation, level of education, proficiency in English, and degree of economic adaptation.

The Prince Rupert *bhangra* dance group at Expo '86, photographed by Siwik Productions (File no. X321A), Vancouver (1986). Courtesy of Pam Nijar.

While Punjabis who moved from the Skeena region to large urban centres often expressed discomfort over the limited interactions with the larger community after relocating, some members of the community also realized that they had limited exposure to the specifics of their own culture and religion. Some children of Punjabi immigrants who moved from Prince Rupert or Terrace to the Lower Mainland found that they did not know as much about their own culture as the Punjabis living in the Lower Mainland did: "I remember the Vaisakhi Parade [in Terrace]. Everyone participated in it, but ours was only twenty minutes long and then everyone went home. Here, the Vaisakhi parade [in Surrey] is much longer and more festive. I brought a Caucasian friend from Terrace to the one in Surrey and she loved it. I did not know about Diwali [and other Punjabi festivals] until I came to the Lower Mainland. I was culturally retarded in Terrace; in the Lower Mainland I have a lot to learn about different cultures."[15]

In contrast to the Skeena region, where Punjabis showcased the general aspects of their culture to educate others (in the context of the desirability of sharing values), Punjabis in the Lower Mainland demonstrated more knowledge about the specifics of their cultural and religious traditions. This was the result of their putting greater emphasis on maintaining, and at times asserting, their Punjabi identity.

A Visible Ethnic Minority Group

The notions of "visible minority" and "racialized groups" mean much the same thing; while the former is generally used by the general population, the latter is employed by social scientists. Social scientists prefer to use the term "racialized groups" because it underscores the social construction of the concept of race, a concept often based on superficial physical variations when in fact there are other underlying issues at play, such as class.[16] Even though there were intercultural tensions in the Skeena region, Punjabis made an effort to be active participants in the mainstream community. This effort was not about being a visible minority; rather, it was about participating as an active contributor to the local socio-political and cultural landscape of the Skeena region. Multiculturalism in the region served as an opportunity to showcase one's heritage before the larger community, while at the same time embracing shared values. Over time, cultural synergy emerged in the larger Skeena community. Cultural synergy was experienced as the "shared" or "common" meeting of various peoples in the public sphere, without anyone's heritage being rejected.

Brian Ray and Valerie Preston[17] put forward the argument that people belonging to a visible minority group experience less ethnic and cultural tension in small towns than in large urban centres.[18] However, while a person of a visible ethnic minority may find it easier to live in a small town than in a metropolis, it is critical to note that the relatively less tense atmosphere in the Skeena region took the Punjabis (and immigrants in general) over two decades to achieve. The intercultural dynamic of being part of the larger local community was not something that was simply handed over to the Punjabis upon their arrival in the region. Note the following comment made by a Punjabi man:

> We had to come to the downtown from the bunkhouse. We would
> go in groups of three to four. People bothered the bunkhouse men.
> We were called "Hindoo" or "Paki," mainly at nighttime. Some
> whites would shout out "Hindoo," but it was mostly the Natives. The
> Natives could get physical but that was mostly at night when under
> the influence of alcohol. Half the men at the bunkhouse were married,
> waiting for their wives to migrate to Canada; the other half were single
> men. We did not go out much at night because it was not really safe.
> In 1972, many people did not know who we were. However, over time,
> by the mid-1980s, I did not have much trouble living in Prince Rupert.
> By then, the Punjabi community was bigger and people knew more
> about us.[19]

Indeed, the Punjabi community had to endure intercultural tension and fend for itself over a significant period of time as it created space for itself in the region. However, in creating space for themselves in the Skeena region, Punjabis also developed a sense of belonging to both the region and the country. Their orientation was towards belonging rather than towards negating where they came from. It is precisely for this reason that many children of Punjabi immigrants find it offensive, and do not like, to be referred to as "Indo-Canadian" in the urban setting; they find it an alienating experience to be labelled as a hyphenated ethnic minority. In the Skeena region, Punjabis referred to themselves as "Canadians of Punjabi heritage." Therefore, after their relocation to large urban centres, they feel that the term "Indo-Canadian" relegates them to "immigrant citizen" status because it differentiates them from the mainstream even though many of them were born and raised in Canada. Moreover, Skeena Punjabis find that while people tend to use the term "Indo-Canadian" for South Asians, they rarely use it for those belonging to a non-visible group; thus, Skeena Punjabis regard the term "Indo-Canadian" as a prejudicial one. In the Skeena region, they were Canadians of Punjabi heritage, just as their friends were Canadians of perhaps Italian, Portuguese, or Chinese background. Shared citizenship was the focus.

Intercultural tension in the Skeena region was undeniably strong at the beginning, but it eased over a couple of decades through a natural process. In the large urban centres, however, there tends to be less space for intercultural interaction, while the sense of belonging tends to be found with a visible minority group. Punjabis who either migrated to the Skeena region or were raised in that region are surprised at how they are perceived by both Punjabis and non-Punjabis in the large urban centres. A Skeena-born Punjabi man who relocated to the Lower Mainland, described his experience: "I cannot be boxed in. The Caucasians and Punjabis in the Lower Mainland look at one another as if in different categories. I am neither."[20] It would seem that the immigrant's tendency to gravitate towards the familiar, the general society's lack of understanding of the Punjabi community in a multicultural setting, and actual or perceived experiences of being discriminated against as a visible ethnic minority within the ethnic-enclave context have played large roles in the Punjabi community's isolation in the large urban areas.

Skeena Punjabis still find themselves grappling with the Punjabi bubble, a contentious phenomenon especially when they have to come to terms with being viewed as a visible minority – a second-time experience for immigrants and a first-time experience for many of the children of immigrants, particularly those in cohort 2. Punjabis who lived in the Skeena region interacted more with other ethnic groups than those who lived in a large urban centre with a large Punjabi community. The degree to which Punjabis interact socially with other ethnic communities is thus closely related to the size of the Punjabi community. Thus, in contrast to the Lower Mainland with its large Punjabi community, the small towns in the Skeena region evidence greater interaction between Punjabis and other communities apparently because of the small size of the Punjabi communities in these towns.

The feeling of being a visible minority – of being unable to blend easily into the mainstream like some other ethno-cultural groups can – poses a problem for Skeena Punjabis who relocated to the Lower Mainland. The issue most frequently raised in regard to this problem concerns the biased and negative portrayal of the Punjabi community in the mainstream media.[21] Like the Lower Mainland Sikhs,[22] the relocated Skeena Punjabis find the manner in which the Punjabi community is depicted in the mainstream media as deeply problematic. Since the events surrounding the Khalistan movement and the Air India tragedy (the largest terrorist attack in Canadian history), the turban has become conflated with terrorism.[23] There is no doubt that the Punjabi, especially the Sikh, community is largely misunderstood in mainstream society, where religion and culture are often misrepresented as having a predisposition for violence.[24]

Both Skeena and Lower Mainland Punjabis (especially Punjabi-Sikhs) are dismayed by the media's negative and biased portrayal of the community. However, the two groups differ in their interpretation of this negative portrayal, and the difference lies in the different frameworks used in viewing inter-group relations in small towns or in large urban centres. The Skeena Punjabis have established themselves in the larger community and consider themselves to be a part of that community, whereas the Lower Mainland Punjabis established themselves within their own community and for the most part function within an ethnic-enclave context. In effect, social fragmentation exists in the Lower Mainland, where non-Punjabis view Punjabis as the "other."[25] A Skeena Punjabi male now living in the Fraser Valley underlines the impact of such fragmentation:

There is a lot of ignorance in the Fraser Valley. It peaked in the 1980s. The community became more visible and a lot more concentrated in the city. Before, the community was more spread out and less noticeable. Racism becomes bad when the community is big. The community becomes the target. We should not segregate ourselves. People have the fear of the unknown. We need to educate others at grassroots level. Punjabis don't take the initiative in the city to educate others. The media inflates cultural negativity and brings up unrelated negative events of the past when reporting news or events of the community.

For example, when the media reports on a peaceful event at the Golden Temple, they always have to bring up 1984 and Air India.[26]

The negative portrayal of the community in the media, especially in the Lower Mainland, perpetuates the social alienation of the Punjabi-Sikhs. Other South Asian groups make a concerted effort to distance themselves from the Punjabi-Sikh community to establish the point that they are different from the negative depictions of this subgroup.[27]

The Heterogeneity of the Punjabi Enclave

Visible minority group identification inevitably, and often erroneously, categorizes a group of people who share a common ancestry as a homogeneous group when in fact the group members are spread along a broad continuum. It really does injustice to Punjabis to speak of them, as the media often does, as if they belong to a distinct homogeneous group. There is no such thing as a specific Punjabi immigrant experience. The Punjabi community is not a single, monolithic entity, and differences in the diaspora relate not only to variables pertaining to the immigrant, such as gender, level of education, proficiency in English, native country location (city, town, or village), and length of residence, but also to less personal variables, such as whether the migration was from another part of the diaspora (e.g., the UK) and the geographical location of settlement in Canada (attitudes towards South Asians vary from region to region).

The heterogeneity of the Punjabi diaspora is further highlighted by the migration of Punjabis from small towns to large urban centres. A relocated Punjabi man shared his observations: "Lower Mainland people are in groups. They stay amongst each other. Everyone in Terrace worked together, lived in the same neighbourhood, and shopped together. Vancouver Punjabi community comprises many groups; there are political ones, religious groups, groups based on caste, village, or region."[28] This different aspect of life in Vancouver had implications for the Skeena Punjabis who had relocated to large urban centres. As a result of the relocation, Skeena Punjabi-Sikhs have been absorbed in the Sikh diaspora of Vancouver while the Skeena Punjabi-Hindus have been similarly absorbed in the Hindu diaspora. However, the Sikh and Hindu Punjabis who moved from the Skeena to the Lower Mainland regularly get together at weddings and other auspicious occasions. These gatherings evoke recollections about the "good old days" in their earlier remote Canadian habitat. However, in contrast, the Skeena Punjabis have difficulty relating to the more recent immigrants from the Punjab. One Punjabi man explained:

We just went to where there was work. New immigrants don't understand Canada; all they know is Toronto, the BC Lower Mainland, and Calgary. In Surrey, there are so many people but no one knows anyone. All the people want is money. There is a lot of greed. A few old school East Indians [who have been here for a while] have become entrepreneurs in development, construction, and farm owners. They are exploiting the new East Indian immigrants. The new immigrants come and don't know how the Canadian system can help them. After some time, they realize that they are being exploited and then they try to do their own business.[29]

Indeed, just as a cohort of Skeena Punjabis have managed to move from working-class positions to property and business ownerships, many of the Punjabi families who arrived in the Lower Mainland from the early 1900s up to the 1970s are well established, at the very least as proprietors, while some have founded businesses (e.g., in forestry, construction, janitorial services, and farming) and others have moved upward by entering the professional sector. As a result of these advancements, a dynamic between established and more recent immigrant families has emerged: Punjabi proprietors rent homes and/or basement suites to new or more recent immigrants, and Punjabi entrepreneurs hire new immigrants for their cheaper labour.

While there are economic disparities between the established and more recent immigrants, it is significant that the concepts of "new" and "old" immigrants are not cut and dried. Many families settled in the Skeena region during the same time period – the 1960s and 1970s – that extended-family members and/or people from their villages settled in the Lower Mainland. The Skeena Punjabis and their Lower Mainland kin have differed in their orientation to Canada even though they arrived in Canada around the same time. Thus, the Skeena Punjabis have differed in their orientation not only from the newer immigrants who have been arriving since the 1990s.

The new or more recent immigrants have arrived in Canada in a different era, one that has seen the formation of ethnic enclaves. Since the 1980s and 1990s, a new kind of ethnic enclave has emerged; ethnic concentration is now located in the metropolitan suburbs.[30] It is important to recognize the underlying factors that have influenced their development. In the Canadian metropolitan context, the ethnic enclave is cited as being the outcome of two intersecting factors: first, immigrants' housing search behaviour (i.e., kinship and clan networks) and, second, the structure of the local housing market.[31] The formation of the ethnic enclave involves a three-stage process: (1) the nucleus of an ethnic group is established in a neighbourhood; (2) households of other ethnic groups withdraw[32] while those of the same ethnicity as the nucleus fill the vacancies; and (3) the consolidation of the enclave takes place through the setting up of services and institutions that cater specifically to the ethnic enclave.[33]

A similar process has been observed in the Lower Mainland, most notably in the formation of the South Asian enclave in South Vancouver and the East Asian enclave in Richmond. However, when analysing the formation of the Punjabi enclave in Surrey's Strawberry Hill and Newton area bordering Delta, it is important to note that the initial stage of the enclave's formation was not voluntary but was rather a result of societal pressures to live apart from the mainstream. The construction of the Guru Nanak Sikh Gurdwara was only tolerated in an undeveloped location, which subsequently led to the development of the surrounding Strawberry Hill and Newton neighbourhoods.

Around 200 Sikh families lived in the Surrey-Delta area during the mid-1970s. The Guru Nanak Sikh Society was registered in 1973 and purchased an old house on 83rd Avenue and 112th Street in North Delta, which it converted into a *gurdwara* in 1975. Non-Sikh residents complained that the *gurdwara* ruined the Delta neighbourhood, especially with respect to the congregation taking up all the street parking space. In February 1977, fire damaged the *gurdwara* beyond repair. Without a temple and the non-availability of a Delta community centre, the Sikhs – without municipal approval – quickly repaired the *gurdwara* for worship. The *gurdwara* was temporarily repaired and re-opened in April 1977. The City of Delta eventually granted the Guru Nanak Sikh Society permission to rebuild it, even as non-Sikh residents near the property lobbied against the project.

Caught between the Guru Nanak Sikh Society and non-Sikh residents, both the City of Delta and the City of Surrey approached the Society to re-locate their temple on Scott Road, which forms the border between Surrey and Delta (at that time an unpaved border). Guru Nanak Sikh Society acquired seven acres of land on the Surrey side of Scott Road in 1973; however, the City of Surrey had previously turned down the Society's proposal to construct a *gurdwara* at that location. This area was undeveloped and had no sewage system. To defuse non-Sikh hostility toward the construction of a *gurdwara* in Delta, the City of Delta assured the Society that if it built the new *gurdwara* on the Surrey side of Scott Road, it would be given access to Delta's sewage system. The Guru Nanak Sikh Gurdwara was built according to traditional temple design and completed in 1981. The location, known as "Scott and 72nd," has since the construction of the Sikh temple become a major shopping district, with many Sikhs living in the surrounding neighbourhoods.[34]

While ethnic enclaves are often critiqued on the grounds that visible ethnic minority immigrants tend to "self-segregate," it is important to keep in mind that visible minorities have not always been welcomed to settle in Anglo- or Euro-Canadian neighbourhoods – that is, the latter preferred that visible minorities live among themselves.[35] The land for non-Christian places of worship has usually only been available in isolated or undeveloped areas. Once the places of worship are built, the surrounding areas often develop into highly concentrated ethnic neighbourhoods.

It is also worthy of mention that Surrey's Strawberry Hill and Newton areas, discussed above, were developed with lax bylaw enforcement, which opened up the area for low-income and visible minority clusters.[36] In a sense, the development of the Strawberry Hill and Newton areas appears to resemble "planned segregation," whereby low-income housing and dense residential developments are kept away from the owner-occupied, single-family-housing neighbourhoods.[37]

Newer Punjabi immigrants can now settle in suburban areas like Surrey as if they were in the Punjab. In neighbourhoods with large Punjabi concentrations, the expectation of interactions between non–South Asians and Punjabis is relatively low. Large concentrations result instead in limited intergroup interaction, while "integration" most often occurs with the pan-ethnic (Indo-Canadian or South Asian) community[38] rather than with the larger Canadian society. While the word "integration" has re-emerged in recent social policy discourse on the management of ethnic diversity, in the 1960s the term suggested conformity with the dominant Anglo culture. Moreover, the word "integrate" has been viewed as offensive to some members of ethnic minorities because it can imply that one ought to be integrated into "the right" system. The term can also erroneously connote the sentiment that immigrants are inherently lacking in the ability to "fit in" with mainstream society. Perhaps, rather than using the concept of integration, it would be more appropriate to use the concept of cultural synergy within the public sphere – different groups using their cultural assets while collaborating on the basis of shared values – something that was achieved by the multi-ethnic Skeena community and serves as an example of how cohesion ought to work in Canada's pluralistic society.

Viewed through an outsider's lens, the Punjabi community may appear to be homogeneous on the basis of its shared ethnicity, history, and language. However, with the ethnic or pan-ethnic boundaries emerging with migration and settlement in ethnic enclaves, intra-group relations sometimes predominate. The internalized sense of belonging with one's ethnic or pan-ethnic group narrows the common ground for a sense of belonging to Canada as a whole. As explored in chapter 9, intra-group factions or rivalries emerge within the enclave environment. Given the heterogeneity of the

Punjabi community alone, this separate pan-ethnic identification can hinder the development of a sense of shared Canadian citizenship. Moreover, pan-ethnic identification within an ethnic enclave can lead to the pan-ethnic communities being used by political parties as potential voting blocs outside a shared Canadian public sphere.

Political Participation and the Ethnic Vote

Punjabis have come from India, which is not only the world's largest democracy, but also a hybrid political system that holds the modern state and traditional society together.[39] Moreover, given the geographical location of the Punjab and its long-standing history of foreign invasions, it is inevitable that Punjabis would have a strong political ethos.[40] Punjabis have therefore brought this aspect of their culture to the Skeena region and to Canada in general. In addition to that common feature, the geographical location of their settlement within Canada also influences their political culture and the local practice of multiculturalism. Punjabi political involvement in the Skeena region therefore differs from that in the Lower Mainland. Indeed, the nature of the political arena in which Punjabis can mobilize political power differs from region to region. In the Skeena region during the period when the resource industries were thriving and unions were strong, Punjabis managed to mobilize political influence via the labour unions. In contrast, in the Lower Mainland, where – unlike in the Skeena – there are large concentrations of Punjabis, political parties sought the Punjabi vote through various religious places of worship.

Punjabi Political Involvement in the Skeena Region

In line with the Sikh concern over socio-political matters in the secular sphere, the *gurdwaras* in British Columbia have been centres for mobilizing political power over issues especially relevant to the BC Punjabi community.[41] This is made evident by the Prince Rupert *gurdwara*'s activities. The *gurdwara* designated one room for discussions of socio-political matters, and committee members would meet with politicians, criminal justice personnel, social workers, and educators. Mayor Lester, who served on the city council from 1958 to 1994, and former lieutenant-governor Iona Campagnolo, who served on the Prince Rupert City Council from 1966 until she turned to federal politics as a Liberal MP in 1974, would regularly meet with the *gurdwara* committee to discuss the Punjabi community's distinctive needs as well as to consult with it on issues regarding the city of Prince Rupert as a whole.[42]

Besides taking part in the temple's socio-political activities, Punjabis exercised their right to vote, whether in union or in municipal, provincial, and federal elections. Punjabi political involvement in the Skeena region, however, related mainly to the unions (PPWC, UFAWU, and IWA) and the municipal government. Punjabis used political leverage primarily through the unions, and some of them were actively involved in the management of unions. For instance, the president of the Pulp, Paper and Woodworkers local from 1995 to 1997 was Kal Sandhu, a Punjabi.[43] Likewise in Terrace, Punjabis mobilized political influence through the International Woodworkers of America. One Punjabi man explained: "Some Punjabi men said we should have a Punjabi union leader ... Surinder Malhotra used to live in Terrace and was union president and business agent for the IWA. The New Democratic Party (NDP) had power in the area and had a link with the gurdwara. There was also a connection that the IWA had with the NDP."[44]

Besides Punjabi involvement in the governance of the labour unions, a couple of Punjabi men also ran for election as alderman. Dave Jatana, a Punjabi who was actively involved with the NDP from 1978 to 1995, ran twice, unsuccessfully, as an independent.[45] Dave Jatana explained how he entered the political arena in Prince Rupert:

> NDP wanted a representative on city council. I was always involved in union politics because it was close to what Sikhism says. Graham Lee ran for NDP provincially. In 1972, he took a leave of absence from the radio station and drove a cab. I also worked part-time as a cab driver and I met Graham Lee who also lived near me. It was through him that I learnt about NDP values and mission. I got involved with NDP. In 1981, I was encouraged by NDP to run as alderman and sit as an independent on city council. I had problems on the campaign: someone burnt a cross on my front lawn. I got a lot of media attention. We didn't know who did it. I did not win. My supporters were labourers and the Punjabi community. Labour union guys were also Native Indians and they helped in the campaign. My family was a lot in Punjab politics (my father was a member of the panchayat [council of the village]). I was interested in writing Punjabi literature and politics. I was the first Punjabi to run in politics in Prince Rupert. My support was union, not business.[46]

Although Dave Jatana was not elected to city council, it is important to note that he drew support from Punjabis and labour. Another Punjabi man, Mohinder Singh Takhar, also ran for municipal office and served as alderman in Terrace for ten years. Takhar provided an account of his entry into municipal politics: "People approached the East Indian community for the vote. The mayor approached East Indians for our vote. In 1982, after he left from the gurdwara, we discussed as to why not have our own Punjabi person

Mohinder Singh Takhar on Terrace City Council (1984). Courtesy of the City of Terrace.

involved in politics. Some people asked me to run for politics. I was on the city council from 1983 to 1993. I ran as an independent, for me as a person, not for any particular party."[47] Takhar, owner of Terrace Precut, drew support from the Punjabi, labour, and business communities. Significantly, he was the first orthodox Sikh to be elected to, and serve in, political office in Canada.

In the Skeena region, politicians went to Sikh temples to canvass for electoral support just as they went to churches. Their platform was centred mainly on the demands of the region's labour and the needs of the resource-based economy. The citizens of Skeena generally focused on job security, since the region was primarily dependent on two resource industries. Although the Punjabi community was relatively small, Punjabi involvement in local politics is a testament to the Punjabi political ethos that they had brought with them to their adopted country.

Today, the relatively small Punjabi communities in the Skeena region have lost much of their political clout because of the decline in union power. Moreover, with the large out-migration of immigrant groups from the Skeena region owing to the decline in the forestry and fishery industries, the presence of the First Nations in the towns has expanded considerably, and they are now the demographic majority. In fact, the primary focus of political parties in the region has become the First Nations: "The Native vote has become key in the campaign and elections."[48] In contrast to the Punjabis remaining in the Skeena region, the Punjabis in large concentrations in metropolitan centres have a voice in politics because politicians view them as potential voting blocs.

Punjabi Politics in an Urban Centre

During the first half of the twentieth century, the Vancouver Punjabi – predominantly Sikh but also Hindu and Muslim – pioneers mobilized for their franchise rights, primarily through the Vancouver Khalsa Diwan Society *gurdwara*.[49] At that time, the Sikh temple was Punjabi space, irrespective of one's religious affiliation. With the right to become Canadian citizens and the right to vote being granted to East Indians in 1947, the *gurdwara*'s function as a locus for mobilizing political power in Canadian society expanded. Initially, as early as the 1940s and with greater vigour from the mid-1960s onwards, Canadian Sikhs had been politically active through labour unions. With the increasing size of the Punjabi community, politicians began to canvass the Sikh vote at the *gurdwara*. In turn, the ethnic vote became a valuable political resource for the established Sikh community in mobilizing support at the municipal, provincial, and federal levels in an effort to influence mainstream politics.

By the 1980s, having observed non-Sikh politicians appeal for the Sikh vote, Sikhs had begun to assert themselves more directly in mainstream politics. The NDP (successor to the CCF in 1960) and the Liberal Party were the first Canadian parties to include Sikhs on their electoral slate.[50] In the late 1990s, Sikh political figures emerged in other parties, such as the Reform Party and later the Conservative Party.[51] Meanwhile, with the changes made to Canada's immigration laws, especially in the 1960s, the Hindu and Muslim populations grew, resulting in the building of their own places of worship (*mandir* and *masjid*). The emerging Punjabi Hindu and Pakistani Punjabi Muslim communities have also begun mobilizing at all three political levels to gain influence in mainstream politics. Since the 1990s, major Canadian political parties have sought out or encouraged visible minority candidates on the premise that such candidates will attract votes in designated ethno-racially mixed ridings.[52]

Punjabis, on the whole, embrace the democratic process even though they tend to vote according to kinship or clan loyalties rather than according to the different parties' political platforms or ideologies. In much the way Punjabi leaders use temples for political purposes in India, Punjabis in Canada participate in temple management as a means to engage with the larger polity. Perhaps it is the traditional political role of the temples that has made it easier for Punjabis to adapt to Canadian politics. Temple administrators involved in Canadian *gurdwara* or *mandir* politics are able to attain political status and derive economic benefits while remaining in familiar Punjabi surroundings where there are minimal language, communication, and cultural barriers.[53] On the other hand, with the intra-group competition in large urban centres, different religious and social factions (Hindu, Sikh, Muslim, caste) jockey for power to position themselves as "community leaders." In fact, there is growing concern that the political divisions in the temples are having a negative impact on the community. In line with the political culture of the Punjab,[54] politics within the ethnic boundaries of the Punjabi community have become very factional.

Given the heterogeneity of the South Asian or even Punjabi community, temple administrators cannot be viewed as representatives of the community. However, the large Punjabi-Sikh and Punjabi-Hindu congregations have come to be viewed as potential voting blocs for political parties, and the prayer halls of the Sikh and Hindu temples have simultaneously become forums for mainstream politicians – both Punjabi and non-Punjabi and of all political stripes – to give campaign speeches. While the appeal for the Punjabi vote has generally been associated with the Liberal Party and its multiculturalism policy, this association has been weakening, however, since all political parties now promise political influence to ethnic voting blocs.

Voting Blocs and the Punjabi Bubble

In the last twenty years or so, the Canadian government has attempted, through its multiculturalism policy, to reduce the barriers between immigrants and the rest of society, even as it has had to contend with the rapid increase in immigration. While social policy over the last two decades has focused on community building, politicians appear to have misused multiculturalism by wooing the ethnic vote with promises of funding to immigrant and ethnic groups that live in large concentrations in metropolitan areas such Vancouver, Surrey, and Abbotsford.

The political appeal for the ethnic vote is evident not only in the actions politicians take in the large urban centres, but also in the inaction of politicians in smaller communities like Prince Rupert and Terrace. The Indo-Canadian Sikh Association of Prince Rupert made efforts to engage in a national dialogue on immigration and multiculturalism issues, but was disappointed with the federal Liberal government's seeming disinterest in engaging with smaller multi-ethnic communities. The following excerpt taken from a brief sent by the association to the Special Joint Committee on Immigration Policy in 1975 makes evident its disappointment: "We regret it very much that the Committee found it unnecessary to hold its hearings in Prince Rupert, BC despite vigorous efforts by our Member of Parliament, Mrs. Iona Campagnolo ... The indication is that the Committee will sit only in large centres as per usual practice. The only inference we can draw from this situation is that this Committee also considers that citizens in large urban centres are the only capable people to present their views on such an important national issue, and that residents of smaller communities have nothing worthwhile to offer!"[55] This brief was sent less than a year after the Liberals, under the leadership of Prime Minister Trudeau, won a majority government (1974).

It appears that politicians – with the hope of winning the ethnic vote – have a greater interest in issues of ethnicity and immigration within the ethnic-enclave context. An example of a blatant effort to canvass for the electoral support of South Asians can be found in the federal Conservative Party's 2011 "ethnic paid media strategy," in which both the South Asian and the Chinese communities were discussed as "markets" in which to garner electoral support.[56] Since immigrants often gravitate towards their respective communities as a means of coping with social and economic challenges, multiculturalism can be misused in the political arena.

The misuse of multiculturalism is more salient where there are appeals for the ethnic vote and for the mobilization of support from ethnic organizations and communities. Multiculturalism funds for ethnic communities are generally provided in areas where ethnic groups live in high concentrations, not in the smaller towns. Indeed, politicians tend to promise such funds to organizations that can seemingly garner electoral support in an ethnically concentrated area. The most recent example of "vote buying" – as voiced by many members of the Punjabi community – is the *Komagata Maru* incident.[57] Following Liberal MP Sukh Dhaliwal's motion brought before the House of Commons on 17 May 2007 that the Conservative government make a formal apology for, and provide compensation to those affected by, the *Komagata Maru* incident,[58] the federal Conservative government made an informal apology to the Indo-Canadian community at Bear Creek Park in Surrey shortly before the 2008 federal election.[59] In addition, the Conservative government promised funding for commemorative and educational initiatives through the Community Historical Recognition Program (CHRP) of the Ministry of Citizenship and Immigration.[60] As part of the CHRP "multicultural initiative," the government allotted a million dollars to the Khalsa Diwan Society to build a museum in commemoration of the *Komagata Maru* incident.[61] The announcement of the funds for the society, which is located in the riding of Vancouver South, was made several months prior to the 2011 federal election. Some community members, especially of the Canadian-born generation, demanded that the funds be used for mainstream multicultural initiatives, such as a permanent exhibition in the National Museum in Ottawa; they also asked that a formal apology be made in the House of Commons, over and above the earlier informal declaration made in an ethnic neighbourhood.[62]

Besides their efforts in the funding of "multicultural initiatives," politicians also involve themselves in intra-ethnic factional politics in their pursuit of electoral support. The 2011 federal election campaign in the riding of Vancouver South is an example of politicians exploiting Sikh factional divisions to achieve their own political goals. The riding was a major battleground, especially because in the previous 2008 election Liberal incumbent Ujjal Dosanjh had held on to his seat by a slight margin of only twenty votes,[63] with Dosanjh capturing 38.49 per cent of the vote and Conservative candidate Wai Young 38.44 per cent.[64] Subsequently, from 2008 to 2011, the federal Conservative government made great efforts to win the "Indo-Canadian vote," such as granting funds to the Khalsa Diwan Society to build a museum and having Jason Kenney (minister of citizenship and immigration) make regular visits to the area.[65] The federal Conservatives also appear to have covertly accepted the support of a controversial Sikh faction in their effort to capture Vancouver South from the Liberal incumbent.

A faction of Sikhs sympathetic to an independent Sikh state (Khalistan) opposed Ujjal Dosanjh,[66] who during the 2011 campaign often spoke out against religious fanaticism and violence, even though, back in 2001, he had made a campaign stop at the pro-Khalistan Sikh temple Dasmesh Darbar (founded by the now banned International Sikh Youth Federation) during his unsuccessful bid to be provincial premier (as leader of the NDP). However, controversy erupted when Ripudaman Singh Malik, one of the two men acquitted in the Air India bombing tragedy, endorsed Conservative candidate Wai Young because of his dislike for Ujjal Dosanjh.[67] Wai Young denied knowing Malik, although she had attended a function at the Vancouver Khalsa School during which Malik (co-founder of the school) had been present. While the controversial faction supported the Conservative candidate in Vancouver South, it also publicly backed several Liberal candidates in a couple of Surrey ridings.[68]

In the course of conducting field research just prior to the 2011 federal election, the present author came across a very revealing conversation between two orthodox Sikhs regarding the Vancouver South riding.[69] Both Sikhs had been raised in Canada, but one was a Skeena native, while the other was a

Vancouver native who worked as a volunteer in Wai Young's campaign and was also sympathetic to the Khalistan movement:

SKEENA SIKH: What's the situation like in Ujjal's riding?
VANCOUVER SIKH: It's tight. We're supporting the Conservatives.
Ujjal is anti-Sikh. He has to be stopped
SKEENA SIKH: You're supporting the Conservatives? But they're a bunch of wanna-be Republican right-wingers.
VANCOUVER SIKH: I'm not a Conservative. I'm supporting the Liberals in Surrey. I'm Liberal too but Ujjal disrespects the Sikhs; we got to get him out ...
SKEENA SIKH: Then fight it in the riding association, not in the damn election ... I'm thinking of Canada, not about *desi pind* (homeland village) politics.

This conversation not only further demonstrates how faction politics is played out in the Lower Mainland ridings, but also underscores how location – whether in a remote town or ethnic enclave – can influence one's orientation to, and participation in, the democratic process, despite the locations' similarities in religious orthodoxy.

The Vancouver South riding case highlights how Sikh faction loyalties – rather than Canadian party platforms – are played out in the political arena of an ethnic enclave. Since politicians use Sikh factionalism to their political advantage, they are, in a sense, exacerbating intra-group conflict as they try to capture the mythic "bloc vote." In fact, while Wai Young defeated incumbent Liberal candidate Ujjal Dosanjh in the 2011 federal election, the results indicate that none of the three immigrant or visible minority candidates could actually rely on ethnic or immigrant solidarity.[70] This also held true for the Surrey Newton-North Delta riding, where incumbent Liberal candidate Sukh Dhaliwal lost his seat to NDP candidate Jinny (Jogindera) Sims.[71] Indeed, the ethnic communities in both ridings did not vote as a bloc,[72] but rather followed the general voting trend of the election, where vote-splitting on the centre-left dimension (Liberal and NDP parties) allowed the Conservative candidate to win.

It is also worthy of mention here that the media erroneously situated the controversial Ripudaman Singh Malik in an ethnic-enclave context when in fact he has been residing in the exclusive Vancouver neighbourhood of Shaughnessy for over thirty years and runs a business in contemporary women's apparel and accessories (Papillon Eastern Imports Ltd) located in Vancouver's trendy Yaletown business core.[73] As an example of erroneous reporting, note CBC senior correspondent Terry Milewski's description of Malik: "Malik is probably the most notorious resident of Vancouver South, bar none."[74] There is no doubt that this type of exaggerated and misleading government-funded reportage reinforces negative stereotypes attached to ethnic enclaves, while at the same time inadvertently maintaining the exclusivity of the Shaughnessy citadel.[75]

In wooing the ethnic vote, mainstream politicians attend cultural centres and places of worship, validating the celebration of particularistic cultures in the socially alienated enclaves. Validation in the ethnic-enclave context is made evident in the speeches made by politicians. Note the observation of a relocated Skeena Punjabi man:

> In 2008, during the federal election campaigns, I went to the *mandir* [Hindu temple] to watch the Ramayana during the Diwali [Festival of Lights] celebrations. Several politicians gave their campaign speeches at the *mandir*. They only talked about more funding for bigger cultural celebrations or expediting the family-sponsorship application process. In the Skeena, politicians went to churches and temples, but their speeches were about our needs in the Skeena community, a resource-dependent region. We were always concerned about Alaskan overfishing and the raw pulp and timber not being processed locally.[76]

Indeed, the speeches in the Lower Mainland ethnic enclaves mainly focus on immigrant citizenship, the celebration of one's culture in the enclave context, and promises about improving the family-sponsorship process. While politicians jockey for power in the ethnic-concentrated neighbourhoods, they appear to make little effort to focus on the socio-economic issues and equal membership concerns relevant to the inhabitants of those neighbourhoods. A relocated Skeena Punjabi male commented on the Punjabi role in politics:

> In the Lower Mainland, the city politicians want the ethnic vote through the *gurdwara*. What makes me sick is that white politicians mention that their forefathers were immigrants, too, and worked in the lumber mills and farms, too. They try to make it seem that they are like us. But none of the political parties in Canada allow Punjabi people [immigrants] into the power broker circles. Punjabis are used as pawns and tokenism. Multiculturalism is supposed to be good. It is good if it is used to do what it is supposed to do. But politicians are buying the ethnic vote. There is no such thing as bloc voting but politicians are desperate for any type of vote. Now Canadian politicians go to India to get votes in Canada. It is all a show for votes. It was totally

unethical when Prime Minister Stephen Harper took a candidate to India and presented him as the next MP of a Brampton riding [in Metro Toronto].[77]

Through their actions, politicians can create the impression that an ethnic group is being celebrated. Yet there also exists the feeling in the Punjabi community that Punjabis are being left behind. In other words, while their ethnicity is celebrated, they are left out of decision-making circles.[78] Similarly, a former organizer for the federal Liberal Party, Sukhi Sandhu, formally issued a letter complaining about the marginalized role South Asians have: "I have heard many horror stories of the promise or wish list of many prominent members in our community as rewards for their contribution in electing the next Liberal leader."[79] Sandhu argues that South Asians, rather than simply serving as mechanisms for signing up large, mass grassroots support, should seek greater influence over policy. While political parties view large Sikh and Hindu congregations as potential voting blocs, many Punjabis of the "silent majority" consider the temple bloc vote to be a myth, given that the community is so heterogeneous.

Summary

Punjabi migration to the Skeena region involved a range of multi-faceted intercultural interactions with people belonging to various other immigrant communities and – more significantly – with people of the First Nations. The ethnic composition of the Skeena region is diverse, and therefore the intercultural dynamic has been complex. A multi-ethnic milieu does not necessarily translate into a multicultural celebration of culture. While the Skeena region was ethnically diverse, there was initially much intercultural tension and hostility. The First Nations people had their own struggle, embedded in a long-standing history of oppression (cultural devastation and unresolved land and water claims), and Anglo-Canadians had a history of being the social elite of the region. Meanwhile, the ethnic immigrants were perceived as a hardworking labour pool.

Punjabi immigrants experienced hostility from the First Nations and discrimination from the Anglo-Canadians. Skeena Punjabis had to invest considerable effort to create religious and cultural space for themselves. With improved socio-economic security, Punjabis asserted themselves and became a social presence in the region, which allowed them to become more engaged in the public sphere. As Punjabis participated more fully in the larger Skeena community, they developed a sense of their own belonging to the region. Ironically, their motivation in maintaining Punjabi culture and language stemmed from the stories they had heard about the cultural and economic dispossession of the First Nations. The cultural synergy that emerged in the Skeena region developed gradually, with the different ethnic groups, including First Nations people, Anglo-Canadians, Euro-Canadians, and Asian-Canadians, taking the initiative to educate others about their cultural heritage as well as to work in collaboration with others on the premise of shared values.

The Punjabi community, with relocation, had to readjust to the Punjabi bubble extant in the large urban centres. The ethnic enclaves in these centres, unlike the communities in the small remote towns, are marked by only limited interactions with non-Punjabis. Interactions are limited to, and more reflective of, pan-ethnicity. According to Punjabis who have come from the Skeena region, the limited intercultural interactions in the large urban centres are problematic, since the ethnic-enclave context can hinder the development of a sense of belonging to a culturally diverse Canadian society. At the same time, in viewing visible minorities as simply ethnic markets, political parties validate the Punjabi bubble as a convenient means to win the (mythic) ethnic bloc vote. Meanwhile, the relocated children of Skeena's Punjabi immigrants feel the contrast in their experiences of multiculturalism as practised in small remote towns and large urban centres. The shift from the cultural synergy of the Skeena region to the ethnic insularity of the urban centres has profoundly altered Punjabis' sense of what it means to be Canadian, the topic of the following chapter.

CHAPTER 9

The Second Journey: From Remote Towns to Urban Centres

Punjabi settlement in the Skeena region entailed a range of multi-faceted intercultural interactions and tensions. While the Punjabi community was collectively establishing itself within the larger Skeena community during the 1970s and 1980s, the children of Punjabi immigrants were forming their own identity based on their ethnicity and their experience of inter-group interactions in the public sphere. For these children, the inter-group experiences occurred primarily in educational and athletic settings. Regardless of the intercultural tensions during this period, these children gradually acquired on the school and athletic playground a sense of "being a part of" the larger Skeena community, without negating or rejecting their Punjabi heritage.

For Punjabis, the complexity of identity formation has been amplified by the Punjabi community being forced, in a sense, to relocate to an urban environment after having established itself in the Skeena region. This relocation, or second journey, of the Punjabi community has involved economic re-adaptation as well as emotional and social readjustment. This second journey has revealed, in effect, significant differences in the ethnic identification of the children of Punjabi immigrants, depending on whether such identification was made in remote towns or in large urban settings. The children who formed their identity in the social context of multiculturalism in the remote towns of the Skeena region have had to renegotiate their ethnic identity after they moved to urban centres, such as BC's Lower Mainland, Calgary, and Metro Toronto. Relocation to urban centres involves a departure from an identity revolving around cultural synergy and a profound shift towards ethnic insularity, where there exists a sense of "being apart from" the broader Canadian society.

This chapter provides an ethnographic narrative of a Canadian-born male of Punjabi immigrant parents who was born in the Skeena region in the early 1970s but had to relocate to Metro Toronto in the late 1980s, as there was growing economic uncertainty in Prince Rupert. Subsequently, in the early 1990s, he moved to the Lower Mainland to pursue post-secondary education, but he returned periodically to the Skeena region to work in a fish cannery during the summer months. This single narrative about the experience of a second-generation Punjabi man – one who, after having been raised in Prince Rupert in the 1970s and 1980s, had moved to a large urban setting – sheds light on two important areas: (1) the experience of children of Punjabi immigrants who grew up in a remote but multicultural town when the initial wave of Punjabi children were entering and proceeding through the educational system (cohort 1); and (2) the experience of those Punjabis who had to renegotiate their ethnic identity when they encountered the Punjabi community in a large urban environment.

This chapter consists of three parts. The first explores the literature on ethnic or minority identity development within a pluralistic environment. The theoretical inquiry in this part is necessary in order to establish external validity for the generalizations that are offered here with respect to the psycho-social processes that children of ethnic minority immigrants experience in Canada.

The second part contains the ethnographic narrative, which is based on the narrator's personal experiences, especially when he began to attend primary and secondary school. It offers important insights into the specific Canadian-born Punjabi experience of inter- and intra-cultural conflicts. This part is based on an analysis of five main types of data: (1) face-to-face, semi-structured interviews conducted in English with the narrator (who, given the sensitive nature of the content, requested to remain anonymous) in August 2009, September 2009, and January 2010; (2) semi-structured interviews conducted with other Canadian-born Punjabi men and women who grew up in the Skeena region in the 1970s, 1980s, and 1990s; (3) semi-structured interviews with two school friends of the narrator's; (4) semi-structured interviews with two educators who taught in Prince Rupert in the 1980s (as corroborative evidence); and (5) analysis of the local *Prince Rupert Daily News* along with Vancouver and Toronto periodicals (as corroborative facts).

Lastly, the third part of the chapter analyses – within the framework of minority identity development – the social challenges that the initial wave of children of Punjabi immigrants experienced as they entered the education system in the Skeena region, as well as the contrasting experiences they had after relocating to large urban centres.

Ethnic Identification and the Children of Immigrants

Adolescence, according to Western psychology, is a developmental stage in life during which youth form and establish their identity.[1] This developmental stage is marked by a conflict between identity formation and role confusion between the ages of twelve and eighteen. The self-differentiation process is said to lead ideally to a developed sense of the self and personal identity, whereas failure in self-differentiation results in role confusion and a weak sense of self.[2] Since self-actualization is founded on the modern ideals of self-orientation and personal autonomy, many immigrant parents from cultures that have a collectivity orientation may not be attentive to the needs that are vital for their children's personal development, even if they have moved to an individualistic milieu.[3]

The children of immigrants undergo a process of personal development where their initial socialization agent is within the home, but as they enter the school system, they are introduced to the values of the dominant culture. Since teachers in Western settings have an individualistic orientation, these children often experience cultural incongruence early in the educational cycle.[4] In effect, there is a lack of synergy between their two primary socializing agents: the home and the school. It is in this environment of contrasting world views that children of immigrants undergo a process of identity development based on their ethnicity and minority status.

Building on Erik Erikson's stage of identity formation during adolescence, African-American psychologist Janet Helms has established a four-stage model of minority identity development: (1) *pre-encounter stage*, when individuals prefer the dominant cultural values to those of their own group; (2) *encounter stage*, when youth encounter societal forces (such as discrimination) that lead to the feeling that they will never be able to become a member of the dominant culture and consequently gradually begin to identify with their own minority group; (3) *immersion/emersion stage*, when individuals completely endorse their minority culture while simultaneously rejecting the values of the dominant society; and (4) *internalization/commitment stage*, when individuals integrate both their personal and their cultural identities. In this last stage, individuals resolve the conflicts and discomforts that arose in the immersion stage; this results in an objective examination of the cultural values held by other ethnic minority individuals and groups as well as cultural values of the dominant group. While the desire to eliminate discrimination or oppression persists, it may manifest itself in the performance of simple acts that are consistent with the individual's minority ethnic identity.[5]

Minority identity development interplays with inter-group relations. Adolescents from different ethnic backgrounds have complex interactions whereby social and contextual factors come into play in identity development. The developmental view holds that there is a correlation between security in ethnic identity and greater acceptance of people belonging to other groups; that is, the more positive the image an ethnic or dominant group has of itself, the more positive the attitude it will have towards other groups.[6] Meanwhile, social structure also influences individuals' sense of their own ethnic group as well as their sense of the out-group. For instance, while equal socioeconomic status makes for positive relations, dissimilar status gives rise to negative relations.[7]

The contact that children and adolescents have with one another outside of school influences inter-group attitudes within the school setting.[8] In fact, young people's contact out of school in their neighbourhood is more important than their contact within their school, since interactions outside of school are voluntary.[9] Moreover, relationships among social groups in existing settings have a history and a future, where individuals can bring prior knowledge to an inter-group situation to affect inter-group relationships positively.[10] On the other hand, if prior interactions are of a negative nature, even in one's neighbourhood, they can give rise to negative relations.

There are many variables – besides self-esteem – that influence inter-group relations. Social status and stereotypes interact with historical and political factors in the social setting. Therefore, one's awareness of the history and culture of any group that one interacts with can enhance understanding and lead to more positive relations. The Skeena region's multi-ethnic makeup and the widely different histories of its social groups resulted in complex inter-group relations. An apparent mutual misunderstanding of one another's histories undeniably adversely affected intercultural relations in the schools in the late 1970s and 1980s (cohort 1), which is made evident in the following ethnographic narrative.

"Being a Part of" or "Being apart from" Society? An Ethnographic Narrative

I was conceived in a trailer park in Terrace, born in Kitimat, and raised in Prince Rupert. My parents migrated to the Skeena region in 1969 through the family-sponsorship system. My father initially worked in the lumber industry and then upgraded his skills by obtaining a trades ticket in metal fabrication. My mother first worked in a poultry farm and then as a motel chambermaid. She told me that she was the first Punjabi woman to work as a chambermaid in Terrace because "in those days dark-skinned people did not work in clean, dry jobs that involved public interaction." My mother said that she got the job because the motel manager mistook her as Italian due to her brown hair, light eye colour, and fair skin. Like others in her family, she later worked in the salmon cannery.

While growing up as a child, I always knew I was different, especially since some of the Anglo-Canadian and First Nations kids would regularly remind me that I was a "f—k'n Hindoo." Sure, I was born in Canada, but I always felt different. As a child, I would try to fit in as best as possible. When I was in kindergarten at Roosevelt Elementary School, I told my mother that some of the students' mothers invited the teacher to their homes for tea and cake. We tried to do the same. My mother invited my teacher; she baked a lemon cake and prepared some Indian tea. At first, I felt good because my teacher had nice things to say about me. However, afterwards I noticed my mother nervously rambling on about how she had made the cake and tea. After the teacher left, I asked my mother what was wrong. She said she felt like a "fool" because she didn't have any "educated things to say." That was the first and last time a teacher came to my home. And looking back, it's not surprising why my mother shied away from interacting with my teachers.

Back in the early seventies, standardized ESL, multicultural, and Aboriginal support programs did not exist like they do today. In grades one and two, I was an ESL student at Seal Cove Elementary School. In the afternoon, a Variety Club minibus would pick up all the ESL kids from different elementary schools. We were a real mixed bag of cultures: Punjabi, Chinese, Japanese, Vietnamese, Italian, and Portuguese. The bus dropped us off at a "central location." For grade one, the central location was actually a room in the remedial high school. It was an intimidating experience, since many of the remedial students had behavioural and substance-abuse problems. In grade two, things were a little better because the central location was a portable classroom at Roosevelt Elementary School. Although I enjoyed interacting with my classmates, I don't remember learning anything. It's all a blur, except for how low I felt when some of the Anglo-Canadian students at my elementary home school called me a "retard" when the Variety Club minibus came to pick me up.

I attended Conrad Elementary School for grades three to seven. Interestingly, I enjoyed grade three, not because I improved my English, but because my teacher was a Japanese immigrant woman. She used to translate stories from a Japanese comic book series. These stories were validating for me because the appearance, behaviour, and attitude of the characters resembled those found in Indian folklore and history. The samurais reminded me of the Khalsa Sikhs with their swords, hair-knots, and disciplined lifestyle.[11]

Grades four to seven were challenging, especially since my English "needed improvement" and I was placed in a classroom with other kids who "needed improvement." These students were mainly from First Nations and low-income Anglo-Canadian backgrounds. Many of the First Nations students were bussed in from Metlakatla.[12] I got along with some, but there were others who always instigated fights by saying, "Hey Hindoo, go back to India." First Nations girls were friendlier than their brothers and cousins. They tended to be shy and had big smiles when joking around. Some kept their hair braided and uncut like the Punjabi girls.

The bullying also occurred off school grounds. Once my father and I went to an Anglo-Canadian bully's house because he would swear at me and periodically throw rocks at our windows. My father tried to converse with the bully's father, but he appeared to be intoxicated and aggressively said, "Get off my property, Hindoo." My father turned to me after leaving their house and said in Punjabi, "You have to punch some sense into him because his father is a sister f—ker bastard." This was my father's advice to me as a fourth-grade student, "you have to fight." And fight we did. Unfortunately, I wasn't much of a fighter, but after a few scraps, the fear of fighting dissipated. Getting into a scrap was no longer a big deal; it was just a part of growing up.

Although I initially reported the bullying to the school administrators, I later refrained from doing so because the "snitches get stitches" attitude prevailed on the playground. My teachers disapproved of me fighting. I think many of them, especially the younger teachers, were too influenced by the Academy Award winning movie *Gandhi*.[13] It seemed like their whole understanding of India was through the movie *Gandhi*, but I was raised in a Punjabi Sikh family. My parents told me stories about Indian freedom fighters, such as Bhagat Singh and Udham Singh,[14] who held the belief that "the use of the sword is justified when all other means have been exhausted." I remember an elder at the Sikh temple giving the same message in his speech during Remembrance Day week: "Hitler was not defeated with non-violence. Canadians lay wreaths on their soldiers' graves, we should put garlands on the pictures of our freedom fighters."

Learning about my cultural background was important to my parents. My mother was more interested in me learning about Sikhism and the Punjabi language, whereas my father tended to like telling stories about Indian historical and political figures. He was a bit of a political buff and would sometimes take me to pro-labour rallies in town. He was a staunch

Sikh scripture (*Japji Sahib*) class at the Indo-Canadian Sikh Temple on Fourth Avenue, Prince Rupert (1983). Courtesy of Surjit Kaur Duley.

NDP supporter at that time. His tool box and lunch kit were plastered with NDP MP Jim Fulton stickers.[15] I think my father's interest in politics was less threatening to him than religion because he cut his unshorn hair and stopped wearing a turban when he arrived in Canada. I never knew he wore a turban until grade three when I was exploring the inside of an old blue trunk and found a lock of human hair and some handwritten Punjabi letters. I asked my mother about my discovery, and she told me that this was my father's hair. She had kept his hair, along with the "romantic" letters he wrote to her prior to marriage, as a reminder of their past. My father never talked about discarding his articles of faith,[16] nor did he encourage us to understand our religious background. For him, Sikh identity was a barrier in Canada. This is why he always instructed Dino, a Greek-Canadian barber on 3rd Avenue, to always give me and my brother a crew cut.

My mother, on the other hand, took me and my brother to the Sikh temple almost every Sunday, and we attended Punjabi language classes two evenings a week. The temple priest taught us how to recite the opening hymn of the Sikh scripture, called *Japji*.[17] Although I didn't appreciate my mother's effort back then – at a time when I'd rather play street hockey with my friends – I am surely grateful for having had that opportunity. Besides, it was nice to bond with the other kids and share our experiences. Many of the older guys started weightlifting and some began taking boxing lessons. The girls tended to be more reserved, and some had the pressure to conform to traditional Punjabi gender expectations. We were often reminded to regard them as our sisters; and we were okay with that because us guys wanted to be tough, and have a "hot" white girlfriend.

We wanted to be the hero. The Italians had "the Stallion" (Sylvester Stallone)[18] and the Chinese had "the Dragon" (Bruce Lee).[19] We had nothing, so we went looking for a hero. That hero was the turbaned Punjabi villain Gobinda, played by Kabir Bedi in the James Bond 007 movie *Octopussy*.[20] We did not see him as the villain, but rather as "the Lion"[21] who everyone dared not disrespect. That's the only film my whole family watched together at the cinema. Kabir Bedi later made several guest appearances in Hollywood productions. Although his character was often that of a wealthy Saudi, we knew he was Punjabi! We were proud to see him respected as an actor and enjoying the luxuries of life, something we all wished we had, even though it wasn't a reality for us. Junior high at Booth Memorial would prove to be a wake-up call to our realities of life.

I shielded myself at junior high by keeping a low profile and making friends with similar students; some were Italian, Portuguese, mixed-blood Natives, and, of course, Punjabi. So long as I didn't venture out of my comfort zone, everything was fine, except for a couple of incidents. These two incidents were unlike anything I had experienced in the past. While attending elementary school, the use of physical force was my means of sticking up for myself; however, in junior high school, I began to fight with hatred and prejudice.

The first incident occurred when I decided to pass by the preppy hangout spot on my way to class. As I walked down the hall, an Anglo-Canadian eighth grader yelled out, "Hey look, it's a Hindoo-Jew." This did not sit well with me, so I challenged him to a fight. When we started to scrap, I could tell he wasn't a fighter and gave him a few punches without using my knuckles. But then I began to hear a chant in the crowd: "fight fight, nigger verses white." That was it. I had to send a message to the crowd. So I gave the kid a knuckle punch to the head. It was over. The chanting stopped and everyone walked away as if nothing had happened. Although I won the fight, I felt I lost the battle because now I was a "nigger." I began to hate "all of them."

The second incident took place when I chose to use the washroom near my classroom, which was situated next to where the First Nations heavy-metal kids would socialize. A tenth grader First Nations student called me a "f—k'n Hindoo," and I reacted by telling him to "f—k off." He didn't like that and pushed my head against a window. The glass shattered and the teachers came rushing to diffuse the situation. We were escorted to the vice principal's office. I was handed the same suspension as the other student, and my father was advised that he would have to pay for half the cost of replacing the glass. I was "pissed off" because I felt wronged by both the bully and the vice principal. My attitude began to change for the worse: when my older cousin offered to beat up the same guy, I told him to "f—k off" and that "I'll kick the shit out of the chug."[22] I was becoming the very thing I hated, that is, prejudiced towards others.

These two incidents were the "highlights" of my first year at junior high school. I basically felt marginalized at school and became disgruntled with the whole education system. My grades plummeted and I stopped caring about trying to succeed at school. I attended another year at Booth Memorial Junior High School, and didn't mind when my family decided to move to Toronto in 1988 as a result of economic uncertainty in Prince Rupert. Even so, I still missed my friends of different backgrounds; we were after all kids who had grown up together. Besides, some of the white girls did not mind asking us brown boys to dance at the school dances.

Toronto was booming. My father quickly found a job because of his training and experience in trades. He was pretty much working six days a week for the first couple of years. My brother, who completed a technical program in British Columbia, eventually found a job in his field; my mother stopped working because of her arthritis and depression. Although finding a job wasn't difficult in Toronto, finding a decent neighbourhood to live in was a challenge. My father found a two-bedroom apartment in Rexdale, in the northwestern region of Metro Toronto. The area was mainly comprised of new immigrants from the Caribbean, South Asia, and Africa. The Italian community had a presence there as well, but they seemed to have been in the area for a longer time and were beginning to shift to new neighbourhoods in Woodbridge. Rexdale pretty much felt like an "inner-city hood."

I attended grade ten at North Albion Collegiate Institute,[23] which is located near Kipling Avenue and Finch Avenue. I experienced culture shock at this school, because, unlike my school experience in Prince Rupert, the Anglo-Canadians were the minority and the ethnic kids were the majority. The different communities pretty much stayed in their own bubble, and within each bubble there were subgroups. For example, in the South Asian bubble there were the new immigrants (or "freshies" as they would be called by their Canadian-born counterparts), Punjabis, Pakistanis, Sri Lankans, and Indian-Caribbeans. It wasn't uncommon to hear a Punjabi kid refer to an Indian from the Caribbean as a "coolie."[24]

The only thing that probably bound all these kids together was their identification with inner-city hip hop and rap culture. I was surprised to hear
Punjabi *bhangra* music being fused with rap and reggae.[25] Unfortunately,
Rexdale had all the hallmarks of an "inner-city hood." The violence and
drug-related themes that are characteristic of some genres of rap, such as
"gangsta rap," were also a reality of life. But I felt different, especially since
I looked like a "small town hick" with my Wrangler jeans, hiking boots,
and John Cougar Mellencamp music albums. Some of the neighbourhood
Punjabi kids jokingly called me a "coconut" or "Oreo."[26] Although they were
Punjabi and clowning around, I didn't like being called "white on the inside"
because I had spent my childhood sticking up for my brownness.

On my first day at North Albion Collegiate Institute, I met with an Anglo-
Canadian school counsellor. I told him I was born and raised in British Columbia and showed him a copy of my school transcript from Booth Memorial
Junior High School. His first question was "Are you a refugee?" My world
was turned upside down as I felt I was being downgraded from a Canadian
to a refugee. He confused me with the Punjabi refugees that arrived off
the shores of Halifax in 1987.[27] Unsurprisingly, I was placed in the non-
academic stream, and my classes comprised of ESL students and juvenile
delinquents.

Unlike Prince Rupert, the culture conflict I witnessed in Rexdale was
more within the group rather than with different groups. I was shocked to
see two Punjabi ESL students fight in the school hallway. It was dishearten-
ing, since one student was an orthodox Sikh, and his turban fell to the floor
and his hair unravelled. Here was the pinnacle of Sikh identity, the turban –
an article of faith for which many Sikhs sacrificed their lives – being
knocked off by a fellow countryman.

After a year in Rexdale, our family moved to Malton, which is an isolated
suburb situated in the northeastern region of Mississauga and bordered
by Rexdale and Brampton. Although Malton was a step up from Rexdale, it
too was composed of new immigrants from South Asia, the Caribbean, and
Africa. Malton had its own share of crime-related problems.[28] We moved
there because it was closer to my father's place of work and the homes
were within our price range.

I completed grades eleven to thirteen at Morning Star Secondary School
(now Morning Star Middle School), which is located near Airport Road and
Morning Star Drive. When I first entered the school, I met with a school
counsellor who was of Caribbean background. This counsellor asked,
"What can we do for you?" I seized the opportunity to tell him my situation,
and that I wanted to be placed in the academic stream. This counsellor

kindly granted my request, and I went on to become a below average student. I was okay with that because at least I was in the "regular" classes. The students at Morning Star Secondary School, for the most part, were motivated to attend post-secondary education. I, for the first time, began to view university as a natural step to take after high school.

From hanging out behind the metalwork shop at Booth Memorial Junior High School, I was now hanging out in the library at Morning Star Secondary School. I felt comfortable at the school library, especially since the librarian, an Anglo-Canadian woman, validated my cultural history. During an orientation at the library, the librarian asked the class if we were familiar with the "Amritsar massacre." The Punjabi students put up their hands and answered, "Operation Blue Star in 1984";[29] however, she was referring to the massacre of 1919.[30] I felt validated, since the library represented a place where my cultural history could be discussed, not discounted, as a worthwhile subject of inquiry. Besides, I met a lovely Jamaican girl whom I enjoyed conversing with.

During my grade twelve year, the hip hop *bhangra* scene began to take off in Mississauga and Brampton. Some enterprising Punjabi youth organized daytime dances at the local clubs as well. These daytime dances coincided with district-wide school PD [professional development] days. It was a clever way for kids to attend a dance without their parents' permission. I was totally immersed in this scene and began to hang out with the hip hop *bhangra* crowd. However, my involvement with this crowd was short-lived since subgroups quickly emerged and kids began to fight each other.

My exit from the hip hop *bhangra* scene did not go unnoticed. One night, a group of Punjabi youth came to a dance with matching shirts saying, "Don't fight brothers, fight others." These words were encircling the Sikh symbol, the *khanda*. I was irritated with their shirts because the words contradicted the meaning of the *khanda*, which represents oneness and unity in all of humanity. We had a heated argument over this. It became clear that these youth were confused about what it meant to be a Sikh. They mistakenly identified the *khanda* as a symbol for Punjabi pride. I soon realized that these youth had a narrow understanding of their cultural history. They were mainly influenced by *bhangra* and Bollywood popular culture. I was searching for something more.

In grade thirteen, I returned to a place that I was familiar with from my childhood – that is, the Sikh temple. The Sri Guru Singh Sabha Gurdwara, located on Airport Road in Malton, is one of the largest Sikh temples in Canada.[31] One morning, I walked into the main hall and bowed before the scripture. The *ragis*[32] were singing Guru Nanak's *Asa Di Var*. I felt at peace while listening to this hymn because my mother had played a cassette recording of *Asa Di Var* in my room so I wouldn't feel lonely when she worked at the fish cannery in Prince Rupert.[33]

After listening to the hymns, I ate in the community kitchen (*langar*) and noticed a familiar quote on the wall, which was, "The use of the sword is justified when all other means have been exhausted." Alongside this quote were several pictures of Sikh separatists holding AK-47s and hand grenades. Banners hung on the wall that read "Long Live Khalistan" and "International Sikh Youth Federation." The administration at this temple misused the teachings of Guru Gobind Singh to legitimize their separatist agenda and fear-mongering campaign.

This movement did not resonate with me because I grew up with seeing pictures of Indian freedom fighters, such as Bhagat Singh, who did not pose with weapons to instil fear in others, but rather worked collectively with Hindus and Muslims to overthrow an oppressive colonial regime. Bhagat Singh, along with his companions at the gallows, Shivaram Rajguru and Sukhdev Thapar,[34] exemplified the totality of Guru Gobind Singh's teachings, such as "God is in Hindu worship as well as in the Muslim prayer. All human beings are the same, though they appear different through our own mistake."[35] I read this quote in a collection of hymns that I received from an elder at the same temple. I had come to learn a simple yet profound life lesson, that is, the universality of humankind.

Near the end of grade thirteen, I received a letter in the mail stating that I did not gain acceptance into university. Feeling disappointed and directionless in Malton, I decided to move back to British Columbia. Several of my cousins still lived in Prince Rupert and invited me to stay with them and work at the salmon cannery during the summer of 1993. It was nice to return to Prince Rupert. Contrary to the past, when the Punjabi community was mainly comprised of labourers, the community had now established itself as successful entrepreneurs and landlords. Many of the Punjabi youth who trained at the gym and/or boxing club forged a solid reputation for themselves and paved the way for the younger generation.

Working at BC Packers was a labour-intensive experience, and after working one season in the cannery I quickly realized the value of pursuing an education. I met with different academic advisers in the Lower Mainland and was pleased to learn that I could apply to university under the "mature student" category and gain admission without having all the entrance requirements. Although I was intimidated at first, I persevered through my studies and became an above-average student. I didn't mind being the first one at the library in the morning and the last one to leave because it sure beat cleaning fish during the night shift. I realized the privilege of having the opportunity to attend university. A lot of my friends were also mature students, most of whom were of Anglo- and Euro-Canadian backgrounds. Our friendship was not based on race, but rather on our common goal to acquire a university education after having worked in a labour environment.

I didn't get involved in the campus social scene because it was too cliquish and tended to be segregated along racial divides; the South Asians, Asians, Anglos, and Euros tended to socialize among themselves. Nor did I get involved in the off-campus Punjabi social scene because there was an emerging Punjabi gang war and, unlike Toronto, the International Sikh Youth Federation in Vancouver used these gangs to maintain control over their temples.[36] Interestingly, most of the Punjabis I got along with at university were from small towns as well, such as Port Alberni, Williams Lake, and Prince George.

University represented not only a place for career-related purposes, but also a place to learn about other cultures. I took a course on Canadian history from an Anglo-Canadian professor who specialized in BC history. I was shocked to learn about the "genocide" of First Nations people by the North West Mounted Police and the residential school program. As he lectured about the residential school experience in BC and the plight of the First Nations peoples, he made reference to the "Metlakatla Natives."

When I walked away from that lecture, I felt both disappointed at myself and anger towards my childhood educators. My personal disappointment was related to me admitting to myself that I held prejudicial views about First Nations people. I felt anger towards my childhood teachers because they never took the time or effort to educate me about the history of First Nations people as well as the history of the Japanese, Chinese, and Indian struggle to become Canadian. Most of my childhood teachers seemed to relish the fact that Canada was not like the United States because Canada was the destination point for the Underground Railroad.[37] I was made to feel indebted to Canada because it was supposedly built on the values of equality, respect, and freedom. But this had not always been the case.

After my first year of university, I still returned to Prince Rupert to work in the salmon cannery during the summer months. I began to have a new-found appreciation for the First Nations people and their culture, and I was able to better empathize with their plight. During one summer long weekend, I travelled to Terrace to visit my cousins. While out jogging, I came across a First Nations man who was heavily intoxicated. He began yelling at me and shouted "you f—k'n Hindoo." I didn't react to his comment, but rather took a moment to empathize with his pain. As I watched him, he began screaming and cursing at himself. When I approached him, I said, "Yo bro, you're gonna be in jail tonight if you keep screaming like that." He looked at me for a moment and said, "Thanks man, you're my brother." Before he went on his way, he gave me a hug. The Anglo-Canadian onlookers appeared to be baffled by what had transpired before them. I wasn't baffled. I felt redeemed.

Working at the salmon cannery also gave me a grassroots understanding of politics. As the salmon industry became volatile due to both Alaskan overfishing and tougher federal conservation policies, Prince Rupert became the centre of controversy in 1997.[38] Our union, the UFAWU, rallied the membership to put pressure on the provincial NDP and federal Liberal governments to stop Alaskan overfishing and to loosen conservation practices. Like my parents before me, I supported the union and NDP because their platform was for the working-class folks.

Glen Clark was the premier of BC and the leader of the NDP during this time.[39] We cheered him on when he told reporters that his government will sue the United States for overfishing BC salmon. David Anderson, former federal Liberal MP and then minister of fisheries and oceans (DFO), was forced to visit Prince Rupert when an Alaskan ferry was blocked by our local fishermen.[40] We felt confident that our efforts would pressure our elected officials to negotiate a solution with the then governor of Alaska, Tony Knowles, and then US president, Bill Clinton. But that didn't happen. It was all political theatre for their urban support base.[41] To add salt to injury, Jimmy Pattison, whom we referred to as the "union buster," finalized the purchase of BC Packers Ltd in 1999 and gradually began outsourcing fish processing to cheaper canneries. That same year, Herb Dhaliwal, a Punjabi Liberal MP from Vancouver, became the DFO minister, but we didn't expect him to act any differently, especially given the fact that the Atlantic cod fishery had collapsed and the federal government was more interested in energy export. Then, in 2002, Glen Clark, our former union ally, joined the Jim Pattison Group of companies. We all felt duped.

I eventually graduated with a bachelor's degree, and after working in several entry-level positions, I found a job in my area of study. I married a Punjabi woman who was also born and raised outside of the Lower Mainland. We initially rented a basement suite in a Surrey neighbourhood that bordered Delta and is referred to as "Sri Delhi" given its large South Asian population. After our children were born, we chose to move to a municipality that is predominantly an Anglo- and Euro-Canadian middle-class neighbourhood. Our decision was based on the rationale that we didn't want our children to be excluded from the mainstream. We wanted them to have access to all the opportunities that we as Canadians are entitled to. And, perhaps it also reminded me of Prince Rupert.

We were the first Punjabi family on our new neighbourhood street. I could tell some of the neighbours felt uneasy about us moving into the neighbourhood because of the stereotypical belief that property values decline when a person of colour moves into an Anglo-Canadian neighbourhood. There is the assumption that all Punjabi people demolish old houses and build "monster homes" with illegal rental suites. After our first week in our home, a city bylaw inspector came by to personally inform us that the neighbourhood was zoned for single-family units only. He also inspected the interior of our house to ensure that there was not an operational illegal secondary suite.

A few weeks later, my wife noticed some graffiti on our driveway. It read "Hindoo." Based on the incorrect spelling and writing style, it appeared that the perpetrator may have been a child. I was surprised that people still held such ignorant attitudes and, more significantly, that these attitudes were being passed on to impressionable children. My wife discretely removed the graffiti and didn't tell our children because we wanted them to feel accepted in our new neighbourhood.

I was disappointed further when my eldest child began kindergarten. I met with the kindergarten teacher for the parent orientation meeting and made it clear at the outset of the meeting that I was born and raised in British Columbia and that I hold a university degree. To my surprise, as the meeting came to an end, the teacher said, "It's going to be different for you because of your schooling in India." A part of me panicked because I was overcome with the fear that my child would be unfairly labelled as an ESL student. I stayed calm and corrected the teacher. She appeared embarrassed and apologized. In spite of that, my children loved their kindergarten experience and enjoyed the opportunity to share their culture and heritage for show and tell.

Even though my children enjoy going to the Sikh Temple, my wife and I decided to take the family to a Christmas play and choir at a nearby church to enhance their interaction with the local community. It was the eve of the 2010 Vancouver Winter Olympics and the Lower Mainland was preparing to host visitors from all around the world. As we sat in the church, I noticed that, besides a few adopted African children, we were the only family of colour in the congregation. Some members of the congregation came by and kindly introduced themselves. My children enjoyed the play and choir, and we also stayed for the sermon afterwards. The lead pastor praised Jesus Christ for being infallible, and continued by saying, "Jesus Christ is not like other gods in the world. I met a pastor from India and he told me that the difference between Indian gods and Jesus Christ is that our Lord never made a mistake!" I felt very awkward, since we were the only family of Indian origin in the congregation. When I turned to my children, they appeared to be uncomfortable with the pastor's remark. My wife and I could not erase this incident like the graffiti on the driveway. My children now had to face the reality that there are people in this country who will judge our religious and cultural background as being "inferior." While driving home, we debriefed the incident, and I was proud to see my children take it in stride when they commented, "We know, Dad. There's good and bad in all communities."

The Second Journey: Renegotiating "Being Canadian"

Janet Helms's four-stage model of minority identity development, discussed earlier, can be used as a framework to shed light on the various stages of minority identity formation. However, it is important to note that this model, along with other models such as that by Jean Phinney, have emerged out of the US environment of white-black binary relations amid a "melting pot" of immigrants. It is, therefore, inevitable that the model does not completely fit an immigrant community that has its own ethnic history, both in the native country and in Canada. Political histories and ethnic geographies are crucial factors in inter-group relations, which, in turn, impact minority identity development. Punjabis have their own history of British colonization, with India eventually gaining its independence in 1947. Although colonialism left a traumatic imprint on the collective Punjabi psyche, the Punjabi experience of political oppression has a different tone than that of the First Nations in Canada. Such differences inevitably influence the minority group's sense of belonging in the dominant culture. Moreover, the aforementioned models do not consider geographical location within a single country as a factor. Such models do not, for example, take into account the difference between the practice of multiculturalism in a remote town and its practice in a large urban centre. Nor do they take into consideration the prevailing ethnic dynamic between the dominant Anglo-Canadian culture and predominant First Nations presence in remote regions.

In the 1960s and 1970s, the Punjabis in the Skeena region were recent immigrants. Since then, the Punjabi community has been going through its own process of consolidation and development in terms of cultural synergy with the larger multicultural population of the region, which rested heavily on labour culture and was predominantly First Nations in its demography. Against this background, the narrative above of a male child of Punjabi immigrants provides important insights into minority identity development, especially in regard to the Skeena region during the 1980s.

The children of Punjabi immigrants who attended school in the 1970s and early 1980s faced the unsettling experience of intense discrimination at an early age. As described in the narrative, Punjabi children experienced discrimination from Anglo-Canadians and hostility from the First Nations. These inter-group relations or clashes undeniably had an impact on their identity formation, especially for cohort 1, the initial group of Punjabi students to enter the education system in the Skeena.

Inter-group Clashes and Resolution

Children of Punjabi immigrants often have to deal with the incongruence between the traditional values they learned within the home and the dominant cultural values that they are exposed to in school.[42] Immigrants from the Punjab have predominantly come from an agricultural society and therefore have brought with them the cultural patterns of a collectivity orientation.[43] Adolescents from Punjabi immigrant families face varying degrees of intrapersonal tension as a result of the lack of congruence between the two socialization agents – home and school.[44] In this situation, there usually takes place a gradual process of differentiation between the values one learns at home and those one learns at school. Instead of preferring the values of the dominant culture (Helms's first stage: pre-encounter), children of Punjabi immigrants experience incongruence between their traditional values learned within the home and the dominant cultural values that they are exposed to in school.[45] Indeed, during the initial phase, as Phinney describes it, ethnicity is in fact unexplored until an encounter that serves as a catalyst for exploration takes place.[46] It is for this reason that critical attention needs to be given to adjustment at school, since school is the principal means by which the children of immigrants adapt to a new country as well as learn to participate in the society.[47]

Inter-group relations were central to the lives of children of Punjabi immigrants in the Skeena region. Along with having their parents stereotyped as "manual labourers unable to speak English," Punjabi children also had to contend with being labelled with terms used for other ethnic or minority groups, like "nigger" or "Jew" – two other minority groups that have had a long-standing history of oppression. In effect, the experience of ethnic discrimination and labelling led many Punjabi children to feel like second-class or minority citizens. A second-generation Punjabi describes the prevailing intercultural dynamic:

> In grade eight, an Italian in my class was bragging that he was related to Mussolini. This kid was desperately trying to fit in. The Anglos con-

gratulated him. They saw it as a cool thing. It was white pride stuff. Anytime they would want to speak derogatorily towards someone they would call them a "nigger" or a "Jew." They would call Punjabis cheap like a "Jew." You could feel the anti-Jew sentiments from the Anglos. We would hear "Hey you f—king Hindoo-Jew." That was only from the Anglos, never the First Nations. Punjabis were thought of as hoarding [saving] money and being cheap and therefore we were like the Jews. One of the supervisors at the fish plant was a Jew. People would refer to him as a "f—king Jew who was cheap and sucking our blood."[48]

The verbal and physical abuse experienced on the playground, as described in the narrative, resulted in feelings of not belonging as well as a growing desensitization to the aggressive nature of inter-group interactions. While some Anglo-Canadians taunted Punjabis with derogatory terms used for other minority groups, the First Nations people only expressed anti-immigrant sentiment by telling Punjabi children to get off their land.

These hostile encounters and feelings of discrimination brought Punjabi children to the realization that membership in the dominant culture was difficult, and this understanding led them to prefer to identify with their own minority group. However, it was not only the Punjabi children who had to contend with discrimination; an Italian-Canadian shared his experience of discrimination: "I went to a private Catholic school until grade ten. Then I joined the public system. It was deadly … I was called 'wop,' other names, and would get into fights. I was put a couple years behind because of my poor English. There was no ESL … When we would go around town, people were not always treating us well. English kids, Native kids, there would be physical fights. After a while we grouped with more Italians in case something developed to protect yourself."[49]

In fact, the experience of discrimination from Anglo-Canadians and hostility from some First Nations people often created a sense of camaraderie among other ethnic groups, especially visible minority groups like the Chinese, Japanese, Italians, and Portuguese. For instance, the Original Foreign Breakdancers, a breakdance group of the mid-1980s, consisted of children of immigrants. One of the original members described the dance team's experience: "In the mid-1980s, we were known as the Foreign Breakers because we all looked like foreigners. No matter how long you have lived in Canada, if you are not white, you will always be seen as a foreigner. The group consisted of one Punjabi, one Japanese, two Chinese, and we had one white guy who justified his membership by the fact that his parents came from Norway, not from England. We competed with other dance teams."[50]

Punjabi children did not, for the most part, fully disclose to their parents the extent of the difficulties they faced in the school setting. Similar to the

Muslim experience in the United States,[51] children of Punjabi immigrants are very aware of burden that their parents have to contend with as immigrants, and therefore they do not always disclose their own experiences of discrimination. One Punjabi father explained: "Our kids were bothered by the Natives at school more than by the white kids, but we did not know about it as much at the time. They did not tell us."[52] The narrator quoted above provided two other examples: he was very aware of his immigrant mother's discomfort in conversing with his teacher and was affected by her feelings of insecurity owing to the language and communication barriers, and while he had a number of physical altercations at school, he only discussed this problem with his father when the vice principal contacted his father to recover the cost of the broken glass.

Notwithstanding their keeping knowledge of such incidents at school from their parents, Punjabi children felt that the prejudices against them were undeserved and they had to stick up for themselves. It is noteworthy here that the parents' reactions further demonstrated to the children that they had to stand up for their rights. With their long-standing historical sense of pride,[53] the Punjabis tend to fight back. The male children of Punjabi immigrants resented being targets of abuse and felt justified in reacting with the use of physical force to assert themselves. In line with the Punjabi warrior culture – a product of centuries of foreign invasions as a result of the Punjab's location on the northwestern gateway to India – the Punjabis developed a "combat ready" orientation to protect their land and way of life. Even though children may have sensed an incongruence between the values learned at home and those learned at school, they nonetheless from a young age selected values, motifs, and images from their own tradition. For instance, the narrator had a "memory of standing up for oneself and freedom" – a sentiment that was cultivated through temple lectures on the freedom fighters as well as through cultural and religious motifs, including swords, pictures of freedom fighters, and portraits of Sikh gurus. Hindus, too, have religious motifs of Hindu warrior gods such as Rama, Hanuman, and Durga. These religious and cultural motifs convey bravery, freedom, and justice, and they are not borrowed from religions imported into India by those who oppressed the Punjabis. Rather, these motifs originated in India's long-standing concept of "just war" expressed in the traditional Indian literature on politics (*Arthasastras*) and were promoted in the ancient Hindu epics (*Mahabharata, Ramayana*). The concept of just war was incorporated into the Sikh religion during the time of Mughal political-military aggression and social oppression. While many Westerners respect Mahatma Gandhi's non-violent resistance to British colonial rule, which was supported by his own interpretation of the *Bhagavad Gita* (a small portion of the war epic *Mahabharata*), it is important to note that the traditional orientation has been to fight back in oppressive situations. Even Rabindranath Tagore disagreed with Gandhi's interpretation of the *Bhagavad Gita* as solely an allegory of the inner struggle between good and evil.[54]

Along with valuing the cultural ethos of protecting oneself and one's community, Punjabi children did not tolerate verbal and non-verbal expressions of discrimination. Importantly, while they undoubtedly believed in standing up for one's self-respect (*izzat*), they did so within the overarching aim of gaining a sense of belonging as a minority group in the dominant culture – that is, of being a part of the Skeena community membership. A Punjabi male remembered how important it was to be proud to be Punjabi: "The older Punjabi guys who had to fight for themselves were proud to stick up for being Punjabi. One day I was at the Sikh temple and as a joke I pretended to be a white guy and said, 'Hey, I'm white.' One of the older and tough Punjabi guys slapped me in the face and said, 'Never call yourself white.'"[55] The male Punjabi children cultivated their sense of being a part of the Skeena community by actively navigating through tense intercultural relations and at the same time asserting themselves in both the educational and the athletic arenas.

Effort in "Being a Part of"

Since Punjabis were relatively new in the Skeena region, they had to make an effort to be known, understood, and accepted as a part of the Skeena community. In the case of the children of Punjabi immigrants, participation in sports became the means by which they could become a part of the community – that is, the playing field was a common and shared space for different groups. For Punjabi males, school-ground scraps and competitive sports were the arenas in which they could organize to assert themselves as "capable, not incapable." Competitive sports provided an even playing field that allowed Punjabi children to prove themselves, at the very least in terms of their physical strength.

Through competitive sports and schoolyard scraps, Punjabi male children gained respect among the youth in the larger Skeena community. For them, the quest for respect was manifested in their strengthening themselves at the gym, engaging in self-defence training, and participating in competitive sports. Children in other immigrant groups also made the effort to fit in by proving that they were "tough": "I had an Italian friend who was teased for being a wop by First Nations and white kids. But when the mafia movies were becoming popular, the Italians inadvertently benefited from it. They were then perceived on the playground as tough, so you better leave them alone. We watched *The Godfather*. So there was a change in the treatment of the Italians, from the kids' perspective, on the playground."[56]

Grade seven Seal Cove Elementary School boys basketball team (1980–81). Punjabi student second from left, middle row. Courtesy of Jesse Sandhu.

The effort to fit in was most evident in the Prince Rupert ball hockey scene.[57] In the mid-1980s, Punjabi males belonging to cohort 1 formed a ball hockey team named "The Big Bad Brown Boys." The name was inspired by the 1970s NHL hockey team the Boston Bruins, also known as the "Big Bad Bruins." Several times a year, the Big Bad Brown Boys played other Punjabi ball hockey teams in the Skeena region, such as teams from Terrace and Kitimat. However, the most intense games were in Prince Rupert, where they played an Anglo- and Euro-Canadian team. These games involved not only Punjabis demonstrating their skill in a Canadian sport, but also Punjabis asserting their physical toughness. Interestingly, the enforcer on the Anglo and Euro ball hockey team was an Italian male who over the years – by winning several schoolyard scraps – had built a reputation for the local Italian community. Meanwhile, the enforcer on the Punjabi ball hockey team was beginning to acquire a reputation for winning schoolyard scraps. A Punjabi male explained how this was a critical moment for Punjabis in Prince Rupert: "This one Punjabi guy beat a Native in grade eight. This put him on the radar. Once on the radar, guys picked on you more. Then, in grade ten he beat an Italian guy in a hockey game. Then, he beat a white guy in a scheduled fight after school. When the Punjabi guy won, he was declared the toughest guy in the school (a title much sought after in a small town like Prince Rupert). That was the first time I was filled with pride and I was proud to be Punjabi."[58]

Another Punjabi male shared his view: "After [—] became known as the toughest guy at Prince Rupert Senior Secondary, the bullying almost immediately stopped at school. The different fighters respected each other, and did not retaliate by ganging up on each other. It is not like the city where if someone loses, they do a drive-by shooting. Up north, the fighters made up and drank beer together."[59]

Boxing was another forum where Punjabi males competed to demonstrate their physical toughness. In fact, ethnic communities have a long history of proving themselves through this sport upon arrival in North America. Note the preamble of the documentary *Facing Ali*: "Let's go back to the beginning. Every race and colour that's ever came to this country has shed their blood in this [boxing] ring. In the 1920s and 1930s, you ask the immigrant nations … Bump! That's why you had all the Jewish fighters, Irish fighters, and Italian fighters. The game hasn't changed. It's just different people playing a part."[60] In this manner, the male Punjabis asserted themselves and were able to demonstrate that they would not tolerate discriminatory abuse; gradually people stopped provoking fights with them. This chain of events in a sense paved the way for future generations of Punjabi boys.

Similarly, First Nations males participated in boxing and were often paired with Punjabi males in the annual Prince Rupert Boxing Association tournament. In line with the goals of martial arts training, these boxers participated in the sport to reach their potential, and they learned to respect their opponents and accept them on equal terms. Note the comment of a Punjabi male:

In the 1980s, Punjabi boys joined the Prince Rupert boxing club and were trained by the late Dick St Louis, a French-Canadian guy who told the First Nations boxers that he had some "Indian" in him. He taught boxing with class. Punjabi boxers sometimes fought the First Nations boxers. Sometimes we won and sometimes we lost. But regardless of the outcome, there was respect … Once a Punjabi boxer overexerted himself in a match against a Nisga'a boxer from the Giskaast (Fireweed/ Killer Whale) clan. By round three, the Punjabi boxer could barely hold his gloves up. The Nisga'a boxer could have easily knocked him out, but he didn't. He let the Punjabi boxer lose with dignity. And for that he had our respect. The Nisga'a boxer's traditional name was HisHiswil-wilgit meaning "He wanted to, but couldn't."[61]

Competitive self-defence training gave these young males a sense of sportsmanship that over time instilled values of respect and dignity that mirrored the values taught in their own traditional cultures.

It is important to mention that while Punjabi youth were propelled to stick up for themselves by participating in Canadian sports, they simultaneously took to other cultural activities, such as learning the Punjabi language and participating in religious services. Their connection with the resiliency aspects of the Punjabi culture served as a source of empowerment [62]

The above narrator described how the male youth navigated through the intercultural dynamic of the Skeena region, but his discourse is gender-specific. A different or double standard applied to the initial wave of female children of Punjabi immigrants. Specifically, Punjabi girls were not encouraged to assert themselves in the public sphere. Punjabi children participated in the same childhood activities as their Canadian counterparts – birthday parties, theme parks, and some sports. However, during adolescence their social activities became more limited in order to discourage dating and partying, in which Punjabi females were not allowed to take part. It was usually not until puberty that Punjabi females actually began to realize that they were different from others, including their brothers. A girl of Punjabi immigrants described the situation for girls: "We were scared as to our parents' reactions with us socializing with others. By grade six and during high school, it was preferred that I socialize with my many East Indian cousins rather than my other friends. We were more scared of getting involved with others because of our parents. There was a double standard with my brothers. My brother had more privileges. Now parents are more open with kids – that is, let them go out with others to socialize."[63]

Notwithstanding the double standard experienced by Punjabi girls from the 1970s to the 1990s, they were allowed to socialize within their family circle of friends: "The East Indian girls mostly socialized only among themselves, with their relatives. The boys socialized much more outside the family circle with their sports. Girls were more protected. There was a double standard for the Punjabi girls in Prince Rupert ... There were more restrictions with regards to not mixing with others when maturing. We were not allowed to cut our hair or wear makeup."[64] As Punjabi boys cultivated respect and built a reputation for themselves and as the local Punjabi community established itself in the Skeena region, fewer restrictions were put on Punjabi females. With improved intercultural relations and the creation of a social space as a result of the Punjabi boys asserting themselves, Punjabi immigrant parents felt more socially secure and thus became more flexible in the social and cultural spheres.

The narrator was part of the first wave of children of immigrants to enter the school system. Concurrent with this wave, the Punjabi community as a whole was going through the process of establishing itself, a process that resulted in cultural synergy between Punjabis and the broader Skeena community, as described in chapter 7. The Punjabi community was relatively new to the Skeena region, and its newness interplayed with the personal development of the narrator. However, once the initial wave of Punjabi children had established themselves among their non-Punjabi peers, their intercultural experience of living in the multi-ethnic small remote towns of the Skeena region improved considerably. A male Punjabi belonging to cohort 2 explained: "Even though we hung out with a multicultural group at school, outside of school we hung out with Punjabi guys who were older than us. They stood up for themselves and gained respect. As they worked out, protected each other like a 'brotherhood,' there were fewer slurs. They paved the way for the other Punjabis. Having gone to Pineridge Elementary, we were also protected. I noticed this when I played on a sports team with kids from the other school. A lot of my friends were First Nations living in Prince Rupert; we established good relations."[65]

The change in intercultural relations is evident among children of Punjabi immigrants raised in the 1990s and first decade of 2000s (cohort 2). These children did not encounter the same kind of discrimination when going through the educational system. A girl of Punjabi immigrant parents born in 1983 provided an account of intercultural relations in Prince Rupert:

> For the longest time I did not have a single East Indian friend. I was
> the only East Indian in my class. My friends were mostly from the First
> Nations, Anglo-Canadian, and Italian-Canadian. There were many
> First Nations. A couple of times I was called "Hindoo" by First Nations
> people. By grade five or seven, I started having East Indian classmates.
> Growing up in a small town made us learn more about other cultures.
> When I was a teenager [1996–2001], if we had a gathering in our house,
> everyone in the Punjabi community would show up. If Punjabis were
> having a party, the Anglo-Canadians would show up. Anyone from
> school would show up.[66]

The nature of intercultural relations is significant in the formation of minority or ethnic identity; once the Punjabi community had become a part of the broader Skeena community, intercultural relations among the various groups became less tense.

Not surprisingly, many of the Punjabi children from the 1990s onwards spoke of having friends from many different groups of people, including First Nations and Anglo-Canadians. A Punjabi girl born in 1988 (cohort 2) described growing up in Terrace:

> We all just hung out together. Our group of friends was tight-knit. They
> are mostly white (Italian, Ukrainian, Portuguese, Greek, Scottish) but

there was also a Vietnamese and two First Nations girls. They know Punjabi words and would say them especially on the field; these are our code words for sports. We never looked at each other as "who are you"; never looked at them being different. We were limited with the people to hang out with ... My group of girlfriends were those that I had grown up with. We were a core group of kids that played together in team sports. It was always the same core group of girls. There is not a whole lot to do in Terrace, so we did a lot of sports.[67]

By the early 1990s, the Punjabi community had established itself within the larger Skeena community, and from the 1990s onwards, the children of Punjabi immigrants generally enjoyed the diversity of their multicultural milieu and at the same time the sense of being a part of the Skeena region. Moreover, the gender divide found in the Punjabi community began to grow less distinct; Punjabi females began playing sports and were less restricted in their social activities. Significantly, Punjabi immigrant parents who experienced discrimination were more protective of their girls than those who felt more secure in their environment and had a greater sense of belonging to the broader Skeena community. Indeed, as immigrants began to feel a greater sense of belonging, respect, and security in their new environment, they started venturing out and mingling with the larger community.

Disorientation at "Being apart from"

Having experienced cultural synergy in the local society – a synergy that had, for the most part, been achieved after the children of Punjabi immigrants in the Skeena region had cultivated a sense of what "being a part of" that society means – the children then had to move to metropolitan centres. They had asserted themselves to become a part of the larger multicultural Skeena community, but after relocating to large urban centres, they found that the orientation of the Punjabi children already resident there was radically different. Rather than trying to "be a part of" the larger Canadian community, their Punjabi urban counterparts were oriented towards "being apart from" that society. Moreover, in contrast to the earlier *inter*-group tensions that cohort 1 had had to contend with in the Skeena region, *intra*-group tensions tended to dominate in the Punjabi or South Asian communities in the larger urban centres. Not surprisingly, both cohort 1 and cohort 2 experienced disorientation when they relocated to urban centres from the 1990s onwards.

The children from the two cohorts who were part of the second journey also experienced much greater differences in socio-economic status in the metropolises than in the predominantly labour towns of the Skeena region.

Earlier, in the Skeena region, they had come to acquire a sense of being Canadian within a multi-ethnic community consisting of immigrants, Anglo-Canadians, and First Nations. Further, as demonstrated in this chapter's narrative, the small towns in the Skeena region had a rough history, with its ethnic minority groups having to assert themselves and contend with much discrimination. The results of their assertiveness, ironically, crystallized into the Punjabis developing the sense that they belonged to the local community that was part of the larger community of Canada.

After relocating to large urban centres, the children of Punjabi immigrants felt pressured to re-examine their ethnic identity. They now had to renegotiate their identity amid intra-group tensions within ethnic enclaves. Leaving the Skeena region resulted in a major shift in cultural synergy; in the Skeena, the narrator had struggled to be a part of the larger community, but after migrating out of the Skeena region to urban Canada (Metro Toronto and Lower Mainland), he found himself entering a new Canadian environment consisting of ethnic enclaves. The narrator's migration to urban Canada meant giving up an identity based on working towards being a part of the broader community and, instead, assuming one based on cultural disorientation as he attempted to adjust to an environment dominated by concerns about being apart from the larger community. A Punjabi female described being surprised by people's concerns over "homeland" regional differences: "I had complete culture shock when I went down to the Lower Mainland. The Punjabis had prejudices against whites. I was called "white wash." My friends [now] were East Indians at college, and they did not have any friends except for Punjabis. They did not mix with people from other groups."[68]

The children of relocated Punjabi immigrants had negative emotions about the ethnic insularity they encountered, initially most often in the context of post-secondary institutions:

I left Prince Rupert to pursue higher education. I went to SFU [Simon Fraser University]. It was strange because the East Indians all stuck together. They were different than me. I came from a small town, where everyone knew each other. Since it was small there was no living a double life. At SFU, the girls raised in Surrey were living double lives in the way that they dressed, socialized. The Surrey girls saw me as a small country girl. They could not see that I was down to earth. Punjabi girls are different here. I was used to socializing with all sorts of people; I could not just be with Punjabis. I also don't like just being with *gore* [whites]. I like diversity.[69]

Interestingly, Skeena Punjabi girls were unaccustomed to the double life they witnessed upon arriving in the large urban centres. Although Skeena Punjabi girls had experienced double standards, they were surprised to encounter Punjabi girls' practising a double life in the Lower Mainland, behaving in the traditional way at home but secretly engaging in Western social behaviour outside.[70]

The relocated Punjabi girls frequently contrasted their earlier experience of not feeling like a minority in the Skeena region to what they found in the urban centres. While they felt that they had come to be accepted in the Skeena region, they remembered being embarrassed when they were singled out as "Punjabi" once they began living in an urban setting. A Punjabi female, born and raised in Prince Rupert, remembered socializing with other Punjabis in the Lower Mainland: "It was like a culture shock. I feel like an outsider. I feel like I am a hillbilly East Indian going there. I feel stared at by Surrey girls. I am used to having friends from all sorts of backgrounds. In Surrey, some schools consist of 80 to 90 per cent East Indian students. In contrast, I only had maximum five East Indian friends."[71] A Punjabi female who was born in 1988 and went through the Terrace school system from the early 1990s until she graduated high school in 2006 described her different experience in the Skeena region: "I see myself as an East Indian girl because there is not many of us. I was not looked upon as an East Indian. I never felt like a minority. I always felt like I was treated like everyone else. There was no difference. We grew up together. People looked at you according to your name and personality."[72]

The relocated Punjabi interviewees, especially the children of Punjabi immigrants, feel that a person may be brown, but he or she is also a member of the broader community. Indeed, the contrasting experiences, which are also underscored in the narrative, comprise a common theme voiced by Punjabi children who relocated to urban settings: rather than having had a sense of being a Canadian of Punjabi background, Punjabi children, once relocated, began to feel that they belonged to a hyphenated, visible ethnic minority group – "Indo-Canadian" – that was seemingly sanctioned by the larger community.

The Intra-group Dynamic in the Metropolis

In the Skeena region, both first- and second-generation Punjabis initially encountered inter-group tension, mainly from the First Nations and Anglo-Canadian communities. In contrast, upon relocating to and re-establishing themselves in large urban centres, the Punjabis encountered intra-group tension. Along with having to adjust to a new life in a large metropolis, where there were neighbourhoods with high concentrations of people from the Punjab or South Asia in general, the former Skeena Punjabis had to adjust to the lack of inter-community relations in their new location. In fact, many of the children of the relocated Punjabi immigrants discovered that some Punjabis practised a "reverse form of racism" against the dominant Anglo-Canadian community. For example, a Punjabi from Prince Rupert described her dismay upon encountering reverse racism:

> I had complete culture shock when I went down to the Lower Main-land. The reverse racism is there. My [Punjabi] friends from Surrey do not interact much with outsiders. They only feel comfortable with *apne* [us]. The mentality is *apne* against *gore* [whites, connotatively "them"]. It is narrow. I value the heritage aspects, which I have been exposed to in the Lower Mainland but you need to interact with everyone and blend with all. When people now come from India, they do not really have to learn English. They go from one India to a smaller one and don't adapt to living in Canada.[73]

In the neighbourhoods with a high Punjabi concentration, a pattern of intra-group tension was apparent to the Skeena Punjabis. For the narrator, it was unsettling to be streamed as an immigrant in an "inner-city hood" because of his Punjabi background, especially since he, along with other Punjabis, had expended considerable effort in being a part of the Skeena region. Regarding the effects of the ghettoization of the Punjabi community, a middle-aged Caucasian Sikh convert commented: "[Because of multiculturalism] there is a 'pickling' effect ... The Punjabi community now does not trust the outside culture. The 'not secure' sentiment is turned inward. It is redirected because of multiculturalism. Its intent is to empower the minority groups and new immigrants, but now it is dangerously keeping the community in the victim mode."[74]

Many of the children of Punjabi immigrants in the Lower Mainland and Toronto had a different orientation from those in the Skeena region; they tended to identify only with their own ethnic group and had limited interactions with others. This inevitably led to insecurity and feelings of not belonging. Indeed, the narrator was branded as an "Oreo" for possessing a strong sense of being a Canadian with a Punjabi heritage. Ironically, in the large urban centres, he was treated as an "other" by other Punjabis. As a consequence of having limited interactions with any group but one's own and feeling insecure within the larger community, people became divided among themselves. Along with this different orientation, there existed, as noted by the narrator, many divisions within the South Asian diaspora, even though there was a stronger emphasis on the fact that a person of colour is a visible minority. In spite of the ethnic cliques on the university campus, the narrator found himself in the company of many Punjabis and people of other backgrounds. In keeping with his Skeena orientation, the binding thread in his relationships was not ethnicity but rather shared labour, a BC small-town experience, and the pursuit of higher education so as to move up the occupational ladder. Indeed, other students from small towns – regardless of ethnic background – also experienced a cultural disorientation in the large urban centres and preferred mingling with "small-town folk."

Interestingly, Helms's four-stage model of minority identity development appears to be more applicable to the children of the earlier Canadian Punjabi pioneers living in large Canadian urban centres, where the Punjabi community is older and evidences greater heterogeneity, than to the Punjabis in the Skeena region. For instance, the third stage, immersion or emersion – when the individual identifies completely with the minority culture – became more pronounced once the narrator shifted to a large Canadian urban centre, where he encountered various groups within the Punjabi community as well as other South Asians from various parts of the world and began participating in "Punjabi pride" cultural events. The intra-group focus is also experienced by females, albeit in the form of pressure to make friends with "one's own kind." Much as the narrator was referred to as an "Oreo" or "coconut," other children of Punjabi immigrants have experienced derogatory labelling because of the collaborative identity that they had formed in the Skeena region. A Punjabi female who was born and raised in Terrace shared her experience of intra-cultural relations in the Lower Mainland:

> Surrey East Indians call me "white wash" as a joke because I have friends from other groups. I don't like how they say it, because they don't step out of their shell. I have more in common with my friend from Castlegar because of the small-town link. My cousins grew up in Surrey, but I don't really hang out with them. I prefer to hang out with some Terrace friends and others from school. I am the only East Indian in my program. East Indian Surrey girls are more into "nursing, sciences, engineering, MD." They say, "Oh, because you are from Terrace." Coming here, I have learnt a lot but not in the way I expected. Everyone is in their own ethnic group, I didn't know it will be separate. [Here] I am a minority.[75]

Another Punjabi female had this to say: "If you have some things in common, then you become friends. I have trouble when people think I should be friends because I am Punjabi or East Indian. East Indians can be hospitable and welcoming, but then you have nothing to say to, or share with, them."[76]

In line with his appreciation of Sikh scripture as universal and with the Punjabi-Sikh history of fighting against oppression, the narrator made efforts to educate not only non-Punjabis but also, significantly, his Punjabi or South Asian counterparts. The narrator took an interest in opposing oppression and enhancing understanding, which is consistent with his Punjabi cultural ethos and the Sikh religion, as well as with the empathy he had developed for the First Nations people.

There is a striking difference between Skeena Punjabis and urban Punjabis with respect to the fourth stage – internalization – which refers to the ethnic group being the primary focus of identity. For Punjabis living in large Canadian urban centres like Toronto and Vancouver, "internalization" had as its referent the dominant Anglo-Canadian culture. On the other hand, for those living in the Skeena region, internalization and the negotiation of personal and ethnic identities were rooted in the individual's relations with both the First Nations and the Anglo-Canadian communities. This difference testifies to the unique intercultural dynamic prevalent in the remote towns of northwestern British Columbia. These discontinuities between the urban centres and the remote small towns underline the importance of geographical location as a pertinent variable. As is apparent, the different geographical locations of Punjabi immigrants have engendered cultural synergy in rural Canada and ethnic insularity in urban Canada.

Unlike what is portrayed in the model put forth by Helms, the resolution of ethnic identity for many children of Punjabi immigrants in the Skeena region was not in reference to the dominant culture, but rather in reference to the First Nations. First Nations played a dominant role in the lives of Punjabi children, especially those of cohort 1, who had physical altercations with the First Nations at school in addition to facing discrimination from the dominant culture. Initially, the larger Skeena community knew little about the Punjabis and only came to know them over time, no doubt thanks to considerable effort on the part of the latter. As with the Skeena community, so with the Punjabis: the Punjabis knew little about the history of other groups, in particular that of the First Nations. However, in due course, Punjabi children learned more of the history of the First Nations and, with this knowledge, came to better understand their situation. In addition to coming to appreciate their cultural similarities and historical differences (i.e., interactions with the colonizers), the Punjabi newcomers developed a feeling of respect for the First Nations.[77] A member of cohort 1 explained: "I am not indebted to Anglo or French Canada. If I am to be indebted to anyone, then it's to the First Nations upon whose land our people have been able to make better lives for themselves. I regret having had altercations with them while growing up as a kid up north. Looking back it feels like someone was playing divide and rule in those days."[78]

The importance of the First Nations in the experience of resolution of ethnic identity is made evident in the narrator's accounts of learning about the

Tsimshian at Metlakatla and feeling "redeemed" after helping a First Nations man who called him "brother." Following these experiences, the narrator developed a greater commitment to his ethnicity and minority identity. It is interesting that the word *taike* (paternal relative) is still used today by first- and second-generation Punjabis and that many First Nations living in the Skeena are familiar with it. If the word is used among Punjabi and First Nations friends, it is used in its original respectful sense of the word; however, when it is used in reference to strangers, it can still carry a derogatory connotation. Surprisingly, many cohort 2 children of Punjabi immigrants use the word *taike* without knowing the literal meaning of the word; that is, rather than "paternal relative," they think it means "Native Indian."[79]

Even though many Skeena Punjabis who resettled in large urban centres have chosen to live near family in Punjabi ethnic enclaves where housing is more affordable, a fair number of them – including the narrator – have made an effort to live in a milieu akin to the Skeena region. In the case of the narrator, he deliberately chose a neighbourhood similar to that of Prince Rupert for his children so that they could experience a multicultural milieu and thus cultivate a sense of being a part of the larger Canadian community, despite some encounters with intercultural discrimination. He preferred this arrangement over living in a highly concentrated Punjabi or South Asian neighbourhood with its tendency to be *apart from* the larger Canadian community and with the accompanying greater intra-group tensions.

Summary

There are different stages in ethnic or minority identity development, and this chapter has focused on them in reference to the children of Punjabi immigrant parents in Canada. While many factors influence ethnic identification, such as socio-economic status and the different histories of the individual ethnic groups, an important and significant variable that emerges in this study is geographical location and the social context of the country's practice of multiculturalism. The narrative in this chapter illustrates the significance of geographical location: inter-group relations predominate in the remote towns of the Skeena region, while intra-group relations are at the fore in the large urban centres like the Lower Mainland and Metro Toronto.

The complexity in ethnic identification is amplified when an ethnic community that had established itself in a remote setting is forced to relocate to an urban centre. This "second journey" entails a shift from cultural synergy with the larger Skeena community to ethnic insularity in the large urban centres. In the course of this shift, the children of Punjabi immigrants – after having formed their identity in the social context of the remote towns of northwestern BC – find themselves renegotiating both their ethnic identity and their identity as Canadians. After having earlier formed a sense of being a part of the larger community, these children have felt disoriented after relocating to the ethnic enclaves in large Canadian urban centres. Their social and cultural disorientation has led members of the Punjabi community in the large urban centres to feel that they are apart from the larger community – which is something that they have great difficulty getting accustomed to, even though the mainstream community generally views them as a visible ethnic minority group. This experience of exclusion is further reinforced with the use of the pan-ethnic label "Indo-Canadian." While the mainstream community tends to look at Punjabis as a homogeneous community, there are in fact many different subgroups within the Punjabi diaspora. As the relocated children renegotiate their ethnicity and identity in the midst of this heterogeneity, one clear question emerges for each of them: "When will I be considered a Canadian?" Or to put it another way, if I am Canadian-born, does ethnic identification with my family history of immigration ever leave me, or can I be seen as just a citizen – not anything else – contributing to Canadian society?

CHAPTER 10

Summary and Conclusions: Resiliency, Cultural Synergy, and Citizenship

This study has examined the patterns of social and cultural transformation that have characterized the Punjabi community, both during its initial settlement in the Skeena region of British Columbia and after its shift to large urban centres as a result of the globalization-driven economic decline of the BC forestry and fishery industries. Even though the second migration has taken place internally, it has been a serious challenge for the Punjabi community, since relocation not only involves socio-economic adaptation, but also requires socio-cultural adjustment to the ethnic enclaves found in the large urban centres. Given the study's complexity, it started with the premise that the most productive framework for delineating the process of social and cultural adaptation and transformation of this community would consist of three key variables: (1) the characteristics of *Punjabi ethnicity*, (2) the circumstances in which *British Columbian labour* was situated, and (3) the policy and practices of *Canadian multiculturalism*. In the course of the research, it was found that to have a fuller understanding of the process of adaptation and the impact of multiculturalism, one should also take into consideration the critical intervening variable of *geographic location* – that is, whether the Punjabis settled in Canada's remote towns or in its urban settings.

Throughout the twentieth century, the socio-economic adaptation of Punjabis in British Columbia was intimately connected with the province's forestry industry, and thus the Punjabis of BC have long been associated with lumber labour. This connection certainly holds true of the Punjabis living in northwestern British Columbia, where the establishment of the Punjabi-owned sawmill in Prince Rupert in 1960 served as a catalyst for the initial migration of Punjabis to the Skeena region. Even after the closure of Prince

Rupert Sawmills, many Punjabis continued to live in the region, as the neighbouring town of Terrace was home to several mills and work also became available at the Columbia Cellulose pulp and paper mill on Watson Island. Although Punjabi immigrants with minimal education could find work in the mills, they were, in a sense, confined to manual or low-skilled labour jobs because of the lack of opportunity to upgrade their education or skills. On the other hand, as a result of Canada's institution of the points system as part of the Immigration Act (1967), some of the Punjabi immigrants arrived with higher levels of education and knowledge of the English language. These educational attributes gave them the opportunity to acquire the necessary skills to work in the trades, and some of them even ventured into business.

With Punjabi men already working in the area, Punjabi women most often migrated to the Skeena region by way of arranged marriages. Although a woman's work has traditionally been within the home, Punjabi women were propelled – out of economic necessity – into the paid workforce during the 1960s and 1970s. They primarily performed seasonal work in the salmon canneries, the same work in which First Nations and other immigrant women were already employed. Since credentials acquired in India were not recognized as equivalent to those acquired in Canada, even educated Punjabi women had to settle for manual labour in the salmon canneries. While the cannery was a place where Punjabi women could earn money, it also served as a base for social networking at a time when they were socially isolated, especially during the early period of Punjabi settlement when a consolidated Punjabi community did not exist. Even though Punjabi women found both economic gain and social benefit in entering the workforce, they had to contend with intercultural hostility while working on the canning lines.

In the 1960s and 1970s, when Punjabis began arriving in the Skeena region, they were, for the most part, not known as an ethnic group to the general community even though various other immigrant communities had already become established in the area. Subsequently, the Punjabis encountered a complex intercultural dynamic in their relations with the First Nations, the Anglo-Canadians, and the more recent immigrant groups. Upon initial contact, the First Nations perceived the Punjabis as immigrants who were "stealing their jobs," while the Punjabis, for their part, made a considerable effort to distance themselves from the First Nations by proving that they, the Punjabis, were both hardworking and reliable. At the same time, some Punjabis experienced discrimination at the hands of Anglo-Canadians, especially when they worked in non-traditional labour jobs that required more education and skill. Although the Punjabis experienced anti-immigrant hostility from the First Nations and felt discriminated against by the Anglo-Canadians, camaraderie emerged at work in their relations with other ethnic immigrant groups, such as the Italians and Portuguese. This intercultural dynamic at the workplace extended into the larger community as well.

During the initial period of settlement, the Prince Rupert Sawmills bunkhouse provided intra-group support and was, in a sense, the centre of the Punjabi community. By the late 1970s, the consolidation of the Punjabi community in the region had begun with the setting up of Sikh places of worship, the purchasing of homes, and the entrance of Punjabi children into the public school system. With the gradual establishment of the Punjabi community, the Punjabis had to contend with anti-immigrant sentiment and discrimination. Rather than excluding themselves from the larger community, however, they made a concerted effort to connect with their fellow Skeena residents. It is noteworthy that their participation in the events of the larger Skeena community grew after Punjabis had developed a sense of socio-economic security and the community had created religious, cultural, and social space for itself. Subsequent to their increased participation in the public sphere, the Punjabis had by the late 1980s and early 1990s begun to feel a sense of belonging to, and synergy with, the Skeena community.

Ironically, in the late 1990s and early 2000s, the globalization-driven decline in BC's forestry and fishery industries, together with the consequential weakening of labour power, coincided with some blurring of ethnic divisions in the Skeena region. Since the decline in the forestry and fishery industries impacted everyone in the region, Skeena residents felt "we're all in it together." However, because local politicians were no longer able to rely on the binding thread of labour, they now had to cater to the First Nations vote, particularly as the region experienced an out-migration of the earlier immigrant families. As in the case of other immigrant communities, the Punjabi community has been undergoing an *internal migration* by relocating to large urban centres. This relocation process has involved both socio-economic re-adaptation and socio-cultural readjustment to life in urban Canada, the nature of which is largely governed by the contrasting location-based immigrant experiences of Canada's practice of multiculturalism, depending on whether it is conducted in small remote towns or in large urban settings.

There is no doubt that social, economic, and political structures constituted one set of determinants in the initial settlement and relocation of the Punjabi community. However, as made evident in this study, Punjabi immigrants have emerged – as they engaged with the new and changing structures of Canadian society – in the foreground as social actors and active contributors to their own social and cultural transformation. In fact, it becomes abundantly apparent that the Punjabis had brought with them from their native country certain cultural assets that have served as an important source of resiliency in their migration, adaptation, and relocation process.

The Enduring Punjabi Community

The Punjabis have been "social actors" in the course of their social and cultural transformation in the Skeena region. This is most evident in the manner in which they have displayed resilience as they navigated through the social structures of Canada in adapting to the Skeena region and then relocating to urban Canada. *Charhdi kala*, an important Punjabi expression that extols fortitude in the face of fear or pain, can be translated as "resilience," as it connotes having or maintaining a positive attitude towards life and the future. In facing the difficult realities of adjusting to a foreign environment, the Punjabis have deployed their own traditional strategies to build their strength and courage. Moreover, Punjabi socio-cultural values and practices have played an important role in fostering resiliency among them.

The narratives of a Punjabi male, a Punjabi female, and an offspring of Punjabi immigrants evidence resiliency and demonstrate how Punjabis, drawing upon their cultural assets, were able to adapt to and assert themselves in the Skeena region. Essentially, each of the three narratives reveals the different arenas in which Punjabis in the Skeena region were able to navigate through the social structures of Canadian society and assert themselves in the public sphere: Punjabi male immigrants showed themselves to be reliable and hardworking, with many of them also being advocates of equal treatment at the workplace; Punjabi women upheld their *izzat*, even as they entered the workforce, by redefining this traditional value; and the children of immigrants, by championing their "Punjabiness" on the school ground, developed a sense of belonging to the Skeena region.

Sawmill Arena

Endowed with an industrious character, the Punjabis were willing to traverse the unfamiliar terrain of northwestern BC under challenging conditions in the hope of finding employment. In their quest for better socio-economic opportunities, however, they experienced many economic and social challenges. In attempting to overcome these challenges, Punjabi male immigrants relied on their Punjabi cultural ethos as a source of enormous adaptive strength. In turn, this ethos played an important role in fostering resilience (*charhdi kala*) among them. Originating in an agricultural society, many Punjabis arrived in Canada with minimal education and poor English-language skills but nonetheless with an enterprising character and a willingness to engage in heavy labour. These latter qualities were foundational in the establishment of the Punjabi community in the Skeena region.

The narrative of a Punjabi man who worked at the sawmill and lived in the bunkhouse (chapter 3) demonstrates how the traditional Punjabi values of hard work, strong kinship ties, and landownership proved to be great cultural assets for Punjabi families and the community at large. Punjabi males, in general, were oriented towards working hard to save money in order to achieve two main goals: (1) to sponsor family members for migration to Canada and (2) to purchase a home and later to invest in rental properties. Kinship and clan relations are very strong among the Punjabis, and this led to a chain of kinship migration to the Skeena region, either through arranged marriages or through Punjabi immigrants already in the area encouraging family members in the Punjab to join them. Moreover, Punjabi families networked creatively among themselves, saving their earnings and pooling their resources to purchase homes and survive economic hardship.

Since agriculture has been the foundation of Punjabi culture, Punjabis have put a high value on landownership. Even when a house has been paid off, Skeena Punjabis have tended to expand their landholdings by acquiring new investment properties. Landownership not only helped Punjabis establish themselves in the Skeena region, but also served as an economic buffer for them during the economic downturn. This is made evident by the fact that many of the early migrants purchased real estate in the Lower Mainland as an investment property that would later be available to their children when they were ready to pursue post-secondary education.

Along with the three central values of hard work, kinship, and landownership, Punjabi men have also relied on other traditional sources of empowerment. According to many Punjabi men, their work in Canada was much more demanding than it had been in the Punjab. However, as discussed with respect to the first narrative, the older immigrants used a traditional communication style of dramatically acting out a situation or telling traditional stories in order to fortify the newer or younger Punjabis for BC labour. Furthermore, while Punjabis relied on the bunkhouse for intra-group support, they also used religious and cultural practices as sources of strength; for example, they turned to their respective warrior gods or gurus for inspiration and engaged in activities reminiscent of the homeland, such as shooting ball and *kabaddi*. Notwithstanding that positive orientation, some of the men turned to maladaptive strategies to cope with their existential situation.

Cannery Arena

Reared with the traditional understanding that a woman's work is within the home, Punjabi women customarily practised *pardah* in relation to the public sphere of Punjab. Migration to the Skeena region, however, served as a catalyst that encouraged Punjabi women to venture out of the private sphere and participate in paid labour outside the home. As demonstrated in the narrative of the first Punjabi immigrant woman to work in the Skeena fisheries (chapter 5), functioning in accord with the traditional custom of fulfilling one's duty (*dharam*) and maintaining one's dignity (*izzat*), the narrator joined the paid workforce in order to improve the economic health of her family. Working in the cannery labour force, however, also came with its challenges of a language barrier, cultural incongruence, and discrimination. For the narrator and many other Punjabi immigrant women, *izzat* – a sense of dignity in relation to one's family and community – served as a source of strength in the face of acculturation stress, intercultural tensions, difficult circumstances (such as widowhood), and inequitable situations (e.g., obstacles to moving up in cannery work).

While the traditional value of *izzat* served as a source of strength and resilience for women, paid labour gave women a new sense of economic self-reliance. The experience of economic independence was a very important step in women's asserting their own autonomy, even as the collectivity remained important in their sense of social connectedness – especially in relation to children and grandchildren. While the traditional value of *izzat* basically applied within the context of a collectivity orientation, it was now extended somewhat to the notion of self-respect in the context of a self-orientation. Women's entry into the Canadian labour force for the sake of economic survival thus had a significant impact on their previous traditional social and cultural patterns of behaviour, as well as on their social and psychological adaptation to the small remote towns in the Skeena region. In other words, as women entered the workforce, they gradually discovered a new kind of respect, one that gave them greater self-confidence.

Labour Union Arena

Some Punjabi men and women arrived in Canada after having received higher education in the Punjab, although their Indian education was not recognized in Canada. Even though their credentials were not transferable, Punjabis with some knowledge of English used that skill to move up in primarily – but not exclusively – in the forestry or fishery industries. However, the Punjabis encountered inequitable conditions and intercultural tensions at the workplace. Although many Punjabis with minimal education or poor English-language skills initially lacked the ability to speak out against inequity, they nonetheless navigated through these barriers by taking advantage of their labour unions, which provided them with a platform from which their voices could be heard. While all workers embraced the union agenda of bargaining for better working conditions and higher wages, union membership for many Punjabis also created, over time, a sense of "brotherhood" and "sisterhood" that transcended ethnicity. Moreover, Punjabi men involved themselves in union politics as a means of addressing socio-political concerns that mattered to them at the municipal, provincial, and federal levels.

Residential Arena

With the consolidation of the Punjabi community during the late 1970s and early 1980s, intercultural tensions emerged when Punjabis began purchasing real estate and their children entered the public school system. The First Nations viewed the Punjabis as "taking their land." Meanwhile, their children – who often shared their parents' mistrust of immigrants and the "white man's" public education system – began to be bussed in from Port Edward or brought in from reservations to attend schools in Prince Rupert. As a consequence, the children of Punjabi immigrants (cohort 1) bore the brunt of intense intercultural tensions in the educational arena.

The third narrative (chapter 9) underscores how the educational arena became the space where children of Punjabi immigrants had to assert themselves in order to develop a "reputation" for the Punjabis. Like their parents, these children also drew upon their heritage – particularly the value of *izzat* – in order to "fight back" or "stick up" for themselves. In response to the hostility of the First Nations and the discrimination of Anglo-Canadians, the children of cohort 1 found themselves not only sticking up for their "Punjabiness," but also simultaneously asserting themselves as equal citizens. In doing so, they developed – as Punjabis – the sense of "being a part of" the larger Skeena community. Significantly, the Punjabis' relations with the First Nations, albeit strained initially, played a role in the Punjabis' comprehension and sense of what it means to be Canadian.

Upon relocating to large urban centres, the children of Punjabi immigrants were surprised to find the Lower Mainland Punjabis perceiving themselves as "being apart from" the larger community. In short, they encountered in their new location an orientation among Punjabi youth that involved an insular form of Punjabi pride, quite foreign to the Skeena Punjabis. The shift from a remote region to an urban centre resulted in a kind of culture shock, and the relocated Skeena Punjabis found themselves having to deal with the unfamiliar milieu of an ethnic enclave.

Multiculturalism and Cultural Synergy

A multi-ethnic milieu does not by itself translate into the celebration or acceptance of ethnic diversity. While the Skeena region has been home to many different groups of people, there was nonetheless at one time much intercultural tension and hostility in the area. The Punjabis initially migrated to the Skeena region when Canada's practice of multiculturalism was in its infancy, while their consolidation as a community (late 1970s) and the process by which the Punjabi community became a full participant in the larger Skeena community (late 1980s) occurred during the initial phases of multiculturalism. The process through which the Punjabis came to experience a sense of shared citizenship reveals the distinctive manner in which multiculturalism operated in the remote Skeena region. No doubt, Canada's policy of multiculturalism allowed the Punjabis to keep their heritage; moreover, it is also apparent that multiculturalism in remote locations – at the very least in the Skeena region – allowed for the development of cultural synergy. This synergy – a combination of the different cultural assets on the basis of shared values – decidedly yields a civic result that is more than the sum of its parts.

Cultural Synergy in the Skeena

When Punjabis first came to the Skeena region, they were, for the most part, unknown to Skeena citizens as an ethnic group. They faced multiple barriers and experienced acculturation stress. To cope with these challenging conditions, the Punjabis initially relied on the intra-group support found at the bunkhouse and then invested considerable effort in creating religious, cultural, social, and political space for themselves.

The policy of multiculturalism facilitated this process in the Skeena region. As noted above, multiculturalism gave Punjabis in the Skeena region the freedom to maintain their heritage while allowing them to meet others on a common ground as equal citizens. Although the acculturation process initially entailed intense intercultural conflict, the Punjabis made a concerted effort to become members of the larger Skeena community. In the process of self-assertion, the Skeena Punjabis sought space in the public sphere and established places of worship in central locations. In doing so, they gradually developed a sense of their own belonging to the region. It is important to highlight here that the acculturation process in the Skeena underlines the crucial point that immigrants have to first feel economically secure and accepted in the public sphere before they can actually experience a shared citizenship. Indeed, the Punjabis had gone through a phase of self-assertion in the common or public sphere before the phenomenon of cultural synergy unfolded before them.

While cultural synergy emerged gradually in the Skeena region, it did occur nonetheless. During this process, the different ethnic groups, including First Nations people and Anglo-Canadians, took the initiative to educate others about their cultural heritage and to collaborate with one another on the basis of shared values. Significantly, as the Punjabis became increasingly engaged in the public sphere and experienced a sense of belonging to the larger community, their reliance on intra-group support waned. The effort the Punjabis made in the Skeena region was carried out with the orientation of being a part of the society. This process led to the unfolding of cultural synergy among the various ethnic groups living in the region, whereby all citizens – without letting go of their heritage – were sustained through a common social link. A relocated Skeena Punjabi male immigrant explained: "We need to find a common thread between Canadian values and the values of ethnic communities. We should not encourage people to celebrate their culture in *isolation*. We should have *unity and diversity*."[1] With multiculturalism practised in this way, Punjabis felt free to keep their heritage even as they participated in the social and political activities of the larger Skeena community; that is, Punjabis experienced a sense of belonging within the entire Skeena community.

The cultural synergy that emerged in the Skeena region can be described by way of the symbolic Canadian maple leaf: "Here in Canada we have a living symbol which every real Canadian loves – the maple leaf in autumn time. One of our great poets has said, 'The scarlet of the maple can move me like a flame.' But actually the maple leaf, sun-treated and frost-tinted, is not plain scarlet. It is a blend of beautiful colours, each distinct in its own sphere, but merging into the other shades without clashing. The different colours help to make the whole not less but infinitely more beautiful, as do the different instruments in the symphony."[2] Just as a musician is an active contributor to a symphony, the symphony, too, relies on the collaboration and contributions of its different musicians. Cultural synergy, in turn, benefits Canadian society, since it maximizes the civic contributions of the various ethnic groups. While the practice of multiculturalism made cultural synergy possible in the Skeena region, the Skeena Punjabis were surprised, upon relocating to the large urban centres, by the lack of such synergy in those new locations.

Ethnic Insularity in the Large Urban Centres

The particular practice of multiculturalism in the Skeena region was further underscored when Punjabis relocated from the remote area to large urban centres. Upon relocation in the large urban centres, the Skeena Punjabis were surprised to find that what they had created for themselves in the Skeena region could not be found in their new locations, especially given the large concentrations of Punjabis in areas like Vancouver, Surrey, and Abbotsford. Indeed, they now had to adjust to living in a Punjabi enclave, which they found a socio-cultural challenge. In examining the Punjabi community after its first migration to the Skeena region and its second migration to urban

Canada, it becomes apparent that the immigrant experiences of multiculturalism differed dramatically depending on whether they occurred in the earlier experience of cultural synergy and or in the contemporary encounter with ethnic insularity.

The ethnic enclaves in the large urban centres, unlike the communities in the small remote towns, are marked by limited interaction between Punjabis and non-Punjabis. According to Punjabis who have come from the Skeena region, this limited intercultural interaction in the large urban centres is a weakness, especially since ethnic enclaves are viewed as an encumbrance to the process of experiencing a sense of belonging to the culturally diverse Canadian society. The Punjabis in the large urban centres are seen as being *apart from* society. Moreover, in contrast to the inter-cultural tensions during the period of the Punjabi immigrants' initial contact with the Skeena community, *intra*-group tensions seem to dominate the South Asian or Punjabi enclave context.

The second migration or shift also involved the unsettling experience of being labelled as a "visible minority" – that is, as being identified and treated as "other." While the media tend to reinforce the notion of visible minorities as "other" by the manner in which they report the news, corporations and political parties also perpetuate "otherness" by viewing visible minorities as "ethnic markets." The Punjabi ethnic-enclave context is further validated by politicians in their appeal to the ethnic vote. However, it is worth recognizing that many of those who live in ethnic enclaves, perhaps constituting the "silent majority," consider the "bloc vote" a myth given the heterogeneity of the community; they are also critical of "self-appointed" leaders who see themselves as the sole representatives of their ethnic community.

The practice of appealing to the ethnic vote is evident not only in the actions politicians take in the large urban centres, but also in their absence in smaller communities like Prince Rupert and Terrace. It appears that political parties manifest a greater interest in issues of ethnicity and immigration within the ethnic-enclave context in the hope of winning the ethnic "bloc vote." In doing so, they are not only misusing multiculturalism but are also playing on intra-group tensions in order to garner electoral support. Moreover, it seems that politicians, in their attempt to win support, set the parameters of the ethnic-enclave arena in which Punjabis might assert themselves in Canada.

Location matters. Depending on the geographic location – a remote region or an urban setting – multiculturalism impacts immigrant communities differently, particularly with respect to how they form their Canadian identity. The contrasting experience of small remote towns and large urban centres is especially felt by the children of Punjabi immigrants. The third narrative (chapter 9) reveals how the shift from the Skeena (a multi-ethnic milieu) to the Lower Mainland (an ethnic-enclave milieu) led the children of Punjabi immigrant parents to re-evaluate what it means to be Canadian. The location-based cultural contrast experienced by the relocated Skeena Punjabis, especially those belonging to the Skeena/Canadian-born generation, raises a significant question: "What does it mean to be a Canadian citizen and what is required of immigrants and their descendants so that they might be regarded – socially and politically, not just legally – as Canadian citizens?"

Citizenship in the Twenty-first Century

With the increase in immigration to Canada and the Western hemisphere in general over the last four decades, along with the terrorist attacks of 9/11 in New York City, concerns over immigration laws and the role of multiculturalism have intensified. Alongside concerns surrounding immigration, there has simultaneously developed a growing apprehension over the lack of a spirit of citizenship in Canada among ethnic groups, who, as a consequence, are perceived as "outsiders." Even though multiculturalism has since the 1990s been increasingly oriented towards fostering an inclusive, civic-oriented society with a shared sense of citizenship, some politicians and scholars continue to hold the perspective that multiculturalism has somehow failed as a result of it allegedly fostering a fragmented pluralism.[3] Since citizenship is not exclusively about legal freedoms, rights, and responsibilities, but also about participation in the public sphere and a felt sense of belonging and attachment to the country, the cultivation of a spirit of citizenship has to be viewed, not as a one-time event like swearing the citizenship oath, but as a process.

As the Punjabis in the Skeena region developed greater socio-economic security, they gained the confidence they needed to enter the common public space, and their doing so has facilitated further interaction with other ethnic communities. Interestingly and unlike the case of the large urban centres, their interactions with the First Nations people not only had an impact on the Punjabis' understanding of what it means to be Canadian, but also inspired them to endeavour to preserve their own culture and language after they learned about the genocide of the First Nations. The question that emerges therefore is not "Do Punjabis have a sense of shared citizenship with other communities in Canada?" but rather "How does the sense of citizenship among the various Punjabis differ and why?"

Immigrants most often choose to migrate to a new country in order to find greater socio-economic opportunity. Placed in a foreign milieu, however, human beings tend to gravitate towards the familiar. Certainly, upon arriving in a new country, immigrants find comfort in the midst of their own ethnic group, for it helps them deal with the many acculturation stresses that they often encounter. Since survival is the driving force for all humans, the natural course to follow in adapting to a new place is first to seek socio-economic security. Because of the common nature of this quest for security, social interaction among different ethnic groups is likely to occur initially at the workplace. The Punjabis who migrated to and settled in the Skeena region, found common ground with other ethnic groups in the area of their work identity. Such was the case with the labourer who typically endured unfair workplace conditions or with the woman who struggled to improve the economic health of her family by entering the paid workforce.

Once people – regardless of ethnicity – become more economically and socially secure, they usually come to possess greater confidence in their ability to meet "others" on a common ground as equal citizens. Such has been the case of the Punjabis in the Skeena region. Greater socio-economic security has allowed for more cultural fluidity among immigrants and their descendants. In contrast, socio-economic insecurity tends to reinforce ethnic identification, with the result that cultural values run the risk of remaining static. In short, insecurity amplifies one's memory of the past, while economic security emboldens the individual to welcome the future. Cultural fluidity, or the lack of it, has a significant impact on the process by which the children of immigrants negotiate their ethnic and national identities.

Geographic location not only plays a large role in the immigrant's experience of Canada's practice of multiculturalism, depending on whether one resides in small remote towns or large urban centres, but it also influences the manner in which immigrants and their children subsequently develop a sense of shared citizenship. This is made evident in this present study as well as in earlier work on the Sikhs in Vancouver,[4] which delineates the various ways in which they relate to the mainstream and to their own ethnic community. Significantly, the process through which immigrants come to experience shared citizenship is much slower in the ethnic-enclave than in the multi-ethnic context. It seems that the very isolation and smallness in population of remote communities compel the many communities to come to terms with one another. While the Punjabis in the Skeena region considered themselves full citizens, the Punjabis in the large urban centres expressed dismay at being regarded as "outsiders" or a minority. This identification as "outsiders" or "immigrant citizens" results in their concluding that they – coming from the outside – have to somehow prove that they can integrate into[5] and actively participate in Canadian society – notwithstanding the tendency of political parties to politically segregate and fragment them.

As visible minorities, the Punjabis are regarded and depicted as "immigrant citizens," regardless of the fact that they have been living in Canada now for over a century. Not only have the Punjabis been in Canada for many generations, but during the 1930s and 1940s they sought to advance their interests by struggling – alongside First Nations, women, labour, and other groups – for equal citizenship rights in Canada. Their lobbying for universal suffrage coincided with the emergence of movements for social equality in Canada at the end of the Second World War. This combined effort contributed to the more recent Canadian socio-political ethos of equality, freedom, and democracy.[6] Despite that, in the large urban centres, the Punjabis are still regarded as "other."

Multiculturalism and ethnicity should not be considered solely responsible for immigrants not feeling a sense of Canadian citizenship. In relation to concerns over the "other," over the rise of an apparently segregated or fragmented pluralism, or over ethnic enclaves in the suburbs of the metropolises, there is something to be said for social equality as an important factor in building a sense of shared citizenship. Greater consideration needs to be given to the socio-economic conditions (e.g., low-wage jobs, lack of job security and benefits, and high housing costs) and adverse intercultural realities (e.g., media stereotyping, inconsistent bylaw enforcement in municipalities, and the tendency of political parties to segregate visible minority groups) faced by the newer immigrants, especially in Canada's large urban centres. If these issues of social inequality were to be adequately addressed, immigrants would be in a better position to move confidently towards a common ground with other citizens.

Multiculturalism has, in part, been based on the implicit assumption that as immigrants become economically secure and prosperous, they will over time move away from the ethnic-enclave context. This assumption does not always apply to visible minorities, most of whom reside in the large urban centres. Concerted effort is therefore necessary to enhance intercultural understanding and to create common spaces for greater interaction, which would prove beneficial both to immigrants in developing a greater sense of shared citizenship and to Canada in building a more socially cohesive nation. If Canada accepts immigrants, it also has the responsibility to foster immigrants' advancement from the status of "immigrant citizens" – who help fill the labour and population needs of the country – to full Canadian citizenship.

Summing Up

The growing theoretical discussion around the issues of heterogeneity in immigrant communities, the greater porosity of borders, and the heightened recognition of the negotiability of identities have contributed to the accordance of greater importance and value to the role of agency in the study of immigrant groups. This study on the twice-migration of the Punjabis in Canada vividly demonstrates the role of human agency. Particularly striking is the important part played by the cultural assets that the Punjabis brought with them, serving as a source of resilience in the adaptation process. At the same time, geographic location emerges as a critical variable in any study of immigrants. Social anthropologists and historians have, for the most part, situated their research in large urban field sites, but the immigrant experience has not been limited to metropolitan areas alone. Many immigrants have, at least initially, settled in small, often remote, communities. Intercultural relations turn out to be very different as a result of whether immigrants have settled in a remote town or a large urban centre. Furthermore, one can fail to appreciate the actual experience of immigrants by focusing only on the interactions between a particular ethnic community and the Anglo-mainstream, as has been made evident in the case of the Punjabis of BC's Skeena region, especially with respect to their interactions with the First Nations.

Ethnic identities, shaped in the course of the immigrants' endeavour to create social space in the host country, emerge as much more complex than generally believed, since the process of identification seems to be negotiable according to the shifting social contexts of immigrant groups. This is evident in the case of the Punjabi community, which, after establishing itself in a remote setting, has been forced by changes in economic circumstances to relocate to an urban site. This second migration has resulted in a shift from being connected – as full citizens – to the larger community in the small remote towns of Canada to a condition of ethnic insularity – as immigrant citizens – in the large urban centres. As a consequence, the children of immigrants, who had formed their identity in the social context of Canada's practice of multiculturalism in remote settings, have found themselves in a position of having to renegotiate both their ethnic and their national identities after moving to metropolitan centres.

The study of the Punjabi immigrants in the Skeena demonstrates that, in spite of the human tendency to gravitate towards the familiar, once immigrants acquire greater socio-economic security, they do have the capacity to participate as equal partners in the public sphere and experience shared citizenship with other members of society. However, the process through which the experience of shared citizenship emerges among immigrants is also dependent on geographic location. Even though an ethnic enclave may provide comfort for immigrants in the process of becoming economically secure, cultural synergy and shared citizenship emerge much more slowly in the ethnic-enclave context of an urban setting than they do in the multi-ethnic milieu of a remote town. This case study of the Skeena Punjabis suggests that in order to foster a spirit of shared citizenship among all Canadians, Canada needs to address and adequately resolve the socio-economic issues pertaining to immigrants and ensure their equal membership in society, thereby enabling immigrants to move away from the experience of being apart from and towards the experience of being a part of Canadian society.

NOTES

CHAPTER ONE

1 It is important to note that not all twice-migrations are a result of economic or political turmoil. Some people may migrate elsewhere for better opportunity, especially with respect to children's secondary and post-secondary education. The following are some well-known cases of twice-migration with respect to South Asians: (1) when Burma gained independence in 1948, Indians' access to Burmese citizenship was restricted, many left, and in 1962 the remaining Indians were expelled; (2) during the 1960s and 1970s, political tensions erupted between native Ugandans and Indians, with the result that many Indians fled, mainly to the United Kingdom (some also went to the United States and Canada); and (3) when Fiji became independent in 1970, Fijian Indians began to leave, and after a political coup in 1987 many fled to Australia, New Zealand, the United States, and Canada. See Judith Brown, *Global South Asians: Introducing the Modern Diaspora* (Cambridge: Cambridge University Press, 2006), 45–50. For an in-depth analysis on the twice-migration of primarily Ramgarhia Sikhs from East Africa to Britain in the late 1970s and early 1980s, see Parminder Bhachu, *Twice Migrants: East African Sikh Settlers in Britain* (London: Tavistock Publications, 1985).

2 Arjun Appadurai, *Modernity at Large: Cultural Dimensions of Globalization* (Minneapolis: University of Minnesota Press, 1996), 33–4; Akhil Gupta and and James Ferguson, eds, *Culture, Power, Place: Explorations in Critical Anthropology* (Durham, NC: Duke University Press, 1997), 1–29.

3 Michael Herzfeld, *Theoretical Practice in Culture and Society* (Oxford: Blackwell Publishers, 2001), 133–51.

4 Franca Iacovetta, *Such Hardworking People: Italian Immigrants in Postwar Toronto* (Montreal & Kingston: McGill-Queen's University Press, 1993), xxiv; Stephen Vertovec, *The Hindu Diaspora: Comparative Patterns* (London, UK: Routledge, 2000), 153–6.

5 Sarah J. Mahler and Patricia R. Pessar, "Gendered Geographies of Power: Analyzing Gender across Transnational Spaces," *Identities: Global Studies in Culture and Power* 7 (2001): 441–59; D. Gabaccia and Franca Iacovetta, eds, *Women, Gender and Transnational Lives: Italian Workers of the World* (Toronto: University of Toronto Press, 2002); Caroline B. Brettell, *Anthropology and Migration: Essays on Transnationalism, Ethnicity and Identity* (New York: Altamira Press, 2003), 185–95.

6 Lila Abu-Lughod, ed., *Remaking Women: Feminism and Modernity in the Middle East* (Princeton, NJ: Princeton University Press, 1998), 3–31; Kamala Elizabeth Nayar, "Sikh Women in Vancouver: An Analysis of Their Psychosocial Issues," in *Women and Sikhism*, ed. Doris Jakobsh, 248–70 (Delhi: Oxford University Press, 2010), 259–66, 269–71.

7 Gerd Baumann, *Contesting Culture: Discourses of Identity in Multi-ethnic London* (Cambridge: Cambridge University Press, 1996); Caroline B. Brettell, "Is the Ethnic Community Inevitable? A Comparison of Settlement Patterns of Portuguese Immigrants in Toronto and Paris," *Journal of Ethnic Studies* 9 (1981): 1–17; Kamala Elizabeth Nayar, *The Sikh Diaspora in Vancouver: Three Generations amid Tradition, Modernity, and Multiculturalism* (Toronto: University of Toronto Press, 2004).

8 Michael Kearney, "The Local and Global: The Anthropology of Globalization and Transnationalism," *Annual Review of Anthropology* 24 (1995): 547–65.

9 Appadurai, *Modernity at Large*; Gupta and Ferguson, *Culture, Power, Place*; Nina Glick Schiller, "Transmigration and Nation-States: Something Old and Something New in the US Immigrant Experience," in *The Handbook of International Migration*, ed. C. Hirchmaan (New York: Russell Sage Publication, 1999), 94–119; Peter Van der Veer, ed., *Nation and Migration: The Politics of Space in the South Asian Diaspora* (Philadelphia: University of Pennsylvania Press, 1995), 1–16.

10 Baumann, *Contesting Culture*; Avtar Brah, *Cartographies of Diaspora* (London, UK: Routledge, 1996), 41.

11 Mahler and Pessar, "Gendered Geographies of Power," 441–59.

12 Nina Glick-Schiller, Linda Basch, and Christina Blanc-Szanton, eds, *Towards a Transnational Perspective on Migration, Race, Class, Ethnicity, and Nationalism Reconsidered* (New York: New York Academy of Sciences, 1992).

13 J.S. Grewal, *The Sikhs of the Punjab* (Cambridge: Cambridge University Press, 1994), 2–3.

14 While the Green Revolution increased agricultural production, it also gave rise to serious problems, such as seasonal rural unemployment, the marginalization of small-scale farmers, and the displacement of poor cultivators, along with over-mechanization and over-utilization of chemical products. Despite these harmful side effects, the Green Revolution can be regarded as having been an economic success in that it drastically increased the region's agricultural production, especially of wheat, the backbone of Punjab's development. For a detailed analysis of the issues related to Punjab's Green Revolution, see Himmat Singh, *Green Revolutions Reconsidered: The Rural World of Contemporary Punjab* (New Delhi: Oxford University Press, 2001).

15 Improvements were made to the older canals (such as the Western Yamuna Canal), while new canals were constructed and canal colonies were established in different parts of the province (such as the Lower Bari Doab Colony project developed during

1910–25). The canal colonies represented not only an effort to expand the province's agricultural economy but also a systematic endeavour to create a modernized rural society. Singh, *Green Revolutions Reconsidered*, 28; Imran Ali, "Canal Colonization and Socio-economic Change," in *Five Punjabi Centuries: Polity, Economy, Society and Culture*, ed. Indu Banga (New Delhi: Manohar Publishers, 1997), 351–2; Khushwant Singh, *A History of the Sikhs*, vol. 2 (Princeton, NJ: Princeton University Press, 1963), 116–20.

16 Grewal, *The Sikhs of the Punjab*, 1–27.

17 Alexander the Great, however, never carried out his plan to conquer northwest India, as his men had refused to go on. Subsequently, Chandragupta Maurya successfully built up a large army that managed to establish the Maurya Empire, which extended across the northern region of the Indian subcontinent by 321 BCE. A.L. Basham, *The Wonder That Was India* (New York: Grove Press, 1954), 48–51; Fred W. Clothey, *Religion in India: A Historical Introduction* (New York: Routledge, 2006), 52.

18 I.S. Sekhon, *The Punjabis: The People, the History, Culture and Enterprise*, vol. 1 (New Delhi: Cosmo Publications, 2000), 3.

19 Ibid.

20 A large portion of the British Indian army consisted of Muslims, many of Punjabi background.

21 Grewal, *The Sikhs of the Punjab*, 137–40.

22 Nayar, *The Sikh Diaspora in Vancouver*, 16; Kamala Elizabeth Nayar, "The Making of Sikh Space in British Columbia: The Central Role of the *Gurdwara*," in *Asian Religions in British Columbia*, ed. Larry DeVries, Don Baker, and Dan Overmyer (Vancouver: University of British Columbia Press, 2010), 44–7.

23 Klaus K. Klostermaier, *A Survey of Hinduism* (Albany: State University of New York Press, 1989), 46–7, 419.

24 Khushwant Singh, *A History of the Sikhs*, vol. 1, 17.

25 Jaswinder Singh Sandhu, "The Sikh Model of the Person, Suffering, and Healing: The Implications for Counselors," *International Journal for the Advancement of Counseling* 26, no. 1 (2004): 36–40.

26 Harjot Singh Oberoi, *The Construction of Religious Boundaries: Culture, Identity and Diversity in the Sikh Tradition* (Chicago: University of Chicago Press, 1994), 381–417.

27 For instance, it was during this time that the Sikhs were successful in removing Hindu images from the Golden Temple in Amritsar (1905), in obtaining legal recognition of the Sikh marriage ceremony (1909), and in establishing the Sikh Code of Conduct (*Sikh Rahit Maryada*) through the Shiromani Gurdwara Parbhandhak Committee in order to codify the religious norms for a Khalsa (orthodox) Sikh (1925).

28 Ramachandra Guha, *India after Gandhi: The History of the World's Largest Democracy* (New York: Ecco, 2007), 31.

29 Ibid.

30 Grewal, *The Sikhs of the Punjab*, 181–3.

31 For further analysis on the Khalistan movement, see Jugdep S. Chima, *The Sikh Separatist Insurgency in India: Political Leadership and Ethnonationalist Movements* (New Delhi: Sage, 2010).

32 Nayar, *The Sikh Diaspora in Vancouver*, 154–5.

33 Statistics Canada, *Population Projections of Visible Minority Groups, Canada, Provinces, and Regions, 2001 to 2017* (2005). Retrieved 4 April 2005 from http://www.statscan.ca.

34 Hugh Johnston, "Patterns of Sikh Migration to Canada 1900–1960," in *Sikh History and Religion in the 20th Century*, ed. Joseph T. O'Connell, Milton Israel, and Willard Oxtoby (Toronto: Centre for South Asian Studies, University of Toronto, 1988), 296–313.

35 In an in-depth study on the formation of the Vancouver Sikh community in the late 1970s, Chadney evaluates the degree to which the Sikh community has integrated into Canadian society. In doing so, he demonstrates how the Sikh community within the "host" society of Canada has transformed its economic patterns while its values pertaining to social and family affairs have remained traditional. James Gaylord Chadney, *The Sikhs of Vancouver* (New York: AMS Press, 1984). Similar studies include Michael M. Ames and Joy Inglis, "Conflict and Change in British Columbia Sikh Family Life," *BC Studies* 20 (1973): 15–49; Norman Buchignani, "Conceptions of Sikh Culture in the Development of a Comparative Analysis of the Sikh Diaspora," in *Sikh History and Religion in the 20th Century*, 276–95; James Gaylord Chadney, "The Formation of Ethnic Communities," in *Sikh History and Religion in the 20th Century*, 185–99; Paramjit S. Judge, *Punjabis in Canada: A Study of Formation of an Ethnic Community* (Delhi: Chanakya Publications, 1994). The ethnography of a single Sikh immigrant who arrived in Canada in the mid-1950s reveals much about the collective experience of immigrants while articulating the voice of a Sikh male mill worker. Tara Singh Bains and Hugh Johnston, *Four Quarters of the Night: The Life Journey of an Emigrant Sikh* (Montreal & Kingston: McGill-Queen's University Press, 1995).

36 Gurcharn Singh Basran and B. Singh Bolaria, *The Sikhs in Canada: Migration, Race, Class, and Gender* (New Delhi: Oxford University Press, 2003).

37 In her study on the Sikhs in Paldi, a mill town situated on Vancouver Island, Verma puts forward the interesting proposition that kinship ties and caste have been a source of strength for Sikhs in coping with alienation and in pursuing upward social mobility. Archana B. Verma, *The Making of Little Punjab in Canada* (New Delhi: Sage, 2002).

38 Darshan Singh Tatla, *The Sikh Diaspora: The Search for Statehood* (Seattle: University of Washington Press, 1999).

39 Margaret Walton-Roberts, "Globalization, National Autonomy and Non-resident Indians," *Contemporary South Asia* 13, no. 1 (2004): 53–69.

40 Harold Coward, John R. Hinnels, and Raymond Brady Williams, eds, *The South Asian Religious Diaspora in Britain, Canada, and the U.S.A.* (Albany: State University of New York Press, 2000); Verne A. Dusenbery, "The Poetics and Politics of Recognition: Diasporan Sikhs in Pluralist Polities," *American Ethnologist* 24, no. 4 (1997): 738–62.

41 Nayar's social-anthropological study – on the multifaceted process of the Vancouver Sikh community's adaptation – delineates social change through an investigation of the tensions among three generations of the community. Significantly, in this study, the Canadian-born generation living in Vancouver whose antecedents had originally

settled in rural BC tended to assess Canada's policy of multiculturalism more critically than those born and raised in BC's Lower Mainland. Nayar, *The Sikh Diaspora in Vancouver.*

42 Norman Buchignani and Doreen M. Indra, *Continuous Journey: A Social History of South Asians in Canada* (Toronto: McClelland and Stewart, 1985)

43 J.F. Unstead, "The Economic Resources of British Columbia," *Geographical Journal* 50, no. 2 (1917): 125–6.

44 Initially, various First Nations accommodated twenty-three small European "settlements" in the region that would become the province of British Columbia. In 1821, the North West Company amalgamated with the Hudson's Bay Company (HBC), giving it a monopoly in the region. These settlements were solely fur-trading posts until 1824, when the settlers began to expand their demands on the First Nations to other activities, such as the provision of food. Victoria – the HBC's headquarters for the west coast since 1846 – became the capital when the colony of Vancouver Island was created in 1849. Robin Fisher, *Contact and Conflict: Indian-European Relations in British Columbia, 1774–1890* (Vancouver: University of British Columbia Press, 1977), 24–5, 49; John S. Lutz, *Makuk: A New History of Aboriginal-White Relations* (Vancouver: University of British Columbia Press, 2008), 165–9; Wilson Duff, *The Indian History of British Columbia: The Impact of the White Man* (reprint, Victoria: Royal British Columbia Museum, 1997), 74–7.

45 Jean Barman, *The West beyond the West: A History of British Columbia* (Toronto: University of Toronto Press, 2007), 80–2; see also Margaret A. Ornsby, *British Columbia: A History* (Toronto: Macmillan of Canada, 1958).

46 There were many "small gold rushes" prior to the Cariboo gold rush. The initial trade of gold occurred with the Haida Nation of the Queen Charlotte Islands in 1851. Lutz, *Makuk*, 173–4.

47 For instance, in 1862 the Bank of British Columbia (which later became the Canadian Imperial Bank of Commerce) was established at Yale, BC, to serve the miners. Moreover, the British government spent millions of dollars building roads and bridges connecting the interior to Vancouver, which facilitated not only trade but also settlement. Barman, *The West beyond the West*, 67–8, 99–128.

48 Lutz, *Makuk*, 166.

49 Prior to joining Canada in 1871, BC comprised the union of the Colony of British Columbia (the mainland colony formed in 1858) and the Colony of Vancouver Island (formed in 1849). The union of these two colonies took place in 1866.

50 Chapters 6 and 7 further discuss Anglo-Canadian and First Nations relations in the twentieth century. For an in-depth discussion of European–First Nations relations during the period of colonization, see Cole Harris, *The Resettlement of British Columbia: Essays on Colonialism and Geographical Change* (Vancouver: University of British Columbia Press, 1997).

51 Alicja Muszynski, *Cheap Wage Labour: Race and Gender in the Fisheries of British Columbia* (Montreal & Kingston: McGill-Queen's University Press, 1996), 15–16, 237–41.

52 Ibid.

53 Ibid., 178–9.

54 Gordon Hak, *Turning Trees into Dollars: The British Columbia Coastal Lumber History, 1858–1913* (Toronto: University of Toronto Press, 2000), 64–7. See also Ken Drushka, *In the Bight: The BC Forest Industry Today* (Madeira Park, BC: Harbour Publishing, 1999), 136.

55 Hak, *Turning Trees into Dollars*, 67–9. See also Drushka, *In the Bight*, 70–1.

56 Hak, *Turning Trees into Dollars*, 21–2; Drushka, *In the Bight*, 70–1.

57 Four railway lines from the Prairies were eventually extended to converge in Vancouver even as the Canadian Northern Railway was built connecting the Prairies and northwestern British Columbia up to Prince Rupert (1908–10). Hak, *Turning Trees into Dollars*, 22–4.

58 Rolf Knight, *Indians at Work: An Informal History of Native Indian Labour in British Columbia 1858–1930* (Vancouver: New Star Books, 1978), 123.

59 Hak, *Turning Trees into Dollars*, 18–28; Drushka, *In the Bight*, 71; Knight, *Indians at Work*, 231–5.

60 Richard A. Rajala, "The Receding Timber Line: Forest Practice, State Regulation, and the Decline of the Cowichan Lake Timber Industry, 1880–1992," in *Canadian Papers in Business History*, vol. 2, ed. Peter A. Baskerville (Victoria: Public History Group, University of Victoria, 1993), 179–81.

61 Hak, *Turning Trees into Dollars*, 95, 114–15; Drushka, *In the Bight*, 33–9.

62 Hak, *Turning Trees into Dollars*, 112; Drushka, *In the Bight*, 71–2.

63 Gordon Hak, *Capital and Labour in the British Columbia Forest Industry, 1934–74* (Vancouver, University of British Columbia Press, 2007), 3; Drushka, *In the Bight*, 74; Lutz, *Makuk*, 226–8.

64 According to Rajala, the government only gave serious consideration to forest conservation when there was a sense of urgency as a result of overcutting in the coastal region. Rajala, *Clearcutting the Pacific Rain Forest*, 154–66. In 1947 the principle of sustained yield forestry was adopted in order to encourage better forest management and thereby secure a steady supply of timber. Under the new system, the larger areas were leased to private firms and municipal bodies for the purpose of (a) harvesting timber and (b) growing future timber crops. Later, the FMLs were renamed as TFLs (Tree Farm Licences). For a detailed analysis of the government's initiatives on tenure over the last one hundred years, see Hak, *Capital and Labour in the British Columbia Forest Industry*, 42–66; Drushka, *In the Bight*, 135–62.

65 Hak, *Capital and Labour in the British Columbia Forest Industry*, 26–41; Drushka, *In the Bight*, 79.

66 Douglas C. Harris, *Landing Native Fisheries: Indian Reserves and Fishing Rights in British Columbia 1849–1925* (Vancouver: University of British Columbia Press, 2008), 187–9; Knight, *Indians at Work*, 179–84; Diane Newell, *Tangled Webs of History: Indians and the Law in Canada's Pacific Coast Fisheries* (Toronto: University of Toronto Press, 1993), 46–65.

67 Newell, *Tangled Webs of History*, 98–112; Lutz, *Makuk*, 205.

68 Stuart Jamieson and Percy Gladstone, "Unionism in the Fishing Industry of British Columbia," *Canadian Journal of Economics and Political Science* 16, no. 1 (1950): 1–11.

69 William K. Carroll and R.S. Ratner. "The NDP Regime in British Columbia, 1991–2001: A Post-mortem," *Canadian Review of Sociology and Anthropology* 42, no. 2 (2005): 169–70.

70 Muszynski, *Cheap Wage Labour*, 180–2; Jamieson and Gladstone, "Unionism in the Fishing Industry of British Columbia," 9–11.

71 Muszynski, *Cheap Wage Labour*, 182.

72 Hak, *Turning Trees into Dollars*, 146, 166; Drushka, *In the Bight*, 73–5.

73 Hak, *Capital and Labour in the British Columbia Forest Industry*, 67–75.

74 Ibid.

75 Ibid., 101–11, 116–21.

76 Ibid., 101–23; Drushka, *In the Bight*, 81.

77 Hak, *Capital and Labour in the British Columbia Forest Industry*, 168–87.

78 Roger Hayter, "The War in the Woods: Post-Fordist Restructuring, Globalization, and the Contested Remapping of British Columbia's Forest Economy," *Annals of the Association of American Geography* 93, no. 3 (2003): 708–10; Roger Hayter, *Flexible Crossroads: The Restructuring of British Columbia's Forest Economy* (Vancouver: University of British Columbia Press, 2000); Drushka, *In the Bight*, 64–6.

79 Hayter, "The War in the Woods," 719–23; Richard A. Rajala, "Forests and Fish: The 1972 Coast Logging Guidelines and British Columbia's First NDP Government," *BC Studies* 159 (2008): 117–20.

80 Carroll and Ratner, "The NDP Regime in British Columbia, 1991–2001," 167–96.

81 "British Columbia Regional District Migration Components: Skeena-Queen Charlottes," BC Statistics, retrieved 6 May 2011 from http://www.bcstats.gov.bc.ca/data/pop/mig/rdcomp.pdf.

82 Augie Fleras and Jean Elliott, *Unequal Relations: An Introduction to Race, Ethnic, and Aboriginal Dynamics in Canada* (Toronto: Pearson, 1996), 297.

83 W. Peter Ward, *White Canada Forever: Popular Attitudes and Public Policy toward Orientals in British Columbia* (Montreal & Kingston: McGill-Queen's University Press, 2002), 36–52; Patricia Roy, *A White Man's Province: British Columbia Politicians and Chinese and Japanese Immigrants, 1858–1914* (Vancouver: University of British Columbia Press, 1989), 91–119.

84 Ward, *White Canada Forever*, 86.

85 Ibid., 142–66; Patricia Roy, *The Oriental Question: Consolidating a White Man's Province, 1914–41* (Vancouver: University of British Columbia Press, 2003), 189–230.

86 Ravi Pendakur, *Immigrants and the Labour Force: Policy, Regulation, and Impact* (Montreal & Kingston: McGill-Queen's University Press, 2000), 78–82; Sarjeet Singh Jagpal, *Becoming Canadians: Pioneer Sikhs in Their Own Words* (Madeira Park, BC: Harbour Publishing, 1994), 147–9.

87 Pendakur, *Immigrants and the Labour Force*, 78–82.

88 Based on pluralistic principles, multiculturalism manages ethnic diversity chiefly through (1) explicitly acknowledging diversity, (2) positively valuing the benefits of diversity to society, and (3) recognizing that minority groups contribute to society.

89 Weaver provides an excellent analysis of the development of this contentious initiative. Sally Weaver, *Making Canadian Indian Policy: The Hidden Agenda, 1968–70* (Toronto: University of Toronto Press, 1981).

90 Fleras and Elliott, *Unequal Relations*, 301–5.
91 For instance, John Porter linked social inequality to ethnic pluralism in Canada. Ethnic pluralism encourages insular and isolationist patterns that, in turn, prevent upward social mobility for ethnic groups. According to Porter, multiculturalism is a distraction from social and political control and economic advancement – that is, ethnic groups should not be bound to ascriptive qualities but rather should have the chance for upward social mobility based on achievement. John Porter, *The Vertical Mosaic: An Analysis of Social Class and Power in Canada* (Toronto: University of Toronto Press, 1965).
92 Schlesinger holds that the lack of a national identity in Canada is related to Canada's policy of multiculturalism. Arthur M. Schlesinger, *The Disuniting of America: Reflections on a Multicultural Society* (New York: W.W. Norton, 1992).
93 Reginald Bibby, *Mosaic Madness: Pluralism without a Cause* (Toronto: Stoddart, 1990), 10.
94 Neil Bissoondath, *Selling Illusions: The Cult of Multiculturalism in Canada* (Toronto: Penguin Books, 1994), 218–19.
95 Will Kymlicka, *Finding Our Way: Rethinking Ethnocultural Relations in Canada* (Toronto: Oxford University Press, 1998).
96 I. Angus, *A Border Within: National Identity, Cultural Plurality and Wilderness* (Montreal & Kingston: McGill-Queen's University Press, 1997), 205.
97 Gérard Bouchard and Charles Taylor, *Building the Future: A Time for Reconciliation* (Montreal: Government of Quebec, 2008).
98 Statistics Canada, *Population Projections of Visible Minority Groups, Canada, Provinces, and Regions, 2001 to 2017* (2005). Retrieved 4 April 2005 from http://www.statscan.ca.
99 Brian Ray and Valerie Preston, "Experiences of Discrimination: The Impact of Metropolitan and Non-Metropolitan Location," power point presentation at CIC Research Network Meeting, Ottawa, 26 February 2009.
100 Marcus nuanced the theoretical concept "multi-sited ethnography," which is often employed in the research of transnational or "de-territorialized" communities. George Marcus, *Ethnography through Thick and Thin* (Princeton, NJ: Princeton University Press, 1998). See also Mark-Anthony Falzon, ed., *Multi-sited Ethnography: Theory, Praxis and Locality in Contemporary Research* (London, UK: Ashgate, 2009).
101 Nayar, *The Sikhs of Vancouver*, 21.
102 Ted Palys, *Research Decisions: Quantitative and Qualitative Perspectives* (Toronto: Harcourt Brace Jovanovich, 1992), 148–9.

CHAPTER TWO

1 Many Punjabi male immigrants were, in fact, married but lived like non-family men because they were unable to bring over their wives and children.
2 Kamala Elizabeth Nayar, *The Sikh Diaspora in Vancouver: Three Generations amid Tradition, Modernity, and Multiculturalism* (Toronto: University of Toronto Press, 2004), 16; James Gaylord Chadney, "The Formation of Ethnic Communities, Lessons from Vancouver Sikhs," in *Sikh History and Religion in the 20th Century*, ed. Joseph

T. O'Connell, Milton Israel, and Willard Oxtoby (Toronto: Centre for South Asian Studies, University of Toronto, 1988), 185–99; Peter W. Ward, *White Canada Forever: Popular Attitudes and Public Policy toward Orientals in British Columbia* (Montreal & Kingston: McGill-Queen's University Press, 2002), 80–1; Paramjit S. Judge, *Punjabis in Canada: A Study of Formation of an Ethnic Community* (Delhi: Chanakya Publications, 1994), 1–17.

3 Gordon Hak, *Capital and Labour in the British Columbia Forest Industry, 1934–74* (Vancouver: University of British Columbia Press, 2007), 32–41.

4 For a discussion of the fishery industries, see chapter 4.

5 Hugh Johnston, "Group Identity in an Emigrant Worker Community: The Example of Sikhs in Early Twentieth-Century British Columbia," *BC Studies* 148 (Winter 2005): 3.

6 Ward, *White Canada Forever*, 81; Hugh Johnston, "Patterns of Sikh Migration to Canada 1900–1960," in *Sikh History and Religion in the 20th Century*, ed. Joseph T. O'Connell, Milton Israel, and Willard Oxtoby (Toronto: Centre for South Asian Studies, University of Toronto, 1988), 296–313.

7 Sarjeet Singh Jagpal, *Becoming Canadians: Pioneer Sikhs in Their Own Words* (Madeira Park, BC: Harbour Publishing, 1994), 52–67; "Hindus employed on railway work," *Province* (Vancouver), 30 November 1906, 1; "Work for Hindus," *Colonist* (Victoria), 12 April 1907, 3. See also the Indo-Canadian Oral History Collection (Burnaby: Simon Fraser University, 1987), items 10, 51, and 53.

8 "How Hindus compare with Chinese as workmen," *Province* (Vancouver), 23 November 1906, 1; "Hindus take Italians' place," *Province* (Vancouver), 30 November 1906, 19. See Audrey Kobayashi and Peter Jackson, "Japanese Canadians and the Racialization of Labour in the British Columbia Sawmill Industry," *BC Studies* 103 (Fall 1994): 33–58.

9 Gordon Hak, *Turning Trees into Dollars: The British Columbia Coastal Lumber History, 1858–1913* (Toronto: University of Toronto Press, 2000), 158.

10 Ibid., 44–7.

11 Johnston, "Patterns of Sikh Migration to Canada 1900–1960," 296–313.

12 See Indo-Canadian Oral History Collection, items 2, 7, 10, 11, 51, and 53.

13 PM 1.18, interview, 20 September 2008, Vancouver.

14 For example, in 1912, spearheaded by Professor Teja Singh, Punjabi-Sikhs banded together in Vancouver and formed the Guru Nanak Mining and Trust Company. Its headquarters were at the Second Avenue Khalsa Diwan Society Gurdwara in Vancouver. According to the company charter of September 1909, its goals were (1) to organize the Guru Nanak Hostel for East Indian Students; (2) to buy land for farming to be settled by unemployed workers; (3) to invest in mining to secure employment for workers; (4) to organize its own trust company to look after the banking needs of the workers; (5) to open its own shopping market for needed goods that it would import from India; (6) to organize a Canadian-Indian supply and trust company; and (7) to organize a company of Canadian homebuilders. The establishment of this company allowed its shareholders to enter the real estate market by purchasing lots and building houses. Jagpal, *Becoming Canadians*, 28–9.

15 Johnston, "Patterns of Sikh Migration to Canada 1900–1960," 296–313.

16 Archana B. Verma, *The Making of Little Punjab in Canada* (New Delhi: Sage, 2002), 116–18. See also Jagpal, *Becoming Canadians*, 66–8.

17 Kapoor Singh Sidhu (1885–1964), a Jat Sikh, came from the village of Kharaudi in Ludhiana district. His clan name is Sidhu; however, upon arriving in Canada, Kapoor Singh chose to spell it as Siddoo. He was an educated man who, following high school, attended a business college in Calcutta. Well versed in English, Kapoor Singh came from India via San Francisco in 1906. Hugh Johnston, *Jewels from the Qila: The Remarkable Story of an Indo-Canadian Family* (Vancouver: University of British Columbia Press, 2011), chaps 2 and 15.

18 Mayo Singh (1888–1955) was a Manhas Rajput Sikh from the village of Paldi in the Hoshiarpur district of the Punjab. He came to Canada in 1906 with little formal education. Upon arrival, he made a great effort to learn English. Joan Mayo, *Paldi Remembered: 50 Years in the Life of a Vancouver Island Logging Town* (Duncan: Paldi History Committee, 1997), 1–2, 119.

19 Doman Singh, a Manhas Rajput Sikh, who had been a partner in the Mayo Lumber Company, left to become foreman at the Hillcrest Lumber Company, near Duncan (Vancouver Island). Doman Singh accumulated funds that served as the capital base for Doman Industries. The sons of Doman Singh – Herb, Ted, and Gordon – founded the Doman Lumber Company in 1953. The company was renamed Doman Industries in 1964, when it became a public traded company, and it grew to become one of British Columbia's major forest companies in the 1970s and 1980s. By the end of the 1980s, Doman Industries had become a lumber giant. In the 1990s, its success began to fade as a result of wrong choices made in reaction to the globalization-driven forces that worked against BC's forestry industry in general and in the face of allegations of insider trading.

20 Verma, *The Making of Little Punjab in Canada*, 118; Johnston, *Jewels from the Qila*, chap. 7.

21 Johnston, *Jewels from the Qila*, chap. 7.

22 Ibid.; Verma, *The Making of Little Punjab in Canada*, 122–6. For an analysis of the development of Paldi, see Mayo, *Paldi Remembered*.

23 Johnston, "Patterns of Sikh Migration to Canada 1900–1960," 296–313; Ward, *White Canada Forever*, 79–80.

24 Jagpal, *Becoming Canadians*, 66.

25 Johnston, "Patterns of Sikh Migration to Canada 1900–1960," 296–313.

26 Verma, *The Making of Little Punjab in Canada*, 216–20.

27 PM 1.18, interview, 20 September 2008, Vancouver.

28 In 1936, fourteen of the Punjabis worked in the day sawmill, while eleven worked in the night sawmill. The twenty-three remaining Punjabis worked on the yard crew. Hak, *Capital and Labour in the British Columbia Forest Industry*, 76.

29 The Japanese primarily worked in the sheds and dry kilns, and the Chinese were distributed throughout the mill, working in power and maintenance, shipping and yard, day mill, planar and kilns. Even though the Japanese had a prominent presence in the mill, by April 1942 the evacuation of the Japanese had changed the ethnic composition of the workforce. Hak, *Capital and Labour in the British Columbia Forest Industry*, 77.

30 Ibid., 76.

31 For instance, in 1959 Kapoor Singh sold his business to the lumber giant BC Forest Products, which started out in 1946 as a logging and sawmilling company but then in the early 1950s expanded into pulp and paper. For a discussion on the role of labour unions and the Punjabi community, see chapter 6.

32 Sohen Singh Gill appears on the list of illegal East Indians who received citizenship in 1947. Personal archive of Jagat Singh (Jack) Uppal, Mitchell Island, Richmond, BC, received 4 December 2009.

33 The Johl brothers – Chanan Singh, Bawa Singh, and Nand Singh – came to Canada in 1905 and 1906. They were among the first to settle in the area near the location where the Second Avenue Gurdwara was built in 1908. After working at the lumber mills in the False Creek area, they started a lumber cartage business. The Johl family was the first Punjabi family to start a fuel-trucking business; the family signed its first contract with Cedar Cove Sawmill on West 6th Avenue in 1918. Jagpal, *Becoming Canadians*, 58–61.

34 PM 1.18, interview, 20 September 2008, Vancouver.

35 See also Indo-Canadian Oral History Collection, items 1, 2, 4, 6, 11, 12, and 51.

36 Jagat Singh (Jack) Uppal, interview, 12 September 2008, Mitchell Island, Richmond, BC.

37 The address for Yukon Lumber Co. was "at the [south] foot of Manitoba" because the mill was on the south side of the Fraser River. The sawmill no longer exists at that location; in fact, Manitoba Street no longer runs through the area, since the main railroad tracks are situated there. Jagat Singh (Jack) Uppal, interview, 12 September 2008, Mitchell Island, Richmond, BC.

38 Jagat Singh (Jack) Uppal, interview, 12 September 2008, Mitchell Island, Richmond, BC.

39 The report included a survey of the forestry potential of the local Skeena region. It was compiled by Prince Rupert's forestry engineer, Marc Gordon. "Equipment ready for start of a new sawmill in Rupert," *Prince Rupert Daily News*, 10 December 1958.

40 According to the British Columbia business registration office, the company was dissolved on 26 September 1988 under Sarjeet K. Gill and Balwant S. Gill, although the actual sawmill was sold in 1966. Personal communication, 5 February 2009.

41 The representatives for Prince Rupert Sawmills Ltd (F.J.G. Johnson and Associates Ltd) co-signed a lease with the Canadian National Railway (CNR) in June 1958 for ten acres of the Old Dry Dock site. It was a twenty-year lease for Prince Rupert's Old Dry Dock (137 George Hills Way) and surrounding area at Cow Bay on the way to Seal Cove.

42 A cannery town on the south bank of the Skeena River called Port Essington was founded in 1871 by Robert Cunningham. Port Essington was the largest settlement in the region, making it the business centre of the North Coast. Dr R.G. Large, *The Skeena: River of Destiny* (1957; reprint, Surrey, BC: Heritage House Publishing, 1996), 32–48.

43 The first train from Winnipeg arrived at its terminus on 8 April 1914. Jean Barman, *The West beyond the West: A History of British Columbia* (Toronto: University of Toronto Press, 2007), 195–6; W.B.M. Hick, *Hays' Orphan: The Story of the Port of*

Prince Rupert (Prince Rupert, BC: Prince Rupert Authority, 2003), 24–5; Large, *The Skeena*, 153.

44 Hays had business relations with financiers like J.P. Morgan in the United States. Mayor Jack Mussallem, personal communication, 2 June 2009, Prince Rupert, BC.

45 The provincial and federal governments had their own political and economic agendas. Both governments wanted to open up the northwest to large-scale expansion and development: for Liberal prime minister Laurier, the creation of a national transportation system was primary; for Conservative premier McBride (1904–15), providing an environment for private sector economic development was central. Prince Rupert is one example of McBride's economic development of rural BC. Barman, *The West beyond the West*, 178–81, 195.

46 Hick, *Hays' Orphan*, 36.

47 It was the only dock that was capable of quickly building a North Sands–class steel freighter of 10,000 tons, which at that time was in urgent demand. Wartime activity peaked in 1943, but the dock was used to repair the many damaged ships up to 1945. Hick, *Hays' Orphan*, 35–7; Large, *The Skeena*, 158.

48 Large, *The Skeena*, 180–8; Hick, *Hays' Orphan*, 37; Reginald H. Roy, "From the Darker Side of Canadian Military History: Mutiny in the Mountains – The Terrace Incident," *Canadian Defence Quarterly* 5 (1976): 42–55. See also Gilbert Norman Tucker, *The Naval Service of Canada, Activities on Shore during the Second World War*, vol. 2 (Ottawa: Minister of National Defence, 1952).

49 Hick, *Hays' Orphan*, 37.

50 Organized Labour 2, interview, 29 May 2007, Prince Rupert, BC.

51 "The Story of Columbia Cellulose," *Canadian Pulp and Paper Industry* 52 (June 1951): 12–2; Bill Stephenson, "Prince Rupert," in *An Account of a Unique Philosophy in Action*, 20–1 (Columbia Cellulose Company Ltd/Chemcell Ltd, 1963).

52 *Pulp and Paper Magazine of Canada* 18 (11 November 1920): 172; *Pulp and Paper Magazine of Canada* 19 (17 February 1921): 197.

53 Hick, *Hays' Orphan*, 38. See also Large, *The Skeena*, 185–8. The coal and grain terminals were built on Ridley Island in the 1950s. The new city of Kitimat was also built during the early 1950s, with the development of the aluminum plant. With the aluminum plant in Kitimat and the pulp mill on Watson Island, regional deep-sea shipping activity increased, delivering and exporting materials. Despite its closer proximity to Asia by 800 kilometres and waters deep enough for docking ships, Prince Rupert became an "overload" port, to be used only when southern (Vancouver, Seattle) terminals could not cope with the volume of exports. Hick, *Hays' Orphan*, 34.

54 Notwithstanding the importance of the fishing industry to the area, the city overlooked pollution issues related to the pulp and paper mill that directly impacted the fisheries. At the municipal level, there appears to have been political preference for the pulp and paper mill.

55 Richard L. Neuberger, "Seattle Ponders a Bad Dream," *Saturday Evening Post*, 7 February 1948. For a Marxist analysis of the "myth" surrounding the development of Prince Rupert, see Ken E. Lukhardt, "Prince Rupert: A 'Tale of Two Cities,'" in *Historical Perspectives on Northern British Columbia*, ed. Thomas Thorner (Prince

George, BC: College of New Caledonia Press, 1989), 309–32. This paper was initially in a series of six articles in the local papers (*Prince Rupert Daily News* and *Northern Times*), published from 3 January 1976 to 30 April 1976.

56 According to Yukon Lumber Co.'s former general manager, Jack Singh (Jack) Uppal, Sohen Gill had a quota of 100 million feet board measure (FBM) per year to run his lumber operation. Along with the crown timber under the Canadian government and BC's TFL (tree farm licence) system for large companies (like Columbia Cellulose, which had a No. 1 licence for logging), small- and medium-size operators took advantage of the railway lands and quota system, whereby they would apply and compete with one another through a bidding process on areas. The quota system required payment per stumpage. Jagat Singh (Jack) Uppal, personal communication, 5 February 2010, Mitchell Island, Richmond, BC.

57 "Equipment ready for start of a new sawmill in Rupert," *Prince Rupert Daily News*, 10 December 1958.

58 PM 1.22, interview, 9 May 2009, Surrey, BC.

59 The company built a band head rig, a gang saw, and a planer mill and installed a new burner on the premises. The sawmill building was 80 by 280 feet, while the green chain or sorting table housing had an area of 80 by 175 feet. Near the dock, and adjacent to the W.H. Malkin Co. Ltd warehouse and offices, stood the 129-foot-high burner for eliminating scraps and sawdust. "Sawmill start seen soon," *Prince Rupert Daily News*, 24 June 1960.

60 "New sawmill to expand facilities," *Prince Rupert Daily News*, 29 August 1960.

61 The sawmill had the capacity to process 175,000 to 200,000 feet board measure (FBM), per shift or 25,000,000 FBM per year. "Strike threat seen only bar to sawmill start," *Prince Rupert Daily News*, 9 July 1958.

62 PM 1.19, interview, 12 September 2008, Richmond, BC.

63 For example, Sohen Gill operated logging camps on the northeast coast of the Queen Charlotte Islands, along the Quottoon Channel, on the Tsimsian Peninsula, and at Stewart, Alice Arm, Kildala Arm, Treston, and Oona River (Porcher Island). Jagat Singh (Jack) Uppal, personal communication, 5 February 2010, Mitchell Island, Richmond, BC. Moreover, Prince Rupert Sawmills had 6,000 acres of timber on the south side of the Skeena River between Prince Rupert and Terrace; Peter Adanack, president of the Windsor Rover Logging Company from Vancouver, had his men fell trees for the sawmill about fifty-one kilometres up the Skeena River. "Sawmill start seen soon," *Prince Rupert Daily News*, 24 June 1960.

64 On 27 November 1958, Robert Duggan, a forest engineer working for Prince Rupert's forest service office, completed a group of timber sales to supply timber to the sawmill. "Equipment ready for start of a new sawmill in Rupert," *Prince Rupert Daily News*, 10 December 1958.

65 By 1962, 19.5 million FBM of rough lumber was shipped to markets in the UK (80%) and Japan (20%); in 1963, production increased to 25.5 million FBM, and in 1964 it grew to 30 million FBM. "Lumber export up and going higher," *Prince Rupert Daily News*, 24 January 1964.

66 Jagat Singh (Jack) Uppal, interview, 12 September 2008, Mitchell Island, Richmond, BC.

67 Hak, *Capital and Labour in the British Columbia Forest Industry*, 65–6.
68 Ken Drushka, *In the Bight: The BC Forest Industry Today* (Madeira Park, BC: Harbour Publishing, 1999), 78–9; Hak, *Capital and Labour in the British Columbia Forest Industry*, 30.
69 Hak, *Capital and Labour in the British Columbia Forest Industry*, 32–41.
70 PM 1.27, interview, 3 August 2009, Surrey, BC.
71 Jagat Singh (Jack) Uppal, interview, 12 September 2008, Mitchell Island, Richmond, BC.
72 PM 1.22, interview, 9 May 2009, Surrey, BC.
73 PM 1.2, interview, 8 May 2006, Terrace, BC; PM 1.9, interview, 10 May 2006, Terrace, BC; PM 1.12, interview, 18 May 2006, Prince Rupert, BC; PM 1.15, interview, 31 May 2007, Prince Rupert, BC; PM 1.22, interview, 9 May 2009, Surrey, BC; PM 1.25, interview, 8 June 2009, Prince Rupert, BC.
74 PM 1.9, interview, 10 May 2006, Terrace, BC.
75 PM 1.31, interview, 2010, Surrey, BC.
76 PM 1.1, interview, 20 February 2009, Langley, BC.
77 PM 1.15, interview, 31 May 2007, Prince Rupert, BC.
78 While the sawmills in Prince Rupert and Vancouver had already been built, these mills would have benefited from some additional machinery so that production could have been more profitable. Jagat Singh (Jack) Uppal, interview, 12 September 2008, Mitchell Island, Richmond, BC.
79 Dr R.G. Large, *Prince Rupert, A Gateway to Alaska and the Pacific*, vol. 2 (Vancouver: Mitchell Press, 1983), 194; Jagat Singh (Jack) Uppal, interview, 12 September 2008, Mitchell Island, Richmond, BC.
80 Hak, *Capital and Labour in the British Columbia Forest Industry*, 26–41; Drushka, *In the Bight*, 79.
81 "Sawmill shuts second shift," *Prince Rupert Daily News*, 29 May 1964.
82 The Pohle Lumber Company was founded in 1952 by Carle Pohle when he moved his operation from Kalum Lake Drive. In 1963, Pohle sold the sawmill to Hans Muehler, but even to this day many mill workers continue to refer to it as the Pohle mill. In 1969 Muehler sold the mill to Columbia Cellulose; in 1973 Columbia Cellulose changed the mill's name to Canadian Cellulose, and the BC government purchased 79 per cent of its shares. In 1980 the BC government purchased the remaining 21 per cent of the shares, and the company was renamed BC Timber. In 1984 BC Timber was sold to Westar Ltd and the name was changed to Skeena Cellulose Inc. "Terrace Lumber Company: Backgrounder," dated 29 August 2005, received from Terrace Lumber Company, Terrace, 6 May 2006.
83 Dumont Sawmill was built by Robert Dumont on Copper River. In the mid-1930s, Clair Giggey built a sawmill to the east of the CNR tracks in Terrace, which he operated until 1947. He sold the sawmill to Ernest Sande and his son, who ran it until they shut it down in 1965. Nadine Asante, *The History of Terrace* (Terrace: Terrace Public Library Association, 1972), 24–6.
84 PM 1.9, interview, 10 May 2006, Terrace, BC; PM 1.22, interview, 9 May 2009, Surrey, BC.
85 Such as PM 1.12, interview, 18 May 2006, Prince Rupert, BC.

86 PM 1.9, interview, 10 May 2006, Terrace, BC; PM 1.22, interview, 9 May 2009, Surrey, BC; husband of PF 1.4, interview, 2005, Terrace, BC.

87 The derelict dock was declared unsafe by the WCB at Terrace in 1968 and was subsequently demolished. Large, *Prince Rupert*, vol. 2, 143; Hick, *Hays' Orphan*, 39; Phylis Bowman, *The City of Rainbows!* (Prince Rupert, BC: author, 1982), 143.

88 PM 1.19, interview, 12 September 2008, Richmond, BC.

89 PM 1.9, interview, 10 May 2006, Terrace, BC.

90 PM 1.27, interview, 3 August 2009, Surrey, BC.

91 PM 1.6, interview, 9 May 2006, Terrace, BC.

92 PM 1.7, interview, 9 May 2006, Terrace, BC.

93 PM 2.13, interview, 17 May 2006, Prince Rupert, BC.

94 Application for a blasting permit to the City Superintendent of Works, Prince Rupert, BC, dated 15 February 1973. The blasting occurred between the dates 15 February 1973 and 28 February 1973 on the cannery site (section WFT) owned by Canadian Fishing Company Ltd on the Dry Dock Road, Cow Bay, Prince Rupert. The site was blasted by Granby Construction Ltd, Seal Cove. Permit archive, City of Prince Rupert, received 12 June 2009.

95 Bowman, *The City of Rainbows!*, 143.

96 PM 1.17, interview, 10 August 2008, Prince Rupert, BC.

97 Prince Rupert was in need of another dock location for a new canning plant, since the original Canadian Fishing Company plant – called "Oceanside" – on the ocean dock burnt down on 10 June 1972. Organized Labour 2, interview, 29 May 2007, Prince Rupert, BC; PM 1.22, interview, 9 May 2009, Surrey, BC.

98 The remaining structures of Prince Rupert Sawmills, including the large yellow office building with the bunkhouse in its south wing, on the Old Dry Dock site were completely dismantled and demolished in January 1977. Bowman, *The City of Rainbows!*, 143.

99 Stephenson, "Prince Rupert," 20–1.

100 Skeena Kraft Company built the Kraft pulp mill. The company was a joint venture between Columbia Cellulose (60%) and Svenska Cellulosa Aktiebolaget of Sweden (40%). In mid-1968, Svenska Cellulosa Aktiebolaget exchanged its shares for shares in Columbia Cellulose. In effect, Columbia Cellulose had total ownership of the Kraft mill. Hak, *Capital and Labour in the British Columbia Forest Industry*, 32.

101 Large, *Prince Rupert*, vol. 2, 194; Hak, *Capital and Labour in the British Columbia Forest Industry*, 32.

102 PM 1.12, interview, 18 May 2006, Prince Rupert, BC; PM 1.15, interview, 31 May 2007, Prince Rupert, BC.

103 PM 1.15, interview, 31 May 2007, Prince Rupert, BC.

104 A third woodroom was subsequently built on the riverside in 1974.

105 Italian-Canadian 2, interview, 12 August 2008, Prince Rupert, BC.

106 PM 1.16, interview, 10 August 2008, Prince Rupert, BC.

107 In the 1960s, immigration policy instituted a two-pronged approach: (1) labour-force requirements (independent skilled immigrants, regardless of country of origin) and (2) family reunification. During this period, barriers to non-European immigration were also lowered. Ravi Pendakur, *Immigrants and the Labour Force: Policy, Regu-*

lation, and Impact (Montreal & Kingston: McGill-Queen's University Press, 2000), 78–82.

108   PM 1.16, interview, 10 August 2008, Prince Rupert, BC.

109   PM 1.17, interview, 10 August 2008, Prince Rupert, BC.

110   PM 1.12, interview, 18 May 2006, Prince Rupert, BC; PM 1.15, interview, 31 May 2007, Prince Rupert, BC.

111   PM 1.33, interview, 15 July 2009, Surrey, BC.

112   Gurcharn Singh Basran and B. Singh Bolaria, *The Sikhs in Canada: Migration, Race, Class, and Gender* (New Delhi: Oxford University Press, 2003), 151–3.

113   Jagpal, *Becoming Canadians*, 100–2; Indo-Canadian Oral History Collection, item 52.

114   Ward, *White Canada Forever*, 81.

115   John Wood, "East Indians and Canada's New Immigration Policy," *Canadian Public Policy* 4, no. 4 (1978): 547–67.

116   Pendakur, *Immigrants and the Labour Force*, 156. Moreover, Basran and Bolaria have noted that while the education profile was higher among non-Sikh Indo-Canadians than among Sikh Indo-Canadians and there was a greater presence of non-Sikh Indo-Canadians in professional or managerial positions, a high proportion of both groups had low-income jobs. Basran and Bolaria, *The Sikhs in Canada*, 163.

117   PM 1.6, interview, 9 May 2006, Terrace, BC.

118   PM 1.1, interview, 20 February 2009, Langley, BC; PM 1.6, interview, 9 May 2006, Terrace, BC; PM 1.27, interview, 3 August 2009, Surrey, BC.

119   PM 1.27, interview, 3 August 2009, Surrey, BC.

120   PM 1.1, interview, 20 February 2009, Langley, BC.

121   Ibid.; PM 1.6, interview, 9 May 2006, Terrace, BC.

122   PM 1.9, interview, 10 May 2006, Terrace, BC; PM 1.15, interview, 31 May 2007, Prince Rupert, BC; PM 1.23, interview, 9 May 2009, Surrey, BC.

123   New Aiyansh was formerly New Aiyansh Indian Reservation No. 1, which was extinguished by the Nisga'a Treaty of 11 May 2000.

124   Taken from http://www.punjabikalma.com/user/ravinderravi (accessed 28 February 2012).

125   See Ravinder Ravi Gill, ed., *Wind Song: An Anthology of Poetry by the School District #92 (Nisgha) Poets of the Nass Valley*, 2 vols (Vancouver: Indo-Canadian Publications, 1984).

126   PM 1.26, interview, 7 June 2009, Prince Rupert, BC.

127   Pendakur, *Immigrants and the Labour Force*, 173–9.

128   Hak, *Capital and Labour in the British Columbia Forest Industry*, 26–41; Drushka, *In the Bight*, 79.

129   PM 1.20, interview, 16 January 2009, Delta, BC.

130   In the 1970s, a number of skilled Punjabi labourers found employment in Kitimat, where a large Alcan aluminum smelter plant was in operation. Even though the work was in Kitimat, a modest number of the Punjabi families lived in Terrace. In the 1950s, after signing the agreement with the BC government for land and water rights, Alcan undertook an engineering project that required not only the damming

and reversal of the Nechako River drainage basin, but also the boring of a sixteen-kilometre hole straight through Mt Dubose to the generating station, also built at Mt Dubose. The Alcan plant at its peak employed over two thousand people, but the number drastically declined after the automation of the plant.

131 PM 1.27, interview, 3 August 2009, Surrey, BC.

132 PM 1.11, interview, 11 May 2006, Prince Rupert, BC; PM 1.33, interview, 15 July 2009, Surrey, BC; PM 1.34, interview, 17 July 2010, Abbotsford, BC; PM 1.35, interview, 9 July 2011, Terrace, BC.

133 PM 1.3, interview, 7 May 2006, Terrace, BC; PM 1.33, interview, 15 July 2009, Surrey, BC; PM 1.35, interview, 9 July 2011, Terrace, BC.

134 Jagpal, *Becoming Canadians*, 79–83.

135 Indo-Canadian Oral History Collection, item 12.

136 Lukhardt, "Prince Rupert: A 'Tale of Two Cities,'" 328.

137 With the growth of Vancouver Punjabi community commercial businesses in the early 1980s, Punjabi merchants commuted annually to the Skeena region to sell their Indian merchandise: that is, commercial businesses of the Punjabi community in the Lower Mainland tapped into the BC small town Punjabi scene. For more information, see chapter 7.

138 Mohinder Singh Takhar, interview, 8 May 2006, Terrace, BC.

139 Jagat Singh (Jack) Uppal, interview, 12 September 2008, Mitchell Island, Richmond, BC.

140 PM 1.15, interview, 31 May 2007, Prince Rupert, BC.

141 PM 1.10, interview, 11 May 2006, Prince Rupert, BC.

142 "BC Timber offers partial start-up," *Prince Rupert Daily News*, 4 March 1983; "Expect temporary shutdowns in May," *Prince Rupert Daily News*, 21 April 1998; "B Line will remain closed," *Prince Rupert Daily News*, 28 April 1998.

143 Mohinder Singh Takhar, interview, 8 May 2006, Terrace, BC.

144 Organized Labour 4, interview, 11 August 2008, Prince Rupert, BC; Organized Labour 5, interview, 12 August 2008, Prince Rupert, BC. See articles such as "Union mood tense at pulp mill," *Prince Rupert Daily News*, 22 May 1998; "It's new deal or no deal, as Local 4 votes," *Prince Rupert Daily News*, 19 August 2002; "Union rejects contract; will present new offer," *Prince Rupert Daily News*, 20 August 2002.

145 The City of Prince Rupert had not received tax revenue from the pulp and paper mill since 1996. Tax revenue once served as the economic core of the city. The pulp and paper mill was to be sold to Sun Wave Forest Products with a promise of tax exemption, made possible through the involvement of the provincial Liberal government. However, the business deal did not go through, and the City of Prince Rupert took control of the mill in September 2009. See "Mill might delay city tax payments," *Prince Rupert Daily News*, 1 June 1998; "City wants unpaid taxes from …," *Prince Rupert Daily News*, 28 November 2003; "Sun Wave, Prince Rupert Mayor talk Watson Island sale, litigation, and possibly bankruptcy," *Northern View*, 23 April 2010.

146 Organized Labour 4, interview, 11 August 2008, Prince Rupert, BC.

147 PM 1.23, interview, 9 May 2009, Surrey, BC.

148 Mayor Jack Mussallem, personal communication, 2 June 2009, Prince Rupert, BC. The Kitwanga Lumber Company was inactive for over two years, but it reopened in April 2011. Retrieved 18 July 2011 from http://www.princegeorgecitizen.com/article/20110709/PRINCEGEORGE0101/307099995/-1/princegeorge/premier-holds-kitwanga-sawmill-grand-reopening.

149 The Pohle mill, under the name of Skeena Cellulose Inc. (Repap Company), went into receivership, one of its major creditors being the government of British Columbia. Although the mill was sold to New Skeena Forest Products in 2002, it remained closed.

150 "From Idle to Active," Logging and Sawmilling Journal, May 2006. Retrieved 22 March 2007 from http://www.forestnet.com/archives/May_06/mill_profile2.htm.

151 Initially, the sawmill was open three days a week. In the winter of 2005–06, it increased its operations to a one-day shift five days a week.

152 Fifty per cent of the northwest timber supply is old and decayed and thus can only be used as pulp logs. The remaining good-quality timber is under a program introduced by the provincial government, which allows contract loggers to export up to 30 per cent of their logs for a premium and then sell their saw logs to the West Fraser mill. Since the pulp mills have ceased to operate, the loggers lost money on the pulp logs.

153 "Last sawmill in Terrace shuts down: West Fraser blames U.S. housing slump, strong Canadian dollar," Vancouver Sun, 25 October 2007. Likewise, on 3 November 2009, Eurocan closed its pulp and paper mill in Kitimat.

154 Ibid.

155 William A. Borgen and Norman E. Amundson, "The Dynamics of Unemployment," Journal of Counseling and Development 66 (1987): 180–4; Norman E. Amundson, William A. Borgen, Sharalyn Jordan, and Anne C. Erlebach, "Survivors of Downsizing: Helpful and Hindering Experiences," Career Development Quarterly 52 (2004): 256–71; Leon Grunberg, Sarah Y. Moore, and Edward Greenberg, "Differences in Psychological and Physical Health among Layoff Survivors: The Effect of Layoff Contact," Journal of Occupational Health Psychology 6, no. 1 (2001): 15–25.

156 This may be comparable to the people of Newfoundland and their experience of the decline in the fisheries. William A. Borgen, Norman E. Amundson, and Jonathan McVicar, "The Experience of Unemployment for Fishery Workers in Newfoundland: What Helps and Hinders," Journal of Employment Counseling 39 (2002): 117–26.

157 PM 1.9, interview, 20 February 2008, Delta, BC.

158 PM 1.25, interview, 8 June 2009, Prince Rupert, BC.

159 PM 1.23, interview, 9 May 2009, Surrey, BC.

160 Pendakur, Immigrants and the Labour Force, 156.

161 PM 1.6, interview, 9 May 2006, Terrace, BC.

162 PM 1.9, interview, 10 May 2006, Terrace, BC.

163 PM 1.25, interview, 8 June 2009, Prince Rupert, BC.

164 PM 1.4, interview, 9 May 2006, Terrace, BC.

165 Amundson, Borgen, Jordan, and Erlebach, "Survivors of Downsizing," 256–71.

166 PM 1.12, interview, 18 May 2006, Prince Rupert, BC.

167 PM 1.6, interview, 9 May 2006, Terrace, BC.

1 Jagat Singh (Jack) Uppal, interview, 12 September 2008, Mitchell Island, Richmond, BC; Dr R.G. Large, *Prince Rupert, A Gateway to Alaska and the Pacific*, vol. 2 (Vancouver: Mitchell Press, 1983), 143.

2 Sarjeet Singh Jagpal, *Becoming Canadians: Pioneer Sikhs in Their Own Words* (Madeira Park, BC: Harbour Publishing, 1994), 61–79. See also the Indo-Canadian Oral History Collection, items 1–5, 8–9, 11–5, and 51–3; and Joan Mayo, *Paldi Remembered: 50 Years in the Life of a Vancouver Island Logging Town* (Duncan, BC: Paldi History Committee, 1997), 16–9.

3 Kamala Elizabeth Nayar, "The Making of Sikh Space in British Columbia: The Central Role of the *Gurdwara*," in *Asian Religions in British Columbia*, ed. Larry DeVries, Don Baker, and Dan Overmyer (Vancouver: University of British Columbia Press, 2010), 45–6.

4 Pioneers have provided descriptions of the bunkhouses and cookhouses at various mills. See Jagpal, *Becoming Canadians*, 62–5, 70.

5 Even though Sohen and Nirmal share the same last name, Sohen Singh Gill, the owner of the mill, was not a relative of Nirmal Singh Gill, the man who provided an account of the bunkhouse experience.

6 Robert K. Yin, *Case Study Research: Design and Methods* (Thousand Oaks, CA: Sage Publications, 2003), 37.

7 John W. Creswell, *Qualitative Inquiry and Research Design: Choosing among Five Traditions* (Thousand Oaks, CA: Sage Publications, 1998), 112.

8 The family members include the case subject's mother (passed away in 2006), middle brother, youngest sister, and wife. Using open-ended questions, three interviews were conducted in English and one in Punjabi.

9 The data gathered were used in the analysis of the narrative in order to determine the reliability and validity of the themes relating to mill bunkhouse experience. Moreover, the data were also used to corroborate facts. Data collection and analysis occurred concurrently; that is, analysis followed the initial gathering of data. Once the data were completely gathered, they were analysed again in order to make sense of the whole picture. Creswell, *Qualitative Inquiry and Research Design*, 213–14.

10 Murray J. Leaf, *Information and Behaviour in a Sikh Village: Social Organization Reconsidered* (Berkeley: University of California Press, 1972), 72; Kamala Elizabeth Nayar, *The Sikh Diaspora in Vancouver: Three Generations amid Tradition, Modernity, and Multiculturalism* (Toronto: University of Toronto Press, 2004), 49.

11 In Hinduism, the four stages of life (*asrama*) are (1) *brahmacarya*, the 'studenthood' stage; (2) *grhastha*, 'householder' stage; (3) *vanaprastha*, 'forest-dweller' stage; and (4) *samnyasa*, 'renunciation' stage. *Manusmrti* 4.1–3, 6.2–45. In Sikhism, the four 'quarters' of the night are (1) infancy, (2) childhood and youth, (3) adulthood, and (4) old age (*Guru Granth Sahib*, 74–8, 137–8).

12 For a discussion on the roles and expectations of females, see chapter 5.

13 See Suresh C. Ghosh, *The History of Education in Modern India 1757–1998* (New Delhi: Orient Longman, 2000).

14 Himmat Singh, *Green Revolutions Reconsidered: The Rural World of Contemporary Punjab* (New Delhi: Oxford University Press, 2001), 24.

15 Imran Ali, "Canal Colonization and Socio-economic Change," in *Five Punjabi Centuries: Polity, Economy, Society and Culture*, ed. Indu Banga (New Delhi: Manohar Publishers, 1997), 344–8; Khushwant Singh, *A History of the Sikhs*, vol. 2 (Princeton, NJ: Princeton University Press, 1963), 116–20.

16 Khushwant Singh, *A History of the Sikhs*, vol. 2, 119.

17 Malcom Lyall Darling, *The Punjab Peasant in Prosperity and Debt* (1928; reprint, Columbia, MO: South Asia Books, 1978).

18 With the East Punjab Holdings Act of 1948, the consolidation of fragmented land not only was based on the wishes of the proprietor body but was also dependent on the consensus of the village advisory committee. Himmat Singh, *Green Revolutions Reconsidered*, 40–3.

19 Punjabi villages have had two basic designs: (1) the nucleated – Jat style – village, in which the houses are built close together at the village centre, forming the nucleus of the village, which is surrounded by fields; and (2) the dispersed village, in which the dwelling places are built in detached groups of three or four houses separated – at a distance – by fields from other groups of several houses. Archana B. Verma, *The Making of Little Punjab in Canada* (New Delhi: Sage, 2002), 77–8.

20 Mridula Mukherjee, *Colonializing Agriculture: The Myth of Punjab Exceptionalism* (New Delhi: Thousand Oaks, 2005), 1–54.

21 A drastic increase in financial debt among landholders also resulted in an increase in land transfers. Moreover, there was a rise in eviction rates, as tenants could no longer pay the high rents, even though they may have been cultivating the land for years. Himmat Singh, *Green Revolutions Reconsidered*, 22–32; Himadri Banerjee, "Changes in Agrarian Society in the Late Nineteenth Century," in *Five Punjabi Centuries: Polity, Economy, Society and Culture*, ed. Indu Banga (New Delhi: Manohar Publishers, 1997), 337–9. For a detailed analysis of the issues surrounding the peasant during colonial Punjab, see Mukherjee, *Colonializing Agriculture*.

22 Reform legislation included the Punjab Security of Land Tenures Act of 1953 and the Tenancy and Agricultural Land Act of 1955. In 1947, only 51.4 per cent of all land was cultivated by its owner. The land reform imposed a ceiling on the total landholding that a family could own and granted ownership rights to tenants-at-will. By 1957, 66.4 per cent of all land was cultivated by its owner; and in 1969–70, it had increased to 80–89 per cent. Himmat Singh, *Green Revolutions Reconsidered*, 39–40.

23 Verma, *The Making of Little Punjab in Canada*, 70.

24 Ibid., 70–3.

25 For more information on remittances made to the Punjab, see Margaret Walton-Roberts, "Globalization, National Autonomy and Non-resident Indians," *Contemporary South Asia* 13, no. 1 (2004): 53–69; Deepak Nayyar, *Migration, Remittances and Capital Flows: The Indian Experience* (Delhi: Oxford University Press, 1994).

26 Many Punjabis have migrated to Western Canada from Dhudike village over the last five decades. In fact, many Punjabis from Dhudike have settled in Abbotsford, BC, where they hold a Dhudike festival annually. Immigrants to Canada have been of

benefit to Dhudike village over the years by upgrading their family homes and the village in general. Dhudike village was large even in the 1950s, consisting of about 400 to 500 extended family homes, but at that time the village did not have a health clinic or hospital. Now it is well developed.

27 Many members of the first generation of immigrants refer to themselves as Sikh or Jat-Sikh and often take traditional customs to mean religion. The narrator refers to himself as "Jat-Sikh," which reflects both his caste and his religious group. A Jat is a person from a specific agriculturalist caste group, while a Sikh is a follower of the world religion Sikhism. Even though ideally Sikhism rejects the caste system and the caste mentality sanctified by the Hindu religion, many Sikhs remain concerned about caste at the time of marriage. Nayar, *The Sikh Diaspora in Vancouver*, 131, 154.

28 If feasible, women are required to return to their natal home for the birth of their first child and then to stay there for up to forty days post-partum before returning to their husband's village.

29 The present narrative reflects an orality mode of thinking that comprises a thought form that is concrete, close to the life situation, and oriented towards the collectivity. Kamala Elizabeth Nayar and Jaswinder Singh Sandhu, "Intergenerational Communication in Immigrant Punjabi Families: Implications for Helping Professionals," *International Journal for the Advancement of Counseling* 28, no. 2 (2006): 142–3. See also Nayar, *The Sikh Diaspora in Vancouver*, 28–33.

30 Land was traditionally cultivated with a plough (*hal*) connected to a bullock; the fields were rolled with a beam of wood attached to the bullock with a man balancing on it; hoeing was done with a trowel (*khurpa* or *rumbah*); and crops were harvested with a sickle (*dati*). Locally produced mechanical technology, such as tractors with low engine capacity, manual and power-operated chaff-cutting machines and threshers, and centrifugal water pumps, had been introduced, even if they were owned by only a very few families. Himmat Singh, *Green Revolutions Reconsidered*, 46–7.

31 *Ramdasia* is a name used for the weaver caste (also known as *julahas*). This man worked all year round, whereas others might be hired during the peak times for harvesting. He ate lunch and supper at the house of the narrator but would go to his own home at night.

32 The Gill family also leased nine acres of land by giving the owner 50 per cent of the crops. They grew mainly wheat and corn in the summer months and sugarcane and cotton during the winter season.

33 Leaf, *Information and Behaviour in a Sikh Village*, 41–4.

34 *Pajama* refers to the traditional Punjabi loose cotton pants drawn with a string.

35 Dharam Dev Pishorimal Anand (1923–2011), better known simply as Dev Anand, is a famous Indian Bollywood actor, director, and film producer. While he had his first movie break in 1948, he was a popular actor and film director from the 1950s to the 1970s. As with Hollywood, Bollywood actresses and actors set the fashions for the youth and young adults.

36 Nirmal Singh Gill was granted Canadian citizenship 12 December 1963 under section 10(5) of the Canadian Citizenship Act.

37 Robby Gill, personal communication, 17 May 2011, Langley, BC.

38 At that time, there was a steady day shift all year round and a second shift that operated only six months of the year. Therefore, he worked for six months and then collected Employment Insurance (EI) during the remaining six months of the year.

39 Guru Nanak (1469–1539 CE) is the first in a succession of ten Sikh gurus who together established the Sikh religion. In Sikhism, Guru means "ultimate reality" or the embodiment of that reality (such as the "sacred word"), but also refers to the ten human gurus, who uttered the sacred word, and the scripture (*Guru Granth Sahib*), which contains the sacred word.

40 Haida 2 worked at "Prince Rupert Sawmills" during 1967–68 and spoke of having been invited to the bunkhouse for lunch. See "Informal Segregation and the Bunkhouse" in chapter 7.

41 The Capitol Theatre on Third Avenue West no longer functions. It has since been transformed into a strip mall called Capitol Mall.

42 At that time, Western spaghetti films, such as *The Good, the Bad and the Ugly* with Clint Eastwood, were shown at the Capitol Theatre.

43 Shooting ball, in general, is the most popular form of "volleyball" in Pakistan and Asia. Unlike in Olympic volleyball, in shooting ball there is no setter (the player who delivers the ball to a player with a high vertical jump who then smashes it over the net). Moreover, the ball is similar in size to a handball. Players hit the ball with both hands. Since the ball is very hard, players tend to develop large calluses and hard hands. While some new players would have to develop tough hands, those working on the green chain perhaps already had hands suited for this game.

44 *Kabaddi* is a team sport that originated in South Asia. Two teams occupy opposite halves of a field. Each team takes turns sending a "raider" into the other half. In order to win points, team members have to tag or wrestle members of the opposing team while returning back to their own half.

45 Nirmal worked at the Dumont Mill (30 May–19 September), the Skeena Forest Mill (20 September–28 November), and the Pohle Lumber Company (9 November–24 December).

46 The "New Canadian Class" was offered to new immigrants in the public school system. At that time, it did not provide ESL classes; rather, the class was conducted in English with the orientation to teach recent immigrants about Canada.

47 The application for his BC driver's licence was signed by the examining officer on 24 November 1966, and his licence was issued for "motor vehicles other than motorcycles," expiration date 2 December 1971. His address was Box 46, c/o Prince Rupert Sawmills, Prince Rupert.

48 The Khalsa Diwan Society established its second *gurdwara* (Sikh temple or place of worship) in Abbotsford in 1911; in 2004 the temple was designated a Canadian historical site by Heritage Canada (under the Ministry of Multiculturalism). In Vancouver in 1906, Sikh migrants established the Khalsa Diwan Society as an offshoot of the Sikh organization founded in the Punjab during the mid-1800s. In 1908 the society bought a church and transformed it into a *gurdwara*; it is referred to as the Second Avenue Gurdwara (in 1970, it was relocated at Ross Street and Southwest Marine Drive).

49 According to the narrator, the Sikh priest at the Abbotsford temple was not registered; therefore, he and his wife had to marry a second time in the court. The second marriage occurred 29 May 1970 at the court house in Prince Rupert. Certificate of Marriage issued by the Division of Vital Statistics, Department of Health Services and Hospital Insurance, Victoria BC, certifying the registration filed with the District Registrar of Births, Deaths, and Marriages at Prince Rupert, BC.

50 Nirmal, along with his father and middle brother, had also been sending money to expand their family farm. Indeed, over time their farm had become twelve acres (about an acre added each year). As the family settled in Canada, the farmland was leased to a cultivator.

51 U.K. Choudhry, "Uprooting and Resettling Experiences of South Asian Women," *Western Journal of Nursing Research* 23, no. 4 (2001): 377; K.J. Arorian, "A Model of Psychological Adaptation to Migration and Resettlement," *Nursing Research* 35 (1990): 5–10.

52 The four general stages have been arrived at from the present study. I prefer to separate coping from adapting, since the former refers to the manner in which a person attenuates psycho-cultural tensions resulting from acculturation stress, while the latter refers to the strategies used to solve acculturation- and adaptation-related problems. However, I have benefited from the four-stage model provided in Khan and Watson, "The Canadian Immigration Experiences of Pakistani Women," 309, which identifies the stages as (1) seeking a better future, (2) confronting reality, (3) grieving and mourning, and (4) gains, remains, and coping.

53 Michael Herzfeld, *Theoretical Practice in Culture and Society* (Oxford: Blackwell Publishers, 2001), 133–51.

54 Franca Iacovetta, *Such Hardworking People: Italian Immigrants in Postwar Toronto* (Montreal & Kingston: McGill-Queen's University Press, 1993), xxiv; Nina Glick Schiller, Linda Basch, and Christina Blanc-Szanton, eds, *Towards a Transnational Perspective on Migration, Race, Class, Ethnicity, and Nationalism Reconsidered* (New York: New York Academy of Sciences, 1992).

55 PM 1.1, interview, 20 February 2009, Langley, BC; PM 1.2, interview, 7 May 2006, Terrace, BC; PM 1.9, interview, Terrace, BC; PM 1.12, interview, Prince Rupert, BC; PM 1.15, interview, 31 May 2007, Prince Rupert, BC; PM 1.16, interview, 10 August 2008, Prince Rupert, BC; PM 1.17, 10 August 2008, Prince Rupert, BC; PM 1.22, interview, 9 May 2009, Surrey. BC.

56 PM 1.15, interview, 31 May 2007, Prince Rupert, BC.

57 D.I. Maraj, "Non-accreditation: Its Impact on Foreign Educated Immigrant Professionals" (MA thesis, University of Toronto, 1996); Salaha Khan and Jeanne Watson, "The Canadian Immigration Experiences of Pakistani Women," *Counseling Psychology Quarterly* 18, no. 4 (2005): 307–8.

58 PM 1.6, interview, May 2006, Terrace, BC; PM 1.9, interview, Terrace, BC; PM 1.10, interview, 11 May 2006, Prince Rupert, BC; PM 1.12, interview, May 2006, Prince Rupert, BC; PM 1.15, interview, 31 May 2007, Prince Rupert, BC; and PM 1.23, interview, 9 May 2009, Surrey. BC.

59 PM 1.23, interview, 9 May 2009, Surrey, BC.

60 PM 1.22, interview, 9 May 2009, Surrey, BC.

61 PM 1.15, interview, 31 May 2007, Prince Rupert, BC.

62 *Charhdi kala* is likewise a central concept in Sikhism, referring to the frame of mind in which one accepts and practices the religion. Therefore, Sikh practice, together with one's dedication and commitment to Guru, cultivates a clear state of mind.

63 While resilience is a process inherent to all societies, there is specificity in the socio-cultural practices and experiences of resiliency building. Rebecca L. Carter, "Understanding Resilience through Ritual and Religious Practice: An Expanded Theoretical and Ethnographical Framework," retrieved on 22 July 2010 from http://www.ehs.unu.edu/file/get/3736.

64 Nayar and Sandhu, "Intergenerational Communication in Immigrant Punjabi Families," 142–3. See also Nayar, *The Sikh Diaspora in Vancouver*, 28–33.

65 M. Abouguendia and K. Noels, "General and Acculturation Related Daily Hassles and Psychological Adjustment in First and Second Generation South Asian Immigrants to Canada," *International Journal of Psychology* 36, no. 3 (2001): 163–73.

66 Robert A. Emmons, "Striving for the Sacred: Personal Goals, Life Meaning, and Religion," *Journal of Social Issues* 61, no. 4 (2005): 731–45.

67 D.N. McIntosh, "Religion as a Schema, with Implications for the Relation between Religion and Coping," *International Journal for the Psychology of Religion* 5 (1995): 1–16.

68 R. Cochrane and S. Bal, "The Drinking Habits of Sikh, Hindu, Muslim, and White Men in the West Midlands: A Community Survey," *British Journal of Addiction* 85 (1990): 759–69.

69 D. Sandhu and R. Malik, "Ethnocultural Background and Substance Abuse Treatment of Asian Indian Americans," in *Ethnocultural Factors in Substance Abuse Treatment*, ed. S.L.A. Straussner (New York: Guildford Press, 2003), 368–92.

70 Jaswinder Singh Sandhu, "A Sikh Perspective on Alcohol and Drugs: Implications for the Treatment of Punjabi-Sikh Patients," *Sikh Formations* 5, no. 1 (2009): 27.

71 The relationships maintained by Punjabi migrants with their home village have been important to India as well. See Walton-Roberts, "Globalization, National Autonomy and Non-resident Indians," 53–69. See also Darshan Singh Tatla and Verne Dusenbery, eds, *Sikh Diaspora Philanthropy in Punjab: Global Giving for Local Good* (New Delhi: Oxford University Press, 2009).

72 Nayar, "The Making of Sikh Space," 45.

73 Nayar, *The Sikh Diaspora in Vancouver*, 59–60.

74 Ibid., 17.

75 Norman Buchignani and Doreen M. Indra, "Key Issues in Canadian-Sikh Ethnic and Race Relations: Implications for the Study of the Sikh Diaspora," in *The Sikh Diaspora: Migration and the Experience beyond the Punjab*, ed. N. Gerald Barrier and Verne A. Dusenbery (Delhi: Chanakya Publishers, 1989), 55.

76 PM 1.22, interview, 9 May 2009, Surrey, BC.

77 T.R. Balakrishnan and Zheng Wu, "Home Ownership Patterns and Ethnicity in Selected Canadian Cities," *Canadian Journal of Sociology* 17, no. 4 (1992): 391.

78 Michael Haan, "The Residential Crowding of Immigrants in Canada, 1971–2001," *Journal of Ethnic and Migration Studies* 37, no. 3 (2011): 443–65.

79 PM 1.25, interview, 8 June 2009, Prince Rupert, BC.
80 PM 1.12, interview, May 2006, Prince Rupert, BC.

CHAPTER FOUR

1 See, for instance, the ethnographic study of a single Sikh immigrant who arrived in Canada in the mid-1950s; the study reveals much about the collective experience of immigrants while articulating the voice of a Sikh male mill worker. Tara Singh Bains and Hugh Johnston, *Four Quarters of the Night: The Life Journey of an Emigrant Sikh* (Montreal & Kingston: McGill-Queen's University Press, 1995).

2 The Code of Manu (*Manusmrti*) justifies the constraint on a woman's autonomy with the belief that women are the essential medium through which the traditional culture can be passed on to the next generation. Josephine C. Naidoo, "Contemporary South Asian Women in the Canadian Mosaic," in *Sex Roles II: Feminist Psychology in Transition*, ed. P. Caplan (Montreal: Eden Press, 1984), 338–50.

3 Lila Abu-Lughod, ed., *Remaking Women: Feminism and Modernity in the Middle East* (Princeton, NJ: Princeton University Press, 1998), 3–31; Kamala Elizabeth Nayar, "Sikh Women in Vancouver: An Analysis of Their Psychosocial Issues," in *Women and Sikhism*, ed. Doris Jakobsh (Delhi: Oxford University Press, 2010), 259–66, 269–71.

4 Kamala Elizabeth Nayar, *The Sikh Diaspora in Vancouver: Three Generations amid Tradition, Modernity, and Multiculturalism* (Toronto: University of Toronto Press, 2004), 47–9; Nayar, "Sikh Women in Vancouver," 248–70.

5 *Manusmrti* 5.148–160.

6 PF 1.8, interview, 14 September 2005, Surrey, BC.

7 Nayar, "Sikh Women in Vancouver," 252–3.

8 Murray J. Leaf, *Information and Behaviour in a Sikh Village: Social Organization Reconsidered* (Berkeley: University of California Press, 1972), 186–92.

9 Ibid., 189. The traditional Indian inheritance laws changed with the Hindu Succession Act (1957), giving women the same rights as men in terms of succession. However, the act has not always been enforced. Women's groups have been agitating for adequate enforcement since the 1980s.

10 Vijay Agnew, ed., *Racialized Migrant Women in Canada: Essays on Health, Violence and Equity* (Toronto: University of Toronto Press, 2009), 16.

11 Prior to the changes in Canadian immigration policy in the 1960s, sisters were often sponsored through marriages arranged with Punjabis already living in Canada.

12 James Gaylord Chadney, *The Sikhs of Vancouver* (New York: AMS Press, 1984), 73–4.

13 PF 1.12, interview, 11 August 2008, Prince Rupert, BC.

14 PF 1.18, interview, 3 June 2009, Prince Rupert, BC.

15 PF 1.12, interview, 11 August 2008, Prince Rupert, BC; PF 1.5, interview, 27 May 2007, Prince Rupert, BC.

16 PF 1.18, interview, 3 June 2009, Prince Rupert, BC.

17 PF 1.14, interview, 23 January 2009, Delta, BC.

18 Paramjit S. Judge, *Punjabis in Canada: A Study of Formation of an Ethnic Community* (Delhi: Chanakya Publications, 1994), 25.

19 Nayar, *The Sikh Diaspora in Vancouver*, 68.

20 The Walia family left Prince Rupert before Prince Rupert Sawmills was sold to Columbia Cellulose in 1966. All three (husband, Gurmail, and their first daughter) have since passed away; the second daughter (Pindy), the second Punjabi to be born in Prince Rupert, now lives in the Lower Mainland. Pindy Kaur Singh, personal communication, 6 September 2008, Surrey, BC.

21 PM 1.1, interview, 20 February 2009, Langley, BC; PM 1.2, interview, 8 May 2006, Terrace, BC; PM 1.12, interview, 18 May 2006, Prince Rupert, BC; PM 1.19, interview, 12 September 2008, Richmond, BC; PF 1.4, interview, 17 July 2000, Terrace, BC.

22 Sarjeet Singh Jagpal, *Becoming Canadians: Pioneer Sikhs in Their Own Words* (Madeira Park, BC: Harbour Publishing, 1994), 61. See also the Indo-Canadian Oral History Collection (Burnaby: Simon Fraser University, 1987), items 35, 37, 43, and 49.

23 Michael M. Ames and Joy Inglis, "Conflict and Change in British Columbia Sikh Family Life," *BC Studies* 20 (1973): 15–49; Nayar, *The Sikh Diaspora in Vancouver*, 62.

24 PF 1.6, interview, 27 May 2007, Prince Rupert, BC.

25 PF 1.11, interview, 11 August 2008, Prince Rupert, BC.

26 PF 1.2, interview, 10 May 2006, Terrace, BC.

27 M. Abouguendia and K. Noels, "General and Acculturation Related Daily Hassles and Psychological Adjustment in First and Second Generation South Asian Immigrants to Canada," *International Journal of Psychology* 36, no. 3 (2001): 163–73; U.K. Choudhry, "Uprooting and Resettling Experiences of South Asian Women," *Western Journal of Nursing Research* 23, no. 4 (2001): 388–9.

28 Nayar, "Sikh Women in Vancouver," 254–5.

29 PF 1.12, interview, 11 August 2008, Prince Rupert, BC.

30 PF 1.14, interview, 23 January 2009, Delta, BC.

31 PF 1.18, interview, 3 June 2009, Prince Rupert, BC.

32 PF 1.12, interview, 11 August 2008, Prince Rupert, BC.

33 PF 1.11, interview, 11 August 2008, Prince Rupert, BC.

34 Chapter 5 provides a narrative about Bunt Kaur Sidhu's Punjabi-Canadian cultural experience of joining the fisheries workforce.

35 Prince Rupert Fishermen's Co-operative (founded in 1931) initially functioned as a local collecting organization to sell its members' fish catches to fish processing plants. However, by 1947, the Co-op began to expand and establish itself as a fish processing plant (by building a cold storage and ice plant). Gladys Young Blyth, *Salmon Canneries: British Columbia North Coast* (Victoria, BC: Trafford Publishing, 2006), 109–10.

36 The Port Edward cannery was built in 1919 by Port Edward Fisheries Ltd. In 1934, BC Packers took ownership of the company. During the Second World War, Nelson Brothers had to vacate their Oceanside location for military activity and therefore shifted to Port Edward and took possession of the Port Edward cannery. BC Packers legally took ownership of the Port Edward cannery in 1970, but it closed in 1981 when the plant was consolidated with the plant at New Oceanside. Blyth, *Salmon Canneries*, 111–14.

37 Organized Labour 2, interview, 29 May 2007, Prince Rupert, BC.

38 PF 1.12, interview, 11 August 2008, Prince Rupert, BC.

39 Seniority List – Women (BC Packers Ltd) as of 1 November 1978, received from UFAWU at Fisherman Hall, Prince Rupert, 29 May 2007.

40 In 1972, the Oceanside (Prince Rupert Fisheries, Canadian Fishing Co.) plant burnt down. It was subsequently rebuilt in 1974 at Prince Rupert's Dry Dock and was referred to as the New Oceanside Cannery. In 1980, BC Packers purchased the company, and consolidated the Port Edward cannery at New Oceanside. Blyth, *Salmon Canneries*, 102.

41 BC Packers at New Oceanside changed back to CANFISCO under the ownership of Jim Pattison in 1999.

42 Canadian Fish and Cold Storage Company Ltd was later known as Rupert Cold Storage and operated out of Seal Cove. The company closed in 1982.

43 Seal Cove Cannery began as a clam canning plant in 1925. However, after a dispute that proceeded through the Canadian courts and the Privy Council in London, it began operations as a salmon cannery. In 1951, BC Packers took over the cannery. Blyth, *Salmon Canneries*, 101.

44 William Babcock purchased a fish market in 1954 and built a plant in 1957. While the company changed ownership throughout the years, in 1977 J.S. McMillan took over the fish plant and by 1982 had transformed it into a modern one. Blyth, *Salmon Canneries*, 105.

45 Organized Labour 1, interview, 16 May 2006, Prince Rupert, BC; Organized Labour 2, interview, 29 May 2007, Prince Rupert, BC.

46 Organized Labour 2, interview, 29 May 2007, Prince Rupert, BC.

47 Amarjit Kaur Pannun, "Pardesan Ka Kam: An Essay on Punjabi-Sikh Women Cannery Workers in Northern British Columbia" (MA thesis, University of British Columbia, 1994), 5–6.

48 It is important to mention here that Punjabis who come from farming villages speak of someone as "educated" if he or she can read and write (*pari-likhi*); however, this may or may not mean that the individual is well enough educated for employment in a high-skill occupation. In the case of those who have received higher education at the college or university level, they would have emigrated from larger towns or cities, since at that time these institutions would not have been accessible in the smaller farming villages.

49 Ravi Pendakur, *Immigrants and the Labour Force Policy, Regulation, and Impact* (Montreal & Kingston: McGill-Queen's University Press, 2000), 156.

50 PM 1.6, interview, 9 May 2006, Terrace, BC.

51 PF 1.18, interview, 3 June 2009, Prince Rupert, BC.

52 PF 1.17, interview, 29 May 2009, Prince Rupert, BC.

53 PF 1.9, interview, 10 August 2008, Prince Rupert, BC.

54 PF 1.7, interview, 28 May 2007, Prince Rupert, BC.

55 Ibid.; PF 1.14, interview, 23 January 2009, Delta, BC; PF 1.6, interview, 27 May 2007, Prince Rupert, BC.

56 Tsimshian 1, interview, 21 February 2012, Prince Rupert, BC.

57 Pendakur, *Immigrants and the Labour Force*, 67.

58 PF 1.16, interview, 27 February 2009, Surrey, BC.
59 PF 1.3, interview, 6 September 2008, Surrey, BC.
60 PF 1.5, interview, 27 May 2007, Prince Rupert, BC.
61 PF 1.14, interview, 23 January 2009, Delta, BC.
62 Ames and Inglis, "Conflict and Change in British Columbia Sikh Family Life," 15–49; Chadney, *The Sikhs in Vancouver*, 91.
63 PF 1.8, interview, 14 September 2005, Surrey, BC.
64 PF 1.6, interview, 27 May 2007, Prince Rupert, BC.
65 PF 1.5, interview, 27 May 2007, Prince Rupert, BC.
66 PF 1.17, interview, 29 May 2009, Prince Rupert, BC.
67 PF 1.9, interview, 10 August 2008, Prince Rupert, BC.
68 PF 1.6, interview, 27 May 2007, Prince Rupert, BC.
69 PF 1.11, interview, 11 August 2008, Prince Rupert, BC.
70 PF 1.12, interview, 11 August 2008, Prince Rupert, BC.
71 PF 1.6, interview, 27 May 2007, Prince Rupert, BC.
72 PF 1.12, interview, 11 August 2008, Prince Rupert, BC.
73 PF 1.14, interview, 23 January 2009, Delta, BC.
74 For example, PF 1.5, interview, 27 May 2007, Prince Rupert, BC; PF 1.14, interview, 23 January 2009, Delta, BC.
75 Although the cohort of Punjabi women working in the cannery began in the 1970s, it was in 1966 that the first woman began working in the Skeena. Chapter 5 provides the narrative of the first Punjabi immigrant woman to work in the fisheries.
76 Business 4, interview, 28 May 2007, Prince Rupert, BC. See also "Wearing the 'Pants' in a Fish Plant: An Ethnographical Narrative" in chapter 5.
77 Nayar, "Sikh Women in Vancouver," 258–9.
78 PF 1.5, interview, 27 May 2007, Prince Rupert, BC.
79 PF 1.11, interview, 11 August 2008, Prince Rupert, BC.
80 PF 1.6, interview, 27 May 2007, Prince Rupert, BC.
81 PF 1.8, interview, 14 September 2005, Surrey, BC.
82 PF 1.7, interview, 28 May 2007, Prince Rupert, BC.
83 Similarly, Mexican women, who worked in food-processing plants, made sexual jokes at the workplace. For analysis of this, see Rafaela Castro, "Mexican Women's Sexual Jokes," *Aztlan: A Journal of Chicano Studies* 13, no. 1–2 (1982), 275–93.
84 PM 2.8, interview, 15 August 2009, Surrey, BC.
85 PF 1.11, interview, 11 August 2008, Prince Rupert, BC. Interestingly, when South Asian immigrant women could not find factory work in poorly industrialized Atlantic Canada, they chose to engage in volunteer work to offset boredom and isolation. Helen Ralston, "Race, Class, Gender and Work Experience of South Asian Immigrant Women in Atlantic Canada," *Canadian Ethnic Studies* 23, no. 2 (1991): 129–39.
86 PF 1.6, interview, 27 May 2007, Prince Rupert, BC.
87 PF 1.12, interview, 11 August 2008, Prince Rupert, BC.
88 PF 1.17, interview, 29 May 2009, Prince Rupert, BC.
89 For more information on the bus petition, see chapter 6.

90 PF 1.8, interview, 14 September 2005, Surrey, BC.

91 PF 1.18, interview, 3 June 2009, Prince Rupert, BC.

92 Organized Labour 1, interview, 16 May 2006, Prince Rupert, BC.

93 PF 1.3, interview, 6 September 2008, Surrey, BC.

94 PF 1.12, interview, 11 August 2008, Prince Rupert, BC.

95 Pannun, "Pardesan Ka Kam," 22.

96 PF 1.12, interview, 11 August 2008, Prince Rupert, BC.

97 For further discussion on politics in the workplace, see chapter 6.

98 The term "aunty" may be used to denote either a blood relation or simply a family friend who falls in the age group of one's mother.

99 PF 1.3, interview, 6 September 2008, Surrey, BC.

100 PF 2.13, interview, 12 August 2008, Prince Rupert, BC.

101 PF 1.12, interview, 11 August 2008, Prince Rupert, BC.

102 The purpose of the treaty was to set up a mechanism that would manage all North American trans-border shared Pacific stocks; it aimed to (a) prevent overfishing and provide optimal production and (b) ensure that each party received benefits equivalent to the production of salmon originating in its waters. For more information, see Geoff Meggs, *Salmon: The Decline of the British Columbia Fisheries* (Vancouver: Douglas & McIntyre, 1995).

103 "Fish boats block Alaska ferry" and "Ferry had nowhere to go," *Prince Rupert Daily News*, 21 July 1997; Dennis Brown, *Salmon Wars: The Battle for the West Coast Salmon Fishery* (Madeira Park, BC: Harbour Publishing, 2005), 182–95.

104 "Prince Rupert Journal; on a menu of despair, salmon is just the starter," *New York Times*, 6 February 1998, section A, 4; Brown, *Salmon Wars*, 213–16.

105 Brown, *Salmon Wars*, 319–20.

106 PF 1.3, interview, 6 September 2008, Surrey, BC.

107 PF 1.6, interview, 27 May 2007, Prince Rupert, BC.

108 PF 1.11, interview, 11 August 2008, Prince Rupert, BC.

109 For example, a Punjabi woman who has worked since 1972 ranks number 28 on the seniority list. In 2009, she still worked during the salmon season. PF 1.18, interview, 3 June 2009, Prince Rupert, BC.

110 PF 1.10, interview, 11 August 2008, Prince Rupert, BC.

111 PF 1.11, interview, 11 August 2008, Prince Rupert, BC.

112 PF 1.6, interview, 27 May 2007, Prince Rupert, BC.

113 Monica Boyd and Jessica Yu, "Immigrant Women and Earnings Equality in Canada," in *Racialized Migrant Women in Canada: Essays on Health, Violence and Equity*, ed. Vijay Agnew (Toronto: University of Toronto Press, 2009), 208–32; Krishna Pendakur and Ravi Pendakur, "The Colour of Money: Earnings Differentials among Ethnic Groups in Canada," *Canadian Journal of Economics* 31, no. 3 (1998): 518–48.

114 PF 1.2, interview, 10 May 2006, Terrace, BC.

115 PF 1.7, interview, 28 May 2007, Prince Rupert, BC.

116 PF 2.13, interview, 12 August 2008, Prince Rupert, BC.

117 PF 1.7, interview, 28 May 2007, Prince Rupert, BC.

118 PF 1.17, interview, 29 May 2009, Prince Rupert, BC.

1 Since Punjab is located on the northwestern frontier of the Indian subcontinent – where there has been a long history of Islamic invasions – the region has widely engaged in *pardah*.

2 Affluent families may or may not have hired a tutor to instruct their girls in the home. See Geraldine Forbes, *Women in Modern India* (Cambridge: Cambridge University Press, 1999), 32–9; Kamala Elizabeth Nayar, *The Sikh Diaspora in Vancouver: Three Generations amid Tradition, Modernity, and Multiculturalism* (Toronto: University of Toronto Press), 50.

3 The Hindu *varna* (social class) system includes (1) *Brahmin*, "priestly" class; (2) *Kshatriya*, "warrior" class; (3) *vaisya*, "agriculturalist" class; and (4) *sudra*, "serving" class. *Bhagavadgita* 18.40–44; *Manusmrti* 1.86–91. Although the Sikh gurus rejected the Hindu class system, many Sikhs continue to practise it, especially at the time of marriage.

4 Traditionally, most widows are not permitted to remarry. In the Punjab (and in India in general), widowhood is regarded as ill-fated, especially if it occurs early in a woman's married life before she has given birth to a son. The social position of the widow is low, as she is viewed as an economic burden for the household. The treatment of a widow can, however, range from hospitable to deplorable, depending on the family. Upon the demise of her husband, the widow comes under the care of – and is, therefore, dependent on – her son(s).

5 Forbes, *Women in Modern India*, 32–63.

6 In accord with the research methodology employed for the ethnographic narratives in this study, the narrative analysis consists of two main components: (1) textual analysis of traditional cultural mores surrounding the role and status of women and (2) fieldwork. The first component relies on theoretical inquiry into the ancient pan-Indian Hindu socio-religious law book (*Manusmrti*) for a general understanding of the pan-Indian societal norms regarding women as well as on secondary sources for specific insights about traditional Punjabi norms and customs concerning women. The second component comprises an analysis of five main types of data: (i) face-to-face semi-structured interviews conducted in English (and some Punjabi) with the narrator in August 2006, September 2008, and June 2009; (ii) semi-structured interviews conducted with other Punjabi women who worked in the fish canneries, about their experience in the Canadian workforce (using open-ended questions, these interviews were conducted in English); (iii) a semi-structured interview with the daughter of the first Punjabi woman to have lived in Prince Rupert; (iv) archival data regarding the Royal Fisheries, Prince Rupert Fishermen's Co-operative, J.S. McMillan Fisheries (previously known as Babcock Fisheries), United Fishermen and Allied Workers' Union (UFAWU), and Prince Rupert Fishermen's Co-operative Association (PRFCA) as corroborative facts; (v) analysis of the local Prince Rupert newspaper (*The Daily*) and secondary literature on the history of Prince Rupert as corroborative facts.

7 Murray J. Leaf, *Information and Behaviour in a Sikh Village: Social Organization Reconsidered* (Berkeley: University of California Press, 1972), 188–9.

8 *Makaan* refers to an ordinary building with four walls that could house a family along with the animals they kept. *Ghar,* on the other hand, means the actual dwelling place, which often has a courtyard (*bera*) with rooms on two or three sides of it.

9 In most cases, the senior men of the immediate joint family (*tabbar*) and extended family (*parivar*) do not come face-to-face with young brides or daughters-in-law for many years. In fact, a sitting room (*sawat*) located on one side of the house's courtyard (*bera*) and completely segregated from the other parts of the house, is meant to be used only by men of the family and their visitors; there they can smoke their *hookah* (hubble-bubble) and discuss politics. Next to the *sawat* is another living room used by both male and female members of the immediate joint family and/or visiting members of the extended family. A bedroom is given only to married couples; it is a place where other members of the family, especially unmarried girls, are forbidden to go. Elderly and young unmarried women sleep in another separate room; meanwhile the older and younger men use the courtyard to sleep. The kitchen is situated out in the open, away from the other rooms, to allow smoke to disperse when food is cooking on the hearth over burning cow dung cakes. Archana B. Verma, *The Making of Little Punjab in Canada* (New Delhi: Sage, 2002), 78–80.

10 Nayar, *The Sikh Diaspora in Vancouver*, 48.

11 The birth date printed on the narrator's passport is 1 April 1935. However, while the narrator is certain of her birth year (1935), she is unsure of the actual month or date. The narrator's parents never formally registered her birth. Nonetheless, her village school certificate states that she was born in 1934; according to the narrator, since her parents wanted her to attend school a year earlier, they changed her birth year from 1935 to 1934.

12 Upon arrival in Canada, the narrator was able to read and write in Punjabi. She therefore tended to possess the literacy mode of thinking; this mode of thinking reflects a shift to differentiating the "self" from the collective. Knowledge is no longer limited to personal life experiences, but also includes concrete facts that have been read or formally learned. Furthermore, while thought continues to be expressed in a concrete form, interpretation is now likely done at the literal level. Kamala Elizabeth Nayar and Jaswinder Singh Sandhu, "Intergenerational Communication in Immigrant Punjabi Families: Implications for Helping Professionals," *International Journal for the Advancement of Counseling* 28, no. 2 (2006): 142–4; Nayar, *The Sikh Diaspora in Vancouver*, 33–8.

13 Royal Fisheries installed an experimental salmon canning line and processed salmon in 1959 and 1960, but it was one of the smaller fish plants in Prince Rupert to operate as a producer of fresh and frozen fish. Gladys Young Blyth, *Salmon Canneries: British Columbia North Coast* (Victoria, BC: Trafford Publishing, 2006), 4.

14 The Sikh scripture – *Guru Granth Sahib* – begins with the sacred concept of *Eko-ankar,* "One Primordial Essence manifest in all." It is popularly translated as "One God," but ontologically is understood as an unstruck sound manifest in all. See Kamala Elizabeth Nayar and Jaswinder Singh Sandhu, *The Socially Involved Renunciate: Guru Nanak's Discourse to the Nath Yogis* (Albany: State University of New York Press, 2007), 72–4.

15 The contemporary Sikh code of conduct (*Sikh Reht Maryada*) requires Sikhs to live according to three fundamental principles: (1) meditation on the Divine Name (*nam-simran*), (2) hard work and honest living (*kirat karo*), and (3) sharing one's earnings with the needy (*vand ke chhako*) (Article 3).

16 Veronica Strong-Boag, "Home Dreams: Women and the Suburban Experiment in Canada, 1945–60," *Canadian Historical Review* 72, no. 4 (1991): 471–9.

17 Veronica Strong-Boag, "Canada's Wage-Earning Wives and the Construction of the Middle Class, 1945–60," *Journal of Canadian Studies* 29, no. 3 (1994): 5–25.

18 Strong-Boag, "Home Dreams," 490–504.

19 Serious shortcomings emerged in idyllic middle-class suburbia, most of which women had to bear – suburban loneliness, social conformity, and the continuation of a patriarchal social arrangement (with respect to employment, pension eligibility, property ownership, and legal rights over children) – not to mention the absence of equity in pay or opportunity. Mona Gleason, "Psychology and the Construction of the 'Normal' Family in Postwar Canada, 1945–60," *Canadian Historical Review* 78, no. 3 (1997): 443–77.

20 Nikky-Guninder Kaur Singh, "Durga Recalled by the Tenth Guru," in *The Sikh Tradition: A Continuing Reality*, ed. S. Bhatia and A. Spencer (Patiala: Punjabi University, 1999), 208–25.

21 Crystal L. Park, "Religion as a Meaning-Making Framework in Coping with Life Stress," *Journal of Social Issues* 61, no. 4 (2005): 707–29.

22 The Sikh practice of praying or reciting scripture (*path*) and singing hymns (*kirtan*) are ideally to be practised in the company of other Sikhs in the form of a congregation (*sangat*).

23 Nayar, *The Sikh Diaspora in Vancouver*, 54–6, 58–60.

24 Kamala Elizabeth Nayar, "Sikh Women in Vancouver: An Analysis of Their Psychosocial Issues," in *Women and Sikhism*, ed. Doris Jakobsh (Delhi: Oxford University Press, 2010), 255–56.

25 Josephine Naidoo and J. Campbell Davis, "Canadian South Asian Women in Transition: A Dualistic View of Life," *Journal of Comparative Family Studies* 19 (1988): 311–27.

26 Nayar, "Sikh Women in Vancouver," 258.

27 Nayar, *The Sikh Diaspora in Vancouver*, 67.

28 In contrast to Punjabi immigrant women in the Skeena region, it was mainly Canadian-born females in the Lower Mainland who had been observed to be generating change. Nayar, "Sikh Women in Vancouver," 266–9.

29 Nayar, *The Sikh Diaspora in Vancouver*, 67–8.

30 PF 1.18, interview, 3 June 2009, Prince Rupert, BC.

31 PF 1.17, interview, 29 May 2009, Prince Rupert, BC.

CHAPTER SIX

1 Gordon Hak, *Capital and Labour in the British Columbia Forest Industry, 1934–74* (Vancouver: University of British Columbia Press, 2007), 145–67; R. Ogmundson and M. Doyle, "The Rise and Decline of Canadian Labour/1960 to 2000: Elites, Power,

Ethnicity and Gender," *Canadian Journal of Sociology* 27, no. 3 (2002): 413–54; Alicja Muszynski, *Cheap Wage Labour: Race and Gender in the Fisheries of British Columbia* (Montreal & Kingston: McGill-Queen's University Press, 1996), 180–222.

2 Dr R.G. Large, *The Skeena: River of Destiny* (1957; reprint, Surrey, BC: Heritage House Publishing, 1996), 6.

3 John S. Lutz, *Makuk: A New History of Aboriginal-White Relations* (Vancouver: University of British Columbia Press, 2008), 165–74; Wilson Duff, *The Indian History of British Columbia: The Impact of the White Man* (reprint; Victoria: Royal British Columbia Museum, 1997), 80, 84–8; Robin Fisher, *Contact and Conflict: Indian-European Relations in British Columbia, 1774–1890* (Vancouver: University of British Columbia Press, 1977), 28–31.

4 James R. Miller, *Shingwauk's Vision: A History of Native Residential Schools* (Toronto: University of Toronto Press, 1996), 90–4.

5 Ibid., 120. For an in-depth analysis on how the First Nations were primary agents in the process of their own acculturation and conversion, see Clarence Bolt, *Thomas Crosby and the Tsimshian: Small Shoes for Feet too Large* (Vancouver: University of British Columbia Press, 1992).

6 Initially, various First Nations accommodated twenty-three small European "settlements" in the region that would become the province of British Columbia. In 1821, the North West Company amalgamated with the Hudson's Bay Company, giving the HBC a monopoly in the region. These settlements were solely fur trading posts until 1824, when the settlers extended their relations with the First Nations to other activities, such as the provision of food. Victoria – the HBC headquarters for the West Coast since 1846 – became the capital when the colony of Vancouver Island was created in 1849. Lutz, *Makuk*, 165–9; Duff, *The Indian History of British Columbia*, 74–7.

7 According to Fisher, the fur trade entailed a reciprocal relationship in which the First Nations were the resource suppliers but "their demands had to be met." Fisher, *Contact and Conflict*, xi. However, it should be noted that Native society experienced a drastic population decline because of disease. Rolf Knight, *Indians at Work: An Informal History of Native Indian Labour in British Columbia 1858–1930* (Vancouver: New Star Books, 1978), 72–3; Diane Newell, *Tangled Webs of History: Indians and the Law in Canada's Pacific Coast Fisheries* (Toronto: University of Toronto Press, 1993), 21; Duff, *The Indian History of British Columbia*, 58–61. After 1919, there was a small increase in the First Nations population even though there continued to be high rates of diseases like tuberculosis. In the 1950s, the First Nations population began to grow rapidly, and this has continued up to contemporary times. Lutz, *Makuk*, 196.

8 Fisher, *Contact and Conflict*, 95–101.

9 Paul Tennant, *Aboriginal Peoples and Politics: The Indian Land Question in British Columbia, 1849–1989* (Vancouver: University of British Columbia Press, 1990), 45–51. The Indian Act underwent many amendments. During the long period from 1876 to 1951, amendments and revisions were made with the single-minded purpose of strengthening the civilizing and assimilating mission (i.e., granting the government powers over the Aboriginals). For more information regarding the reforms and revisions made to the Indian Act, see http://www.inac.gc.ca.

10 Muszynski, *Cheap Wage Labour*, 93–7; Fisher, *Contact and Conflict*, 175–211.

11 There were at least thirty nations or ethnic groups, together speaking a total of twenty-six distinct languages. Lutz, *Makuk*, 165. For the classification of the Aboriginal groups, see Duff, *The Indian History of British Columbia*, 20–52.

12 Contrary to popular or romanticized views about the communal living of the First Nations, the people suffered hardships stemming from tribal economies as well as from warfare between the various First Nations. Knight, *Indians at Work*, 69–72.

13 Status was not based on the extent of the wealth a family possessed; the potlatch was a custom whereby clan members acquired status by redistributing their wealth. Lutz, *Makuk*, 93–6; Tennant, *Aboriginal Peoples and Politics*, 51–2. For more information on the potlatch and the ban, see Douglas Cole and Ira Chaikin, *An Iron Hand upon the People: The Law against the Potlatch on the Northwest Coast* (Vancouver: Douglas & McIntyre, 1990).

14 In 1927, an amendment was enacted prohibiting anyone from soliciting funds for Aboriginal legal claims without special licence from the superintendent general; that is, the government assumed control over the Aboriginals' ability to pursue land claims. This ban was quietly lifted in the revision of the Indian Act in 1951. Tennant, *Aboriginal Peoples and Politics*, 111–12.

15 Muszynski, *Cheap Wage Labour*, 88–9.

16 Percy Gladstone, "Native Indians and the Fishing Industry of British Columbia," *Canadian Journal of Economics and Political Science* 19, no. 1 (1953): 23.

17 Douglas Hudson, "Traplines and Timber: Social and Economic Change among the Carrier" (PhD diss., University of Alberta, Edmonton, 1983), 145.

18 The western red cedar was the most important tree species for the coastal people. Cedar was easily split and worked, and was therefore usable – its bark for clothing and its timber for housing, utensils, boats, and ceremonial carvings.

19 The first commercial cannery plant in BC was opened on the Fraser River in 1871, and by 1876, it had become well established with the development of the canning process. The first cannery on the Skeena River was built in 1877; likewise, the first one on the Nass River began operations in 1881. Knight, *Indians at Work*, 179–84.

20 See Douglas C. Harris, *Landing Native Fisheries: Indian Reserves and Fishing Rights in British Columbia 1849–1925* (Vancouver: University of British Columbia Press, 2008), 189–9; Newell, *Tangled Webs of History*, 46–65.

21 Newell, *Tangled Webs of History*, 66–97; Gladstone, "Native Indians and the Fishing Industry of British Columbia," 21–4.

22 Newell, *Tangled Webs of History*, 52–5, 75–87; Gladstone, "Native Indians and the Fishing Industry of British Columbia," 20.

23 For information about the Arrandale Cannery, see Gladys Young Blyth, *Salmon Canneries: British Columbia North Coast* (Victoria, BC: Trafford Publishing, 2006), 70–1.

24 Nisga'a 1, interview, 16 June 2009, Prince Rupert, BC; Nisga'a 1, interview, 12 July 2011, Prince Rupert, BC.

25 Lutz, *Makuk*, 205; Newell, *Tangled Webs of History*, 103–4.

26 Lutz, *Makuk*, 261–4.

27 Tennant, *Aboriginal Peoples and Politics*, 114–24; Newell, *Tangled Webs of History*, 116; Gladstone, "Native Indians and the Fishing Industry of British Columbia," 26–33.

28 Muszynski, *Cheap Wage Labour*, 202–7.
29 See Daniel Raunet, *Without Surrender, without Consent: A History of the Nishga Land Claims* (Vancouver: Douglas & McIntyre, 1984).
30 The Chinese first set foot on BC soil in the mid-1800s. They began to migrate in the hope of finding employment during a challenging time for workers in their homeland as China struggled to hold its empire together. The federal government imposed the head tax on the Chinese (in effect from 1885 to 1923), and in 1923 the Exclusion Act further barred Chinese people from migrating to Canada. W. Peter Ward, *White Canada Forever: Popular Attitudes and Public Policy toward Orientals in British Columbia* (Montreal & Kingston: McGill-Queen's University Press, 2002), 51–76; Patricia Roy, *A White Man's Province: British Columbia Politicians and Chinese and Japanese Immigrants, 1858–1914* (Vancouver: University of British Columbia Press, 1989), 185–226; Patricia Roy, *The Oriental Question: Consolidating a White Man's Province, 1914–41* (Vancouver: University of British Columbia Press, 2003), 73–7.
31 Japanese immigration began during a period of economic transition in Japan (the change from feudal society to modern society), when many Japanese were searching for work. Japanese migration to Canada can be delineated into four periods: (1) from 1877 up to the Lemieux Agreement of 1908; (2) from 1908 up to the advent of the Second World War; (3) from the evacuation of Japanese to internment camps during the Second World War up to 1949; and (4) from 1950s up to the present. During the Second World War, the Japanese were categorized as "alien," and the Canadian government forced them to live in internment camps. Roy, *A White Man's Province*, 209–13; Patricia Roy, *The Triumph of Citizenship: The Japanese and Chinese in Canada, 1941–67* (Vancouver: University of British Columbia Press, 2007), 16–66.
32 Muszynski, *Cheap Wage Labour*, 178–9.
33 See Audrey Kobayashi and Peter Jackson, "Japanese Canadians and the Racialization of Labour in the British Columbia Sawmill Industry," BC *Studies* 103 (Fall 1994): 33–58.
34 Ross Lambertson, "The BC Court of Appeal and Civil Liberties," BC *Studies* 162 (Summer 2009): 82.
35 Sarjeet Singh Jagpal, *Becoming Canadians: Pioneer Sikhs in Their Own Words* (Madeira Park, BC: Harbour Publishing, 1994), 78–9.
36 Gordon Hak, *Turning Trees into Dollars: The British Columbia Coastal Lumber History, 1858–1913* (Toronto: University of Toronto Press, 2000), 155.
37 Jagpal, *Becoming Canadians*, 65. See also the Indo-Canadian Oral History Collection (Burnaby: Simon Fraser University, 1987), item 13.
38 Hak, *Turning Trees into Dollars*, 157.
39 PM 1.18, interview, 20 September 2008, Vancouver, BC.
40 Muszynski, *Cheap Wage Labour*, 73.
41 Nisga'a 2, interview, 15 June 2009, Prince Rupert, BC.
42 The United Fishermen Allied Workers Union (UFAWU) also contributed to the elimination of the Chinese labour force and its contract system in the fishery industry. Muszynski, *Cheap Wage Labour*, 194–8.
43 Nisga'a 1, interview, 16 June 2009, Prince Rupert, BC.
44 Muszynski, *Cheap Wage Labour*, 73.

45 Hak, *Turning Trees into Dollars*, 159.
46 For instance, Chicano women traditionally worked seasonally in the fruit canneries of the Santa Clara Valley. Patricia Zavella, *Women's Work & Chicano Families: Cannery Workers of the Santa Clara Valley* (Ithaca, NY: Cornell University Press, 1987), 1–2, 57–62.
47 Gladstone, "Native Indians and the Fishing Industry of British Columbia," 22–3.
48 Dr R.G. Large, *Prince Rupert, A Gateway to Alaska and the Pacific*, vol. 2 (Vancouver: Mitchell Press, 1983), 58–61.
49 Gladstone, "Native Indians and the Fishing Industry of British Columbia," 29–31; Newell, *Tangled Webs of History*, 106–12.
50 Muszynski, *Cheap Wage Labour*, 178–9.
51 In 1886, the North Pacific Cannery was built in Port Edward. It is now a national historic site, as it is the oldest completely preserved cannery still in existence. Its labour force was multi-ethnic, with Europeans, First Nations, Japanese, and Chinese working as fishers, canners, and boat builders. Prior to the closure of canning lines at the cannery in the 1970s, some Punjabis also worked in the cannery. The plant was permanently closed in 1981. Blyth, *Salmon Canneries*, 121–3.
52 Nisga'a 3, interview, 10 June 2009, Prince Rupert, BC.
53 The Chinese men were regarded as the cannery's butchers. When fifty butchers were displaced as a result of the introduction of the butchering machine in 1905, the name given to the machine was the "Iron Chink." Since the 1970s, the machines have been referred to as the "Iron Butcher." Muszynski, *Cheap Wage Labour*, 168–9.
54 Organized Labour 2, interview, 29 May 2007, Prince Rupert, BC.
55 Tsimshian 1, interview, 21 February 2012, Prince Rupert, BC.
56 Muszynski, *Cheap Wage Labour*, 95, 129–44; Knight, *Indians at Work*, 192–3.
57 Anglo-Canadian 5, interview, 18 June 2009, Prince Rupert, BC.
58 Nisga'a 1, interview, 16 June 2009, Prince Rupert, BC.
59 Muszynski, *Cheap Wage Labour*, 88–9; Lutz, *Makuk*, 8–9.
60 Roy, *A White Man's Province*, 229–63. See also Roy, "The Oriental 'Menace' in British Columbia," 243–55.
61 Ward, *White Canada Forever*, 36–52.
62 Political 3, interview, 2 June 2009, Prince Rupert, BC.
63 Jagat Singh Uppal, personal communication, 5 February 2010, Mitchell Island, Richmond, BC; Jagpal, *Becoming Canadians*, 724.
64 PM 1.1, interview, 20 February 2009, Langley, BC.
65 PM 1.19, interview, 12 September 2008, Richmond, BC.
66 Large, *Prince Rupert*, vol. 2, 55–7.
67 Haida 2, interview, 1 June 2009, Prince Rupert, BC.
68 Social Service 2, interview, 13 May 2009, Delta, BC. See Jo-Anne Fiske, "Placing Violence against First Nations Children: The Use of Space and Place to Construct the (In)credible Violated Subject," in *Healing Traditions: The Mental Health of Aboriginal Peoples in Canada*, ed. Laurence J. Kirmayer and Gail Gutherie Valaskakis (Vancouver: University of British Columbia Press, 2009), 140–63.
69 Organized Labour 3, interview, 11 August 2008, Prince Rupert, BC.

70 Organized Labour 2, interview, 29 May 2007, Prince Rupert, BC; Organized Labour 4, interview, 12 August 2008, Prince Rupert, BC; Business 1, interview, 8 May 2006, Terrace, BC; Business 5, interview, 4 November 2009, Vancouver, BC.

71 PF 1.14, interview, 23 January 2009, Delta, BC.

72 PF 1.6, interview, 27 May 2007, Prince Rupert, BC.

73 PF 1.8, interview, 14 September 2000, Surrey, BC.

74 PF 1.3, interview, 6 September 2008, Langley, BC.

75 PF 1.18, interview, 3 June 2009, Prince Rupert, BC.

76 Tsimshian 3, interview, 12 June 2009, Prince Rupert, BC.

77 PM 1.19, interview, 12 September 2008, Richmond, BC.

78 PM 1.23, interview, 9 May 2009, Surrey, BC.

79 Ruth M. Hallock, "A Letter from Fort St. James," in *Issues in Cultural Diversity*, ed. Harold Martin Tripper (Toronto: Ontario Institute for Studies in Education, 1976), 58.

80 PM 1.32, interview, 3 April 2010, Abbotsford, BC.

81 PM 1.21, interview, 16 January 2009, Surrey, BC.

82 Nisga'a 1, interview, 15 August 2008, Prince Rupert, BC.

83 Nisga'a 1, interview, 16 June 2009, Prince Rupert, BC.

84 Haida 2, interview, 1 June 2009, Prince Rupert, BC.

85 Nisga'a 2, interview, 15 June 2009, Prince Rupert, BC; Nisga'a 2, interview, 3 June 2009, Prince Rupert, BC.

86 Nisga'a 1, interview, 15 August 2008, Prince Rupert, BC.

87 PF 1.3, interview, 6 September 2008, Langley, BC.

88 Tsimshian 3, interview, 12 June 2009, Prince Rupert, BC.

89 PF 1.17, interview, 29 May 2009, Prince Rupert, BC.

90 Nisga'a 1, interview, 15 August 2008, Prince Rupert, BC; Nisga'a 2, interview, 15 June 2009, Prince Rupert, BC; Haida 2, interview, 1 June 2009, Prince Rupert, BC; Tsimshian 2, interview, 6 June 2009, Prince Rupert, BC.

91 PF 1.18, interview, 3 June 2009, Prince Rupert, BC.

92 Organized Labour 1, interview, 16 May 2006, Prince Rupert, BC; Organized Labour 2, interview, 29 May 2007, Prince Rupert, BC.

93 Zavella, *Women's Work & Chicano Families*, 119.

94 Italian-Canadian 2, interview, 12 August 2008, Prince Rupert, BC.

95 PM 1.1, interview, 20 February 2009, Langley, BC; PM 1.20, interview, 16 January 2009, Delta, BC; PM 1.26, interview, 7 June 2009, Prince Rupert, BC; PM 1.32, interview, 3 April 2010, Abbotsford, BC; PM 1.34, interview, 21 July 2008, Abbotsford, BC.

96 PM 1.6, interview, 9 May 2006, Terrace, BC; PM 1.20 interview, 16 January 2009, Delta, BC; PM 1.24, interview, 4 June 2009, Prince Rupert, BC; PM 1.32, interview, 3 April 2010, Abbotsford, BC; PM 1.33, interview, 15 July 2009, Surrey, BC; PM 1.34, interview, 21 July 2008, Abbotsford, BC.

97 PM 1.26, interview, 7 June 2009, Prince Rupert, BC.

98 PM 1.24, interview, 4 June 2009, Prince Rupert, BC.

99 This has been the case for middle-class South Asian immigrant women in Atlantic Canada. See Helen Ralston, "Race, Class, Gender and Work Experience of South

Asian Immigrant Women in Atlantic Canada," *Canadian Ethnic Studies* 23, no. 2 (1991): 129–39.

100 PF 1.16, interview, 27 February 2009, Surrey, BC.
101 Business 4, interview, 28 May 2007, Prince Rupert, BC.
102 Muszynski, *Cheap Wage Labour*, 182.
103 Ogmundson and Doyle, "The Rise and Decline of Canadian Labour/1960 to 2000," 415–22.
104 Jagpal, *Becoming Canadians*, 125–46; Indo-Canadian Oral History Collection, items 3, 4, and 52.
105 Political 6, interview, 1 August 2008, Surrey, BC; Organized Labour 3, interview, 18 July 2008, Surrey, BC; Jagat Singh Uppal, interview, 3 February 2009, Vancouver, BC; Hak, *Capital and Labour in the British Columbia Forest Industry*, 82.
106 PM 1.18, interview, 20 September 2008, Vancouver, BC.
107 Indo-Canadian Oral History Collection, item 52.
108 PM 1.1, interview, 20 February 2009, Langley, BC.
109 PM 1.18, interview, 20 September 2008, Vancouver, BC.
110 PM 1.27, interview, 3 August 2009, Surrey, BC.
111 PF 1.3, interview, 6 September 2008, Surrey, BC.
112 Kamala Elizabeth Nayar, *The Sikh Diaspora in Vancouver: Three Generations amid Tradition, Modernity, and Multiculturalism* (Toronto: University of Toronto Press, 2004), 173–4. As the South Asian community grew, each religious group created its own place of worship, such as the Hindu *mandir* and Muslim *masjid*, for mobilizing political clout.
113 Organized Labour 3, interview, 18 July 2008, Surrey, BC.
114 PM 1.20, interview, 16 January 2009, Delta, BC.
115 PM 1.12, interview, 18 May 2006, Prince Rupert, BC.
116 PM 1.17, interview, 10 August 2008, Prince Rupert, BC.
117 PF 1.9, interview, 10 August 2008, Prince Rupert, BC.
118 For example, PF 1.3, interview, PF 1.5, interview, May 27, 2007, Prince Rupert, BC; PF 1.6, interview, May 27, 2007, Prince Rupert, BC; PF 1.7, interview, 28 May 2007, Prince Rupert, BC; PF 1.8, interview, 14 September 2000, Surrey, BC; PF 1.14, interview, 23 January 2009, Delta, BC; Organized Labour 1, interview, 16 May 2006.
119 PF 1.17, interview, 29 May 2009, Prince Rupert, BC.
120 PF 1.14, interview, 23 January 2009, Delta, BC.
121 Ibid.
122 PF 1.12, interview, 11 August 2008, Prince Rupert, BC.
123 Ibid.; PF 1.18, interview, 3 June 2009, Prince Rupert, BC.
124 PF 1.18, interview, 3 June 2009, Prince Rupert, BC.
125 Organized Labour 2, interview, 29 May 2007, Prince Rupert, BC.
126 PF 1.14, interview, 23 January 2009, Delta, BC.
127 PF 1.12, interview, 11 August 2008, Prince Rupert, BC.
128 PM 1.8, interview, 18 July 2008, Surrey, BC.
129 Organized Labour 5, interview, 12 August 2008, Prince Rupert, BC.
130 PM 1.26, interview, 7 June 2009, Prince Rupert, BC.
131 PF 1.18, interview, 3 June 2009, Prince Rupert, BC.

132　Organized Labour 2, interview, 29 May 2007, Prince Rupert, BC.

133　Ibid.

134　Conversely, some First Nations workers from the Port Edward plant were dissatisfied because they felt that they were being demoted as a result of the merging of the two seniority lists. Nisga'a 4, interview, 25 June 2010, Prince Rupert, BC.

135　Business 4, interview, 28 May 2007, Prince Rupert, BC.

136　PF 1.6, interview, 27 May 2007, Prince Rupert, BC.

137　PF 1.3, interview, 6 September 2008, Langley, BC; PF 1.6, interview, 27 May 2007, Prince Rupert, BC; Organized Labour 1, interview, 16 May 2006; Organized Labour 2, interview, 29 May 2007, Prince Rupert, BC.

138　Tsimshian 3, interview, 12 June 2009, Prince Rupert, BC.

139　Nisga'a 4, interview, 25 June 2010, Prince Rupert, BC.

140　Nisga'a 1, interview, 16 June 2009, Prince Rupert, BC; Nisga'a 2, interview, 15 June 2009, Prince Rupert, BC; Nisga'a 4, interview, 25 June 2010, Prince Rupert, BC.

141　Nisga'a 2, interview, 15 June 2009.

142　William K. Carroll and R.S. Ratner, "The NDP Regime in British Columbia, 1991–2001: A Post-mortem," *Canadian Review of Sociology and Anthropology* 42, no. 2 (2005): 167–96.

143　PM 1.12, interview, 18 May 2006, Prince Rupert, BC.

144　Political 6, interview, 1 August 2008, Surrey, BC.

145　PM 1.18, interview, 20 September 2008, Vancouver, BC.

146　PF 1.12, interview, 11 August 2008, Prince Rupert, BC.

147　PM 1.23, interview, 9 May 2009, Surrey, BC.

148　PM 1.20, interview, 16 January 2009, Delta, BC.

149　PM 1.25, interview, 8 June 2009, Prince Rupert, BC.

150　Political 4, interview, 12 May 2006, Prince Rupert, BC; Political 8, interview, 12 June 2009, Prince Rupert, BC.

151　Nisga'a 2, interview, 3 June 2009, Prince Rupert, BC.

CHAPTER SEVEN

1　The operational definition used here is built on the definition in Wallace V. Schmidt, Roger N. Conway, Susan S. Easton, and William J. Wardrope, "The Concept of Cultural Synergy and the Global Organization," in *Communication Globally: Intercultural Communication and International Business* (Thousand Oaks, CA: Sage Publications, 2007), 41–59.

2　*Qur'an* declares that Sakeena descends from the sky on to the hearts of true believers (*mu'mineen*).

3　Dr R.G. Large, *Prince Rupert, A Gateway to Alaska and the Pacific*, vol. 2 (Vancouver: Mitchell Press, 1983), 35.

4　For example, in the discussion about "The People" of Prince Rupert in the most popular book on the local history of the town, Dr Large (a respected local resident who died in 1988) does not discuss the Punjabi or East Indian community, even though there is mention of a church that was later made into a Sikh temple. Large, *Prince Rupert*, vol. 2, 83.

5 Organized Labour 2, interview, May 2008, Prince Rupert, BC.
6 For example, "Multicultural Character on Display," *Province* (Vancouver), 20 May 2010, Vancouver, BC.
7 PM 1.18, interview, 16 July 2010, Vancouver, BC.
8 PM 1.1, interview, 20 February 2009, Langley, BC; PM 1.10, interview, 11 May 2006, Prince Rupert, BC; PM 1.14, interview, 28 May 2007, Prince Rupert, BC; PM 1.16, interview, 10 August 2008, Prince Rupert, BC; PM 1.19, interview, 12 September 2008, Richmond, BC; PM 1.20, interview, 16 January 2009, Delta, BC; PF 1.3, interview, 6 September 2008, Surrey, BC; PF 1.4, interview, 17 July 2000, Terrace, BC; PF 1.5, interview, 27 May 2007, Prince Rupert, BC; PF 1.6, interview, 27 May 2007, Prince Rupert, BC; PF 1.7, interview, 28 May 2007, Prince Rupert, BC.
9 Italian-Canadian 4, interview, 12 August 2008, Prince Rupert, BC.
10 Interestingly, during the field research conducted for the present study, it became apparent that the oral history of both the Prince Rupert Sawmills and the bunkhouse on the grounds by the Old Dry Dock is vanishing. While the history of the Old Dry Dock has been well preserved in archival literature, there is very little documented account of the sawmill and its adjoining bunkhouse. For instance, in the most recent book on Prince Rupert, a photo of the Prince Rupert Sawmills is included, but there is no mention of it having been built by a Punjabi man or that Punjabi workers lived in the bunkhouse on the mill grounds. See Prince Rupert City and Regional Archives Society, *Prince Rupert: An Illustrated History* (Prince Rupert, 2010), 89.
11 PM 1.17, interview, 10 August 2008, Prince Rupert, BC.
12 For instance, PM 1.12, interview, 18 May 2006, Prince Rupert, BC; PM 1.17, interview, 10 August 2008, Prince Rupert, BC; PF 1.16, interview, 27 February 2009, Surrey, BC; husband of PF 1.17, interview, 29 May 2009, Prince Rupert, BC; wife of PM 1.33, interview, 15 July 2009, Surrey, BC.
13 France Iacovetta, *Such Hardworking People: Italian Immigrants in Postwar Toronto* (Montreal & Kingston: McGill-Queen's University Press, 1993), 3–19.
14 Nisga'a 3, interview, 10 June 2009, Prince Rupert, BC.
15 Haida 2, interview, 1 June 2009, Prince Rupert, BC.
16 PM 1.19, interview, 12 September 2008, Richmond, BC.
17 PM 1.9, interview, 10 May 2006, Terrace, BC; PM 1.12, interview, 18 May 2006, Prince Rupert, BC; PM 1.15, interview, 31 May 2007, Prince Rupert, BC.
18 Nisga'a 3, interview, 10 June 2009, Prince Rupert, BC.
19 PM 1.22, interview, 9 May 2009, Surrey, BC.
20 PM 1.12, interview, 18 May 2006, Prince Rupert, BC. See also Ruth M. Hallock, "A Letter from Fort St. James," in *Issues in Cultural Diversity*, ed. Harold Martin Tripper (Toronto: Ontario Institute for Studies in Education, 1976), 56.
21 The derogatory term widely used for First Nations at that time was "siwash," which is Chinook jargon for a savage or wild man. PM 1.18, interview, 20 September 2008, Vancouver, BC.
22 PM 1.1, interview, 20 February 2009, Langley, BC.
23 PM 1.12, interview, 18 May 2006, Prince Rupert, BC.
24 Italian-Canadian 1, interview, 16 May 2006, Prince Rupert, BC; Italian-Canadian 2, interview, 12 August 2008, Prince Rupert, BC; Italian-Canadian 3, interview, 8 June 2009, Prince Rupert, BC.

25 Italian-Canadian 2, interview, 12 August 2008, Prince Rupert, BC.

26 Hallock, "Letter from Fort St. James," 58.

27 PM 1.22, interview, 9 May 2009, Surrey, BC.

28 PM 1.23, interview, 9 May 2009, Surrey, BC.

29 PM 1.32, interview, 3 April 2010, Abbotsford, BC.

30 No single date marks the institution of the residential school system for First Nations people (though such schools existed prior to Confederation); however, Native educational policy was backed by the assimilationist orientation of the Indian Act adopted in 1876. For more information about the residential schools, see James R. Miller, *Shingwauk's Vision: A History of Native Residential Schools* (Toronto: University of Toronto Press, 1996).

31 Social Service 2, interview, 13 May 2009, Delta, BC. See Rod McCormick, "Aboriginal Approaches to Counselling," in *Healing Traditions: The Mental Health of Aboriginal Peoples in Canada*, ed. Laurence J. Kirmayer and Gail Gutherie Valaskakis (Vancouver: University of British Columbia Press, 2009), 337–54.

32 Tsimshian 2, interview, 6 June 2009, Prince Rupert, BC.

33 Social Service 2, interview, 13 May 2009, Delta, BC.

34 PF 1.14, interview, 23 January 2009, Delta, BC.

35 PF 1.16, interview, 27 February 2009, Surrey, BC.

36 Haida 2, interview, 1 June 2009, Prince Rupert, BC.

37 Tsimshian 1, interview, 21 February 2012, Prince Rupert, BC.

38 Haida 1, interview, 30 May 2009, Prince Rupert, BC.

39 Ken E. Lukhardt, "Prince Rupert: A 'Tale of Two Cities,'" in *Historical Perspectives on Northern British Columbia*, ed. Thomas Thorner (Prince George, BC: College of New Caledonia Press, 1989), 329.

40 Euro-Canadian, interview, 25 September 2009, Surrey, BC.

41 The term "nigger" refers to people who seem black in colour and/or demeanour. Prashad interprets this as white power determining who fits the category at specific times for various reasons. Vijay Prashad, *The Karma of Brown Folk* (Minneapolis: University of Minnesota Press, 2000), 159.

42 PM 2.8, interview, 15 August 2009, Surrey, BC.

43 Jamillah Karim, *American Muslim Women: Negotiating Race, Class, and Gender within the Ummah* (New York: New York University Press, 2009), 28; Nicholas De Genova, *Working the Boundaries: Race, Space and "Illegality" in Mexican Chicago* (Durham, NC: Duke University Press, 2005), 207.

44 Herbert Hill, "Black-Jewish Conflict in the Labor Context: Race, Jobs, and Institutional Power," in *Strangers and Neighbors: Relations between Blacks & Jews in the United States*, ed. Maurianne Adams and John Bracey (Amherst: University of Massachusetts Press, 1999), 596–619.

45 PM 2.8, interview, 15 August 2009, Surrey, BC; PM 2.25, interview, 8 June 2009, Prince Rupert, BC; PM 2.28, interview, 8 September 2009, Surrey, BC; PF 2.15, interview, 20 February 2009, Langley, BC; PF 2.20, interview, 13 June 2010, Prince Rupert, BC.

46 Italian-Canadian 2, interview, 12 August 2008, Prince Rupert, BC.

47 PF 1.17, interview, 29 May 2009, Prince Rupert, BC.

48 PF 1.3, interview, 6 September 2008, Surrey, BC.

49 It has been noted that a small number of Sikhs who had migrated to Canada attended church and sent their children to Sunday school so as to socially integrate. Kamala Elizabeth Nayar, *The Sikh Diaspora in Vancouver: Three Generations amid Tradition, Modernity, and Multiculturalism* (Toronto: University of Toronto Press, 2004), 135. On the other hand, many Chinese immigrants built relations with Manitoban society through informal partnerships with Christian and missionary groups; these partnerships served them well in terms of survival, social adaptation, and business success. Alison R. Marshall, *The Way of the Bachelor: Early Chinese Settlement in Manitoba* (Vancouver: University of British Columbia Press, 2011), 21–57.

50 Kamala Elizabeth Nayar, "The Making of Sikh Space in British Columbia: The Central Role of the *Gurdwara*," in *Asian Religions in British Columbia*, ed. Larry DeVries, Don Baker, and Dan Overmyer (Vancouver: University of British Columbia Press, 2010), 44.

51 Nayar, "The Making of Sikh Space," 48.

52 The guiding principles of the Indo-Canadian Association were "to improve and promote the ethnic, social, cultural, religious, economic and the general well-being of the members. The association also provides full information about the East Indian community and its events, helps to provide professional and social contacts and also acts as a liaison between the East Indians and the governmental and social agencies." *FolkFest '74 Indo-Canadians Special Newsletter to Honour Canada's Multicultural Birthday*, brochure received from a participant.

53 PM 1.1, interview, 20 February 2009, Langley, BC.

54 The church was originally built in 1926 as a meeting place for the Oddfellow's Lodge. Later, it became a meeting place for members of the Bethel Church and then for the Bethel-Baptist Church. When the First Baptist and the Bethel-Baptist congregations merged, they built a new building on India Avenue. "The Sikh Temple at 200 Fourth Avenue East," *Prince Rupert Daily News*, 19 July 1991.

55 PM 1.32, interview, 3 April 2010, Abbotsford, BC.

56 Nayar, "The Making of Sikh Space," 48.

57 PM 1.1, interview, 20 February 2009, Langley, BC.

58 Ibid.

59 Harbhajan Singh Bhamrah, personal communication, 16 January 2009, Delta, BC.

60 With the steady growth of the Punjabi community in Terrace, an extension was built and completed in 1979.

61 PM 1.35, interview, 9 July 2011, Terrace, BC.

62 Nayar, *The Sikh Diaspora in Vancouver*, 194–9.

63 Nayar, "The Making of Sikh Space," 51–2.

64 PF 1.3, interview, 6 September 2008, Surrey, BC.

65 PM 1.32, interview, 3 April 2010, Abbotsford, BC.

66 PF 1.18, interview, 3 June 2009, Surrey, BC.

67 Operation Bluestar refers to the Indian military storming of the Golden Temple complex in Amritsar on 3 June 1984 in reaction to the fortification of the Akal Takht Temple complex by Jarnail Singh and other Sikh militants. Ramachandra Guha, *India after Gandhi: The History of the World's Largest Democracy* (New York: Ecco,

2007), 563–5; J.S. Grewal, *The Sikhs of the Punjab* (Cambridge: Cambridge University Press, 1994), 235–8.

68 The so-called split between fundamentalists and moderates that occurred in the Lower Mainland's Sikh community in 1997 over the use of tables and chairs in Surrey's Guru Nanak Gurdwara's community dining hall (*langar*) did have repercussions in some remote BC towns. It is now common to find two *gurdwaras* – one traditionalist, the other moderate – in smaller centres, such as Terrace, Prince George, and Kamloops. As a consequence of the edict about sitting on mats in the *langar*, issued in 1998, the traditional Sikhs in Terrace established the Skeena Gursikh Society in 2000 and transformed an old church into a *gurdwara*. Meanwhile, the Skeena Valley Guru Nanak Gurdwara continued to allow the use of tables and chairs in the *langar*. Nayar, "The Making of Sikh Space," 49–50. Worthy of mention here is that a second *gurdwara* was created in Prince Rupert in 1987. A visiting charismatic preacher named Karnail Singh Gareeb and his congregation established the Prince Rupert Sikh Missionary Society and transformed a house on McNicholl Avenue into a *gurdwara*. Soon after, when allegations surfaced that Gareeb was involved in an extramarital affair in Vancouver, he fled to the United States. While most Sikh families returned to the Prince Rupert Indo-Canadian Sikh Association *gurdwara*, a few families sympathized with Karnail Singh Gareeb and continued to manage his *gurdwara*.

69 T.R. Balakrishnan and Zheng Wu, "Home Ownership Patterns and Ethnicity in Selected Canadian Cities," *Canadian Journal of Sociology* 17, no. 4 (1992): 391.

70 Tsimshian 1, interview, 21 February 2012, Prince Rupert, BC.

71 PM 2.25, interview, 8 June 2009, Prince Rupert, BC.

72 PM 1.26, interview, 7 June 2009, Prince Rupert, BC.

73 Ibid.

74 The four Nisga'a villages are Gitlakdamix (New Aiyansh), Gitwinksihlkw (Canyon City), Laxgalts'ap (Greenville), and Gingolx (Kincolith). While the construction of the Nisga'a Highway involved upgrading an existing logging road that connected Lavelle Lake to Greenville (92 km), the project also included building a completely new road between Greenville and Kincolith (24 km). The route was designated Provincial Highway 113 in 2006. The number 113 is historically significant to the Nisga'a Nation: in 1887, a Nisga'a chief travelled to Victoria to meet with provincial government representatives, demanding self-government, which came 113 years later when the Nisga'a Treaty came into effect on 11 May 2000. George Peter Lomas, Regional Project Manager, Skeena District, BC Ministry of Transportation and Infrastructure, telephone communication, 5 August 2011.

75 PM 1.7, interview, 9 July 2011, Terrace, BC; PM 1.12, interview, 18 May 2006, Prince Rupert, BC; PM 1.35, interview, 9 July 2011, Terrace, BC. The First Nations population in Terrace was 10.02 per cent of the total population in 1996, 17.8 per cent in 2001, and 21 per cent in 2006. "Profile of Diversity in BC Communities" for 1996, 2001, and 2006, retrieved 3 August 2011 from http://www.welcomebc.ca/wbc/communities/facts_trends/profiles/index.page?WT.svl=LeftNav.

76 PM 2.8, interview, 15 August 2009, Surrey, BC.

77 In contrast to the situation in the Skeena region, there has continued to be more residential crowding among immigrants than among Anglo-Canadian groups in large urban centres like Toronto and Vancouver, even with their economic adaptation. Michael Haan, "The Residential Crowding of Immigrants in Canada, 1971–2001," *Journal of Ethnic and Migration Studies* 37, no. 3 (2011): 443–65.

78 Nayar, *The Sikh Diaspora in Vancouver*, 58–60.

79 PM 1.9, interview, 10 May 2006, Terrace, BC.

80 In Terrace, cohort 1 consisted of children who started school in the 1970s and the early 1980s and cohort 2 included children who entered the public school system from the mid-1980s onwards. Cohort 1 primarily endured discrimination from "white boys" at Skeena Secondary School.

81 PM 2.25, interview, 8 June 2009, Prince Rupert, BC.

82 Metlakatla is a small Tsimshian village situated on the Metlakatla Pass north of Prince Rupert. Today, Metlakatla is one of the smallest Tsimshian communities and is dependent on Prince Rupert.

83 PM 2.8, interview, 15 August 2009, Surrey, BC.

84 Educator 2, interview, 30 May 2009, Prince Rupert, BC; Educator 3, interview, 25 September 2009, Surrey, BC; Educator 4, interview, 6 June 2009, Prince Rupert, BC Social Service 2, interview, 13 May 2009, Delta, BC.

85 Political 3, interview, 2 June 2009, Prince Rupert, BC.

86 "Indian Education at Skeena School," *Prince Rupert Daily News*, 21 April 1971.

87 Educator 3, interview, 25 September, Surrey, BC.

88 Educator 2, interview, 30 May 2009, Prince Rupert, BC. See also Peter Cowley, Stephen Easton, and Michael Thomas, *Report Card on Aboriginal Education in British Columbia 2011, Studies in Education Policy* (Vancouver: Fraser Institute, 2011). More recently, the Prince Rupert's Aboriginal Education Council presented data that demonstrates an increase in Aboriginal student success. "Aboriginal Education Council's annual report shows improvements in Prince Rupert's Aboriginal learners," *Northern View*, 13 April 2012.

89 The Punjabi immigrants residing in Terrace primarily interacted with the First Nations at the workplace (i.e., sawmills and canneries) from the 1960s to the 1990s. As mentioned previously, in contrast to Prince Rupert, there was minimal interaction between the Punjabis and the First Nations in the residential areas of Terrace in the 1970s and 1980s. Greater interaction in the residential areas and schools only emerged in the late 1990s. However, at that time, intercultural tension was less pronounced because it occurred when the First Nations were gaining more recognition in general and while the Nisga'a Nation land claim was being negotiated in particular. The Nisga'a Treaty was passed in the BC Legislature on 23 April 1999 and in Parliament on 13 April 2000; the Nisga'a Final Agreement came into effect on 11 May 2000.

90 In Terrace, the Punjabis initially settled on or near Straume Street in central Terrace. However, in the mid-1980s, many Punjabis began to settle in newly developed areas (northwest or south of the railroad tracks that run through Terrace).

91 This fits in with the model of socio-economic integration, which postulates that residential space changes with economic adaptation and progress.

92 PM 2.28, interview, 8 September 2009, Surrey, BC.
93 PF 2.20, interview, 13 June 2010, Prince Rupert, BC.
94 For instance, see "Harnek Singh Brar presented the Indo-Canadian Society Archery Award," *Prince Rupert Daily News*, 31 March 1986.
95 "The plight of Indo-Canadian children," *Prince Rupert Daily News*, 19 December 1978; "Status of the Indo-Canadian Sikh women," *Prince Rupert Daily News*, January 1979.
96 PM 1.1, interview, 20 February 2009, Langley, BC.
97 PF 1.16, interview, 27 February 2009, Surrey, BC.
98 Folkfest Program of 1977, Prince Rupert, Prince Rupert Regional Archives, received 15 June 2010.
99 Vaisakhi (or Baisakhi) is the Punjabi festival celebrating the harvest at the advent of the month Vaisakh (between April and May). Although Vaisakhi is a traditional agricultural festival for Punjabis, it has greater importance for Sikhs. According to tradition, Guru Gobind Singh created the Khalsa Order on the first day of Vaisakh in 1699.
100 PF 1.16, interview, 27 February 2009, Surrey, BC.
101 Ibid.
102 "Ethnic groups prepare for ARTstravaganza," *Prince Rupert Daily News*, 11 May 1983; "ARTstravaganza praise," *Prince Rupert Daily News*, 24 May 1983; PF 1.16, interview, 27 February 2009, Surrey, BC.
103 "The Northcoast on stage," *Prince Rupert Daily News*, 2 April 1986.
104 Pam Nijar, personal communication, 17 April 2012, Surrey, BC.
105 For instance, "Credit Union wins parade contest," *Prince Rupert Daily News*, 15 June 1998; "Thank you," *Prince Rupert Daily News*, 23 July 2000.
106 Nisga'a 1, interview, 16 June 2009, Prince Rupert, BC.
107 Nisga'a 2, interview, 3 June 2009, Prince Rupert, BC.
108 Jaswinder S. Sandhu and Kamala Elizabeth Nayar, "Studying the Sikh Diaspora: First Year University Experience of Punjabi Sikh Students," *Sikh Formations* 4, no. 1 (2008): 40–2.
109 PM 1.27, interview, 3 August 2009, Surrey, BC.
110 Political 1, interview, 8 May 2006, Terrace, BC; Political 2, interview, May 2006, Terrace, BC; Business 1, interview, May 2006, Terrace, BC.

CHAPTER EIGHT

1 PM 1.22, interview, 9 May 2009, Surrey, BC.
2 PM 1.32, interview, 3 April 2010, Abbotsford, BC.
3 South Asians (predominantly Punjabi Sikhs), who in the late 1970s and 1980s were concentrated in South Vancouver and Burnaby, have since shifted primarily to Surrey. Even so, the South Asian presence in Vancouver has increased to 9.9 per cent of the city's total population. Meanwhile, Surrey has the second-largest proportion of South Asians in a single Canadian municipality, with over 27.5 per cent of its current population being South Asian. Meanwhile, many South Asians have also shifted to Abbotsford in the Fraser Valley, where they comprise 16.3 per cent (25,600) of the

city's total population. Statistics Canada 2006, Canada's ethnocultural mosaic, 2006 census: Canada's major census metropolitan areas: Vancouver four in ten belonged to a visible minority group, retrieved 25 March 2006 from http://www12.statcan.gc.ca/census-recensment/2006/as-sa/97-562/p24-eng.cfm.

4 Michael Haan, "The Residential Crowding of Immigrants in Canada, 1971–2001." *Journal of Ethnic and Migration Studies* 37, no. 3 (2011): 448.

5 Ibid., 443–65; Michael Haan, "Is Recent Immigrant Clustering in Montréal, Toronto and Vancouver Part of the Reason behind Declining Immigrant Neighbourhood Quality?," in *Demographic Aspects of Migration*, ed. Barry Edmonston, Thomas Saltzmann, and James Raymer (Berlin: Springer Verlag, 2010), 263–79.

6 PM 1.17, interview, 17 August 2008, Prince Rupert, BC.

7 PM 1.1, interview, 20 February 2009, Langley, BC.

8 PF 2.19, interview, 5 September 2009, Delta, BC.

9 PF 1.16, interview, 27 February 2009, Surrey, BC.

10 For instance, "Bhangra.me: Vancouver's Bhangra Story" was featured at the Museum of Vancouver from 5 May 2011 to 23 October 2011. The display was organized by Vivian Gosselin (curator of contemporary issues) and Naveen Girn (guest curator).

11 "The Northcoast on Stage," *Prince Rupert Daily News*, 2 April 1986.

12 For instance, see Harry Bains, "Opening ceremonies missed opportunity to show-case true beauty of BC: Our cultural diversity," *Indo-Canadian Voice* (Surrey, BC), 13 February 2010, 1; "Sukhi Sandhu letter regarding Olympic opening," *Vancouver Sun*, 16 February 2010.

13 Nayar, *The Sikh Diaspora in Vancouver: Three Generations amid Tradition, Modernity, and Multiculturalism* (Toronto: University of Toronto Press, 2004), 208.

14 PF 2.20, interview, 13 June 2010, Prince Rupert, BC.

15 PF 2.19, interview, 5 September 2009, Delta, BC.

16 For instance, see Floya Nathias and Nira Yuval-Davis, *Racialized Boundaries: Race, Nation, Gender, Colour, Class and the Anti-racist Struggle* (London: Routledge, 1992), 1–22.

17 Brian Ray and Valerie Preston, "Experiences of Discrimination: The Impact of Metropolitan and Non-metropolitan Location," power point presentation, CIC Research Network Meeting, 26 February 2009, Ottawa.

18 Forty-six per cent of visible minorities in large urban centres felt ethnic-related discomfort, compared to 40 per cent of visible minorities living in communities of ten thousand people or fewer. "Small towns offer visible minorities less ethnic friction," *Vancouver Sun*, 28 October 2008.

19 PM 1.17, interview, 10 August 2008, Prince Rupert, BC.

20 PM 2.29, interview, 17 July 2010, Abbotsford, BC.

21 A long-standing problem has been the news media's negative and unbalanced portrayal of South Asians. See Doreen M. Indra, "South Asian Stereotypes in the Vancouver Press," *Ethnic and Racial Studies* 2, no. 2 (April 1979): 166–89.

22 Nayar, *The Sikh Diaspora in Vancouver*, 207, 215–18.

23 Kamala Elizabeth Nayar, "Misunderstood in the Diaspora: The Experience of Orthodox Sikhs in Vancouver," *Sikh Formations* 4, no. 1 (2008): 17–32.

24 For further analysis of the role of the media and the Canadian South Asian community, see Yasmin Jiwani, *Discourses of Denial: Mediations of Race, Gender, and Violence* (Vancouver: University of British Columbia Press, 2006). Interestingly, Jiwani analyses two case studies, both of which involve Sikhs in British Columbia.

25 PF 1.17, interview, 29 May 2009, Prince Rupert, BC.

26 PM 1.32, interview, 3 April 2010, Abbotsford, BC.

27 Nayar, "Misunderstood in the Sikh Diaspora," 26–8.

28 PM 1.27, interview, 3 August 2009, Surrey, BC.

29 PM 1.3, interview, 7 May 2006, Terrace, BC.

30 John Zucchi, *A History of Ethnic Enclaves in Canada*, Canada's Ethnic Group Series 31 (Ottawa: Canadian Historical Association, 2007), 18.

31 Mohammad Qadeer, "Ethnic Segregation in a Multicultural City," in *Desegregating the City: Ghettos, Enclaves, and Inequality*, ed. David P. Varady (Albany: State University of New York Press, 2005), 56–7.

32 "White flight" is a term used to describe the withdrawal of others from an ethnic nucleus. Christopher Caldwell, *Reflections on the Revolution in Europe: Immigration, Islam, and the West* (New York: Anchor Books, 2009), 49–51.

33 Qadeer, "Ethnic Segregation in a Multicultural City," 57.

34 Nayar, "The Making of Sikh Space," 49.

35 For instance, in the 1950s, there was a heated dispute over Punjabis living in South Vancouver. Seven South Vancouver residents held a meeting to explain their reasons for trying to prevent the sale of a house. See "It's not racial prejudice, but – Turbans and things" and "Sikhs' seven neighbors say: 'We just don't want them,'" *Vancouver Sun*, 29 September 1958, 1, 3; cited in Kamala Elizabeth Nayar, "Religion, Resiliency and Citizenship: The Journey of a Vancouver Sikh Pioneer," in *Sikh Diaspora: Theory, Agency, and Experience*, ed. Michael Hawley (Leiden, Netherlands: Brill Academic Publishers, under review).

36 For instance, see Harold Munro, "Neighbors battle creeping invasion of 'monsters,'" *Vancouver Sun*, 2 November 1994, A3; Kent Spencer, "Neighbours are against neighbours: Monster homes that violate bylaws leave many people calling for change," *Province* (Vancouver), 1 November 2009, A4.

37 N. Ariel Espino, "Inequality, Segregation, and Housing Markets: The U.S. Case," in *Desegregating the City: Ghettos, Enclaves, and Inequality*, ed. David P. Varady (Albany: State University of New York Press, 2005), 151.

38 Pan-ethnic refers to the wider group of ethnic or "racialized" subgroups that are interconnected by superficial physical features and place of origin. Pan-ethnic categories are often used for the measurement and statistical analysis of various aspects of immigrant groups. Ann H. Kim and Michael J. White, "Panethnicity, Ethnic Diversity and Residential Segregation," *American Journal of Sociology* 115, no. 5 (2010): 1568–70.

39 Subrata K. Mitra, "Democracy's Resilience: Tradition, Modernity, and Hybridity in India," *Harvard International Review* 32, no. 4 (2011): 46–7.

40 Paramjit S. Judge, *Punjabis in Canada: A Study of Formation of an Ethnic Community* (Delhi: Chanakya Publications, 1994), 84–7.

41 Nayar, "The Making of Sikh Space," 55.

42 PM 1.1, interview, 20 February 2009, Langley, BC; PM 1.32, interview, 3 April 2010, Abbotsford, BC.

43 Organized Labour 5, interview, 12 August 2008, Prince Rupert, BC.

44 PM 1.27, interview, 3 August 2009, Surrey, BC.

45 "Nine vying for alderman seats," *Prince Rupert Daily News*, 26 October 1981; "Few new issues raised in aldermanic race," *Prince Rupert Daily News*, 18 November 1981; "Candidates examine projects," *Prince Rupert Daily News*, 19 November 1981; "Council winners," *Prince Rupert Daily News*, 23 November 1981.

46 Dave Jatana, interview, 3 April 2010, Abbotsford, BC.

47 Mohinder Singh Takhar, interview, 8 May 2006, Terrace, BC.

48 Political 4, interview, 26 May 2006, Prince Rupert, BC.

49 In the 1940s, the CCF (Co-operative Commonwealth Federation) and Communist parties attended public meetings to discuss the East Indian right to vote in Canada and the end British colonial rule in India. See Nayar, "Religion, Resiliency and Citizenship."

50 For instance, in 1986, Munmohan Singh (Moe) Sihota was the first Sikh elected to the British Columbia legislature for the NDP. Following suit, in 1991, Ujjal Dosanjh and Harry Lalli were elected as members of the provincial legislature for the NDP. Meanwhile, in 1988, Gulzar Singh Cheema won a seat in the Manitoba legislature as a Liberal; in 1993, Harbance Singh (Herb) Dhaliwal in South Vancouver and Gurbax Malhi in Malton (Greater Toronto) were elected as Liberal members of Parliament.

51 For instance, Gurmant Singh Grewal was elected as a Reform member of the Canadian Parliament in 1997.

52 Jerome H. Black, "The 2006 Federal Election and Visible Minority Candidates: More of the Same?," *Canadian Parliamentary Review* 31, no. 3 (2008): 33. See also Jerome H. Black and Bruce M. Hicks, "Visible Minority Candidates in the 2004 Federal Election," *Canadian Parliamentary Review* 29, no. 2 (2006): 26–31; Livianna S. Tossutti and Tom Pierre Najem, "Minorities and Elections in Canada's Fourth Party System: Macro and Micro Constraints and Opportunities," *Canadian Ethnic Studies* 34, no. 1 (2002): 85–112.

53 Nayar, *The Sikh Diaspora in Vancouver*, 172–4.

54 Joyce Pettigrew, Robber Noblemen: A Study of the Political System of Sikh Jats (Boston: Routledge and Kegan Paul, 1975), 57, 187–98.

55 Indo-Canadian Sikh Association of Prince Rupert, "Brief submitted to the Special Joint Committee on Immigration Policy, PO Box 728, Parliament, Ottawa, Ontario" (Prince Rupert, BC, May 1975).

56 Conservative Party, "Breaking Through – Building the Conservative Brand in Cultural Communities" (Ottawa: Ministry of Immigration and Citizenship, 2011), accessed 4 March 2011, http://www.sribd.com/doc/49973469/Breaking-Through-Building-the-Conservative-Brand-in-Cultural-Communities.

57 The *Komagata Maru* incident of 1914 evidences how Canada aimed, through the "continuous journey" rule, to prevent East Indians from migrating to Canada. A Japanese ship, the *Komagata Maru*, had been chartered by Gurdit Singh to bring 376 prospective Punjabi immigrants to British Columbia. Having the immigrants

embark in Hong Kong was an attempt to work around the Canadian continuous journey restriction. When the ship was refused the right to dock at Burrard Inlet, Vancouver, the Khalsa Diwan Society raised funds to take legal action in support of the prospective immigrants. However, the attempt was unsuccessful, and the ship was sent back to Hong Kong by court order. See Hugh Johnston, *The Voyage of Komagata Maru: The Sikh Challenge to Canada's Colour Bar* (Delhi: Oxford University Press, 1979). There is tragic irony in the experience of "East Indian" immigrants: the continuous journey rule made it impossible for "East Indians" from a colony of the British Empire to migrate to another part of the empire – Canada – even as many "East Indians" served in the British Indian army during the First and Second World Wars.

58 "Sukh Dhaliwal on *Komagata Maru*," 17 May 2007, retrieved 4 May 2011 from http://openparliament.ca/hansards/316/99/only/.

59 However, despite the Conservative government's gesture, the Liberal Party's Sukh Dhaliwal was re-elected in the Surrey Newton-North Delta riding with 36.42 per cent of the vote.

60 Harshia Walia, "*Komagata Maru* and the Politics of Apologies," *Dominion* 54, no. 11 (September 2008), retrieved 3 March 2010 from http://www.dominionpaper.ca/articles2014; Veeno Deewan, "Local Sikhs claim *Komagata Maru* government funding is blood money – Back door deal is wrong." *Indo-Canadian Voice* (Surrey), 25 December 2010, 2. The apology itself turned into a contentious issue because it was not made in the House of Commons, though it was subsequently debated as an issue in the House. Jeremy Hainsworth, "Sikhs don't accept apology for *Komagata Maru*," 3 August 2008, retrieved 3 March 2010 from http://www.theglobeandmail.com/news/national/article702064.ece.

61 The CHRP also administered funds for "multicultural initiatives" that commemorate those communities affected by the head tax, internment of "alien enemies" during the First and Second World Wars, and the MS *St Louis* incident of 1939.

62 "South Asian community raise questions on *Komagata Maru* 'Payout,'" *Indo-Canadian Voice* (Surrey), 15 January 2011, 9.

63 Dennis Wong, "Vancouver South expected to be a battleground again," 2 April 2011, retrieved from http://www.news1130.com/news/local/article/206832-Vancouver South-expected-to-be-a-battleground-again; Ian Austin, "Vancouver South incumbent Ujjal Dosanjh in fight for political life," 7 April 2011, retrieved 29 April 2011 from http://www.globaltvbc.com/incumbent+ujjal+dosanjh+fight+political+life/4582875/story.html.

64 "Official voting result, fortieth general election 2008," retrieved 29 April 2011 from http://www.elections.ca/script/OVR2008/default.html.

65 Paul Wells, "Jason Kenney: Harper's secret weapon," retrieved 29 April 2011 from http://www2.macleans.ca/2010/11/29/harper%e2%80%99s-secret-weapon.

66 Opposition to Ujjal Dosanjh also involves those who are against the Indian Congress Party for "short changing the Sikhs," who allege that Dosanjh deliberately conflates Sikh identity with terrorism, and who feel Dosanjh has been silent on issues pertaining to human rights violations in the Punjab.

67 Mark Kennedy, "Conservatives, supporters circle the wagons on Air India link to BC candidate," 23 April 2011, retrieved from http://www2.canada.com/edmonton journal/news/story.html?id=8013cd39-80f8-4e5b-8722-480263ab1209; Kim Bolan, "Dosanjh files complaint over publicly funded school's boost to rival," 23 April 2011, retrieved from http://www.canada.com/vancouversun/news/westcoastnews/ story.html?id=19955790-efa2-45d4-9953-7e8986221f31.

68 Kim Bolan, "Former Air India accused defends support of Vancouver South Conservative candidate," 25 April 2011, retrieved from http://www.globalnews.ca/ former+air+india+accused+defends+support+of+vancouver+south+conservative +candidate/271232/story.html.

69 Field observation, 15 April 2011, Surrey, BC.

70 According to Elections Canada, Conservative Wai Young was elected with 19,504 votes (43.3%); Liberal candidate Ujjal Dosanjh had 15,605 votes (34.7%); and NDP candidate Meena Wong had 8,554 votes (18%). The 2006 Canada census reports that the Vancouver South riding included 51,940 Chinese (43.2%) and 17,990 South Asians (15%). "Federal Electoral District Profile of Vancouver South, British Columbia (2003 Representation Order), 2006 Census," retrieved 3 August 2011 from http://www12.statcan.gc.ca/census-recensement/2006/dp-pd/prof/92-595/P2C.cfm? TPL=RETR&LANG=E&GC=59034.

71 According to Elections Canada, NDP Jinny Sims was elected with 15,413 votes (33.4%); Liberal candidate Sukh Dhaliwal had 14,510 votes (31.5%); and Conservative candidate Mani Fallon had 14,434 votes (31.3%). The 2006 census reports that the Newton-North Delta riding included 50,510 South Asians (42.5%) and 5,975 Chinese (5%). "Federal Electoral District Profile of Newton – North Delta, British Columbia (2003 Representation Order), 2006 Census," retrieved 3 August 2011 from http://www12.statcan.gc.ca/census-recensement/2006/dp-pd/prof/92-595/P2C.cfm? TPL=RETR&LANG=E&GC=59016.

72 Robert Matas, "Conservative Wai Young beats Dosanjh in rematch," 3 May 2001, retrieved 3 May 2011 from http://www.theglobeandmail.com/news/politics/ conservative-wai-young-beats-dosanjh-in-rematch/article2007655/.

73 Ripudaman Singh Malik, telephone communication, 2 May 2011, Papillon Eastern Imports Ltd, Vancouver, BC.

74 Terry Milewski, "Harper's controversial candidate," 22 April 2011, retrieved 29 April 2011 from http://www.cbc.ca/news/politics/canadavotes2011/story/2011/04/22/ cv-election-dosanjh.html#.

75 A citadel encompasses an area of spatial concentration of a particular population group defined by its members' superior position of power, wealth, or status. Peter Marcuse, "The Enclave, the Citadel, and the Ghetto: What Has Happened in the Post-Fordist U.S. City," *Urban Affairs Review* 33, no. 3 (1997): 228–64.

76 PM 2.8, interview, 15 August 2009, Surrey, BC.

77 PM 1.32, interview, 3 April 2010, Abbotsford, BC.

78 There is low ethnic representation in Parliament, and according to some, the political process is in need of reform. See, for example, Brian Tanguay and Steven Bittle, "Parliament as a Mirror to the Nation: Promoting Diversity in Representation through Electoral Reform," *Canadian Issues*, Summer 2005, 61–3; Jerome H. Black and Bruce

M. Hicks, "Visible Minorities and Under-Representation: The Views of Candidates," *Electoral Insight* 8, no. 2 (2006): 17–23.

79 "Indo-Canadians urged to exert more influence over Grit policy," 1 December 2006, retrieved 23 March 2011 from http://www.nationalpost.com/news/story.html?id= 9597a449-614c-4b62-886c-86927b2aec9f.

CHAPTER NINE

1 Erik H. Erikson, *Identity and the Life Cycle* (New York: Norton, 1980).

2 Jean S. Phinney, Anthony Ong, and Tanya Madden, "Cultural Values and Intergenerational Value Discrepancies in Immigrant and Non-immigrant Families," *Child Development* 71, no. 2 (2000): 528–39; Jean S. Phinney and Linda L. Alipuria, "At the Interface of Cultures: Multiethnic/Multiracial High School and College Students," *Journal of Social Psychology* 136, no. 2 (1996): 139–58.

3 Kamala Elizabeth Nayar, *The Sikh Diaspora in Vancouver: Three Generations amid Tradition, Modernity, and Multiculturalism* (Toronto: University of Toronto Press, 2004), 80–2; J.W. Berry, "Immigration, Acculturation, and Adaptation," *Applied Psychology: An International Review* 46 (1997): 5–68.

4 G. Bhattacharya, "The School Adjustment of South Asian Immigrant Children in the United States," *Adolescence* 35, no. 137 (2000): 77–85.

5 John Santrock, *Adolescence* (7th ed.; Boston: McGraw Hill, 1998), 329–30.

6 J.W. Berry, "Cultural Relations in Plural Societies: Alternatives to Segregation and Their Socio-psychological Implications," in *Groups in Contact: The Psychology of Desegregation*, ed. N. Miller and M. Brewer (Orlando, FL: Academic Press, 1984), 11–29; Jean S. Phinney, "The Multi-group Ethnic Identity Measure: A New Scale for Use with Adolescents and Young Adults from Diverse Groups," *Journal of Adolescent Research* 7, no. 2 (1992): 156–76.

7 Socio-economic status relates to education level as well as income. R. Ben-Ari and Y. Amir, "Contact between Arab and Jewish Youth in Israel: Reality and Potential," in *Contact and Conflict in Intergroup Encounters*, ed. M. Hewstone and R. Brown (Oxford: Blackwell, 1986), 45–58.

8 Jean S. Phinney, Debra L. Ferguson, and Jerry D. Tate, "Intergroup Attitudes among Ethnic Minority Adolescents: A Causal Model," *Child Development* 68, no. 5 (1997): 955–69.

9 D. Dubois and B. Hirsch, "School and Neighbourhood Friendship Patterns of Black and Whites in Early Adolescence," *Child Development* 61 (1990): 524–36.

10 R. Brown and G. Ross, "The Battle for Acceptance: An Investigation into Dynamics of Intergroup Behaviours," in *Social Identity in Intergroup Relations*, ed. H. Tajfel (Cambridge: Cambridge University Press, 1982), 155–78; M. Brewer and R. Kramer, "The Psychology of Intergroup Attitudes and Behaviour," *Annual Review of Psychology* 36 (1985): 219–43.

11 "Khalsa Sikhs" is another term for "orthodox Sikhs." According to tradition, the Khalsa Order was established by the tenth and last Sikh human guru, Guru Gobind Singh (1666–1708) to fight for social justice. In reaction to Mughal oppression and aggression, Guru Gobind Singh established the Khalsa ("the pure" or "the elect")

Sikh brotherhood. Guru (ultimate reality) was now to be worshipped in the form of the sword, the symbol for the inner battle with the ego and the external battle, as the last resort, for social and political justice.

12 Metlakatla is a small Tsimshian village situated on the Metlakatla Pass north of Prince Rupert. In 1862, Anglican minister William Duncan established a "utopian" Christian community, which comprised around 350 Tsimshians from Port Simpson (Lax Kw'alaams), along with members from other Tsimshian tribes. Today, Metlakatla remains one of the smallest of the Tsimshian communities and is dependent on Prince Rupert.

13 *Gandhi* (1982) is a biographical film directed by Richard Attenborough. The film is based on the life of Mahatma Gandhi, who led the non-violent resistance movement against British colonial rule. The film won eight Academy Awards, including one for best picture.

14 Bhagat Singh (1907–1931) is considered to be one of the most influential revolutionaries of the Indian independence movement. He was born into a Jat Sikh family that had previously been involved in revolutionary activity against British colonial rule. Associated with many organizations, he became a leader of the Hindustan Republican Association, which then became the Hindustan Socialist Republican Association. He gained popular support for a sixty-four-day fast during his imprisonment. Bhagat Singh was arrested for the death of a police officer (J.P. Saunders), killed in retaliation for the killing of another freedom fighter (Lala Lajpat Rai). As a consequence, Bhagat Singh was hanged on 23 March 1931.

Uddam Singh is another well-known Indian freedom fighter. About twenty-one years after the Amritsar massacre of 1919, Uddam Singh shot Michael O'Dwyer in London. O'Dwyer had been the governor of the Punjab in 1919 when Colonel Reginald Dyer ordered British troops to fire on unarmed Punjabi protestors at Jallianwala Bagh in Amritsar.

15 James Ross (Jim) Fulton (1950–2008) was a former NDP member of Parliament. He was first elected as MP for the Skeena riding in the 1979 federal elections. He was re-elected in three subsequent elections before retiring from politics prior to the 1993 federal election. While MP, he served as the NDP's small business critic (1979) and environmental critic (1980–93). He also served as forestry critic and spoke on Aboriginal affairs.

16 The articles of the Sikh faith are the five Ks (*kakkars*): comb (*kanga*), sword (*kirpan*), undershorts (*kachera*), cast iron bangle (*kara*), and uncut and covered hair (*kes*). Not all Sikhs bear the five articles of faith; however, all ritually baptized Sikhs (*amritdhari*) do. Sikhs who are not ritually baptized are of two types: (1) those who keep the articles of faith (particularly the *kes*), referred to as "bearer of the hair" (*kesdhari*); and (2) those who do not keep the hair, referred to as "slow adopter" (*sahajdhari*).

17 *Japji Sahib* is the first hymn in the Sikh scripture (*Guru Granth Sahib*). It was composed by Guru Nanak and is meant to be recited every morning.

18 Sylvester Stallone is a Hollywood actor known for his machismo and action heroism. His two major roles – as Rocky Balboa (a boxer who overcomes the odds to fight for love and glory) and John Rambo (a courageous soldier who specializes in violent

rescue missions) – brought him much popularity at the movie box office in the 1970s through to the 2000s.

19 Bruce Lee's Hong Kong and Hollywood produced films brought the traditional Hong Kong martial arts film to a new and popular level. In fact, his films *Way of the Dragon* (1972) and *Enter the Dragon* (1973) sparked great interest in Chinese martial arts in the West during the 1970s.

20 *Octopussy* (1983) is the thirteenth spy film of the James Bond series. In the film, James Bond is assigned the task of following a general who is stealing jewels from the Russian government. His investigation leads him to an Afghan prince named Kamal Khan and his associate Octopussy. The prince's strong and loyal bodyguard – Gobinda – is played by Kabir Bedi.

21 Sikh men carry the name Singh, which means "lion."

22 While "chug" means to quickly drink alcohol without breathing, it is also a prejudicial slang word for First Nations people.

23 The student body at North Albion Collegiate Institute, which faces significant socioeconomic challenges, received attention for a couple of violent events at the school in the 1990s. See "Student stabbed near school: Security guards put on duty daily," *Toronto Star*, 15 October 1994, A3; "Racism denied in free-for-all: Etobicoke fight about respect, students say," *Toronto Star*, 11 February 1997, A6; "The kids are all right, says cop," *Toronto Star*, 11 January 2009, A4.

24 "Coolie" literally means a cheaply hired, unskilled Asian labourer and was a derogatory term used for East Indians in South Africa. It continues to be a derogatory term used for an East Indian within the diaspora.

25 *Bhangra* is Punjabi folk music and dance traditionally performed by farmers, especially during the time leading up to Vaisakhi and the celebration of a good harvest. The dance has taken hybrid forms – especially as fusion with pop music – in the South Asian diaspora and has become very popular in the West.

26 "Coconut" and "Oreo" (cookie) are derogatory terms used by people of colour to refer to people who they consider as "brown on the outside" and "white on the inside"; that is, people with dark skin who act and live as if they were white. See Nayar, *The Sikh Diaspora in Vancouver*, 209.

27 See "Ocean search for refugee ship," *Sydney Morning Herald*, 15 July 1987.

28 For instance, see "Malton battles its demons," *Toronto Star*, 31 October 2008.

29 Operation Bluestar refers to the Indian government's storming of the Golden Temple complex in Amritsar on 3 June 1984 in reaction to the fortification of the Akal Takht (the place for governing over social and political matters) in the temple complex by Jarnail Singh Brar (Bhindrawale) and other Sikh militants.

30 The massacre of 1919 refers to the attack on unarmed Punjabis gathered at a pro-Indian nationalist rally in Jallianwalla Bagh (Amritsar) during British colonial rule. General Dyer commanded his troops to block all entries to the garden area and then to fire on the unarmed people, including women and children.

31 Sri Guru Singh Sabha Gurdwara at this time was under the political administration of members of the International Sikh Youth Federation (ISYF). The ISYF is an offshoot of the World Sikh Organization (WSO), a politically moderate organization. The ISYF was more radical and uncompromising in its single-minded goal of a sep-

arate Sikh state (Khalistan) and raised funds in the West for the Khalistan movement in the 1980s and early 1990s. In 2003, the federal government banned the ISYF as a terrorist organization.

32 *Ragis* are musicians who sing *gurbani* (Sikh scripture) or religious literature. The main scripture (*Guru Granth Sahib*) has been composed according to musical measure, indicating that scripture is meant to be sung.

33 *Asa Di Var* is a prayer meant to be recited on a daily basis in the morning.

34 Shivaram Rajguru (1908–1931) and Sukhdev Thapar (1907–1931) were both Indian freedom fighters and accomplices of Bhagat Singh. All three of them were hanged on 23 March 1931 in Lahore.

35 *Akaal Ustat* 16.86.

36 Salim Jiwa, "Slain Sikh activist was marked for death," *Kingston Whig-Standard*, 21 April 1994, 8.

37 The Underground Railroad was an informal network of secret routes and safe houses for African-American slaves to escape slave-holding states to other (free) states and Canada.

38 For details on the 1997 salmon fishery crisis, see Dennis Brown, *Salmon Wars: The Battle for the West Coast Salmon Fishery* (Madeira Park, BC: Harbour Publishing, 2005), 182–95.

39 Glen David Clark (b. 1957) is a former NDP member of the BC Legislature. He was first elected in the 1986 provincial election and served as finance minister under the NDP Harcourt government. When Harcourt resigned in 1995 after a scandal, Clark became the party leader and premier of British Columbia. In 1996, the NDP narrowly won a majority of seats, albeit with fewer votes than the BC Liberal Party.

40 "No pain, no gain: Putting the fish first," *Vancouver Sun*, 18 July 1998.

41 "Premier makes no promises," *Prince Rupert Daily News*, 15 July 1998.

42 Nayar, *The Sikh Diaspora in Vancouver*, 78–80, 111–12.

43 Ibid., 28.

44 Jaswinder S. Sandhu and Kamala Elizabeth Nayar, "Studying the Sikh Diaspora: First Year University Experience of Punjabi Sikh Students," *Sikh Formations* 4, no. 1 (2008): 36.

45 Nayar, *The Sikh Diaspora in Vancouver*, 78–80, 111–12.

46 Jean S. Phinney has established a three-stage model of ethnic identity formation: (1) unexamined ethnic identity, characterized by a lack of exploration and an acceptance of the values and attitudes of the majority culture (including internalized negative views of their own group held by the majority culture); (2) ethnic identity search of moratorium, regarded as the period of exploration initiated by an encounter or situation; and (3) ethnic identity achievement, marked by the outcome of the identity process whereby one has an acceptance and internalization of one's own ethnicity. Phinney, "The Multi-group Ethnic Identity Measure," 156–76.

47 Jean S. Phinney, Gabriel Horenczyk, Karmela Liebkind, and Paul Vedder, "Ethnic Identity, Immigration, and Well-Being: An Interactional Perspective," *Journal of Social Issues* 57, no. 3 (2001): 493–510.

48 PM 2.8, interview, 15 August 2009, Surrey, BC.

49 Italian-Canadian 2, interview, 12 August 2008, Prince Rupert, BC.

50 PM 2.29, interview, 17 July 2010, Abbotsford, BC.

51 Selcuk R. Sirin and Michelle Fine, "Hyphenated Selves: Muslim American Youth Negotiating Identities on the Fault Lines of Global Conflict," *Applied Developmental Science* 11, no. 3 (2007): 151–63.

52 PM 1.32, interview, 3 April 2010, Abbotsford, BC.

53 Vijay Prashad, *The Karma of Brown Folk* (Minneapolis: University of Minnesota Press, 2000), 158.

54 See T.S. Rukhmani, "Tagore and Gandhi," in *Indian Critiques of Gandhi*, ed. Harold Coward (Albany: State University of New York, 2003), 107–30; Robert N. Minor, "Sri Aurobindo's Dismissal of Gandhi and His Non-violence," in *Indian Critiques of Gandhi*, 87–106.

55 PM 2.29, interview, 17 July 2010, Abbotsford, BC.

56 PM 2.8, interview, 15 August 2009, Surrey, BC.

57 In Terrace, the Punjabi males of cohort 1 asserted their toughness primarily by playing ice hockey. By the mid-1980s, thanks to their physical ability, they built a reputation for Punjabis at school in particular and in the town in general. PM 1.22, interview, 9 May 2009, Surrey, BC; PM 1.35, interview, 9 July 2011, Terrace, BC.

58 PM 2.29, interview, 17 July 2010, Abbotsford, BC.

59 PM 2.8, interview, 15 August 2009, Surrey, BC.

60 *Facing Ali*, directed by Pete McCormack (Santa Monica, CA: Lionsgate and SPIKE TV, 2009).

61 PM 2.8, interview, 15 August 2009, Surrey, BC.

62 PM 2.25, interview, 8 June 2009, Prince Rupert, BC; PM 2.28, interview, 8 September 2009, Surrey, BC; PM 2.30, interview, 28 March 2010, Surrey, BC; PM 2.29, interview, 17 July 2010, Abbotsford, BC.

63 PF 2.13, interview, 12 August 2008, Prince Rupert, BC.

64 PF 2.15, interview, 20 February 2009, Langley, BC.

65 PM 2.28, interview, 8 September 2009, Surrey, BC.

66 PF 2.13, interview, 12 August 2008, Prince Rupert, BC.

67 PF 2.19, interview, 5 September 2009, Delta, BC.

68 PF 2.20, interview, 13 June 2010, Prince Rupert, BC.

69 PF 2.15, interview, 20 February 2009, Surrey, BC.

70 Nayar, *The Sikh Diaspora in Vancouver*, 103–5. See also Helen Ralston, "Identity and Lived Experience of Daughters of South Asian Immigrant Women in Halifax and Vancouver," prepared for International Migration and Ethnic Relations Conference "Youth in the Plural City: Individualized and Collectivized Identities," Norwegian Institute, Rome, 25 to 28 May 1999.

71 PF 2.13, interview, 12 August 2008, Prince Rupert, BC.

72 PF 2.19, interview, 5 September 2009, Delta, BC.

73 PF 2.20, interview, 13 June 2010, Prince Rupert, BC.

74 Gora Sikh 2.1, cited in Nayar, *The Sikh Diaspora in Vancouver*, 204.

75 PF 2.19, interview, 5 September 2009, Delta, BC.

76 PF 2.15, interview, 20 February 2009, Surrey, BC.

77 PM 2.8, interview, August 15, 2009, Surrey, BC; PM 2.25, interview, 8 June 2009, Prince Rupert, BC; PM 2.28, interview, 8 September 2009, Surrey, BC; PM 2.29, interview, 17 July 2010, Abbotsford, BC.
78 PM 2.8, interview, 15 August 2009, Surrey, BC.
79 PF 2.19, interview, 5 September 2009, Delta, BC.

CHAPTER TEN

1 PM 1.21, interview, 16 January 2009, Surrey, BC; emphasis added.
2 Elmore Philpott, editorial director of the *Vancouver News-Herald* and the first Liberal to openly support East Indians for franchise rights in BC, wrote a letter ("My Friends, the Sikhs") that was used as the foreword to a booklet about why the Sikhs should be given the franchise. See Sadhu Singh Dhami, *The Sikhs and Their Religion: A Struggle for Democracy* (Vancouver and Victoria: Khalsa Diwan Society, 1943), 4.
3 While critiques about multiculturalism creating ethnic ghettos emerged in the early 1990s, more recently there have been objections to multiculturalism based on the newer debates on inclusion and accommodation in pluralistic societies, especially in Europe. For example, see Steven Vertovec and Susanne Wessendorf, eds, *The Multiculturalism Backlash: European Discourses, Policies and Practices* (London: Routledge, 2010).
4 Kamala Elizabeth Nayar, *The Sikh Diaspora in Vancouver: Three Generations amid Tradition, Modernity, and Multiculturalism* (Toronto: University of Toronto Press, 2004).
5 Tariq Ramadan, *The Quest for Meaning: Developing a Philosophy of Pluralism* (New York: Allen Lane, 2010), 169.
6 Kamala Elizabeth Nayar, "The Sikhs: Citizenship and the Canadian Experience," in *Perspectives on Faith and Citizenship: Issues, Challenges and Opportunities*, ed. Paul Bramadat, commissioned report for the Department of Citizenship and Immigration of Canada (Victoria: University of Victoria, 2011), 126–8.

BIBLIOGRAPHY

Abouguendia, M., and K. Noels. "General and Acculturation Related Daily Hassles and Psychological Adjustment in First and Second Generation South Asian Immigrants to Canada." *International Journal of Psychology* 36, no. 3 (2001): 163–73.

Abu-Lughod, Lila, ed. *Remaking Women: Feminism and Modernity in the Middle East.* Princeton, NJ: Princeton University Press, 1998.

Adams, Maurianne, and John Bracey, eds. *Strangers and Neighbors: Relations between Blacks & Jews in the United States.* Amherst: University of Massachusetts Press, 1999.

Agnew, Vijay, ed. *Racialized Migrant Women in Canada: Essays on Health, Violence and Equity.* Toronto: University of Toronto Press, 2009.

Ali, Imran. "Canal Colonization and Socio-economic Change." In *Five Punjabi Centuries: Polity, Economy, Society and Culture,* ed. Indu Banga, 341–57. New Delhi: Manohar Publishers, 1997.

Ali, Mehrunnisa Ahmad. "Second-Generation Youth's Belief in the Myth of Canadian Multiculturalism." *Canadian Ethnic Studies* 40, no. 2 (2008): 89–107.

Ames, Michael M., and Joy Inglis. "Conflict and Change in British Columbia Sikh Family Life." *BC Studies* 20 (1973): 15–49.

Amundson, Norman E., William A. Borgen, Sharalyn Jordan, and Anne C. Erlebach. "Survivors of Downsizing: Helpful and Hindering Experiences." *Career Development Quarterly* 52 (2004): 256–71.

Anderson, Cameron D. and Laura B. Stephenson, eds. *Voting Behaviour in Canada.* Vancouver: University of British Columbia, 2010.

Angus, I. *A Border Within: National Identity, Cultural Plurality and Wilderness.* Montreal & Kingston: McGill-Queen's University Press, 1997.

Appadurai, Arjun. *Modernity at Large: Cultural Dimensions of Globalization.* Minneapolis: University of Minnesota Press, 1996.

Archer, Keith. *Political Choices and Electoral Consequences: A Study of Organized Labour and the New Democratic Party.* Montreal & Kingston: McGill-Queen's University Press, 1990.

Arorian, K.J. "A Model of Psychological Adaptation to Migration and Resettlement." *Nursing Research* 35 (1990): 5–10.

Asante, Nadine. *The History of Terrace.* Terrace, BC: Terrace Public Library Association, 1972.

Bains, Tara Singh, and Hugh Johnston. *Four Quarters of the Night: The Life Journey of an Emigrant Sikh.* Montreal & Kingston: McGill-Queen's University Press, 1995.

Balakrishnan, T.R., and Zheng Wu. "Home Ownership Patterns and Ethnicity in Selected Canadian Cities." *Canadian Journal of Sociology* 17, no. 4 (1992): 389–403.

Banerjee, Himadri. "Changes in Agrarian Society in the Late Nineteenth Century." In *Five Punjabi Centuries: Polity, Economy, Society and Culture*, ed. Indu Banga, 333–40. New Delhi: Manohar Publishers, 1997.

Banga, Indu. *Agrarian System of the Sikhs: Late Eighteenth and Early Nineteenth Centuries.* New Delhi: Manohar Publications, 1978.

– ed. *Five Punjabi Centuries: Polity, Economy, Society and Culture.* New Delhi: Manohar Publishers, 1997.

Barker, John. "Tangled Reconciliations: The Anglican Church and the Nisga'a of British Columbia." *American Ethnologist* 25, no. 3 (1998): 433–51.

Barman, Jean. *The West beyond the West: A History of British Columbia.* Toronto: University of Toronto Press, 2007.

Basham, A.L. *The Wonder That Was India.* New York: Grove Press, 1954.

Basran, Gurcharn Singh, and B. Singh Bolaria. *The Sikhs in Canada: Migration, Race, Class, and Gender.* New Delhi: Oxford University Press, 2003.

Baumann, Gerd. *Contesting Culture: Discourses of Identity in Multi-ethnic London.* Cambridge: Cambridge University Press, 1996.

Ben-Ari, R., and Y. Amir. "Contact between Arab and Jewish Youth in Israel: Reality and Potential." In *Contact and Conflict in Intergroup Encounters*, ed. M. Hewstone and R. Brown, 45–58. Oxford: Blackwell, 1986.

Bernard, H. Russell. *Research Methods in Anthropology: Qualitative and Quantitative Approaches.* New York: Altamira Press, 2002.

Berry, J.W. "Cultural Relations in Plural Societies: Alternatives to Segregation and Their Socio-psychological Implications." In *Groups in Contact: The Psychology of Desegregation*, ed. N. Miller and M. Brewer, 11–29. Orlando, FL: Academic Press, 1984.

– "Immigration, Acculturation, and Adaptation." *Applied Psychology: An International Review* 46 (1997): 5–68.

Bhachu, Parminder. *Twice Migrants: East African Sikh Settlers in Britain.* London: Tavistock Publications, 1985.

Bhattacharya, G. "The School Adjustment of South Asian Immigrant Children in the United States." *Adolescence* 35, no. 137 (2000): 77–85.

Bibby, Reginald. *Mosaic Madness: Pluralism without a Cause.* Toronto: Stoddart, 1990.

Bissoondath, Neil. *Selling Illusions: The Cult of Multiculturalism in Canada*. Toronto: Penguin Books, 1994.

Black, Jerome H. "Ethnoracial minorities in the 38th Parliament: Patterns of Change and Continuity." In *Electing a Diverse Canada: The Representation of Immigrants, Minorities, and Women*, ed. C. Andrew, J. Biles, M. Siemiatycki, and E. Tolley, 229–54. Vancouver: University of British Columbia Press, 2008.

– "The 2006 Federal Election and Visible Minority Candidates: More of the Same?" *Canadian Parliamentary Review* 31, no. 3 (2008): 30–6.

Black, Jerome H., and Bruce M. Hicks. "Visible Minorities and Under-Representation: The Views of Candidates." *Electoral Insight* 8, no. 2 (2006): 17–23.

– "Visible Minority Candidates in the 2004 Federal Election." *Canadian Parliamentary Review* 29, no. 2 (2006): 26–31.

Blyth, Gladys Young. *Salmon Canneries: British Columbia North Coast*. Victoria, BC: Trafford Publishing, 2006.

Bolt, Clarence. *Thomas Cosby and the Tsimshian: Small Shoes for Feet Too Large*. Vancouver: University of British Columbia Press, 1992.

Borgen, William A., and Norman E. Amundson. "The Dynamics of Unemployment." *Journal of Counseling and Development* 66 (1987): 180–4.

Borgen, William A., Norman E. Amundson, and Jonathan McVicar. "The Experience of Unemployment for Fishery Workers in Newfoundland: What Helps and Hinders." *Journal of Employment Counseling* 39 (2002): 117–26.

Bouchard, Gerard, and Charles Taylor. *Building the Future: A Time for Reconciliation*. Montreal: Government of Quebec, 2008.

Bowman, Phylis. *The City of Rainbows!* Prince Rupert, BC: author, 1982.

Boyd, Monica, and Jessica Yu. "Immigrant Women and Earnings Equality in Canada." In *Racialized Migrant Women in Canada: Essays on Health, Violence and Equity*, ed. Vijay Agnew, 208–32. Toronto: University of Toronto Press, 2009.

Brah, Avtar. *Cartographies of Diaspora*. London, UK: Routledge, 1996.

Brettell, Caroline B. *Anthropology and Migration: Essays on Transnationalism, Ethnicity and Identity*. New York: Altamira Press, 2003.

– "Is the Ethnic Community Inevitable? A Comparison of Settlement Patterns of Portuguese Immigrants in Toronto and Paris." *Journal of Ethnic Studies* 9 (1981): 1–17.

Brewer, M., and R. Kramer. "The Psychology of Intergroup Attitudes and Behaviour." *Annual Review of Psychology* 36 (1985): 219–43.

Brown, Dennis. *Salmon Wars: The Battle for the West Coast Salmon Fishery*. Madeira Park, BC: Harbour Publishing, 2005.

Brown, Judith. *Global South Asians: Introducing the Modern Diaspora*. Cambridge: Cambridge University Press, 2006.

Brown, R., and G. Ross. "The Battle for Acceptance: An Investigation into Dynamics of Intergroup Behaviours." In *Social Identity in Intergroup Relations*, ed. H. Tajfel, 155–78. Cambridge: Cambridge University Press, 1982.

Buchignani, Norman. "Conceptions of Sikh Culture in the Development of a Comparative Analysis of the Sikh Diaspora." In *Sikh History and Religion in the 20th*

Century, ed. Joseph T. O'Connell, Milton Israel, and Willard Oxtoby, 276–95. Toronto: Centre for South Asian Studies, University of Toronto, 1988.

Buchignani, Norman, and Doreen M. Indra. *Continuous Journey: A Social History of South Asians in Canada*. Toronto: McClelland and Stewart, 1985.

– "Key Issues in Canadian-Sikh Ethnic and Race Relations: Implications for the Study of the Sikh Diaspora." In *The Sikh Diaspora: Migration and the Experience beyond the Punjab*, ed. N. Gerald Barrier and Verne A. Dusenbery, 141–84. Delhi: Chanakya Publishers, 1989.

Cairns, Alan C., John C. Courtney, Peter MacKinnon, Hans J. Michelmann, and David E. Smith, ed. *Citizenship, Diversity and Pluralism: Canadian and Comparative Perspectives*. Montreal & Kingston: McGill-Queen's University Press, 1999.

Caldwell, Christopher. *Reflections on the Revolution in Europe: Immigration, Islam, and the West*. New York: Anchor Books, 2009.

Carroll, William K., and R.S. Ratner. "The NDP Regime in British Columbia, 1991–2001: A Post-mortem." *Canadian Review of Sociology and Anthropology* 42, no. 2 (2005): 167–96.

Carter, Rebecca L. "Understanding Resilience through Ritual and Religious Practice: An Expanded Theoretical and Ethnographical Framework." Retrieved 22 July 2010 from http://www.ehs.unu.edu/file/get/3736.

Castro, Rafaela. "Mexican Women's Sexual Jokes." *Aztlan: A Journal of Chicano Studies* 13, nos 1–2 (1982): 275–93.

Chadney, James Gaylord. "The Formation of Ethnic Communities, Lessons from Vancouver Sikhs." In *Sikh History and Religion in the 20th Century*, ed. Joseph T. O'Connell, Milton Israel, and Willard Oxtoby, 185–99. Toronto: Centre for South Asian Studies, University of Toronto, 1988.

– *The Sikhs of Vancouver*. New York: AMS Press, 1984.

Chima, Jugdep S. *The Sikh Separatist Insurgency in India: Political Leadership and Ethnonationalist Movements*. New Delhi: Sage, 2010.

Choudhry, U.K. "Uprooting and Resettling Experiences of South Asian Women." *Western Journal of Nursing Research* 23, no. 4 (2001): 388–9.

Ciprut, Jose V., ed. *The Future of Citizenship*. Cambridge, MA: MIT Press, 2009.

Clothey, Fred W. *Religion in India: A Historical Introduction*. New York: Routledge, 2006.

Cochrane, R., and S. Bal. "The Drinking Habits of Sikh, Hindu, Muslim, and White Men in the West Midlands: A Community Survey." *British Journal of Addiction* 85 (1990): 759–69.

Cole, Douglas, and Ira Chaikin. *An Iron Hand upon the People: The Law against the Potlatch on the Northwest Coast*. Vancouver: Douglas & McIntyre, 1990.

Coward, Harold., ed. *Indian Critiques of Gandhi*. Albany: State University of New York Press, 2003.

Coward, Harold, John R. Hinnels, and Raymond Brady Williams, eds. *The South Asian Religious Diaspora in Britain, Canada, and the U.S.A.* Albany: State University of New York Press, 2000.

Cowley, Peter, Stephen Easton, and Michael Thomas. "Report Card on Aboriginal Education in British Columbia 2011." In *Studies in Education Policy*. Vancouver: Fraser Institute, 2011.

Creswell, John W. *Qualitative Inquiry and Research Design: Choosing among Five Traditions*. Thousand Oaks, CA: Sage Publications, 1998.

Darling, Malcolm Lyall. *The Punjab Peasant in Prosperity and Debt*. 1928; reprint, Columbia, MO: South Asia Books, 1978.

De Genova, Nicholas. *Working the Boundaries: Race, Space and "Illegality" in Mexican Chicago*. Durham, NC: Duke University Press, 2005.

Dhami, Sadhu Singh. *The Sikhs and Their Religion: A Struggle for Democracy*. Vancouver and Victoria: Khalsa Diwan Society, 1943.

Dib, Kamal, Ian Donaldson, and Brittany Turcotte. "Integration and Identity in Canada: The Importance of Multicultural Common Spaces 1." *Canadian Ethnic Studies* 40, no. 1 (2008): 161–87.

Di Leonardo, Micaela. *The Varieties of Ethnic Experience: Kinship, Class, and Gender among California Italian-Americans*. Ithaca, NY: Cornell University Press, 1984.

Driedger, Leo, ed. *The Canadian Ethnic Mosaic: A Quest for Identity*. Toronto: McClelland and Stewart, 1978.

– *Multi-ethnic Canada: Identities and Inequalities*. Toronto: Oxford University Press, 1996.

Drushka, Ken. *In the Bight: The BC Forest Industry Today*. Madeira Park, BC: Harbour Publishing, 1999.

Dubois, D., and B. Hirsch. "School and Neighbourhood Friendship Patterns of Black and Whites in Early Adolescence." *Child Development* 61 (1990): 524–36.

Duff, Wilson. *The Indian History of British Columbia: The Impact of the White Man*. 1965; reprint, Victoria: Royal British Columbia Museum, 1997.

Dusenbery, Verne A. "The Poetics and Politics of Recognition: Diasporan Sikhs in Pluralist Polities." *American Ethnologist* 24, no. 4 (1997): 738–62.

Emmons, Robert A. "Striving for the Sacred: Personal Goals, Life Meaning, and Religion." *Journal of Social Issues* 61, no. 4 (2005): 731–45.

Erikson, Erik. *Identity and the Life Cycle*. 1959; reprint, New York: Norton, 1980.

Espino, N. Ariel. "Inequality, Segregation, and Housing Markets: The U.S. Case." In *Desegregating the City: Ghettos, Enclaves, and Inequality*, ed. David P. Varady, 145–57. Albany: State University of New York Press, 2005.

Fairlie, Robert W., and Alicia M. Robb. *Race and Entrepreneurial Success*. Cambridge, MA: MIT Press, 2010.

Falzon, Mark-Anthony, ed. *Multi-sited Ethnography: Theory, Praxis and Locality in Contemporary Research*. London, UK: Ashgate, 2009.

Findlay, Andrew. "'The Nisga'a's Private Struggle: Home Ownership Comes to the Nisga'a Nation, Along with Concerns about Erosion of Traditional Values." *BC Business* 38, no. 3 (2010): 68–71.

Fisher, Robin. *Contact and Conflict: Indian-European Relations in British Columbia, 1774–1890*. Vancouver: University of British Columbia Press, 1977.

Fiske, Jo-Anne. "Placing Violence against First Nations Children: The Use of Space and Place to Construct the (In)credible Violated Subject." In *Healing Traditions: The Mental Health of Aboriginal Peoples in Canada*, ed. Laurence J. Kirmayer and Gail Gutherie Valaskakis, 140–63. Vancouver: University of British Columbia Press, 2009.

Fleras, Augie, and Jean Elliot. *Multiculturalism in Canada*. Scarborough, ON: Nelson, 1992.

– *Unequal Relations: An Introduction to Race, Ethnic, and Aboriginal Dynamics in Canada*. Toronto: Pearson, 1996.

Foley, Janice R., and Patricia L. Baker, eds. *Unions, Equity, and the Path to Renewal*. Vancouver: University of British Columbia Press, 2010.

Foley, Pamela F., and John E. Smith. "A Model Psycho-educational Group for Survivors of Organizational Downsizing." *Journal for Specialists in Group Work* 24, no. 4 (1999): 354–68.

Foner, Nancy. *Islands in the City: West Indian Migration to New York*. Berkeley: University of California Press, 2001.

Fong, Mary, and Rueyling Chuang, eds. *Communicating Ethnic and Cultural Identity*. Lanham, MD: Rowman & Littlefield Publishers, 2004.

Forbes, Geraldine. *Women in Modern India*. Cambridge: Cambridge University Press, 1999.

Gabaccia, D., and Franca Iacovetta, eds. *Women, Gender and Transnational Lives: Italian Workers of the World*. Toronto: University of Toronto Press, 2002.

Ghosh, Suresh C. *The History of Education in Modern India 1757–1998*. New Delhi: Orient Longman, 2000.

Gill, Ravinder Ravi, ed. *Wind Song: An Anthology of Poetry by the School District #92 (Nisgha) Poets of the Nass Valley*. Vols 1–2. Vancouver: Indo-Canadian Publications, 1984.

Gjerde, Per F. "Culture, Power, and Experience: Toward a Person-Centered Cultural Psychology." *Human Development* 47 (2004): 138–57.

Gladstone, Percy. "Native Indians and the Fishing Industry of British Columbia." *Canadian Journal of Economics and Political Science* 19, no. 1 (1953): 20–34.

Gleason, Mona. "Psychology and the Construction of the 'Normal' Family in Postwar Canada, 1945–60." *Canadian Historical Review* 78, no. 3 (1997): 443–77.

Glick Schiller, Nina. "Transmigration and Nation-States: Something Old and Something New in the US Immigrant Experience." In *The Handbook of International Migration*, ed. C. Hirchmaan, 94–119. New York: Russell Sage Publication, 1999.

Glick Schiller, Nina, Linda Basch, and Christina Blanc-Szanton, eds. *Towards a Transnational Perspective on Migration, Race, Class, Ethnicity, and Nationalism Reconsidered*. New York: New York Academy of Sciences, 1992.

Gough, Barry M. "Pioneer Missionaries to the Nishga: The Crosscurrents of Demon Rum and British Gunboats, 1860–1871." *Journal of the Canadian Church Historical Society* 26, no. 2 (1984): 81–97.

Grewal, J.S. *The Sikhs of the Punjab*. Cambridge: Cambridge University Press, 1994.

Grunberg, Leon, Sarah Y. Moore, and Edward Greenberg. "Differences in Psychological and Physical Health among Layoff Survivors: The Effect of Layoff Contact." *Journal of Occupational Health Psychology* 6, no. 1 (2001): 15–25.

Guha, Ramachandra. *India after Gandhi: The History of the World's Largest Democracy*. New York: Ecco, 2007.

Gupta, Akhil, and James Ferguson, eds. *Culture, Power, Place: Explorations in Critical Anthropology*. Durham, NC: Duke University Press, 1997.

Haan, Michael. "The Homeownership Hierarchies of Canada and the United States: The Housing Patterns of White and Non-white Immigrants of the Past Thirty Years." *International Migration Review* 41, no. 2 (2007): 433–65.

– "The Place of Place: Location and Immigrant Economic Wellbeing in Canada." *Population Research and Policy Review* 27, no. 6 (2009): 751–71.

– "The Residential Crowding of Immigrants in Canada, 1971–2001." *Journal of Ethnic and Migration Studies* 37, no. 3 (2011): 443–65.

– "Is Recent Immigrant Clustering in Montréal, Toronto and Vancouver Part of the Reason behind Declining Immigrant Neighbourhood Quality?" In *Demographic Aspects of Migration*, ed. Barry Edmonston, Thomas Saltzmann, and James Raymer, 263–79. Berlin: Springer Verlag, 2010.

Hage, Ghassan. "A Not So Multi-sited Ethnography of a Not So Imagined Community." *Anthropological Theory* 5, no. 4 (2005): 463–75.

Hak, Gordon. *Capital and Labour in the British Columbia Forest Industry, 1934–74.* Vancouver: University of British Columbia Press, 2007.

– *Turning Trees into Dollars: The British Columbia Coastal Lumber History, 1858–1913.* Toronto: University of Toronto Press, 2000.

Hallock, Ruth M. "A Letter from Fort St. James." In *Issues in Cultural Diversity*, ed. Harold Martin Tripper, 52–60. Toronto: Ontario Institute for Studies in Education, 1976.

Harris, Cole. *The Resettlement of British Columbia: Essays on Colonialism and Geographical Change.* Vancouver: University of British Columbia Press, 1997.

Harris, Douglas C. *Fish, Law, and Colonialism: The Legal Capture of Salmon in British Columbia.* Toronto: University of Toronto Press, 2001.

– *Landing Native Fisheries: Indian Reserves and Fishing Rights in British Columbia 1849–1925.* Vancouver: University of British Columbia Press, 2008.

Hayter, Roger. *Flexible Crossroads: The Restructuring of British Columbia's Forest Economy.* Vancouver: University of British Columbia Press, 2000.

– "The War in the Woods: Post-Fordist Restructuring, Globalization, and the Contested Remapping of British Columbia's Forest Economy." *Annals of the Association of American Geography* 93, no. 3 (2003): 706–29.

Heibert, Daniel, Nadine Schuurman, and Heather Smith. "Multiculturalism 'On the Ground': The Social Geography of Immigrant and Visible Minority Populations in Montreal, Toronto, and Vancouver, Projected to 2017." Vancouver: Metropolis British Columbia (Working Paper Series 07-12), 2007.

Heibert, Daniel, and Kathy Sherrell. "The Integration and Inclusion of Newcomers in British Columbia." Vancouver: Metropolis British Columbia (Working Paper Series 09-11), 2009.

Helin, Calvin. *Dances with Dependency: Indigenous Success through Self-Reliance.* Vancouver: Orca Spirit Publishing, 2006.

Herzfeld, Michael. *Theoretical Practice in Culture and Society.* Oxford: Blackwell Publishers, 2001.

Hick, W.B.M. *Hays' Orphan: The Story of the Port of Prince Rupert.* Prince Rupert, BC: Prince Rupert Authority, 2003.

Hill, Herbert. "Black-Jewish Conflict in the Labor Context: Race, Jobs, and Institutional Power." In *Strangers and Neighbors: Relations between Blacks & Jews in the United States*, ed. Maurianne Adams and John Bracey, 596–619. Amherst: University of Massachusetts Press, 1999.

Hols, Grace. *Marks of a Century: A History of Houston, BC, 1900–2000*. Houston, BC: District of Houston, 1999.

Hudson, Douglas. "Traplines and Timber: Social and Economic Change among the Carrier." PhD diss., University of Alberta, Edmonton, 1983.

Iacovetta, Franca. *Such Hardworking People: Italian Immigrants in Postwar Toronto*. Montreal & Kingston: McGill-Queen's University Press, 1993.

Indo-Canadian Oral History Collection. Burnaby: Simon Fraser University, 1987.

Indra, Doreen M. "South Asian Stereotypes in the Vancouver Press." *Ethnic and Racial Studies* 2, no. 2 (1979): 169–89.

Ishin, Engin F., ed. *Recasting the Social in Citizenship*. Toronto: Toronto University Press, 2008.

Israel, Milton, ed. *The South Asian Diaspora in Canada: Six Essays*. Toronto: Multicultural History Society of Ontario, 1987.

Jagpal, Sarjeet Singh. *Becoming Canadians: Pioneer Sikhs in Their Own Words*. Madeira Park, BC: Harbour Publishing, 1994.

Jamieson, Stuart, and Percy Gladstone. "Unionism in the Fishing Industry of British Columbia." *Canadian Journal of Economics and Political Science* 16, no. 1 (1950): 1–11.

Jiwani, Yasmin. *Discourses of Denial: Mediations of Race, Gender, and Violence*. Vancouver: University of British Columbia Press, 2006.

Johnston, Hugh. "Group Identity in an Emigrant Worker Community: The Example of Sikhs in Early Twentieth-Century British Columbia." *BC Studies* 148 (Winter 2005): 3–23.

– *Jewels from the Qila: The Remarkable Story of an Indo-Canadian Family*. Vancouver: University of British Columbia Press, 2011.

– "Patterns of Sikh Migration to Canada 1900–1960." In *Sikh History and Religion in the 20th Century*, ed. Joseph T. O'Connell, Milton Israel, and Willard Oxtoby, 296–313. Toronto: Centre for South Asian Studies, University of Toronto, 1988.

– *The Voyage of Komagata Maru: The Sikh Challenge to Canada's Colour Bar*. Delhi: Oxford University Press, 1979.

Judge, Paramjit S. *Punjabis in Canada: A Study of Formation of an Ethnic Community*. Delhi: Chanakya Publications, 1994.

Karim, Jamillah. *American Muslim Women: Negotiating Race, Class, and Gender within the Ummah*. New York: New York University Press, 2009.

Kearney, Michael. "The Local and Global: The Anthropology of Globalization and Transnationalism." *Annual Review of Anthropology* 24 (1995): 547–65.

Keddie, Vincent. "Class Identification and Party Preference among Manual Workers: The Influence of Community, Union Membership and Kinship." *Canadian Review of Sociology and Anthropology* 17 (1980): 24–36.

Kessinger, Tom G. *Vilyatpur, 1848–1968: Social and Economic Change in a North Indian Village*. Berkeley: University of California Press, 1974.

Khan, Salaha, and Jeanne Watson. "The Canadian Immigration Experiences of Pakistani Women: Dreams Confront Reality." *Counseling Psychology Quarterly* 18, no. 4 (2005): 307–17.

Kim, Ann H., and Michael J. White. "Panethnicity, Ethnic Diversity and Residential Segregation." *American Journal of Sociology* 115, no. 5 (2010): 1558–96.

Klostermaier, Klaus K. *A Survey of Hinduism.* Albany: State University of New York Press, 1989.

Knight, Rolf. *Indians at Work: An Informal History of Native Indian Labour in British Columbia 1858–1930.* Vancouver: New Star Books, 1978.

Kobayashi, Audrey, and Peter Jackson. "Japanese Canadians and the Racialization of Labour in the British Columbia Sawmill Industry." *BC Studies* 103 (Fall 1994): 33–58.

Kymlicka, Will. *Finding Our Way: Rethinking Ethnocultural Relations in Canada.* Toronto: Oxford University Press, 1998.

Lambertson, Ross. "The BC Court of Appeal and Civil Liberties." *BC Studies* 162 (Summer 2009): 81–109.

– *Repression and Resistance: Canadian Human Rights Activists, 1930–1960.* Toronto: University of Toronto Press, 2005.

Large, Dr R.G. *Prince Rupert, A Gateway to Alaska and the Pacific,* vol. 1. Vancouver: Mitchell Press, 1973.

– *Prince Rupert, A Gateway to Alaska and the Pacific,* vol. 2. Vancouver: Mitchell Press, 1983.

– *The Skeena: River of Destiny.* 1957; reprint, Surrey, BC: Heritage House Publishing, 1996.

LaViolette, F.E. *The Struggle for Survival: Indian Cultures and the Protestant Work Ethic in British Columbia.* Toronto: University of Toronto Press, 1961.

Leaf, Murray J. *Information and Behaviour in a Sikh Village: Social Organization Reconsidered.* Berkeley: University of California Press, 1972.

Lukhardt, Ken E. "Prince Rupert: A 'Tale of Two Cities.'" In *Historical Perspectives on Northern British Columbia,* ed. Thomas Thorner, 309–32. Prince George, BC: College of New Caledonia Press, 1989.

Lutz, John S. *Makuk: A New History of Aboriginal-White Relations.* Vancouver: University of British Columbia Press, 2008.

McCormick, Rod. "Aboriginal Approaches to Counselling." In *Healing Traditions: The Mental Health of Aboriginal Peoples in Canada,* ed. Laurence J. Kirmayer and Gail Gutherie Valaskakis, 337–54. Vancouver: University of British Columbia Press, 2009.

McIntosh, D.N. "Religion as a Schema, with Implications for the Relation between Religion and Coping." *International Journal for the Psychology of Religion* 5 (1995): 1–16.

McLeod, W.H. *Sikhs of the Khalsa: A History of the Rahit Maryada.* New Delhi: Oxford University Press, 2003.

McRoberts, K. *Misconceiving Canada: The Struggle for National Unity.* Oxford: Oxford University Press, 1997.

Madan, T.N. "The Double-Edged Sword: Fundamentalism and the Sikh Religious Tradition." In *Fundamentalisms Observed*, ed. M. Marty and R.S. Appleby, 594–627. Chicago: University of Chicago Press, 1991.

Mahler, Sarah J., and Patricia R. Pessar. "Gendered Geographies of Power: Analyzing Gender across Transnational Spaces." *Identities: Global Studies in Culture and Power* 7 (2001): 441–59.

Manusmrti. Transl. M.N. Dutt. Varanasi: Chowkhamba Press, 1979.

Maraj, D.I. "Non-accreditation: Its Impact on Foreign Educated Immigrant Professionals." MA thesis, University of Toronto, 1996.

Marcus, George. *Ethnography through Thick and Thin.* Princeton, NJ: Princeton University Press, 1998.

Marcuse, Peter. "The Enclave, the Citadel, and the Ghetto: What Has Happened in the Post-Fordist U.S. City." *Urban Affairs Review* 33, no. 3 (1997): 228–64.

Marshall, Alison R. *The Way of the Bachelor: Early Chinese Settlement in Manitoba.* Vancouver: University of British Columbia Press, 2011.

Mayo, Joan. *Paldi Remembered: 50 Years in the Life of a Vancouver Island Logging Town.* Duncan, BC: Paldi History Committee, 1997.

Meggs, Geoff. *Salmon: The Decline of the British Columbia Fisheries.* Vancouver: Douglas & McIntyre, 1995.

Mendez, Pablo. "Immigrant Residential Geographies and the 'Spatial Assimilation' Debate in Canada, 1997–2007." *International Journal of Migration and Integration* 10 (2009): 89–108.

Miller, James R. *Shingwauk's Vision: A History of Native Residential Schools.* Toronto: University of Toronto Press, 1996.

Miller, Joy, and Carol M. Eastman, eds. *The Tsimshian and Their Neighbours of the North Pacific Coast.* Seattle: University of Washington Press, 1984.

Milloy, J. *National Crime: The Canadian Government and the Residential School System.* Winnipeg: University of Manitoba Press, 1999.

Minor, Robert N. "Sri Aurobindo's Dismissal of Gandhi and His Non-violence." In *Indian Critiques of Gandhi*, ed. Harold Coward, 87–106. Albany: State University of New York, 2003.

Mitra, Subrata K. 2011. "Democracy's Resilience: Tradition, Modernity, and Hybridity in India." *Harvard International Review* 32, no. 4 (2011): 46–52.

Morton, Desmond. *Working People: An Illustrated History of the Canadian Labour Movement.* Montreal & Kingston: McGill-Queen's University Press, 1998.

Mukherjee, Mridula. *Colonializing Agriculture: The Myth of Punjab Exceptionalism.* New Delhi: Thousand Oaks, 2005.

Muszynski, Alicja. *Cheap Wage Labour: Race and Gender in the Fisheries of British Columbia.* Montreal & Kingston: McGill-Queen's University Press, 1996.

Naidoo, Josephine C. "Contemporary South Asian Women in the Canadian Mosaic." In *Sex Roles II: Feminist Psychology in Transition*, ed. P. Caplan, 338–50. Montreal: Eden Press, 1984.

Naidoo, Josephine C., and J. Campbell Davis. "Canadian South Asian Women in Transition: A Dualistic View of Life." *Journal of Comparative Family Studies* 19 (1988): 311–27.

Narayanan, Vasudha. "The Hindu Tradition." In *World Religions: Eastern Traditions*, ed. Willard G. Oxtoby, 12–125. New York: Oxford University Press, 2002.

Nathias, Floya, and Nira Yuval-Davis. *Racialized Boundaries: Race, Nation, Gender, Colour, Class and the Anti-racist Struggle*. London: Routledge, 1992.

Nayar, Kamala Elizabeth. "Ethnic Identity Formation in Canada." Report for the Canada and Cultural Diversity Website Project. Montreal: National Film Board of Canada, 2007.

– "The Intersection of Religious Identity and Visible Minority Status." In *Religion in the Public Sphere: Interdisciplinary Perspectives across the Canadian Provinces*, ed. Lori Beaman and Solange Lefebvre. Toronto: University of Toronto Press, in press.

– "The Making of Sikh Space in British Columbia: The Central Role of the *Gurdwara*." In *Asian Religions in British Columbia*, ed. Larry DeVries, Don Baker, and Dan Overmyer, 43–63. Vancouver: University of British Columbia Press, 2010.

– "Misunderstood in the Diaspora: The Experience of Orthodox Sikhs in Vancouver." *Sikh Formations* 4, no. 1 (2008): 17–32.

– "Religion, Resiliency and Citizenship: The Journey of a Vancouver Sikh Pioneer." In *Sikh Diaspora: Theory, Agency, and Experience*, ed. Michael Hawley. Leiden: Brill Academic Publishers, in press.

– *The Sikh Diaspora in Vancouver: Three Generations amid Tradition, Modernity, and Multiculturalism*. Toronto: University of Toronto Press, 2004.

– "The Sikhs: Citizenship and the Canadian Experience." In *Perspectives on Faith and Citizenship: Issues, Challenges and Opportunities*, ed. Paul Bramadat, 116–40. Commissioned report for the Department of Citizenship and Immigration of Canada. Victoria: University of Victoria, 2011.

– "Sikh Women in Vancouver: An Analysis of Their Psychosocial Issues." In *Women and Sikhism*, ed. Doris Jakobsh, 248–70. Delhi: Oxford University Press, 2010.

Nayar, Kamala Elizabeth, and Jaswinder Singh Sandhu. "Intergenerational Communication in Immigrant Punjabi Families: Implications for Helping Professionals." *International Journal for the Advancement of Counseling* 28, no. 2 (2006): 139–52.

– *The Socially Involved Renunciate: Guru Nanak's Discourse to the Nath Yogis*. Albany: State University of New York Press, 2007.

Nayyar, Deepak. *Migration, Remittances and Capital Flows: The Indian Experience*. Delhi: Oxford University Press, 1994.

Newell, Diane, ed. *Development of the Pacific Salmon-Canning Industry: A Grown Man's Game*. Montreal & Kingston: McGill-Queen's University Press, 1989.

– *Tangled Webs of History: Indians and the Law in Canada's Pacific Coast Fisheries*. Toronto: University of Toronto Press, 1993.

Oberoi, Harjot Singh. *The Construction of Religious Boundaries: Culture, Identity and Diversity in the Sikh Tradition*. Chicago: University of Chicago Press, 1994.

Ogmundson, R., and M. Doyle. "The Rise and Decline of Canadian Labour/1960 to 2000: Elites, Power, Ethnicity and Gender." *Canadian Journal of Sociology* 27, no. 3 (2002): 413–54.

Ornsby, Margaret A. *British Columbia: A History*. Toronto: Macmillan of Canada, 1958.

Palys, Ted. *Research Decisions: Quantitative and Qualitative Perspectives.* Toronto: Harcourt Brace Jovanovich, 1992.

Pannun, Amarjit Kaur. "Pardesan Ka Kam: An Essay on Punjabi-Sikh Women Cannery Workers in Northern British Columbia." MA thesis, University of British Columbia, 1994.

Park, Crystal L. "Religion as a Meaning-Making Framework in Coping with Life Stress." *Journal of Social Issues* 61, no. 4 (2005): 707–29.

Pendakur, Krishna, and Ravi Pendakur. "Colour My World: Have Earnings Gaps for Canadian-Born Ethnic Minorities Changed over Time?" *Canadian Public Policy* 28, no. 4 (2002): 489–512.

– "The Colour of Money: Earnings Differentials among Ethnic Groups in Canada." *Canadian Journal of Economics* 31, no. 3 (1998): 518–48.

Pendakur, Ravi. *Immigrants and the Labour Force: Policy, Regulation, and Impact.* Montreal & Kingston: McGill-Queen's University Press, 2000.

Pettigrew, Joyce. *Robber Noblemen: A Study of the Political System of Sikh Jats.* Boston: Routledge and Kegan Paul, 1975.

Phinney, Jean S. "The Multi-group Ethnic Identity Measure: A New Scale for Use with Adolescents and Young Adults from Diverse Groups." *Journal of Adolescent Research* 7, no. 2 (1992): 156–76.

Phinney, Jean S., and Linda L. Alipuria. "At the Interface of Cultures: Multiethnic/Multiracial High School and College Students." *Journal of Social Psychology* 136, no. 2 (1996): 139–58.

Phinney, Jean S., Debra L. Ferguson, and Jerry D. Tate. "Intergroup Attitudes among Ethnic Minority Adolescents: A Causal Model." *Child Development* 68, no. 5 (1997): 955–69.

Phinney, Jean S., Gabriel Horenczyk, Karmela Liebkind, and Paul Vedder. "Ethnic Identity, Immigration, and Well-Being: An Interactional Perspective." *Journal of Social Issues* 57, no. 3 (2001): 493–510.

Phinney, Jean S., Anthony Ong, and Tanya Madden. "Cultural Values and Intergenerational Value Discrepancies in Immigrant and Non-immigrant Families." *Child Development* 71, no. 2 (2000): 528–39.

Porter, John. *The Vertical Mosaic: An Analysis of Social Class and Power in Canada.* Toronto: University of Toronto Press, 1965.

Prashad, Vijay. *Everybody Was Kung Fu Fighting.* Boston: Beacon Press, 2001.

– "How the Hindus Became Jews: American Racism after 9/11." *South Atlantic Quarterly* 104, no. 3 (2005): 583–606.

– *The Karma of Brown Folk.* Minneapolis: University of Minnesota Press, 2000.

– "Second-Hand Dreams." *Social Analysis* 49, no. 2 (2005): 191–8.

Prince Rupert City and Regional Archives Society. *Prince Rupert: An Illustrated History.* Prince Rupert, 2010.

Qadeer, Mohammad. "Ethnic Segregation in a Multicultural City." In *Desegregating the City: Ghettos, Enclaves, and Inequality,* ed. David P. Varady, 49–61. Albany: State University of New York Press, 2005.

Qadeer, Mohammad, Sandeep K. Agrawal, and Alexander Lovell. "Evolution of Ethnic Enclaves in the Toronto Metropolitan Area, 2001–2006." *International Journal of Migration and Integration* 11 (2010): 315–39.

Rajala, Richard A. *Clearcutting the Pacific Rain Forest: Production, Science and Regulation.* Vancouver: University of British Columbia Press, 1998.
– "Forests and Fish: The 1972 Coast Logging Guidelines and British Columbia's First NDP Government." *BC Studies* 159 (2008): 81–120.
– "The Receding Timber Line: Forest Practice, State Regulation, and the Decline of the Cowichan Lake Timber Industry, 1880–1992." In *Canadian Papers in Business History*, vol. 2, ed. Peter A. Baskerville. Victoria: Public History Group, University of Victoria, 1993.
Ralston, Helen. "Identity and Lived Experience of Daughters of South Asian Immigrant Women in Halifax and Vancouver." Prepared for International Migration and Ethnic Relations Conference "Youth in the Plural City: Individualized and Collectivized Identities." Norwegian Institute, Rome, 25 to 28 May 1999.
– "Race, Class, Gender and Work Experience of South Asian Immigrant Women in Atlantic Canada." *Canadian Ethnic Studies* 23, no. 2 (1991): 129–39.
Ramadan, Tariq. *The Quest for Meaning: Developing a Philosophy of Pluralism.* New York: Allen Lane, 2010.
Raunet, Daniel. *Without Surrender, without Consent: A History of the Nishga Land Claims.* Vancouver: Douglas & McIntyre, 1984.
Ray, Brian, and E. Moore. "Access to Homeownership among Immigrant Groups in Canada." *Canadian Sociology Review* 28, no. 1 (1991): 1–29.
Ray, Brian, and Valerie Preston. "Experiences of Discrimination: The Impact of Metropolitan and Non-metropolitan Location." Power point presentation on 26 February 2009, CIC Research Network Meeting, Metropolis, Ottawa.
Rodriguez-Garcia, Dan. "Beyond Assimilation and Multiculturalism: A Critical Review of the Debate on Managing Diversity." *International Journal of Migration and Integration* 11 (2010): 251–71.
Roy, Patricia. "The Oriental 'Menace' in British Columbia." In *Historical Essays on British Columbia*, ed. J. Friesen and H.K. Ralston, 243–55. Toronto: McClelland & Stewart, 1976.
– *The Oriental Question: Consolidating a White Man's Province, 1914–41.* Vancouver: University of British Columbia Press, 2003.
– *The Triumph of Citizenship: The Japanese and Chinese in Canada, 1941–67.* Vancouver: University of British Columbia Press, 2007.
– *A White Man's Province: British Columbia Politicians and Chinese and Japanese Immigrants, 1858–1914.* Vancouver: University of British Columbia Press, 1989.
Roy, Reginald H. "From the Darker Side of Canadian Military History: Mutiny in the Mountains – The Terrace Incident." *Canadian Defence Quarterly* 5 (1976): 42–55.
Rukhmani, T.S. "Tagore and Gandhi." In *Indian Critiques of Gandhi*, ed. Harold Coward, 107–30. Albany: State University of New York, 2003.
Sandhu, D., and R. Malik. "Ethnocultural Background and Substance Abuse Treatment of Asian Indian Americans." In *Ethnocultural Factors in Substance Abuse Treatment*, ed. S.L.A. Straussner, 368–92. New York: Guildford Press, 2001.
Sandhu, Jaswinder Singh. "The Sikh Model of the Person, Suffering, and Healing: The Implications for Counselors." *International Journal for the Advancement of Counseling* 26, no. 1 (2004): 33–46.

- "A Sikh Perspective on Alcohol and Drugs: Implications for the Treatment of Punjabi-Sikh Patients." *Sikh Formations* 5, no. 1 (2009): 23–37.

Sandhu, Jaswinder S., and Kamala Elizabeth Nayar. "Studying the Sikh Diaspora: First Year University Experience of Punjabi Sikh Students." *Sikh Formations* 4, no. 1 (2008): 33–46.

Santrock, John. *Adolescence*. 7th ed. Boston: McGraw Hill, 1998.

Schlesinger, Arthur M. *The Disuniting of America: Reflections on a Multicultural Society*. New York: W.W. Norton, 1992.

Schmidt, Wallace V., Roger N. Conway, Susan S. Easton, and William J. Wardrope. *Communication Globally: Intercultural Communication and International Business*. Thousand Oaks, CA: Sage Publications, 2007.

Sekhon, I.S. *The Punjabis: The People, the History, Culture and Enterprise*, vol. 1. New Delhi: Cosmo Publications, 2000.

Singh, Himmat. *Green Revolutions Reconsidered: The Rural World of Contemporary Punjab*. New Delhi: Oxford University Press, 2001.

Singh, Khushwant. *A History of the Sikhs*, vols 1–2. Princeton, NJ: Princeton University Press, 1963.

Singh, Narinder. *Canadian Sikhs, History, Religion, and Culture of Sikhs in North America*. Ottawa: Canadian Sikhs' Studies Institute, 1994.

Singh, Nikky-Guninder Kaur. "Durga Recalled by the Tenth Guru." In *The Sikh Tradition: A Continuing Reality*, ed. S. Bhatia and A. Spencer, 208–25. Patiala: Punjabi University, 1999.

- "The Mahatma and the Sikhs." In *Indian Critiques of Gandhi*, ed. Harold Coward, 171–91. Albany: Stature University of New York Press, 2003.

Sirin, Selcuk R., and Michelle Fine. "Hyphenated Selves: Muslim American Youth Negotiating Identities on the Fault Lines of Global Conflict." *Applied Developmental Science* 11, no. 3 (2007): 151–63.

Statistics Canada. *Population Projections of Visible Minority Groups, Canada, Provinces, and Regions, 2001 to 2017*. Retrieved 4 April 2005 from http://www.statscan.ca.

Stephenson, Bill. "Prince Rupert." In *An Account of a Unique Philosophy in Action*, 20–1. Columbia Cellulose Company Ltd/Chemcell Ltd, 1963.

Strong-Boag, Veronica. "Canada's Wage-Earning Wives and the Construction of the Middle Class, 1945–60." *Journal of Canadian Studies* 29, no. 3 (1994): 5–25.

- "Home Dreams: Women and the Suburban Experiment in Canada, 1945–60." *Canadian Historical Review* 72, no. 4 (1991): 471–504.

Talbani, Aziz, and Parveen Hasanali. "Adolescent Females between Tradition and Modernity: Gender Role Socialization in South Asian Immigrant Culture." *Journal of Adolescence* 23, no. 5 (2000): 615–27.

Tanguay, Brian, and Steven Bittle. "Parliament as a Mirror to the Nation: Promoting Diversity in Representation through Electoral Reform." *Canadian Issues*, Summer 2005, 61–3.

Tatla, Darshan Singh. "The Morning After: Trauma, Memory and the Sikh Predicament since 1984." *Sikh Formations* 2, no. 1 (2006): 57–88.

– *The Sikh Diaspora: The Search for Statehood.* Seattle: University of Washington Press, 1999.

Tatla, Darshan Singh, and Verne A. Dusenbery, eds. *Sikh Diaspora Philanthropy in Punjab: Global Giving for Local Good.* New Delhi: Oxford University Press, 2009.

Tennant, Paul. *Aboriginal Peoples and Politics: The Indian Land Question in British Columbia, 1849–1989.* Vancouver: University of British Columbia Press, 1990.

Tossutti, Livianna S., and Tom Pierre Najem. "Minorities and Elections in Canada's Fourth Party System: Macro and Micro Constraints and Opportunities." *Canadian Ethnic Studies* 34, no. 1 (2002): 85–112.

Unstead, J.F. "The Economic Resources of British Columbia." *Geographical Journal* 50, no. 2 (1917): 125–43.

Van der Veer, Peter, ed. *Nation and Migration: The Politics of Space in the South Asian Diaspora.* Philadelphia: University of Pennsylvania Press, 1995.

Varady, David P., ed. *Desegregating the City: Ghettos, Enclaves, and Inequality.* Albany: State University of New York Press, 2005.

Verma, Archana B. *The Making of Little Punjab in Canada.* New Delhi: Sage, 2002.

Vertovec, Steven. *The Hindu Diaspora: Comparative Patterns.* London, UK: Routledge, 2000.

Vertovec, Steven, and Susanne Wessendorf, eds. *The Multiculturalism Backlash: European Discourses, Policies and Practices.* London: Routledge, 2010.

Walton-Roberts, Margaret. "Globalization, National Autonomy and Non-resident Indians." *Contemporary South Asia* 13, no. 1 (2004): 53–69.

– "Transnational Geographies: Indian Immigration to Canada." *Canadian Geographer* 47, no. 3 (2003): 235–50.

Wang, Shuguang, and Lucia Lo. "What Does It Take to Achieve Full Integration? Economic (Under)Performance of Chinese Immigrants in Canada." In *Interrogating Race and Racism*, ed. Vijay Agnew, 172–205. Toronto: University of Toronto Press, 2007.

Ward, W. Peter. *White Canada Forever: Popular Attitudes and Public Policy toward Orientals in British Columbia.* 3rd ed. Montreal & Kingston: McGill-Queen's University Press, 2002.

Waters, Mary C. "Growing Up West Indian and African American: Gender and Class Differences in the Second Generation." In *Islands in the City: West Indian Migration to New York*, ed. Nancy Foner, 193–215. Berkeley: University of California Press, 2001.

Waters, Mary C., and Karl Eschbach. "Immigration and Ethnic and Racial Inequality in the United States." *Annual Review of Sociology* 21 (1995): 419–46.

Weaver, Sally. *Making Canadian Indian Policy: The Hidden Agenda, 1968–70.* Toronto: University of Toronto Press, 1981.

Widdowson, Frances, and Albert Howard. *Disrobing the Aboriginal Industry: The Deception behind Indigenous Cultural Preservation.* Montreal & Kingston: McGill-Queen's University Press, 2008.

Wilson, J. *Talk and Log: Wilderness Politics in British Columbia.* Vancouver: University of British Columbia Press, 1998.

Wong, Lloyd. "Multiculturalism and Ethnic Pluralism in Sociology: An Analysis of the Fragmentation Position Discourse." *Canadian Ethnic Studies* 40, no. 1 (2008): 11–32.

Wood, John. "East Indians and Canada's New Immigration Policy." *Canadian Public Policy* 4, no. 4 (1978): 547–67.

Wulff, Maryann, Tom Carter, Rob Vineberg, and Stephen Ward. "Attracting New Arrivals to Smaller Cities and Rural Communities: Findings from Australia, Canada and New Zealand." *International Journal of Migration and Integration* 9 (2008): 119–24.

Yin, Robert K. *Case Study Research: Design and Methods.* Thousand Oaks, CA: Sage Publications, 2003.

Zavella, Patricia. *Women's Work & Chicano Families: Cannery Workers of the Santa Clara Valley.* Ithaca, NY: Cornell University Press, 1987.

Zucchi, John. *A History of Ethnic Enclaves in Canada.* Canada's Ethnic Group Series 31. Ottawa: Canadian Historical Association, 2007.

– *Italians in Toronto: Development of a National Identity 1875–1935.* Montreal & Kingston: McGill-Queen's University Press, 1988.

INDEX

Cedar Cove Sawmill, 31, 293n33
Chadney, James Gaylord, 88, 286n35
charhdi kala, 76–7, 272, 306n62
Charter of Rights and Freedoms (1982),
16
Cheam Lumber Company, 29
Chinese, 21, 179, 189, 193, 198, 203, 206,
241, 244, 254, 317n30, 324n49; as cheap
labour, 28, 60, 142–4; in fisheries,
143–7, 155, 317n42, 318n53; in forestry,
142–3; franchise rights, 15, 249; head
tax, 15, 317n30; in railways, 152; and
the union, 13
Christianity, 193, 324n49
Church of England, 137
citizenship: concept of, 279; "immigrant," 220, 234–5, 263, 280–1; negotiating, 219–20, 236, 267–8, 278–82;
shared, 19, 178, 214, 220, 277–82. *See
also* cultural synergy
Clark, Glen, 53, 250, 336n39
Clinton, Bill, 110, 250
Columbia Cellulose, 35, 39; pulp and
paper mill (Watson Island), 39–40,
42–4, 49, 52–3, 58, 72–3, 101–2, 149–50,
162, 164, 173, 270, 295n56
Community Historical Recognition
Program (CHRP), 231–2, 331n61
Confederation, 10, 139
Conrad Elementary, 71, 200–1, 203, 241
Conservative Party (federal), 229, 231–5,
332n70–1
coping, 76–7, 105–6, 130–2, 305n52; maladaptive, 77–8
Crosby, Thomas, 138
cultural: barriers, 73–6, 137; synergy,
178, 204–11, 213–4, 217–20, 225–6, 236,
275–7, 282, 321n1; validation, 210

Davis, J. Campbell, 129
Delta, 224, 233, 250
Dhaliwal, Herb, 250, 330n50
Dhaliwal, Sukh, 231, 233, 332n71
dharma, 64, 86, 118–19, 129–31
diaspora, 3–5, 222, 281–2

discrimination: gender-based, 95–7, 114,
159–60; in residential areas, 198–200,
219–20, 240, 251, 275, 329n35; in
schools, 200–4, 241–2, 244–7, 253–5,
262–3, 275; at workplace, 137, 142–7,
156–60, 167–71, 190
Dosanjh, Ujjal, 232–3, 331n66, 332n70-1
Dry Dock ("Old"), 32, 35, 36, 42, 60, 70,
297n87, 322n10
Dryland Fuels, 31
Dumont Sawmill, 40, 296n83
Duncan, William, 139, 334n12
duty. See *dharma*

East Indian, 9, 15–16, 143, 169, 189, 191,
194, 205. *See also* Punjabi
education, 309n48; lack of, 39, 72, 74,
113–4; non-transferability of, 45–9,
97–100; upgrading 48–50, 114–5; value
of, 74, 80, 96
employment: barriers, 45–9, 137; decline
and loss, 53–8, 111–13. *See also* women
in labour force; occupation
Employment Equity Act (1986), 16
Employment Insurance (EI), 55, 57,
102–4
English as Second Language (ESL), 200,
241, 246, 254, 304n46
English skills, 44, 46–7, 51, 58, 70, 213,
217, 274; lack of, 165–6, 170. *See also*
language barrier
Erikson, Erik, 239
ethnic: bloc vote, 230–6, 278; diversity,
15, 177–80, 329n38; enclave, 214–15,
222–6, 234–6, 245–6; insularity, 17, 178,
213–18, 234–6, 249, 261–7, 277–8; markets, 217, 231, 236, 281; relations. *See
also* race relations; minority group,
visible
Expo '86, 207, 217

Filipino, 179, 205, 206
First Nations: anti-immigrant hostility, 69, 127, 135, 150–7, 175, 183–9, 235,
275; as cheap labour, 141–2, 144–7;

colonization of, 10–12, 139–42, 175, 197, 206–7, 235, 249, 279, 287n44, 315n6, 315n9, 316n14; discrimination against, 149–50, 175, 183–9, 190–1, 266, 315n7, 316n14, 336n22; education, 202–3, 323n, 326n88; and fisheries, 12, 138–44, 145, 149–57, 172, 185, 321n134; and forestry, 140, 149, 172; land claims 142, 185–6, 198, 315n9, 316n14; and respect, 171–2, 182, 266–7; wage employment 141, 145–7, 154–5

fisheries, 12–13, 139–41, 316n19; decline in, 109–12, 137–8, 172, 271, 300n156, 311n102; and Punjabi women, 93–104, 113–15, 117–18, 123–4; and Punjabi youth, 96, 108–9

FolkFest, 205

Fordist model, 13–14, 137

forestry, 11–12, 28, 288n64; decline in, 52–5, 72–3, 137–8, 172, 245, 271, 300n152

Free Trade Agreement, 14

French, 21; language, 16; Canada, 16

Fulton, Jim, 227, 243, 334n15

gender, 4; changing roles in English Canada, 129, 314n19; changing roles among Skeena Punjabis, 100–1, 129–36, 203–4, 259–61, 314n28; traditional roles in village India, 63–4, 85–7, 137, 307n2, 307n9, 312n2, 312n3, 313n9. *See also* women

Germans, 145, 183, 195

gidda, 207

Gill, Nirmal Singh, 61, 303n32, 305n50; narrative, 65–73

Gill, Ravinder, 47–8

Gill, Sohen Singh, 27, 31–2, 36, 38–9, 50, 60, 70–1, 148–9

Gitxan, 139

gold rushes, 10, 139, 287n46

Grand Trunk Pacific Railway (GTPR), 32

Great Central Sawmills, 30

Great Depression, 11–12, 29–30, 141, 143, 148

Greeks, 200, 243

Guru Nanak Sikh Gurdwara, 234

Haan, Michael, 81

Haida, 21, 146, 148, 149, 154–5, 181, 189, 207

Haisla, 21, 139

Hays, Charles Melville, 32, 179, 294n44

Helms, Janet, 239, 252–3, 265–6

Hillcrest Lumber Company, 26, 148

Hindu: politics, 229–30; religion, 7, 130–1, 197, 301n11, 307n2, 312n3

Hindus: in Lower Mainland, 222; in Skeena, 194–5, 197–8

honour. See *izzat*

Hudson's Bay Company, 139, 287n44, 315n6

Hungarian, 21

identity, 4; Canadian, 5, 213, 226, 262, 282; ethnic, 5, 222–3, 225–6, 236–7, 239–40, 260–1, 279–82. *See also* minority identity, formation

immigration policies, 14–15, 45–6, 87–8, 97, 270, 297n107, 317n30, 317n31

Indian Act, 16, 139–40, 315n9, 323n30

Indian residential school system, 21–2, 156, 186–7, 203, 323n30

Indo-Canadian Arts Club, 207–8

Indra, Doreen Marie, 79

Inglis, Joy, 91

integration, 15–16, 178, 225. *See also* cultural synergy

inter-group conflict, 190–3, 237–9, 241–2, 244–5, 250–61, 276; over language, 16, 127, 135, 156, 169, 170–1, 188–9

inter-group support, 130, 171–2, 174–5, 190–3, 249

International Woodworkers of America (IWA), 13, 71, 78, 160–2, 163–4, 174, 227

intra-group conflict, 230, 233, 245–7, 261–8, 278; support, 76–8, 194–8, 213–14

Italians, 21, 70, 127, 144, 148, 179, 180–3, 184, 191–2, 198, 200, 203, 205, 241, 244, 254, 256